THE ROLE AND FUNCTION OF
REPENTANCE IN LUKE-ACTS

Society of Biblical Literature

Academia Biblica

Saul M. Olyan,
Old Testament Editor

Mark Allan Powell,
New Testament Editor

Number 4

The Role and Function of
Repentance in Luke-Acts

THE ROLE AND FUNCTION OF REPENTANCE IN LUKE-ACTS

Guy D. Nave, Jr.

Society of Biblical Literature
Atlanta

THE ROLE AND FUNCTION OF REPENTANCE IN LUKE-ACTS

Copyright © 2002 by the Society of Biblical Literature

All rights reserved. No part of this work may be reproduced or transmitted in any form or by any means, electronic or mechanical, including photocopying and recording, or by means of any information storage or retrieval system, except as may be expressly permitted by the 1976 Copyright Act or in writing from the publisher. Requests for permission should be addressed in writing to the Rights and Permissions Office, Society of Biblical Literature, 825 Houston Mill Road, Atlanta, GA 30329, USA.

Library of Congress Cataloging-in-Publication Data

Nave, Guy D.
  The role and function of repentance in Luke-Acts/ by Guy D. Nave, Jr.
    p. cm. — (Academia Biblica ; no. 4)
  Includes bibliographical references.
   ISBN 1-58983-031-8 (pbk. : alk. paper)
 1. Repentance—Biblical teaching. 2. Bible. N.T. Luke—Criticism, interpretation, etc. 3. Bible. N.T. Acts—Criticism, interpretation, etc. 4. Bible. N.T. Luke—Socio-rhetorical criticism. 5. Bible. N.T. Acts—Socio-rhetorical criticism. I. Title. II. Academia Biblica (Series) ; 4.
  BS2589.6.R45 N38 2002b
  226.4'06—dc21
                                     2002003320

07 06 05 04 03 02   5 4 3 2 1

Printed in the United States of America
on acid-free paper

CONTENTS

Acknowledgments	vii
Chapter One: History of Research regarding New Testament Repentance	1
The Problem	1
Repentance within the New Testament	2
Repentance within Luke-Acts	3
Repentance and New Testament Theology	5
Solution	5
Chapter Two: Repentance within the Narrative Structure of Luke-Acts	7
Authorial Intention	7
Authorial Intention of Luke-Acts: The Plan of God	11
Salvation as the Plan of God in Luke-Acts	25
Repentance as Part of the Plan of God	29
Chapter Three: The Meaning of Repentance	39
Μετανοέω and Μετάνοια in Classical and Hellenistic Greek Literature	40
Μετανοέω and Μετάνοια in Hellenistic Jewish Literature	70
Μετανοέω and Μετάνοια in the New Testament and Other Early Christian Literature	119
Chapter Four: The Role and Function of Repentance in Luke-Acts	145
Repentance in the Preaching of John the Baptist	146
Repentance in the Preaching of Jesus	159
Repentance in the Preaching of the Disciples	191
Summary	220
Appendix	225
Selected Bibliography	227

Acknowledgments

Pursuing and completing a graduate degree like the one this dissertation finalizes, requires an invaluable amount of support and assistance. While it is impossible for me to formally acknowledge everyone who helped bring this dissertation to fruition, there are those who deserve formal recognition. First and foremost, I must acknowledge God, not only for the strength to persevere but for the grace that allowed me to do so.

No one individual has sacrificed more in order to support my academic pursuits than my friend and wife, Darla Payne Nave. Her enduring love and support throughout this endeavor has and continues to play an instrumental role in my life. My desire to spend more time with her and my newborn daughter, Cydney Hope Nave, motivated me to work even harder to complete this dissertation.

I am extremely grateful for the financial support of the Fund for Theological Education (FTE), Yale University, and A Fund for Theological Education (AFTE). This dissertation marks the initial return on their investment. Their investment in my life as a scholar, teacher, and minister has and will continue to enable me to invest in the lives of countless others, and for that I say, "Thank you!"

It is common knowledge that the rewards of teaching are in no way monetary. There are certain teachers who can never be paid enough for the contributions they have made to my own intellectual development. As my advisor, Professor Wayne Meeks has not only provided guidance and direction for this dissertation, but his own scholarship has raised for me the bar of excellence after which I strive. The scholarship and friendship of Yale Professors Bentley Layton, Leander Keck, and David Bartlett have also proven both invaluable and rewarding.

Others along the way who have contributed to my development include my Princeton Theological Seminary mentors and friends, the late J. Christiaan Beker, Peter Paris and Geddes Hanson, as well as Cornel West, who during my Seminary years was Professor of Religion at Princeton University. I also wish to acknowledge my undergraduate English teacher Mrs. Ruth Givens, my high school home room teacher Mrs. Shoemaker, my middle school English teacher Mrs. Sweeney and elementary school teachers, Mrs. Lackey and Mrs. Ford.

Working on a Ph.D. can often be a lonely endeavor; therefore, I acknowledge the personal friendships of my colleagues, Jamie Clark-Soles, Warren Smith, Steven Davis, and Regina Plunkett-Dowling. I also acknowledge the friendship of the department registrar, Roz Ferguson, who always "had my back" and encouraged me to hang in there when I felt like giving up. I acknowledge my brothers and sisters from Bethel A.M.E. Church in New Haven, CT, North Stelton A.M.E. Church in Piscataway, NJ and Allen Chapel A.M.E. Church in Anderson, IN for the unwavering love and support shown to both me and my family. I acknowledge the friendships of Priscilla and Dave Mac Innis, Nancy Lyall, Nan Cook, and all those involved with the Madison A Better Chance Program in Madison, CT. I acknowledge my parents, Judith Pearson Nave and Guy D. Nave, Sr for their unconditional love. They have traveled all over the country to attend **EVERY** graduation, including this most recent one. This dissertation is the fruit of their love and support.

I have to acknowledge Clint Davis, without whom I would not have been able to submit this dissertation in time for my December 2000 graduation. Clint helped me put my dissertation back together after a computer systems failure destroyed all but nine pages from both my hard drive and my floppy disk one week before the dissertation was due. I would still be sitting at my desk in tears today without his help.

I wish to acknowledge my friends and colleagues at Luther College for the support they have shown me as a new faculty member in the Religion and Philosophy Department. Accepting a teaching position at a liberal arts college in Decorah, IA required some major "change in thinking" (i.e. repentance) on the part of both my wife and I. Having been at Luther now for four months, we are convinced we made the right decision.

Lastly, I wish to thank my new friends at the Society of Biblical Literature for accepting my manuscript for publication in the SBL Dissertation Series. I greatly appreciate the help and support of both Mark Allan Powell, New Testament Dissertation Series Editor, and Leigh C. Andersen, SBL Managing Editor. I also wish to acknowledge Gene Lovering for taking the time to help me prepare the camera-ready version of this manuscript.

Chapter One

History of Research regarding New Testament Repentance

The Problem

The fundamental problem with much of the research that claims to examine repentance within the New Testament is that most of it attempts to arrive at **THE** New Testament meaning of repentance. There is very little research that examines how specific New Testament authors utilize and incorporate the notion of repentance within their own individual writings. Many—if not most—New Testament scholars make the mistake of assuming that there is one comprehensive definition of repentance that governs how the notion of repentance is used and understood throughout the New Testament.[1] However, treating repentance as a New Testament theme that can be examined longitudinally ignores the diversity among the various New Testament writings. Such a thematic approach seeks an overarching unity within the New Testament, while violating the individuality of the various Christian writers and communities present during the formative years of Christianity. The results of redaction criticism have clearly demonstrated that the New Testament canonizes a far-reaching diversity.

---

[1] A. H. Dirksen, *The New Testament Concept of Metanoia* (Washington: The Catholic University of America, 1932); H. Pohlmann, *Die Metanoia als Zentralbegriff der christlichen Frömmigkeit* (Leipzig: J. C. Hinrichs, 1938); W. D. Chamberlain, *The Meaning of Repentance* (Philadelphia: Westminster Press, 1943); C. E. Carlston, *Metanoia and Church Discipline in the New Testament* (Ph.D. Dissertation, Harvard University, 1958); R. Wilkes, *Repentance as a Condition for Salvation in the New Testament* (Ph.D. Dissertation, Dallas Theological Seminary, 1985).

Furthermore many scholars, especially New Testament scholars, have made the mistake of assuming that the early Christian conception of repentance is so special that there is nothing like it in pre-Christian Greek usage. These scholars boldly—but erroneously— assert that there is little or no affinity between the usage of μετανοέω and μετάνοια in non-Christian Greek literature and its usage in Christian literature.[2]

Repentance within the New Testament

Over half a century ago William Chamberlain wrote:

> This formula, "Repent ye; for the kingdom of heaven is at hand," is not only a trumpet blast, but also the keynote of the New Testament message. Not only does it break the stillness of the Judean wilderness, but its reverberations are heard throughout the New Testament, reaching their climax in the thunders of the Apocalypse.
>
> If these words do constitute the keynote, we must understand them before we understand the New Testament.[3]

Chamberlain's words echo the sentiments of several scholars who preceded him,[4] and reflect the sentiments of several more who have followed him.[5] These scholars approach the motif of repentance as if it is the leitmotif of the New Testament.[6] Chamberlain's assertion implies that in order to understand the New Testament, readers must first understand the significance of the demand for repentance.[7] For Chamberlain, understanding the demand for repentance serves as the key for unlocking the meaning of the entire New Testament. Thorough examination of the New Testament, however, reveals not only how infrequently the demand for repentance occurs within the New Testament, but also how infrequently the words "repent" and "repentance" occur within English translations of the New Testament.

---

[2] This position will be examined and refuted in Chapter Three of this study.
[3] *The Meaning of Repentance*, 17.
[4] A. H. Dirksen, *The New Testament Concept of Metanoia*; Hans Pohlmann, *Die Metanoia als Zentralbegrif der christlichen Frömmigkeit*; Otto Michel, "Die Umkehr nach der Verkündigung Jesu," *EvT* 5 (1938) 403–413; Behm and Würthwein, "μετανοέω, μετάνοια," *TDNT*, 4.975–1008.
[5] E. Roche, "Pénitence et Conversion dans l'evangile et la vie Chrétienne," *NRT* 79 (1957) 113–134; C. E. Carlston, *Metanoia and Church Discipline*; Robert Koch, "Die religiöse-sittliche Umkehr nach den drei ältesten Evangelien und der Apostelgeschichte," *Anima* 14 (1959) 296–307; Jürgen Goetzmann, "μετάνοια," *NIDNTT*, 1.357–359.
[6] For a review of the modern literature on repentance, see Jon N. Bailey, *Repentance in Luke-Acts* (Ph.D. Dissertation, University of Notre Dame, 1993) 6–22.
[7] See Rudolf Schnackenburg, "The Demand for Repentance," *The Moral Teaching of the New Testament* (Trans. J. H. Smith and J. W. J. O'Hara; New York: Herder and Herder, 1962) 25–33.

Outside of Luke-Acts and the Book of Revelation, the Greek verb μετανοέω, which is commonly translated "to repent," occurs only eight times in the entire New Testament. Seven of those occurrences are found in Matthew and Mark.[8] Similarly, outside of Luke-Acts the noun μετάνοια, which is commonly translated "repentance," occurs only 11 times in the entire New Testament. Both μετανοέω and μετάνοια occur a combined total of four times in the entire Pauline corpus.[9] The demand for repentance is clearly a far cry from being "the keynote of the New Testament message." It is, however, a keynote of the message in Luke-Acts.

Repentance within Luke-Acts

The principal Greek words for "repent" and "repentance" occur 25 times in Luke-Acts. That is more than 45 percent of all the occurrences in the entire New Testament.[10] Only Luke presents John the Baptist defining what the "fruits worthy of repentance" look like. Only Luke tells stories of Jesus calling on people to repent. Only Luke depicts Jesus persuading the wicked to repent and pay back their ill-gotten gains. Only Luke-Acts gives explicit accounts of people responding to the calls for repentance issued by John the Baptist, Jesus and the apostles. Only Acts portrays Peter echoing John the Baptist by urging the people to "Repent and be baptized. . . so that your sins may be forgiven" (Acts 2:38). It is Acts, rather than the Pauline epistles, that records Paul declaring (on two occasions) that his ministry included proclaiming a message of repentance. Repentance is without question a fundamental aspect of Luke-Acts.

Although repentance clearly has a prominence in Luke-Acts that it does not have in the rest of the New Testament, it was not until recently that anyone ever attempted an examination of the role and function of repentance in Luke-Acts.[11] During the 1960's Jacques Dupont made the first contribution to a study of repentance in the Lukan writings with the publication of two articles on the subject of repentance and conversion in the Book of Acts.[12] While making important contributions toward understanding the broader concept of conversion in the book of Acts, Dupont never explicitly defines the notion of repentance, and he frequently uses "conversion" and "repentance" interchangeably. Furthermore, Dupont's focus

---

[8] Most of the occurrences in Matthew and Mark are found merely in summary statements about the preaching of Jesus, John the Baptist, or the twelve disciples. The words play a minimal role in the message and purpose of these two gospels.

[9] Romans 2:4; 2 Corinthians 7:9, 10; 12:21.

[10] Another 22 percent of the occurrences are found in Revelation, leaving less than 33 percent of the occurrences in the rest of the New Testament. The Book of Revelation is the only other New Testament writing in which the concept of repentance plays a significant role. (Cf. Appendix, Table 3).

[11] John Bailey's dissertation, *Repentance in Luke Acts*, is the first work dedicated to an examination of repentance in Luke-Acts.

[12] J. Dupont, "Repentir et conversion d'après les Actes des Apôtres," *ScEccl* 12 (1960) 137–173; "La conversion dans les Actes des Apôtres," *Lumière et Vie* 9 (1960) 48–70.

is solely on the book of Acts; therefore, there is no discussion of repentance within Luke. Four years later R. Michiels published an article devoted to the Lukan concept of conversion.[13] Like Dupont, however, Michiels also devotes much space to the concept of conversion without ever clearly defining conversion and without ever making a clear distinction between repentance and conversion. Both of these scholars subsume the concept of repentance within the concept of conversion. Such a practice, however, complicates all endeavors to arrive at an understanding of repentance in Luke-Acts. Dupont and Michiels work with a preconceived definition of conversion that obscures the nuances of the Lukan use of repentance.

The most recent attempt at examining the concept of repentance in the Lukan writings is the 1993 dissertation by Jon Nelson Bailey.[14] Bailey asserts that the purpose of his work is "to explain the significance of repentance in Luke-Acts."[15] He goes on to say that he seeks to provide an understanding of "the origin, development, and function of repentance for Luke."[16] Unfortunately, however, Bailey's work is little more than a word study of μετανοέω/μετάνοια (with some attention also given to ἐπιστρέφω). Bailey's philological emphasis leads to a very narrow understanding of repentance. An exploration of the Lukan understanding of repentance involves not only a study of particular words but also an examination of the varying imagery for repentance, as well as an examination of the communicative context reflected within the author's narrative design. Bailey's work fails to demonstrate how the concept of repentance functions within the narrative design and the narrative world of Luke-Acts. Bailey fails to examine repentance as a concept understood through and within the progressive development of the author's narrative. Bailey's work also fails to show how repentance is related to the overall purpose of the author's two volume work, and how it meshes with other Lukan themes. Finally, while Bailey states that he will suggest "ways in which repentance defined the social identity of the Lucan community,"[17] Bailey's work fails to adequately consider what the social reality may have been that gave rise to the notion of "repentance" as depicted by the author in the narrative world of Luke-Acts.

By far Bailey has made the most significant contributions to understanding the notion of repentance in Luke-Acts; however, Bailey's inattention to the relationship between repentance and the narrative design of Luke-Acts is a major weakness of his work. Bailey's isolated examination of selected passages in Luke-Acts where the theme of repentance occurs fails to provide an understanding of repentance shaped by the progressively developing communicative context of Luke-Acts. As with most motifs within well crafted narratives, the meaning and purpose of repentance is

---

[13] R. Michiels, "La conception lucanienne de la conversion," *ETL* 41 (1965) 42–78.
[14] *Repentance in Luke-Acts*.
[15] Ibid., 4.
[16] Ibid., 26.
[17] Ibid., 2.

revealed through progressive development.[18] What is needed, therefore, is a narrative-critical examination of repentance in Luke-Acts.

Repentance and New Testament Theology

In addition to the problem of looking for a comprehensive definition of repentance throughout the New Testament, most scholarly treatments of repentance also limit their focus exclusively to the role of repentance within New Testament theology. In general, scholars have been concerned with developing a systematic theology of repentance. Of the few scholarly examinations of repentance in Luke-Acts, Bailey's being the most extensive, virtually every study has been concerned primarily with the contributions being made to New Testament theology, or at least with uncovering the theology reflected in the author's use of repentance.[19] Even Bailey asserts that "The primary argument of this dissertation is that Luke's understanding of repentance is unique in its religio-historical context and significant in its contribution to his theology."[20] He goes on to assert that "There is a need to examine the theme of repentance as a distinctively Lucan theological motif."[21] The author of Luke-Acts, however, is not writing a theological treatise. The author has written a narrative (i.e. a story), and repentance must be examined and understood within the context of the author's narrative.

The Solution

In an attempt to correct the problems and address the weaknesses found in much of the research that claims to examine repentance within the New Testament, this work will focus on examining how the author of Luke-Acts utilizes and incorporates the notion of repentance within his two-volume narrative. This work will also examine the various usages of μετανοέω and μετάνοια within the time and culture relevant to Luke-Acts, as well as historical usages—especially pre-Christian Greek usages—of the terms that might have influenced Luke-Acts, in order to determine how the terms might have been heard by the author's audience.

---

[18] Cf. R. L. Brawley, "Progressive Discovery: Truth in the Narrative World," *Centering on God: Method and Message in Luke-Acts* (Louisville, KY: Westminster/John Knox, 1990) 34–57.

[19] Cf. R. Michiels, "La conception lucanienne de la conversion," 42–78; Francis Hezel, "'Conversion and 'Repentance' in Lucan Theology," *The Bible Today* 37 (1968) 2596–2602; François Bovon, *Luke the Theologian. Thirty-Three Years of Research (1950–1983)* (tran. K. McKinney; Allison Park, PA: Pickwick, 1987) 271–289; I. Howard Marshall, *Luke: Historian and Theologian* (Grand Rapids, MI: Zondervan, 1971) 192–196; J. A. Fitzmyer, *The Gospel According to Luke* (Anchor Bible 2 vols; Garden City, NY: Doubleday, 1981–1985) 1:237; Robert F. O'Toole, *The Unity of Luke's Theology: An Analysis of Luke-Acts* (Wilmington, DE: Glazier, 1984) 118.

[20] *Repentance*, 5.

[21] Ibid., 26.

In my analysis of the Lukan narrative, I will utilize a literary-critical methodology, employing predominantly narrative and redaction criticism. I will also subject this literary-critical methodology to sociological analysis, in an attempt to arrive at a descriptive sociological interpretation of the narrative world of Luke-Acts. I will examine the narrative structure and plot development of Luke-Acts for clues revealing not only the role and significance of repentance within the author's two-volume work but also the religious, social, political, and economic realities reflected in the author's narrative world. I will then examine how the concept of repentance interacts with these realities. As a result of my efforts, I will highlight the dialectical relationship between the social reality reflected in the author's narrative world and the author's use of the concept of repentance.[22]

An examination of the narrative structure of Luke-Acts will reveal that the author has not only significantly shaped the gospel traditions at his disposal but also the prevailing concepts of repentance at that time—most likely in response to the social pressures experienced by his own community. Specific social, moral, ethical, financial, and religious inequities are challenged in Luke-Acts, and repentance is presented as the method of correcting them. In Luke-Acts repentance is not merely a theological principle; repentance addresses and seeks to correct communal inequities. Any examination of repentance in Luke-Acts that focuses primarily on drawing theological conclusions while overlooking the relationship between repentance and the specific inequities reflected in the narrative world of Luke-Acts fails to recognize the impact of the narrative structure on the meaning of repentance, as well as the impact of repentance on the narrative structure. Repentance addresses and confronts the inequities promoted by the symbolic universe that has shaped the way the author's audience thinks and lives. The use of repentance in Luke-Acts grows out of a specific context that must be understood, and that is depicted in the narrative structure of Luke-Acts. It is impossible to fully understand the role and function of repentance in Luke-Acts without recognizing the relationship between repentance and the social, moral, ethical, financial, and religious inequites depicted in the narrative structure of Luke-Acts. That is why this study will use a literary rather than a theological approach to understanding repentance in Luke-Acts: examining how the theme of repentance functions in both the narrative structure of Luke-Acts and in the social reality of the narrative world created by Luke-Acts.

Finally, this work will show how repentance serves as the means for establishing and resocializing the Christian community identified in the Lukan narrative and for transforming traditional world views that often prohibit diverse individuals from living together as a community of God's people. In Luke-Acts, individuals are transformed and Christian communities are established as a result of repentance.

---

[22] Peter Berger was instrumental in drawing attention to the dialectical relationship between religion and society in his classis work, *The Sacred Canopy: The Social Reality of Religion* (London: Farber, 1969).

Chapter Two

Repentance within the Narrative Structure of Luke-Acts

In addition to being the longest narrative in the New Testament, Luke-Acts is without question one of the most skillfully and rhetorically crafted pieces of narrative literature in the New Testament. This chapter will briefly examine the issue of intentionality within the narrative structure of literature in general and within the narrative structure of Luke-Acts in particular. The ultimate purpose will be to examine the role of repentance within the narrative structure of Luke-Acts.

Authorial Intention

The author of Luke-Acts is without doubt a storyteller.[1] He explicitly identifies his work with the accounts (or narratives; διήγησις) of his predecessors. Since others had given accounts concerning the things that had been accomplished, it seemed like a good idea to the author for him to do likewise. The author reveals that he is a very deliberate and purposeful storyteller, who stresses the accurate and orderly telling of events in his narrative (Luke 1:1–3). According to Seymour Chatman,[2] the events of a narrative help comprise what Chatman identifies as the

---

[1] Cf. Robert Karris, *Luke: Artist and Theologian. Luke's Passion Account as Literature* (New York: Paulist, 1985); Robert Tannehill, *The Narrative Unity of Luke-Acts. A Literary Interpretation* (2 vols; Philadelphia: Fortress, 1986–1990).

[2] Chatman's *Story and Discourse: Narrative Structure in Fiction and Film* (Ithaca, NY: Cornell University Press, 1978) has without question had the greatest impact on

"what" of a narrative. The *what* of a narrative is comprised of the events and the characters of that narrative. The what of the narrative, Chatman calls its "story."[3] The story is simply the substance or content that is depicted in the narrative. After identifying the *what*, Chatman further identifies the "way" of a narrative. The *way* of a narrative, Chatman calls its "discourse."[4] The discourse is nothing more than the *way* in which the *what* of a narrative is expressed. In other words, the discourse is how the story is told.

What Chatman does not identify, however, is the **why** of a narrative. Chatman outlines steps, methods and procedures for unpacking and better understanding the *what* and the *way* of a narrative, but he offers no suggestions for identifying, unpacking or understanding the **why** of a narrative. For Chatman, the *what* and the *way* are the only necessary components of a narrative. Chatman writes, "Taking poetics as a rationalistic discipline, we may ask, as does the linguist about language: What are the necessary components—and only those—of a narrative? Structuralist theory argues that each narrative has two parts: a story. . . and a discourse."[5] Since Chatman is "less concerned with interpreting individual narratives than with developing general theories. . . which would make explicit the system of narrative (its constituent parts, techniques, conventions, etc.) that enables individual narratives to function intelligibly,"[6] he gives no clues for uncovering and understanding the *why* of a narrative. The *why* represents the intention of a narrative; it contributes to interpreting and understanding individual narratives. The *why* reveals the author's reason(s) for writing his or her narrative. The *why*, therefore, is not only a necessary component that enables narratives to function intelligibly, it is also a necessary component that gives meaning to individual narratives.[7]

---

narrative criticism (Cf. Mark A. Powell, *What is Narrative Criticism* (Minneapolis, MN: Fortress Press, 1990) 23–34; Stephen Moore, *Literary Criticism and the Gospels: The Theoretical Challenge* (New Haven, CT: Yale University Press, 1989) 43 ff).

[3] *Story and Discourse*, 15–145.
[4] Ibid. 146–262.
[5] Ibid. 19.
[6] Stephen Moore, *Literary Criticism*, 43.
[7] As a narratologist rather than a narrative critic, Chatman is not concerned about the meaning of texts (for a brief discussion of the differences between narratology and narrative criticism see Moore, *Literary Criticism*, 51–55). Unfortunately, Rhoads and Michie—who are considered by most scholars as narrative critics rather than narratologists—also focus exclusively on the "what" and "how" of narrative in their critical analysis of Mark (David Rhoads and Donald Michie, *Mark as Story: An Introduction to the Narrative of a Gospel* (Philadelphia: Fortress Press, 1982)). They write, "The story refers to 'what' a narrative is about—the basic elements of the narrative world—events, characters, and settings. Rhetoric refers to 'how' that story is told in a given narrative in order to achieve certain effects upon the reader. Thus we can distinguish between 'what' the story is about and 'how' the story is told" (p. 4). However, as scholars seeking to explicate texts, narrative critics should also be concerned with revealing "why" the story is told, because why the story is told greatly impacts the meaning of the story.

The *what* of a narrative (i.e. the events and characters) can very easily be identified. Similarly, with a little more effort, one can easily identify the *way* in which a narrative is expressed. However, unless an author explicitly states his or her reason(s) for writing a narrative, discovering the *why* of a narrative can be much more complicated. Nevertheless, discovering the *why* is extremely important, because failing to recognize the *why* of a narrative can often contribute to a reader missing the point or intended meaning of that narrative.

The notion of authorial intention began to be challenged in the 1920s with the rise of New Criticism.[8] Prior to New Criticism, English and Classical literature had been taught in universities with a strongly historical and philological emphasis.[9] New Criticism, however, insisted on the autonomy of literature. It insisted that meaning is conveyed by the literary work itself. New Critics asserted that literature must be allowed to speak on its own terms.

New Criticism was the dominant mode of literary criticism in America from the late 1930s through the 1950s.[10] In 1954 two New Critics fired the proverbial 'shot heard around the (literary) world' with the publication of an essay entitled "The Intentional Fallacy."[11] In the essay, W. K. Wimsatt and Monroe Beardsley asserted that the notion of going behind the text and using the intention of the author as a criterion of meaning rested on a fallacy. For the New Critics, meaning was inherent within the narrative itself and in no way dependent upon the intentions of the author. According to New Critics, the author's intention is "irrelevant to literary critics, because meaning and value reside within the text of the finished, free-standing, and public work of literature itself."[12]

Although it is true that the narrative itself may possess or engender meaning beyond and in addition to what the author may have intended,[13] discovering the intentions of an author is without a doubt one of the most powerful interpretive tools for understanding the meaning of individual narratives (at least biblical narratives).[14] In their pioneering narrative-critical analysis of Mark's gospel, Rhoads

---

[8] Originating with I. A. Richards and T. S. Eliot (See Robert Morgan and John Barton, *Biblical Interpretation* (New York: Oxford University Press, 1988) 217).

[9] Morgan, *Biblical Interpretation*, 217.

[10] See Lynn Poland, *Literary Criticism and Biblical Hermeneutics: A Critique of Formalist Approaches* (Chico, CA: Scholar's Press, 1985) 65–105; René Wellek and Warren Austin, *Theory of Literature* (3d ed.; San Diego: Harcourt Brace, Jovanovich, 1975).

[11] William Wimsatt and Monroe Beardsley, "The Intentional Fallacy," *The Verbal Icon: Studies in the Meaning of Poetry* (New York: Noonday, 1954).

[12] Meyer Howard Abrams, *A Glossary of Literary Terms* (4th ed.; New York: Holt, Rhinehart and Winston, 1981) 83.

[13] See E. D. Hirsch, Jr. *The Aims of Interpretation* (Chicago: University of Chicago Press, 1976) 74–92; Anthony Thiselton, *New Horizons in Hermeneutics* (Grand Rapids, MI: Zondervan, 1992) 471–550.

[14] Stephen Moore, in his discussion of narrative criticism asserts that, "Narrative criticism. . . tends to hold strongly (if implicitly) to the view that the gospel text has a primary, recoverable meaning: what its author intended. This is its unbroken link with traditional biblical criticism." (*Literary Criticism*, 12). It is of course this notion of authorial

and Michie write, "the [Markan] writer has told the story in such a way as to have certain effects on the reader.... The author... developed the characters and the conflicts, and built suspense with deliberateness, telling the story in such a way as to generate certain emotions and insights in the reader."[15] Narratives are designed to create certain expectations, evoke certain responses, and produce specifiable effects within the reader. These expectations, responses, and effects originate in an author's intentions. Although Rhoads and Michie implicitly stress the intentions of the author within the Markan narrative, it is important to recognize the marked affinities between the conceptions of the text in *Mark as Story* and those of New Criticism.[16] In their analysis of Mark, Rhoads and Michie imply that the author's intention is accessible only through the text itself.[17] It is difficult, if not impossible, to go outside of the text (or as Wimsatt and Beardsley asserted, "behind the text") in order to determine the author's state of mind, or to discover some private unexpressed intention of the author. The author's intention is revealed within the text. This is why Robert Tannehill, who contributed a similar narrative-critical analysis of Luke-Acts speaks of the "implied author" rather than the actual author.[18] The actual author is the person external to the work, while the implied author is reconstructed by the reader from the narrative.[19] The implied author's point of view can be determined without considering anything extrinsic to the narrative. The (implied or actual) author's intention can only be discovered in and through the "story line," for it is found only there.[20] While New Criticism's absolute disregard

---

intention, prevalent within biblical criticism, that most literary critics have been uncomfortable with for over half a century (cf. David De-Newton Molina, *On Literary Intention* (Edinburgh: Edinburgh University Press, 1976); Timothy J. Bagwell, *American Formalism and the Problem of Interpretation* (Houston: Rice University Press, 1981); Derrida, *Margins of Philosophy* (trans. Alan Bass; Chicago: University of Chicago Press, 1982) 307–30).

[15] *Mark as Story*, 1.

[16] The *implicit* stressing of the author's intention by Rhoads and Michie is somewhat confusing in light of the fact that in an article published that same year Rhoads included the approach to Mark "as a story which reveals the author's intention" in his list of extrinsic approaches, which, according to Rhoads, it is narrative criticism's business to bracket ("Narrative Criticism," 413).

[17] Ricoeur suggests that a text unfolds a world, and that world—not the author's intention—is the reference of the literary work (Ricoeur, "Toward a Hermeneutic of the Idea of Revelation," *Harvard Theological Review* 70 (1977) 1–37). Although I agree that the literary world provides the reference for understanding a text, ultimately the author is the one responsible for creating that literary world. Therefore, that literary world possess the keys for understanding the author's intentions, even if those intentions are not explicitly identified by the reader. A well written narrative should guide the reader through the narrative world created by the author without the reader consciously recognizing that he or she is being guided, or that this world has been created by the author. The reader is not supposed to be able to consciously identify the author's intention; the reader is supposed to **experience** the narrative, unlike the critic whose job it is to **analyze** the narrative.

[18] Robert Tannehill, *Narrative Unity*, 1:6–9.

[19] Wayne Booth, *The Rhetoric of Fiction* (2d ed.; Chicago: University of Chicago Press, 1983) 66–77.

[20] N. Frye, *Anatomy of Criticism* (Princeton, NJ: Princeton University Press, 1957).

for authorial intention has been abandoned by most literary critics, a lasting contribution of New Criticism has been the emphases on literary autonomy and close readings of individual narratives.

Nothing is more important for understanding the "why" of a narrative than a close reading of that narrative. Often readers—especially critical readers—of a narrative will turn to the social, political, cultural, religious, *et. al.* historical factors of the author's milieu in order to determine the *why* of a narrative. However, it is the narrative itself that produces expectations, responses and effects within the reader; therefore, it is the narrative itself that reveals the *why* of the narrative. While recognizing the social, political, cultural, religious, *et. al.* historical factors of the author's milieu often proves helpful in understanding the meaning of a narrative, ultimately the reader must learn to mine the narrative itself for reliable indicators of the *why*. It is also important for a reader to realize that there may be a number of reasons why an author writes a narrative. The discovery of one *why* does not prohibit there being other reasons why an author may have written a narrative. A narrative may have a multiplicity of meanings because there may be numerous reasons why the author has written the narrative.[21]

Authorial Intention of Luke-Acts: The Plan of God

In our efforts to understand the role and function of repentance within Luke-Acts, it will first be necessary to recognize the *why* of Luke-Acts, and then examine the relationship that exists between repentance and the why of Luke-Acts. Through the voice of the narrator, the implied author of Luke-Acts divulges his purpose for writing this two volume collection.[22] The narrator informs the implied reader that this narrative has been written as an accurate (ἀκριβῶς) and orderly (καθεξῆς) account of the things having been accomplished, in order that the reader might have assurance concerning those things of which he has been informed (Luke 1:1–4).[23]

---

[21] There may of course be meanings present within a narrative that were unintended by the author. Such meanings, however, should be recognized as secondary meanings rather than as the primary meaning of the narrative.

[22] Although James Dawsey, *The Lukan Voice. Confusion and Irony in the Gospel of Luke* (Macon, GA: Mercer, 1987), has proposed an interpretation of the Lukan narrator as unreliable, there are no indicators in Luke-Acts that the Lukan narrator is an unreliable narrator (See Tannehill, *Narrative Unity*, 1:7 for a critique of Dawsey's claim). Therefore, like Tannehill, "I will use the terms narrator and implied author without implying a major distinction between them" (*Narrative Unity*, v.1 p.7).

[23] The importance to this author of accuracy and orderliness in the conveying and understanding of information, as well as in the occurrence of events, is clearly seen in the author's use of ἀκριβῶς and καθεξῆς. Of the nine occurrences of ἀκριβῶς in the New Testament, six occur in Luke-Acts (Luke 1:3; Acts 18:25, 26; 23:15, 20; 24:22). Furthermore, every occurrence of καθεξῆς in the New Testament occurs in Luke-Acts (Luke 1:3; 8:1; Acts 3:24; 11:4; 18:23). See also the author's use of ἀκρίβεια (Acts 22:3) and ἀκριβής (Acts 26:5).

Although the accuracy and orderliness of the author's[24] account may provide the reader with a degree of assurance, it is the message conveyed through the author's accurate and orderly account that is meant to provide the reader with this so-called assurance.[25] The message that is conveyed through the author's accurate and orderly account is that there is a divine plan or purpose at work within history, particularly the redemptive history of humanity.

The author attempts to provide the reader with assurance concerning those things of which he has been informed by demonstrating to the reader how everything that has been accomplished is in accordance with God's divine plan and purpose. In discussing the purpose of Luke-Acts, Henry J. Cadbury states that "One of the features of Luke's whole work that might be conscious **intention**... is the evidence of divine guidance and control that pervades it."[26] It is the author's intention to demonstrate to the reader how there has been and continues to be a divine plan at work within history.[27] The author seeks to convince the implied reader of this divine plan at work, in order to persuade the implied reader that he can be assured of the appropriateness of everything that has been accomplished.[28] For the author, providing assurance (ἀσφάλεια; Luke 1:4) to the implied reader is crucial.[29] The author seeks to assure the reader that those things about which he

---

[24] Unless otherwise indicated, my use of the word "author" when referring to Luke-Acts will always represent the implied author.

[25] Because of the author's emphasis on the message conveyed through his narrative, the author's concern with accuracy and orderliness most likely does not refer to accurate chronological order, but rather "a literary order" that seeks to convey a message and create a narrative representation of reality (cf. Tannehill, *Luke* (Nashville, Abingdon, 1996) 35). This is supported by the fact that the term καθεξῆς in Luke 1:3 has a close parallel in Acts 11:4 where it likewise refers to the technique of narration. Acts 10 clearly indicates that Peter's narration of events in Acts 11 is neither chronological nor complete. "Rather, Peter creates a narrative world in which he invites his detractors to participate. When they do, they adopt a new construct of world and agree with Peter" (Brawley, *Centering*, 39; cf. M. Vökel, "Exegetische Erwägungen zum Verständnis des Begriffs κατεξῆς im lukanischen Prolog." *New Testament Studies* 20 (1973–74) 293–95).

[26] H. J. Cadbury, *The Making of Luke-Acts* (2d ed. London: SPCK, 1958) 303 [emphasis added].

[27] This idea of a divine plan at work represents what narrative critics call the evaluative point of view. The evaluative point of view refers to the "general worldview that the implied author establishes as operative for the story" (Powell, *Narrative Criticism*, 23–26). For detailed discussion concerning the notion of *point of view* see Moore, *Literary Criticism*, 25–40; Booth, *The Rhetoric of Fiction*; and Gérard Genette, *Narrative Discourse: An Essay in Method* (trans. J. Lewin; Ithaca, NY: Cornell University Press, 1980) chs. 4, 5.

[28] John Squires, *The Plan of God in Luke-Acts* (Cambridge: Cambridge University Press, 1993) 21 demonstrates how providing such assurance was a common objective in the Hellenistic histories of antiquity.

[29] The emphatic position of ἀσφάλειαν in the phrase ἵνα ἐπιγνῷς... τὴν ἀσφάλειαν is noted by both R. J. Maddox, *The Purpose of Luke-Acts* (Edinburgh: Clark, 1982) 22 and Fitzmyer, *The Gospel*, 1:289. W. C. van Unnik asserts that providing assurance to the implied reader is the author's purpose for writing ("Remarks on the Purpose of Luke's Historical Writing," *Sparsa Collecta. The Collected Essays of W. C. van Unnik*, I (Leiden: E. J. Brill, 1973) 8–14).

has been informed have happened according to God's plan, even as Peter sought to assure (ἀσφαλῶς) the "house of Israel" that what had happened among them was according to God's plan (Acts 2:36).³⁰ The author, through his narrative, seeks to reveal God's plan, even as Paul through his apostolic preaching revealed God's plan. In Acts 20:27, Paul tells the Ephesian elders that through his preaching he has declared to them "the entire plan of God."³¹

According to Robert C. Tannehill, "The author of Luke-Acts consciously understands the story as unified by the controlling purpose of God and wants readers to understand it in the same way."³² This idea of a divine plan at work is expressed by the author in two ways: a) explicitly through specific Lukan terminology, and b) implicitly through literary devices employed by the author.

Lukan Terminology Employed to Express a Divine Plan

In his examination of the literary standard of Luke's vocabulary,³³ Henry J. Cadbury wrote, "Probably half of every writer's vocabulary is made up of words of such frequent occurrence that any other writer is likely to use them. It is only the unusual or uncommon words that can be expected to have much significance."³⁴ Cadbury cautions, however, against searching for such words among New Testament writers "in the list of words peculiar to each writer, i.e., not found elsewhere in the New Testament." Cadbury's reason for this is: "In a collection like the New Testament the occurrence of a word in only one writer is often merely an accident, and the words so distinguished are not characteristic of him."³⁵ Despite the various dangers that Cadbury addresses with regard to the study of Luke's vocabulary, Cadbury does assert that an examination can be safely made, "if the

---

³⁰ The ἀσφάλ- word group occurs 15 times in the New Testament, with eight of those occurrences in Luke-Acts. In Luke-Acts the word group frequently designates in the literal sense the certainty or stability of a thing (cf. Acts 21:34; 22:30; 25:26). The author emphasizes for the reader the certainty and reliability of what has occurred and has been declared. The Lukan construction, λόγων τὴν ἀσφάλειαν (Luke 1:4) is similar in form and meaning to the construction found in Xenophon *Mem.* iv. 6,15: ἀσφάλεια λόγου. ἀσφάλεια is also used as a juridical t.t. for "certainty" in Epictetus *Diss.* ii. 13,7. The prevalence of the word group in Luke-Acts emphasizes the author's concern with creating a sense of assurance for the reader. Even God gives "assurance" (although the author uses πίστις rather than ἀσφάλεια) of God's divine plan by raising Jesus from the dead (Acts 17:31b).
³¹ According to Tannehill, one way of emphasizing a divine plan at work is through the use of statements by reliable characters. This will be discussed in more detail below when I examine Tannehill's presentation of the literary devices employed by the author to emphasize the presence of a divine plan.
³² *The Narrative Unity of Luke-Acts*; 2.
³³ Without prejudice concerning actual authorship, I shall refer to the author of Luke-Acts as "Luke."
³⁴ Cadbury, *The Style and Literary Method of Luke* (2 vols; Cambridge, MA: Harvard University Press, 1919–20) 1:6.
³⁵ Ibid.

method of procedure is selected with some care, and if the results are not treated too mathematically or made to prove too much."³⁶ The following examination of Luke's vocabulary is not intended to examine or make conclusions about the literary standing of Luke. The objective is to demonstrate how the Lukan emphasis on a divine plan is supported by a wide array of terms and or phrases employed by the author in order to express the idea of a divine plan at work in his narrative. Luke's use of such terms and phrases is not the result of Luke's dependence on synoptic sources, but rather the result of Luke's own deliberate literary composition.

In his monograph, Squires asserts that "The plan of God is a distinctively Lukan theme which undergirds the whole of Luke-Acts."³⁷ No New Testament writer other than the author of Luke-Acts makes explicit references to the "plan of God" (ἡ βουλὴ τοῦ Θεοῦ).³⁸ In his gospel, the author explicitly identifies two plans at work: there's the "plan of God," which the religious leaders rejected (Luke 7:30), and there's the "plan" of most of the religious leaders and the religious council (βουλευτής), which one of its own members—Joseph of Arimathea—did not consent to because he was looking for the kingdom of God (Luke 23:50–51).³⁹ In Acts, there is another member of the religious council who also refuses to consent to the desire (βούλομαι) of the council, and who warns the council of the dangers of opposing the "plan" (βουλή) of God (Acts 5:33–39). Ultimately it is the plan of God that defeats the plan of the religious leaders as well as every other plan.⁴⁰

In the first reported sermon of both Peter (which is the first recorded sermon in Acts) and Paul, the "plan of God" is a central motif.⁴¹ Furthermore, of the 37 times that βούλομαι is used in the New Testament, 16 of those occurrences are

---

³⁶ Ibid., 8.
³⁷ *The Plan of God*, 1. Squires convincingly demonstrates the programmatic role of providence in Luke-Acts in particular and in Hellenistic historiography in general. Squires shows throughout his monograph how Hellenistic readers would have easily recognized the motif of providence at work.
³⁸ See Luke 7:30; Acts 2:23; 13:36; 20:27; Cf also Acts 4:28; 5:38–39. The importance of the phrase in the overall structure of Luke-Acts was recognized by Paul Schubert in his article "The Final Cycle of Speeches in the book of Acts," *JBL* 87 (1968) 235–61. The phrase also has currency within Hellenistic mysticism (cf. Corp. Herm., I 8b, 14, 18, 31). Furthermore, of the 13 uses of βουλή in the New Testament, 10 of them occur in Luke-Acts
³⁹ It is worth noting that even though Mark and Matthew both tell the story of Joseph of Arimathea, neither make reference to the "plan" of the religious council (Matthew of course makes no reference to Joseph being a member of the council).
⁴⁰ This contrast between the plan of God and the plan of men is also conveyed through the author's use of the word χείρ—"hand." On a number of occasions the author uses the phrase "χείρ κυρίου" to suggest a divine plan at work (e.g. Luke 1:66; 3:17; 23:46; Acts 4:28, 30; 7:50; 11:21; 13:11). The "hands of men," however, work against the plan of God. Peter declared, "this Jesus, delivered up according to the definite plan and foreknowledge of God, you crucified and killed by the **hand of lawless men**." (Acts 2:23; cf Luke 9:44; 24:7; Acts 12:1, 11). In Acts, the "hands of the apostles" continue the plan of God (5:12; 8:17; 9:17; 11:30; 14:3; 19:6, 11).
⁴¹ Acts 2:23 and 13:6.

found in Luke-Acts. The intentionality behind the author's use of βούλομαι is clearly revealed in the author's telling of Jesus' going out to the Mount of Olives to pray before his betrayal. The incident is recorded in all three synoptic gospels. Both Matthew and Mark record Jesus as praying, "**if it is possible** (εἰ δυνατόν ἐστιν; Mk 14:35; Mt 26:39) let this cup pass from me." Luke, however, records Jesus as praying, "Father **if you are willing** (εἰ βούλει) remove this cup from me" (Luke 22:42). The author wants to clearly identify the events taking place as being part of God's will (i.e. plan).[42] It is evident that the author's use of βουλή and βούλομαι is intentional and not accidental, especially in light of the fact that 22 of the 26 occurrences in Luke-Acts are found in Luke's original composition, i.e. Acts,[43] and in light of the fact that in the New Testament the use of θέλω has virtually supplanted the use of βούλομαι.[44]

In addition to the use of βούλομαι, the author employs an assortment of other terms to convey the idea of a divine plan at work. Prevalent among the terms are the many προ- compounds.[45] According to Conzelmann, "The fact that they are so numerous is symptomatic for Luke."[46] These προ- compounds indicate a sense of predetermination. The things accomplished during the time of the author and his implied reader did not just happen inadvertently, rather they were predetermined beforehand. It is not a coincidence that all of the Lukan προ- compounds occur in Acts. The time of Acts represents the time of the author and his implied reader. It is the time of the missionary expansion of the Church beyond the people of Israel. Acts represents the location from which the author and his reader have to make sense of all that has happened prior and all that is currently happening. It is from this location that the author seeks to assure the reader that the Christ event was determined beforehand. It was determined by God beforehand that Jesus would come and be rejected, that he would suffer and be crucified, and that he would be resurrected and preached among all nations. Such predetermination is indicative not only of a divine plan but of a carefully thought out divine plan.[47] God is not merely

---

[42] Furthermore, only Luke at this point uses the noun θέλημα rather than the verb θέλω; thereby explicitly identifying the plan as God's will (Matthew does, however, use θέλημα within the second prayer of Jesus; 26:42).

[43] See Table 1 in Appendix.

[44] The use of βούλομαι predominated from the time of Herodotus. Even though βούλομαι was preferred by the prose writers during the time of Herodotus, and predominated the writings of historians such as Thucydides and later historians such as Josephus and Diodorus (cf. Schrenk, *TDNT*, I:630.), this does not negate the intentionality behind Luke's use of the word; especially in light of the frequent occurrence of θέλω in Luke-Acts and its near absence in the writings of Diodorus and Thucydides.

[45] See Table 2 in Appendix

[46] H. Conzelmann, *The Theology of St. Luke* (trans. Geoffrey Buswell; Philadelphia: Fortress, 1961) 151.

[47] According to David P. Moessner, "The 'script' of the Scriptures in Acts: suffering as God's plan (βουλή) for the world for the 'release of sins'," *History, Literature, and Society in the Book of Acts* (ed. Ben Witherington, III; Cambridge: Cambridge University Press, 1996), it is "the suffering or death of Jesus that is the fulfillment of Scripture tied most

reacting to recent developments, but rather God is fulfilling[48] the "plan" (βουλή) determined by God "beforehand" (πρόγνωσις) (Acts 2:23).

God foretold (προκαταγγέλλω), by the mouth of prophets, the events of this plan (Acts 3:18; 7:52).[49] Not only did God foretell the events of this plan, God also "appointed" certain individuals to perform certain functions in order to fulfill this predetermined plan of God. Luke is the only New Testament author to use the word προχειρίζομαι to refer to divine appointment. Jesus was appointed (or destined) by God to be the Christ (Acts 3:20). Likewise, Paul was appointed (or destined) by God to serve as a witness and apostle (Acts 22:14; 26:16).[50] As can clearly be seen in these verses (especially the verses pertaining to Paul's appointment), the emphasis of this verb is not only on the predetermination of the appointment, but also on the function to which the subject of the verb is appointed. Paul has been appointed by God to serve as a witness and apostle, and Jesus has been appointed by God to serve as the Christ. In Luke-Acts, one of the ways God is fulfilling God's plan is through the appointing[51] or "commissioning"[52] of individuals for specific functions.[53]

The author of Luke-Acts makes frequent use of the term ὁρίζω[54] (as well as its cognates)[55] to convey the idea of God having determined or ordained the things that have taken place: "For the Son of Man is going as it has been determined" (Luke 22:22). Jesus is preached as the one determined by God to be judge of the living and the dead (Acts 10:42; cf 17:26, 31). It is this sense of predetermination implied throughout Luke-Acts that provides the implied reader with a sense of assurance concerning the things about which he has been informed. As Conzelmann asserts, "Because God alone ordains, the course of events is hidden from us, but on

---

closely to the 'plan of God." (249).

[48] The frequent use of πληρόω by the author indicates how important the idea of "fulfillment" is within the narrative of Luke-Acts. The gospel of Matthew is the only book in the New Testament that compares with Luke-Acts in its frequent use of πληρόω. In Matthew, however, the term is used primarily in the context of the fulfillment of Jewish scripture, in order to prove that Jesus is the promised Jewish Messiah. In Luke-Acts, on the other hand, the word is used in the larger context of demonstrating the fulfillment of a controlling divine plan.

[49] The Holy Spirit also "spoke beforehand (προεῖπον) by the mouth of David." (Acts 1:16).

[50] See also the only use of the word προχειροτονέω (Acts 10:41) in the New Testament, as well as the use of χειροτονέω (which occurs only in Acts 14:23 and 2 Cor 8:19).

[51] See also the author's use of the word τάσσω to refer to the idea of appointment (Luke 7:8, Acts 13:48; 15:2; 18:2; 22:10; 28:23). Acts 22:10 is the only use that implies a divine appointment rather than a human appointment.

[52] See the discussion below about the author's use of commissioning.

[53] See also the author's use of τίθημι for the idea of divine appointment, e.g., "It is not for you to know the times or seasons which the Father has **appointed** by his own authority." (Acts 1:7). Cf. Luke 20:43 ≈ Acts 2:35; 12:47; 20:28.

[54] Of the eight uses of ὁρίζω in the New Testament, six of them occur in Luke-Acts (Luke 22:22; Acts 2:23; 10:42; 11:29; 17:26, 31).

[55] Cf Luke 6:22; Acts 4:28; 13:2; 19:9.

the other hand for the very same reason we can be **certain** that the plan will be carried through."[56] Finally, not only is everything that has been accomplished among the author and his reader in accordance with God's divine plan, but God's plan has predestined (προορίζω) these events to take place (Acts 4:28). In Luke-Acts the plan of God was predetermined by God, and the plan itself has predetermined the events that have taken place.

Before turning to the literary devices employed by the author to express the idea of a divine plan at work, one more uniquely Lukan term needs to be examined. According to Joseph Fitzmyer, it is the idea of a divine plan at work that "underlies the **necessity** often associated in the Lukan story with what Jesus does or says, with what happens as the fulfillment of Scripture, and with the activities of various Christians."[57] In Luke 4:43, Luke records Jesus as saying, "**It is necessary** that I preach the good news of the kingdom of God to the other cities also; for I was sent for this purpose."[58] In Luke 24:44, Jesus says to his disciples after his resurrection, "**it is necessary** that everything written about me in the law of Moses and the prophets and the psalms be fulfilled." Acts 5:29 records Peter and the other apostles saying, "**It is necessary** that we obey God rather than man." Because there is a divine plan at work, it is necessary that certain things take place. This necessity in Luke-Acts is expressed by the impersonal verb δεῖ.

Throughout Luke-Acts δεῖ is used as a term to express divinely ordained necessities. These necessities are unconditional necessities. Nothing can stand in the way of what God has predetermined. There is a deterministic character inherent within the use of this verb.[59] In Luke-Acts, the verb is used as a general expression for the will or plan of God, a plan that cannot be deterred. The first words spoken by Jesus in Luke's gospel is the question he asks his parents as a twelve-year-old boy when his parents are searching for him in Jerusalem—"How is it that you sought me? Did you not know that I must be (δεῖ) in my Father's house?" (Luke 2:49).[60] From the very beginning Jesus indicated that there was a divine necessity compelling his every action, and nothing would get in the way of his submitting to that divine necessity.[61] Because there is a divine plan governing the events taking

---

[56] *Theology*, 152; [emphasis added].

[57] *The Gospel*, 1:179 [emphasis added].

[58] The characteristic Lukan additions of δεῖ and ἀπεστάλην emphasize the presence of a divine plan at work (see Fitzmyer, *The Gospel*, 1.557).

[59] See W. Popkes, "δεῖ," *Exegetical Dictionary of the New Testament* (3 vols; Grand Rapids, MI: Eerdmans, 1990–93) 1:279–280.

[60] This verse might also be translated, "I must be about my Father's affairs," which stresses the idea of divine necessity even more. Marshall rejects such a translation (*Luke*, p. 129) and Brown considers it possible but unlikely (*Birth of the Messiah: A Commentary on the Infancy Narratives in Matthew and Luke* (New York: Doubleday, 1993) 475–7). Fitzmyer states, however, that "It is not easy to say which is the best sense in the Lucan context." (*The Gospel*, 1:443). For linguistic parallels; see P. J. Temple, '"House" or "Business" in Luke 2.49?', *CBQ* 1 (1939) 342–52.

[61] On the importance of divine necessity in Luke-Acts, see Squires, *The Plan*, 166–185.

place, virtually everything that happens in Luke-Acts is the result of divine necessity. According to Conzelmann, δεῖ is the most prominent indication of the conceptual framework of Luke-Acts.[62] Unlike the author's use of προ- compounds, the use of δεῖ is not limited to volume two of the author's work. The verb occurs 42 times in Luke-Acts,[63] with 18 of those occurrences in Luke's gospel, in contrast to only 8 occurrences in Matt and 6 occurrences in Mark.[64]

Lukan Literary Devices Employed to Express a Divine Plan

In his seminal narrative-critical analysis of Luke-Acts, Tannehill presents at least four literary devices employed by the author to underscore the author's presentation of a divine plan.[65] The first literary device is what Tannehill calls "previews" of future events and "reviews" of past events.[66] These previews and reviews are used in such a way as to interpret events as fulfillment of a divine purpose. The most obvious examples of Lukan previews consists of the angelic and prophetic announcements within the birth narratives of John the Baptist and Jesus.[67] These announcements clearly indicate that events yet to occur in the narrative are to be understood as fulfillment of a divine plan. Another preview consists of the time when the apostles are questioned before the high priest, the council, and all the senate of Israel. The people become enraged by the apostles' response, and desire to kill them; however, a Pharisee in the council named Gamaliel persuades the crowd not to kill the apostles and tells the council that if the plan (βουλή) or undertaking of the apostles "is of men, it will fail; but if it is of God, you will not be able to overthrow them. You might even be found opposing God!" (Acts 5:21b–39). The statement serves as a preview of the success of the apostolic mission, and as an indicator that the mission is according to God's plan and not merely man's plan. Examples of reviews include the narrator's statement that the baptism of John represented the purpose (βουλή) of God (Luke 7:29–30), Paul's statements concerning the baptism of John (Acts 13:24; 19:4), and Peter's

---

[62] *Theology*, 151–154. On the importance of δεῖ in Luke-Acts, see also Grundmann, "δεῖ," *TDNT* 2:23–24; C. Cosgrove, "The Divine ΔΕΙ in Luke-Acts. Investigations into the Lukan understanding of God's Providence," *NovT* 26 (1984) 190; E. Richard, "The Divine Purpose: The Jews and the Gentile Mission (Acts 15)," in *Luke-Acts: New Perspectives from the Society of Biblical Literature Seminar* (ed. C. H. Talbert; New York: Crossroad Publishing Co., 1984) 192.

[63] Outside of Luke-Acts the word only occurs 52 times in the entire New Testament.

[64] In addition to the author's frequent use of δεῖ to the depict the unfolding of the plan of God throughout his story, the author also occasionally uses μέλλω for this same purpose (see Luke 9:31, 44; 22:23; 24:21; Acts 17:31; 26:22, 23).

[65] *Narrative Unity*, 1:21.

[66] Gérard Genette conducts an extensive analysis of previews and reviews in narratives in his *Narrative Discourse*, 35–83.

[67] Squires classifies these particular previews as "epiphanies," which for Squires serves as one of the literary devices used by the author to describe the execution of the plan of God (cf *The Plan*, 2, 27, 103–120).

declaration that Jesus was delivered up according to the plan (βουλή) of God (Acts 2:22–23).

The second literary device discussed by Tannehill is the author's use of Old Testament quotations that express a divine plan being fulfilled.[68] The narrator frequently finds God's plan revealed in Scriptures, especially in certain key texts of the Septuagint which appear repeatedly in Luke-Acts or are given prominent positions in it. The two programmatic Isaian quotations found in Luke 3:4–6 and 4:18–19 are obvious examples. These scriptural passages indicate a present fulfillment of a divine plan, and they provoke the attentive reader to read the narrative carefully to see if and how God's plan is actually being realized in the narrative.

The third device is the use of commission statements regarding specific individuals commissioned by God as chosen instruments to carry out God's divine plan.[69] Throughout Luke-Acts there are statements pertaining to the commissions received by certain individuals. As Tannehill points out, these statements of commission serve as disclosures of a divine plan at work.[70] The prime example is the commission statement received by Paul after his Damascus road experience. So important is this experience and its resulting commission, that the author reports it three times. The first reporting of the commission is done by the narrator, and it is reported as having been spoken directly by the Lord (Acts 9:15). The next two times, Paul himself declares the commission he received from the Lord (Acts 22:12–15; 26:16–18).[71] The purpose of the Pauline recapitulation is not simply to recall the event, "but to interpret it within the overall context of the plan of God."[72]

Finally, the author indicates a divine plan at work through statements made by reliable characters within the story. These characters are portrayed by the author as reliable in their judgments and discerning in their statements. These characters serve as spokespersons for the author by interpreting events and disclosing God's plan in

---

[68] See also discussions of the motif of fulfilled prophecies in Squires, *The Plan*, 121–154; Navone, "The Way;" Fitzmyer, *The Gospel*, 1:179–81.

[69] For more detail about the standard elements involved in commissioning episodes, see B. J. Hubbard, "Commissioning Stories in Luke-Acts: A Study of Their Antecedents, Form and Content," *Semeia* 8 (1977) 103–26, and "The Role of Commissioning Accounts in Acts," *Perspectives on Luke-Acts* (ed. Charles H. Talbert; Danville, VA: Association of Baptist Professors of Religion, 1978) 187–98.

[70] *Narrative Unity*, 1:22.

[71] The last two references contain two of the three Lukan uses of the verb προχειρίζω (22:14; 26:16). This verb is found in the New Testament only in Luke-Acts, and its importance has already been discussed above.

[72] According to Squires, these latter two accounts serve as an apologetic defense of Paul's entire career. "Luke makes it quite clear to his Hellenistic readers, in their own terms, that Paul's conversion (and the ensuing events) was no surprise, but rather an integral and inevitable part of the plan of God." (*The Plan*, 33).

the story.[73] Their statements can be prophetic declarations (e.g. Luke 1:68 ff; 2:25–35), instructions (e.g. Luke 3:10–14; Acts 2:38), mission statements (e.g Luke 4:43; 19:10); apostolic assertions (e.g. Acts 10:34–35; Acts 28:28), or various other forms of declarations or proclamations—especially preaching. According to the narrator of Luke-Acts, Paul informed the Ephesian elders that through his preaching he had declared to them "the entire plan of God" (Acts 20:27). Paul acknowledges that there is a divine plan at work, and that the specifics of that plan are revealed in the content of his preaching.

This idea of the author using preaching as an indicator of a divine plan at work helps to explain the prominence of preaching within the author's narrative. Preaching good news is a central motif in Luke-Acts. As a matter of fact, stressing the **preaching** of good news is actually more important in Luke-Acts than specifically identifying the news as good. The noun εὐαγγέλιον—commonly translated as "good news"—occurs twelve times in Matthew and Mark but does not occur at all in Luke, and only occurs twice in Acts. However, the verb, εὐαγγελίζω (-ομαι), occurs 25 times in Luke-Acts; with no occurrences in Mark and only one occurrence in Matthew. This is because the author is more concerned with emphasizing the **preaching**[74] of the good news than with emphasizing the **goodness** of the news.[75] It is the act of preaching good news that is according to God's plan, and it is the act of preaching that indicates that there is a divine plan at work. Only in Luke's gospel is Jesus recorded as saying, "I must preach the good news of the kingdom of God. . . for I was sent for this purpose" (4:43). The plan of God requires that Jesus preach. Not only does the plan of God require that Jesus preach, but it is actually God who preaches through Jesus. In Acts 10:36 Peter declares, "You know the word which he [i.e. God] sent to Israel, preaching good news (εὐαγγελιζόμενος) of peace by Jesus Christ." Preaching is part of the plan of God. It was God who sent the angel Gabriel to preach good news to Zechariah (Luke 1:19). It was God who called Paul to preach good news to the Macedonians (Acts 16:10). By demonstrating that the act of preaching is according to the plan of God, the author forces the reader to identify the content of the preaching as that which God intended to be preached. Those who preach are fulfilling God's divine plan, and, as shall be discussed later, the content of the preaching reflects the nature of the divine plan.

According to Tannehill, it is through the use of these four literary devices—1) previews and reviews, 2) Old Testament quotations, 3) commission statements, and 4) statements by reliable characters—that the author stresses the presence of a

---

[73] According to W. Booth, *The Rhetoric of Fiction*; 18, "The author is present in every speech given by any character who has had conferred upon him, in whatever manner, the badge of reliability."

[74] See also the prominence of κηρύσσω in Luke-Acts.

[75] Fitzmyer asserts that Luke's use of the verb εὐαγγελίζω "by and large has the meaning of 'preach, announce, proclaim'. . . rather than 'announce the good news.'" (*The Gospel*, 1.174).

divine plan at work. In addition to the four literary devices presented by Tannehill, there are at least three other literary devices used by the author that are just as important for stressing the presence of a divine plan at work: 1) the orchestrating role of the Holy Spirit, 2) the role of God as an active character in Luke-Acts, and 3) the deliberate geographical development of Luke's two volume work.[76]

Much attention has been given to the role of the Holy Spirit in Acts. "Acts has appropriately been called the Book of the Holy Spirit."[77] However, much less attention has been given to the role of the Holy Spirit in volume one of this two volume work. It is important to notice that virtually every reference to spirit ($\pi\nu\epsilon\hat{\upsilon}\mu\alpha$) in the first four chapters of Luke's gospel is connected to the Holy Spirit's orchestrating of and involvement in the events occurring. Of the sixteen occurrences of $\pi\nu\epsilon\hat{\upsilon}\mu\alpha$ up to Luke 4:18, only two of them do not refer to the Holy Spirit.[78] All of the events recorded in the gospel up to this point have been divinely coordinated by the Holy Spirit. The Holy Spirit serves as an active agent intervening in the progress of God's mission, both impelling and guiding it. Furthermore, of the 14 references to the Holy Spirit, 13 of them are in some way connected to the mission and ministry of Jesus.

The author leads up to the programmatic episode of Luke 4:16–30 by emphasizing the intimate relationship between the Holy Spirit and Jesus. However, prior to the episode, no explicit statement is made as to why or for what purpose the Spirit is so intimately connected with Jesus. The reader cannot help but be aware that the impelling and guiding nature of the Holy Spirit in the life of Jesus reflects a divine plan at work, but the reader has yet to be made aware of the specific function of the Holy Spirit in the life of Jesus. The "bodily" descending of the Holy Spirit upon Jesus (3:22) highlights the intimacy between the Holy Spirit and Jesus, as well as the physical involvement of the Holy Spirit in the events occurring in the life of Jesus. After the Holy Spirit's descent, Jesus is permeated and led by the Spirit (4:1, 14). The fact that everything Jesus does is the result of the Holy Spirit's leading indicates that there is a divine plan at work.

The words of the prophet Isaiah cited in Luke 4:18–19 declare why the Holy Spirit is so intimately connected to Jesus. It is the Spirit that has empowered and enabled Jesus to fulfill God's plan for him as revealed in the prophecy of Isaiah. Now that the author has explicitly identified the Holy Spirit's role as empowering Jesus to fulfill God's plan, the author drastically changes his use of $\pi\nu\epsilon\hat{\upsilon}\mu\alpha$ after

---

[76] In *The Plan*, Squires analyzes five literary devices used by the author to express a divine plan at work: 1) God as the primary actor in human history; 2) the performance of signs and wonders by God in human history; 3) epiphanies as inspired indications of the plan of God; 4) the foretelling and fulfilling of prophecy; 5) fate, i.e. the presence of the theme of "necessity."

[77] Luke Johnson, *The Writings*, 207.

[78] Luke 1:17, 47 (cf. 1:15, 35, 41, 67, 80; 2:25, 26, 27; 3:16, 22; 4:1 (x2), 14, 18). Although 1:17 is not a reference to the Holy Spirit, it does have divine overtones in that it is a reference to the "spirit and power of Elijah."

this episode. Of the 21 occurrences of πνεῦμα after 4:18, only four of them are references to the Holy Spirit,[79] and none of the four involve the Spirit's leading and guiding of Jesus. Only 23:46, which is the last use of πνεῦμα and "Jesus" together, reflects the use of πνεῦμα found in the first four chapters. Just as the Spirit had been given to Jesus at the beginning of his earthly ministry in order to empower him to fulfill God's plan, now at the end of his earthly ministry Jesus commits the Spirit back into the hands of God. Only Luke places upon the lips of Jesus the words, "Father, into your hands I commend my spirit" (23:46).[80] The Spirit descended upon Jesus, enabling him to fulfill God's divine plan. Now that Jesus had done his part in fulfilling that divine plan, the Spirit ascends back to God.

The story does not end there, however; the same Spirit that anointed Jesus and enabled him to fulfill God's divine plan, now also anoints the followers of Jesus. Luke ends volume one by having Jesus declare to his disciples, "Behold I send the promise of my Father upon you; but stay in the city, until you are clothed with power from on high" (24:49). In the opening chapter of volume two the reader quickly discovers that the "promise of the Father" is the Holy Spirit (Acts 1:4 ff).[81] Just as the Holy Spirit empowered, impelled and guided Jesus in fulfilling God's plan, so also the Holy Spirit empowers, impels and guides the followers of Jesus, enabling them also to fulfill God's plan. The continued involvement of the Holy Spirit testifies to the continued fulfillment of God's plan, and assures the reader of the reliability of Luke's narrative. As Shepherd writes concerning Acts 2:14–47, "The presence of the Spirit establishes the reliability not only of Peter's speech, but of Luke's narrative.[82]

The role of God as an active character in Luke-Acts is also indicative of a divine plan at work.[83] God is clearly portrayed as an active character in Luke-Acts. The use of the word θεός in Luke-Acts far surpasses its use in the other synoptic gospels (as well as in John) and its use anywhere else in the New Testament. Θεός is used 42 times in Mark and 47 times in Matthew (and 71 times in John). It is used 117 times, however, in Luke's gospel, and 165 times in Acts (more than in any other New Testament book). When comparing Luke with Matthew and Mark, it should be noticed that in Luke God is identified as the one who sends angels to speak (Luke 1:19, 26). God gives the throne of David to Jesus (Luke 1:32). God is Mary's savior (Luke 1:47). God "has visited and redeemed his people" (Luke 1:68; cf. 7:16). As indicated earlier, God is credited with having a distinct purpose (7:30; cf. Acts 2:23; 13:36; 20:27; see also Acts 4:28; 5:38–39). Only in Luke does Jesus

---

[79] 10:21; 11:13; 12:10, 12.
[80] Mark and Matthew simply state that Jesus gave a loud cry (Mk 15:37; Mt 27:50).
[81] See Mikeal Parsons, *The Departure of Jesus in Luke-Acts: The Ascension Narratives in Context* (Sheffield: JSOT Press, 1987) for a detailed discussion of the literary devices used by the author in the ending of the gospel and the beginning of Acts.
[82] William H. Shepherd, Jr., *The Narrative Function of the Holy Spirit as a Character in Luke-Acts* (Atlanta: Scholars Press, 1994) 167.
[83] See Squires' discussion of "God at work in human history," *The Plan*, 37–77.

declare that God is the one responsible for healing the demoniac (Luke 8:39; cf Mk 5:19; Mt 8:28–34). By the finger of God Jesus casts out demons (Luke 11:20; cf Mt 12:28, Mk 3:20). God chastises the rich fool for building larger barns (Luke 12:20). God knows the heart (Luke 16:15; cf Acts 15:8). Twice it is declared that God is able to do the impossible (Luke 1:37; 18:27; cf. Mt 19:26; Mk 10:27). God is not only able to raise up children to Abraham (Luke 3:8), but in Luke God does so (Luke 13:16; 16:22; 19:9). In Luke God is clearly an active character, working to fulfil God's plan. The one active role attributed to God in Matthew and Mark is noticeably absent from Luke. Matthew and Mark both record Jesus crying out on the cross, "My God, my God, why have you forsaken me?" (Mk 15:34; Mt 27:46). God in no way forsakes Jesus in Luke.[84]

The author continues his depiction of God as an active character in volume two of his work. In Acts, the replacement apostle for Judas is chosen by God (1:24); God has performed mighty works (2:11). What happens on the day of Pentecost is the result of God's initiative (2:17–21). God is the one who did signs and wonders through Jesus (2:22). God raised Jesus from the dead (2:24, 32; 4:10; 5:30; 10:40; 13:30, 33). God exalted Jesus to Lord, Christ, and Savior (2:36; 5:31). God calls people to Godself (2:39). The healing of the lame man is an act of God (3:1–10). God foretold by the prophets that Jesus would suffer (3:18). God sent Jesus (3:26). God gives the Holy Spirit (5:32; 11:17). From the time of Abraham, God has been orchestrating salvation history (7:2–56; 13:17). God speaks through visions (10:15; 28). God answers prayer (10:31). God shows no partiality (10:34). God preaches through Jesus (10:36). God anointed Jesus with the Holy Spirit and with power (10:38). God chooses those who are to be witnesses (10:41). God ordained Jesus to be judge of the living and the dead (10:42). God is fulfilling the promises made to the fathers (13:32). God called Peter to go to the Gentiles (15:7). God visited the Gentiles (15:14; 21:19). God called Paul to preach to the Macedonians (16:10). God did miracles through Paul (19:11). God obtained the church by the blood of Jesus (20:28). God appointed Paul to know God's will (22:14). God protects people from death (27:24). God is without a doubt the most active character in Luke-Acts.

The deliberate geographical development of Luke's two volume work also points to a divine plan at work.[85] Luke begins Jesus' public ministry with his rejection at Nazareth (Luke 4:16–30). Luke intentionally moves this scene from later on in the gospel tradition to the beginning of Jesus' public ministry. Prior to this episode the author explicitly reveals that Jesus is conceived and reared in Nazareth. The city of Nazareth is mentioned four times in the first two chapters of Luke's gospel alone.[86] The author explicitly identifies Nazareth[87] as the locale of the

---

[84] As was indicated above, even the crucifixion was part of God's plan.

[85] Conzelmann, *Theology*, 18–94.

[86] See Luke 1:26; 2:4, 39, 51. These four occurrences specifically refer to Nazareth as a geographical locale and not as an identifier for Jesus (e.g. "Jesus of Nazareth") as it is commonly used in Mark's gospel. The frequency so early in Luke's gospel of "Nazareth" as a geographical locale is contrasted to only one such occurrence in the entire gospel of

initial rejection of Jesus in order to underscore the rejection of Jesus by 'his own,' and to provide a concrete starting point for the dissemination of the gospel. The rejection at Nazareth serves as the catalyst for the "preaching of the good news" to others. Since Nazareth is the place where Jesus grew up, it is the natural starting point for the geographical development which Luke traces throughout his two volume work. This author is not merely concerned with a particular event on a particular day at a particular locale, rather he is concerned with the meaning of Jesus' mission as a whole and its consequences. The author seeks to demonstrate that Jesus' mission is to "preach good news" to all people (especially the dispossessed), and that the rejection of Jesus only provides an opportunity for the preaching of the good news to others. The rejection at Nazareth sets in motion the geographical development which is so prominent in Luke-Acts and vital for the fulfillment of God's plan.[88]

The rejection at Nazareth is the first of six pericopes in Luke-Acts having a common pattern and theme of confrontation and rejection.[89] What is common to each pericope is that the confrontation with and rejection of God's agent is always followed by a forward movement of that agent and the continuation of God's plan.[90] The deliberate geographical development of Luke's two volume work, the emphasis on the orchestrating role of the Holy Spirit, and the portrayal of God as an active character all function in the same manner as the literary devices presented by Tannehill: they help to stress the presence of a divine plan at work.

Mark and three such occurrences in the gospel of Matthew. It should also be noted that the prominent use of "Nazareth" in the first two chapters of Luke-Acts cannot simply be considered the natural result of creating an infancy narrative, especially since "Nazareth" only occurs once in Matthew's infancy narrative.

[87] Neither Mark nor Matthew explicitly identify the place of Jesus' rejection as Nazareth. The locale is simply identified as his hometown.

[88] After 4:16–30, Nazareth never again serves as a locale for any other episodes in the gospel. Jesus has moved beyond Nazareth once and for all, and it is the other cities of Israel which benefit from his work. As a matter of fact Nazareth is only mentioned three other times in the entire gospel, and each time it is used simply as an identifier to remind the reader that Jesus is from Nazareth (e.g. *Jesus of Nazareth*; cf Luke 4:34; 18:37; 24:19), as is the case in six of the seven uses in Acts (2:22; 3:6; 4:10; 6:14; 22:8; 26:9).

[89] The other five pericopes include Luke 20:9–19; Acts 3:1–4:31; 5:12–42; 13:13–52; 18:1–18.

[90] Cf. N. Petersen, *Literary Criticism for New Testament Critics* (Philadelphia: Fortress, 1978) 88.

Salvation as the Plan of God in Luke-Acts

The author clearly seeks to convince the reader that there is a divine plan at work. What, however, is this divine plan? What does the author of Luke-Acts understand the plan of God to be? From start to finish—from the announcement that "all flesh shall see the salvation of God" (Luke 3:6) to Paul's declaration, "that this salvation of God has been sent to the Gentiles" (Acts 28:28)—the extension of "the salvation of God" (τὸ σωτήριον τοῦ θεοῦ) to all people clearly represents the plan of God that unites the entire narrative of Luke-Acts. The author uses "τὸ σωτήριον τοῦ θεοῦ" to form an inclusio for Luke's two volume work. The phrase is introduced in a quote from the prophet Isaiah (Luke 3:4–6), and it is used the second time in connection with a quote from the prophet Isaiah (Acts 28:25b–28).[91] The prophetic identification with τὸ σωτήριον τοῦ θεοῦ bears witness to the fact that "the salvation of God" represents a predetermined plan of God, and its use as an inclusio for the entirety of Luke's two volume work indicates that it is the plan that unites the entire narrative of Luke-Acts. The author seeks to assure the implied reader that, despite the separation and unfair treatment of people on the basis of ethnic identity, economic status, occupation, power, gender, and all other social barriers, the extension of salvation to and the inclusion of all people within the family of God has been and continues to be the plan of God. This universal saving purpose of God is the chief moving force behind the entire narrative.[92]

Salvation has a prominence in Luke-Acts that it does not have in the writings of the other synoptic authors. Luke alone uses the noun σωτηρία, as well as the adjective σωτήριον[93]—both of which are translated "salvation" in Luke-Acts. Luke is also the only one among the synoptic authors who uses the title "Savior."[94] Furthermore, Luke utilizes two programmatic quotations from Isaiah in such a way that salvation becomes the climax of both quotations. All three synoptic gospels

---

[91] While the infancy narrative (1:5–2:52) is the first major section of Luke's account (contra. H. Conzelmann, *Theology*, 118; C. H. Talbert, "Prophecies of Future Greatness: The Contributions of Greco-Roman Biographies to an Understanding of Luke 1:5–4:15," *The Divine Helmsman* (eds. J. L. Crenshaw and S. Sandmel; New York: KTAV, 1980) 129–41), the emergence of John the Baptist as a preacher of repentance (ch. 3) represents the beginning of the Lukan gospel proper (While most biblical scholars agree that the New Testament infancy narratives—as a literary genre—represent the latest part of the gospel tradition to take shape, Fitzmyer asserts that Luke composed his infancy narrative after his gospel proper, and that 3:1–2 was at one time a formal introduction to the work; *The Gospel*, 1:310–12). Luke's infancy narrative serves to prepare the reader for the gospel proper. Salvation plays a prominent role within Luke's infancy narrative, and it's prominence foreshadows the importance it will play throughout the gospel. Of the 17 explicit references to salvation in Luke-Acts, 6 of those references are found in Luke's infancy narrative.

[92] Conzelmann asserts that "God's plan is primarily concerned with the saving events as a whole," more so than with Jesus individually or with his destiny (*Theology*, 154).

[93] Luke 1:69, 71, 77; 2:30; 3:6; 19:9; Acts 4:12, 7:25; 13:26, 47, 16:17; 27:34; 28:28. See also the author's extensive use of σῴζω and its verbal cognates (e.g. διασῴζω, ἐκσῴζω).

[94] Luke 1:47; 2:11; Acts 5:31; 13:23.

contain the Isaian quotation which refers to John the Baptist as: "The voice of one crying out in the wilderness: 'Prepare the way of the Lord, make his paths straight.'" Luke alone, however, continues the quotation, "Every valley shall be filled, and every mountain and hill shall be made low, and the crooked shall be made straight, and the rough ways made smooth; and all flesh shall see the salvation of God" (Luke 3:4–6). For Luke, "the salvation of God" is the object of this Isaian prophecy.[95]

In the second quotation, cited by Jesus in the self-identification of his ministry, salvation is also the climax. Jesus declares that he has been anointed by the Spirit of the Lord "to preach good news to the poor. . . to proclaim release (ἄφεσις) to the captives and recovery of sight to the blind, to send the oppressed away released (ἄφεσις), to proclaim the acceptable year of the Lord" (Luke 4:18–19). The author's repeated use of "release" (ἄφεσις) in these two verses stresses the author's concern with salvation. For Luke, the "release" or "setting free" of God's people is one of the motifs intimately related to the content of salvation. Earlier, in the prophecy of Zechariah, it was declared that John the Baptist would "go before the Lord. . . to *give knowledge of salvation to his people* **by means of the release (*ἄφεσις*) from their sins**." (1:76b–77). The first motif associated with salvation in Luke-Acts is the release of God's people from their sins.[96]

The importance of this release motif is revealed by the author's repeated use of the noun ἄφεσις. The noun occurs only once in Matthew and twice in Mark. It occurs ten times, however, in Luke-Acts.[97] The noun ἄφεσις is used by Luke in two contexts. First, the word is used to refer to a physical setting free, such as a release from blindness, captivity, and demon possession. This is how the term is used by Luke in Jesus' self-identification of his ministry. The author also uses the term in the construction "release from sins," which is more commonly translated "remission (or forgiveness) of sins."[98] In both contexts ἄφεσις represents a setting free, i.e. a liberation, from that which enslaves. In Paul's speech in the synagogue at Antioch Luke writes, "Let it be known to you therefore, brethren, that through this man (i.e. Jesus) **release from sins** is proclaimed to you, and by him every one that believes is freed from everything from which you could not be freed by the law of Moses" (Acts 13:38–39).

---

[95] This prophecy has already been examined in closer detail above.
[96] The first use of ἄφεσις in Luke-Acts is used in connection with salvation, and the first use of salvation (σωτηρία) is used in connection with release (specifically, release from sins). Fitzmyer claims that the abstract form of the verbal expression "To forgive sins," which is ἄφεσις ἁμαρτιῶν, is a uniquely Lukan way of expressing the effects of the Christ event (*The Gospel*, 1.224).
[97] The word occurs five times in Luke's gospel and five times in Acts. The word is only found four times in the rest of the New Testament.
[98] Eight of the ten occurrences of ἄφεσις in Luke-Acts occur in the context, "remission of sins" (cf. Luke 1:77; 3:3; 24:47; Acts 2:38; 5:31; 10:43; 13:38; 26:18).

The emphasis on salvation in Luke 4:18–19 is also revealed through the manner in which the author has constructed the passage. The verses represent a patchwork of materials which have been brought together by the author in order to emphasize the importance of "release." The quotation from Isaiah is actually a conflation of Isaiah 61:1a,b,d; 58:6d; 61:2a, which demonstrates a deliberate and conscious literary reworking by Luke in order to achieve a desired emphasis. The phrase "to send away the oppressed released" (v. 18d) comes from Isaiah 58:6d, and has been added to Isaiah 61:1–2, in order to emphasize the term ἄφεσις. Furthermore, that Luke intentionally makes salvation the climax of this particular quotation is emphasized by that fact that Luke ends the quotation where he does. Unlike the first Isaian quotation, where Luke extended the quote to include a direct reference to the salvation of God, here Luke ends the quotation in the middle of the sentence. In its earlier literary context, the sentence "to proclaim the acceptable year of the Lord" continues—"*and the day of vengeance of our God.*" In its original context, the author of the prophecy is announcing both salvation and judgment. However, by ending the quotation where he does, Luke makes the reference to the time of salvation the climax of the quotation.[99]

The author also attempts to assure the implied reader that as a result of Jesus, God is now bringing this plan of universal salvation to fulfillment in the reader's time. Like the inclusio that defines Luke's two volume work, Simeon's oracle now also reveals the purpose which unites the entire narrative and constitutes its central meaning. Simeon declares that he has seen 'God's salvation' (τὸ σωτήριόν σου), which God has "prepared in the presence of all peoples, a light for revelation to the Gentiles and for glory to your people Israel" (Luke 2:29–32). For Luke the life and ministry of Jesus marks the arrival of God's salvation. Jesus not only marks the arrival of God's salvation, but he actually brings God's salvation through his presence and work. Jesus' assertion, "**Today** this scripture has been fulfilled in your ears" (Luke 4:21) indicates that it is Jesus who is responsible for bringing salvation. In the last of three significant mission statements made by Jesus,[100] Jesus declares, after announcing the coming of salvation to the household of Zacchaeus, "For the Son of Man came to seek and to save (σῶσαι) the lost" (Luke 19:10).[101] That salvation is realized in the ministry and person of Jesus is also proclaimed by the disciples. In Acts 4:12, Peter declares, "There is salvation in no one else, for there is no other name under heaven given among mortals by which we must be saved."

---

[99] Similarly, the quotation in Acts 2:17–21 from Joel 3:1–5a (in most English translations, the passage is found in Joel 2:28–32) makes salvation the climax. The author omits the word "terrible" from the identification of the "day of the Lord." Furthermore the author does not continue the passage in Joel to make mention of "those who escape" and "the survivors" (Joel 3:5b). The focus of the quotation as cited in Acts is on the promise, "whoever calls on the name of the Lord shall be saved."

[100] See Luke 4:43; 5:32; 19:10.

[101] In addition to the author's exclusive use of σωτήρ, σωτηρία and σωτήριον among the synoptic authors, see also the prevalent use of σώζω within Luke-Acts.

The reality of salvation in Luke-Acts is revealed in the life, words and deeds of Jesus.[102] Simeon, while holding the baby Jesus in his arms and praising God, declares: "Master, now you are dismissing your servant in peace, according to your word; for my eyes have seen your salvation" (Luke 2:30; cf. 3:4ff). It was not in the cross that Simeon saw the salvation of God but rather in life of the baby Jesus himself.[103] For Luke there was no need to wait for the cross, salvation was present in the life of Jesus. Simeon did not have to wait until the crucifixion to die in peace and declare God's salvation. The birth of Jesus marked the arrival of God's salvation. In Luke-Acts, God's salvation is linked primarily to the birth (Luke 2:11), life and ministry (Luke 19:9–10), and exaltation (Acts 5:31) of Jesus. Luke does not stress the atoning nature of the death of Jesus, because for Luke salvation is connected to a **living** savior.[104] Even when Luke does allude to or specifically mention the death of Jesus, it is always in connection with the resurrection and exaltation. Luke points not to the death of Jesus but to the life of Jesus—both the life that preceded the cross and the life after the cross. It is Luke alone who places on the lips of the angels who greet the women at the empty tomb, "Why do you look for the **living** among the dead?" (Luke 24:5b). It is as a **living savior** that Jesus brings salvation. Salvation is present in the life and ministry of Jesus, who is God's salvation to all people.

According to the author of Luke-Acts, the plan of God has always been for salvation to be made available to all flesh, and it was also God's plan to make that salvation available through Jesus. Through Jesus salvation is offered to all flesh.[105] However, according to the author, God's plan requires the appropriate human

---

[102] This is one of the reasons why there is such an emphasis on both "seeing and hearing" in Luke-Acts.

[103] The diminished role of the cross in the theology of Luke-Acts is one of the points for which Conzelmann severely criticizes the work (*Theology*, 199–202; see also Joseph B. Tyson, *The Death of Jesus in Luke-Acts* (Columbia, SC: University of South Carolina Press, 1986).

[104] This does not necessarily mean that the author of Luke-Acts opposes the notion of the atoning nature of Jesus' death; it simply means that the author is not as concerned with this aspect of Christian theology as are most modern Christians and theologians (Moessner asserts, "Luke configures the death of Jesus as an atoning event through the interweaving of the stories of Israel's rejection of their Messiah and of God's overarching purpose for this rejection in God's plan (βουλή) for all humanity ("The 'script,'" 249). For an attempt to demonstrate a salvific interpretation of the cross in Luke-Acts, see Fitzmyer, *Luke the Theologian* (London: Geoffrey Chapman, 1989) 203–233; Joel B. Green, "'Salvation to the End of the Earth' (Acts 1347): God as Savior in the Acts of the Apostles," *The Book of Acts in its Theological Setting* (Grand Rapids, MI: Eerdmans, 1997) 97–99).

[105] It is important to realize that although salvation comes *through* Jesus, it is *from* God. The phrase "τὸ σωτήριον τοῦ θεοῦ" in Luke-Acts indicates that salvation originates with God. God *alone* initiates salvation. Jesus is the agent of God's salvation. In Luke-Acts, God is the first one called Savior (Luke 1:47). Furthermore, Jesus is exalted as Savior by God (Acts 5:31), and God is the one who promised and brought to Israel a Savior, who happened to be Jesus (Acts 13:23). The emphasis on God as the initiator of salvation highlights the fact that the saving plan of God was operative prior to Jesus' birth (cf. J. Green "Salvation to the End of the Earth," 97).

response to the offer of salvation in order for human beings to receive God's salvation. In Luke-Acts, the coming of Jesus does not guarantee that everyone will be a recipient of salvation. Jesus is the salvation of God, but his coming does not automatically bestow salvation upon everyone. God's plan extends salvation to all flesh, and allows for the inclusion of all people within the family of God, but God's plan also requires appropriate human responses. In Luke Acts, the offer of salvation requires a human response, and one of the responses prescribed by God for the acceptance of salvation is the response of repentance.

Repentance as Part of the Plan of God

In Luke-Acts the extension of salvation to and the inclusion of all people within the family of God represents the plan of God. Furthermore, the human response of repentance to the offer of salvation comprises a vital part of that plan. After comparing Luke's gospel with the other synoptic gospels, it is clear that the author's use of repent/repentance is conscious. The author is intentionally emphasizing the concept of repentance for a specific reason. Just as "the salvation of God" (τὸ σωτήριον τοῦ θεοῦ) forms an inclusio for the entirety of Luke's two volume work—uniting the entire narrative and constituting its central meaning—the motif of repentance also forms an important inclusio for this two volume work. Within the inclusio formed by τὸ σωτήριον τοῦ θεοῦ (Luke 3:6; Acts 28:28) resides another inclusio formed by the theme "fruits/deeds worthy of repentance" (καρποὺς ἀξίους τῆς μετανοίας / ἄξια τῆς μετανοίας ἔργα; Luke 3:8/Acts 26:20). Paul's statement to King Agrippa that he had declared to the Gentiles "that they should repent and turn to God and **perform deeds worthy of repentance**" (Acts 26:20) is clearly meant to echo John the Baptist's declaration to the crowds that they should "**Bear fruits worthy of repentance**" (Luke 3:8). That the author is intentionally connecting these two scenes is further confirmed by the fact that immediately before John the Baptist's declaration to the crowds that they should "Bear fruits worthy of repentance," the author makes reference to John the Baptist preaching a baptism of repentance for the **remission of sins** (ἄφεσιν ἁμαρτιῶν; Luke 3:3); likewise, immediately before Paul's statement to King Agrippa that he had declared to the Gentiles that they should "perform deeds worthy of repentance," the author makes reference to Paul being sent to the Gentiles in order that they might receive **remission of sins** (ἄφεσιν ἁμαρτιῶν; Acts 26:18). Like John the Baptist, Paul has been sent so that others might receive remission of sins through the act of repentance.[106]

---

[106] Since the author understood the preaching of John as "the beginning of the gospel" (Luke 16:16; Acts 1:22; 10:37; 13:24) and since the speech given by Paul before King Agrippa is the last major address in Luke-Acts, the author clearly seeks to convey to the reader that repentance is at the heart of the gospel.

Just as the "salvation of God" is a theme uniting the entire narrative and constituting its central meaning, so also the theme of "bearing fruits/ performing deeds worthy of repentance" is a theme uniting the entire narrative and constituting its central meaning.[107] Deeds worthy of repentance demonstrate one's repentance and acceptance of God's salvation, but deeds unworthy of repentance demonstrate one's failure to repent and the rejection of God's salvation.[108] In Luke-Acts salvation and repentance work hand in hand, and these two themes unite the entire narrative and constitute its central meaning.

The first explicit reference to repentance in Luke-Acts occurs in the episode describing the preaching of John the Baptist. Although Mark sums up John's message as "baptism of repentance for the remission of sins," Luke emphasizes John's message of "repentance for the remission of sins" by rearranging his material.[109] Both Mark and Matthew make John the Baptist the focal point of the Baptist preaching unit; Luke, however, makes the "baptism of repentance for the remission of sins" the focal point. It is not John the Baptist that the author is concerned with, instead it is John's message of "repentance for the remission of sins." In Mark and Matthew the people are attracted to John the Baptist, and they come from all over Jerusalem, Judea and along the Jordan to come to John (cf. Mk 1:5; Mt 3:5);[110] however, in Luke it is the "baptism of repentance." not John that is central,[111] and instead of people coming to John, John goes into all the region around the Jordan proclaiming the "baptism of repentance." It is the message of

---

[107] Immediately after Jesus commanded a group of followers to either repent or perish, he shared with them a parable about a fig tree that produced no fruit (Luke 13:1–9). After being cultivated and given another opportunity, if the tree continued to be fruitless it was to be cut down (cf. Luke 3:9). Once again repentance is closely associated with bearing fruit. Bultmann considers the passage on repentance (vv. 1–5) a "unitary composition" which serves as an introduction to the parable about the importance of bearing fruit (*The History of the Synoptic Tradition* (rev. ed.; trns. John Marsh; New York: Harper & Row, 1963) 23; see also Fitzmyer, *The Gospel*, 2:1004–06; J. Denney, "Three Motives to Repentance, Luke XIII. 1–9," *Expos* 4/7 (1893) 232–237).

[108] In Luke, during the crucifixion of Jesus, two criminals hang on crosses next to Jesus, and one of the criminals states that he and the other criminal are being justly punished because they are receiving what is worthy (ἄξιος) for what they have done (πράσσω; cf Acts 26:20) (Luke 23:41). This idea of doing (πράσσω/ποιέω) something worthy (ἄξιος) of something is a common theme in Luke-Acts (cf. Luke 3:8, 13; 12:48; 15:19, 21; 23:15, 41; Acts 25:11, 25; 26:20, 31).

[109] Matthew shifts the emphasis of John's preaching away from "repentance for remission of sins" to the idea of repenting because "the kingdom of heaven is at hand."

[110] This depiction of John the Baptist as a prominent figure drawing large crowds is confirmed by the only extant extrabiblical testimony to the career of John the Baptist, found in Josephus' *Antiquities* (18.5,2 §§ 116–119). Josephus writes, "Herod put to death this good man who was exhorting the Jews to live upright lives. . . . When still others joined the crowds around him, because they were quite enthusiastic in listening to his words, Herod became frightened that such persuasiveness with the people might lead to some uprising; for it seemed that they might go to any length on his advice."

[111] Conzelmann writes, "Thus John has a clearly defined function. . . it is his ministry rather than his person that serves as a preparation for Jesus." (*Theology*, 24).

repentance that is the author's focus. The message of repentance is not restricted to being proclaimed simply in the wilderness, but the message is proclaimed throughout all the region around the Jordan.[112]

The Markan construction, "As it is written in the prophet Isaiah. . . **John the baptizer appeared**." (1:2–4) clearly makes John the Baptist the object of prophetic fulfillment. The Markan inclusion of the non-Isaian phrase, "See, I am sending my messenger ahead of you, who will prepare your way;"[113] within the Isaian quote is clearly meant to point to John the Baptist as the object of the prophecy. Similarly, the Matthean preface, "This is the one of whom the prophet Isaiah spoke when he said, . . . ", explicitly makes John the Baptist the object of the Isaian prophecy. The Lukan passage, however, makes the "baptism of repentance" the object of the Isaian prophecy.

In Mark's gospel, the passage about John the Baptist "proclaiming a baptism of repentance for the remission of sins" follows the Isaian prophecy; however, in Luke's gospel the passage has been moved immediately before the introduction of the Isaian prophecy. The result is that the "baptism of repentance for the remission of sins" becomes the object of the prophecy rather than John the Baptist being the object.[114] By following the reference to John "proclaiming a baptism of repentance for the remission of sins," with the citation formula: "as it is written in the book of the words of the prophet Isaiah," Luke depicts John's baptism and, more importantly, his preaching of "repentance for the remission of sins" as the fulfillment of Isaiah's prophetic message.[115] The author of this gospel is asserting that the Isaian prophecy is fulfilled through the preaching of "a baptism of repentance for the remission of sins." It is more so the "preaching of repentance," rather than the coming of John the Baptist, that was foretold by the prophet Isaiah.[116] Therefore, the preaching of "repentance for the remission of sins" was and

---

[112] C. H. Kraeling suggests that John went to the highways to preach his message of repentance (*John the Baptist* (New York: Scribner, 1951) 64), while W. R. Brownlee suggests that John "found places in the wilderness where he could meet people" in villages and towns and preach his message of repentance ("John the Baptist in the Light of Ancient Scrolls," in *The Scrolls and the New Testament* (eds. Krister Stendahl and James Charlesworth; New York: Crossroad, 1992) 33–53).

[113] Cf Exodus 23:20; Malachi 3:1.

[114] Although the reference has been moved before the Isaian prophecy in Matthew's gospel, the passage has been significantly redacted and is followed by the Matthean summary statement, "This is the one of whom the prophet Isaiah spoke." So in Matthew, the focus is not on the baptism of repentance (which is not even mentioned), but on John the Baptist.

[115] Fitzmyer states that "The introductory conj. *hōs*, "as," shows that Luke regards John's baptism and preaching as a fulfillment of Isaiah's prophetic message." (*The Gospel*, 1:460).

[116] Tannehill makes reference not only to the preceding of the Isaian quote by the phrase "a baptism of repentance for the remission of sin," he also points out that "Following the quotation, we are given a sample of John's call to repentance. Thus the quotation is framed by John's preaching of repentance and is partly interpreted by this context. Preparing the Lord's way means preparing the people through repentance, as 1:17 indicated." (*Narrative Unity*, 48).

is part of God's divine plan.[117] Repentance is not merely a human response, it is **the** human response foretold by God's prophet and ordained by God.

Not only does the author of Luke-Acts make the baptism of repentance the object of the Isaian prophecy, and therefore part of God's divine plan, he also increases the attention given to John's preaching of repentance by identifying John the Baptist with God's "holy prophets of old" (Luke 1:70; Acts 3:21). Although early Christian tradition recognized John the Baptist as a prophet,[118] Luke alone, employing the prophetic utterance of the angel Gabriel, identifies John the Baptist before his birth with the prophet Elijah (1:17). Similarly, John's father, while under the influence of the Holy Spirit, prophetically declares that John shall "be called the prophet of the Most High" (1:76).[119] Finally, in this passage announcing the preparation for the public ministry of Jesus, Luke alone introduces John the Baptist using the formulaic prophetic introduction, which includes both the traditional synchronism relating the prophet's call and ministry to contemporary history[120] and the call of John the Baptist in the form of an Old Testament prophetic vocation.[121] Whereas Mark and Matthew simply portray John the Baptist as preaching in the wilderness, Luke depicts his activity as the result of a "call" from God. Through all of this prophetic identification, the author portrays the words and deeds spoken and performed by John the Baptist as those in response to "the word of God" which "came to John son of Zechariah in the wilderness" (Luke 3:2b).

Typical Old Testament prophetic introductions were designed not to direct one's attention to the prophet, but rather to direct one's attention to the "word of God" spoken to the prophet, as well as to the deeds performed and words spoken by the prophet in response to the word of God spoken to the prophet.[122] The reader recognizes the prophet's behavior and speech as either consistent or inconsistent with the word of God, but either way the behavior and speech of the prophet is always understood in relationship to the "word of God" received by that prophet. If the prophet is a true prophet, he or she ultimately does and says what God commands through the "word of God." The attention is always on the "word of God" spoken to and fulfilled by the prophet. The deeds performed and words

---

[117] Once again the author uses an Old Testament quotation to express a divine purpose being fulfilled.

[118] Cf. Mk 11:32, par.; Mt 11:9, par.

[119] Both of these statements serve as typical Lukan "previews."

[120] Luke 3:1–2 (cf Jer 1:1–3; Ezk 1:1–3; Dan 9:1–2; Hos 1:1; Mic 1:1; Zeph 1:1; Hag 1:1; 2:10; Zec 1:1, 7; 7:1). Such synchronism was also used by Greek historians (cf Thucydides *History of the Peloponnesian War* 2.2.1; Polybius *The Histories* 1.3; Dionysius of Halicarnassus *Roman Antiquities* 9.61). See also Cadbury, *The Making of Luke-Acts*, 204–209.

[121] Luke 3:2b (cf. 1 Sam 15:10; 2 Sam 7:4; 24:11; 1 Kg 12:22; 18:1; Isa 38:4; Jer 1:4, 13; 2:1; 13:3; 33:1; Ezk 1:3; 6:1; 25:1; Jon 1:1; Hag 1:3; Zec 7:8).

[122] During the Prophetic Period in Israel, the formula: "The word of the Lord came unto X" was used to draw the readers attention to the words given and the acts performed by the one receiving the word.

spoken by the prophet were always more important than the prophet, because the deeds performed by the prophet were in obedience to the word of God, and the message spoken by the prophet represented the word of God to the people.

By introducing John as a prophet receiving a word from the Lord, the author implies that the act of "preaching a baptism of repentance for the remission of sins" is done in fulfillment of the word of God which came to John. John's baptism functions in the category of the symbolic actions of the prophets.[123] Furthermore, the prophetic introduction of John the Baptist causes the reader to recognize the words declared by John in vv 7–14 to be words proclaimed by the prophet in response to the word he received from God. The words are not simply the words of John the Baptist, but they are the words given to John by God. Therefore, John's call for repentance is actually a call from God. The call for repentance in Luke-Acts is indeed part of the plan of God.

As stated earlier, the motif of "remission of sins" (ἄφεσις ἁμαρτιῶν) is intimately related to the content of salvation. In Luke 3:1–6, the author clearly asserts that it is the "baptism of repentance" that secures the "remission of sins."[124] Therefore, the "baptism of repentance" serves as a prerequisite for this motif that is intimately related to the content of salvation. This identification of the "baptism of repentance" as the means for securing the "remission of sins" serves a pivotal function in the unfolding of the narrative of Luke-Acts.[125] Through the infancy narrative, the author has spawned a number of expectations within the implied reader.[126] A number of these expectations have to do with John the Baptist. The implied reader has been informed that John "will turn many of the sons of Israel to the Lord their God" (Luke 1:16). John will "turn the hearts of the fathers to the children, and the disobedient to the wisdom of the just, to make ready for the Lord a people prepared" (1:17). John will "go before the Lord to prepare his ways, to give knowledge of salvation to his people by means of the remission of their sins" (1:76c–77). Through foreshadowing, the author has told the reader what John is going to do and accomplish. Such foreshadowing has created an immediate sense of suspense and expectation within the author's narrative. According to Robert Brawley, "Suspense pulls readers forward in narrative. . . . Suspense is usually achieved by foreshadowing even though foreshadowing may give away the ending. When foreshadowing and outright predictions make the ending a foregone conclusion, the narratives enticement shifts from what will happen to how it will

---

[123] J. Barton, *Oracles of God: Perceptions of Ancient Prophecy in Israel after the Exile* (London: Darton, Longman and Todd, 1986).

[124] Matthew (3:5–6) neglects saying that John's baptism was for the remission of sins

[125] With regard to the "unfolding" of Luke's narrative, see Brawley, *Centering*, 34–54 for a discussion of the progressive development within narratives.

[126] For an examination of the points of contact between the birth stories and the rest of Luke-Acts, see Paul Minear, "Luke's Use of the Birth Stories," *Studies in Luke Acts* (eds. Leander Keck and J. Louis Martyn; Nashville, Abingdon, 1966) 111–30.

happen."[127] The reader is concerned not with **what** John will do, but with **how** he will do what he's been sent to do. The author partly fulfills the readers' anticipation in Luke 3:1–14 by showing **how** John gives "knowledge of salvation to [God's] people by means of the remission of their sins." The knowledge of salvation by means of the remission of sins is accomplished through John's "baptism of repentance." Furthermore, the author now makes a connection between "baptism of repentance," "remission of sins," and "salvation" by extending the Isaian quote to include the phrase, "and all flesh shall see the salvation of God." By extending the quote, the author again identifies the remission of sins as part of the content of salvation.[128] In addition, the author now connects the "baptism of repentance" with the "salvation of God." The "remission of sins" serves as the common denominator connecting the "baptism of repentance" and "the salvation of God."

In Luke it is most likely the act of repentance rather than the ritual of baptism that secures the remission of sins. After all in Jesus' resurrection appearance to the disciples, Jesus opens the disciples' understanding to the scriptures that assert, "repentance for the remission of sins" shall be preached to all nations in Jesus' name.[129] Furthermore, in Peter's speech before the religious council, remission of sins is associated with repentance not with baptism (Acts 5:31).[130] The emphasis on repentance rather than baptism as the means of securing the remission of sins is a notion found in the writings of the Qumran community.[131] The Essenes at Qumran

---

[127] *Centering on God*, 34; cf. Shlomith Rimmon-Kenan, *Narrative Fiction: Contemporary Poetics* (London: Methuen, 1983) 48; Chatman, *Story and Discourse*, 59–63.

[128] As was the case in Luke 1:77. In Luke-Acts, "remission of sins" often appears in balanced apposition with "salvation," however, the two expressions should not be considered synonymous. Salvation includes the remission of sins (cf Luke 7:48–50); however, salvation should not be defined simply as remission of sins. (See Joel Green, "'Salvation to the ends of the earth,'" 89–94).

[129] Luke 24:45–47. In the finale of the Matthean gospel (28:19–20a) and in the Markan appendix (16:15–16) baptism is commanded of the disciples; however, in the Lukan commission statement there is no mention of baptism. Furthermore, Luke alone in his commission statement records Jesus instructing the disciples to preach repentance for the remission of sins to all nations.

[130] While "remission of sins" appears intimately connected with baptism in Peter's response to the crowd on the day of Pentecost (Acts 2:38), Peter's response, "Repent, and be baptized every one of you *in the name of Jesus* for the remission of sins" is clearly meant to echo Jesus' post-resurrection instructions to his disciples that "repentance for the remission of sins should be preached *in his name* to all nations" (Luke 24:47). Peter is preaching "**Repentance** for the remission of sins," as instructed by Jesus.

[131] While it cannot be proved (nor can it be disproved), it is plausible that John the Baptist spent some time in the desert among the Essenes of Qumran (cf. Luke 1:80; see J. A. T. Robinson, "The Baptism of John and the Qumran Community," *HTR* 50 (1957) 175–194). After all Isaiah 40:3, which explains the reason why John was in the desert, is also used in the Essene Rule Book to explain why the Essenes were in the desert (1QS 8:12–16). The baptism which John preached, therefore, could have been a development of the ritual washing of the Essenes. It is very unlikely that John's baptizing activity should be understood in relation to Jewish proselyte baptism (cf. W. Michaelis, "Zum jüdischen hintergrund der Johannestaufe," *Judaica* 7 (1951) 81–121 (especially 94–121); see also D. Smith, "Jewish Proselyte Baptism and the Baptism of John *ResQ* 25 (1982) 13–32).

suggested that ritual washing itself had no cleansing power. The cleansing was contingent upon a change of behavior: "They shall not enter the water to share in the pure meal of the saints, for they shall not be cleansed unless they turn from their evil doings."[132] Concerning a man who showed no signs of repentance, the Community Rule declares: "He shall not be reckoned among the perfect; he shall neither be purified by atonement, nor cleansed by purifying waters nor sanctified by seas and rivers, nor washed clean with any ablution."[133] Similarly, it was most likely the repentance associated with John's baptism rather than the baptism itself that secured the remission of sins.[134] In Luke, John's baptism represents the arrival of a time of repentance when God cleanses God's people of all of their sins (1:76–77), enabling them to return to the Lord their God (1:16–17). Sin separates the sinner from God, but the remission of sins enables the sinner to be reunited with God and with the community of God's people.[135]

By ending the Isaian quote in Luke 3:4–6 with the words "and all flesh shall see the salvation of God," the author makes the connection between "repentance," "remission of sins" and "the salvation of God." This connection is the ultimate and final point that the author is seeking to make in this passage. There is no need for the author to discuss John's physical appearance or to discuss the baptism process (cf Mk 1:5b–6; par.), because neither John the Baptist[136] nor the baptism itself is the focus. Salvation, resulting from repentance for the remission of sins, is the focus. In the prophecy of Zechariah, the implied reader is informed that John's purpose is to prepare the way of the Lord by giving "knowledge of salvation" to God's people "by means of the remission of their sins" (Luke 1:77). Zechariah's prophecy serves as a preview of John's ministry. In Luke-Acts, the only episodic depiction of John's ministry is found here in Luke 3:1–14. Thus, the implied reader is forced to understand John's preaching of a baptism of repentance for "the remission of sins" as the fulfillment of Zechariah's prophecy.[137] John is giving to God's people "knowledge of salvation. . . by means of the remission of their sins," which is accomplished through repentance. Because of the preview given through Zechariah's prophecy, the reader is compelled to see the connection between

---

[132] 1QS 5:13–14.

[133] 1QS 3:3–12. The emphasis is on repentance rather than on the physical act of baptism, because it is repentance that reckons one "among the perfect."

[134] Josephus, in his depiction of John the Baptist, observed that John baptized people as a outward sign of an inward cleansing (*Ant* 18.5.2. § 117). Josephus clearly understood that inward cleansing to be the result of repentance, not baptism.

[135] Cf. *Jub.* 1:22–25; 1 QS 4:18–23. John's call for the repentant ones to come to the Jordan to be baptized was an action symbolic of their return to God. Their baptism also marked their entitlement to be received into the community of God's people.

[136] The author of Luke-Acts even omits the story of John's execution by Herod (after 9:7–9), because it is John's purpose not his person that the author is concerned with.

[137] In addition, all the summary statements in Luke-Acts about the ministry of John the Baptist refer to events depicted in this episode (Luke 7:29–30; Acts 13:24; 18:25; 19:4). John fulfills his ordained purpose by preaching a baptism of repentance for the remission of sins.

36   The Role and Function of Repentance

"baptism of repentance," "remission of sins" and "the salvation of God." The focus of this passage is salvation, resulting from repentance for the remission of sins. It is the human response of repentance that secures the remission of sins, and it is the remission of sins that gives knowledge of salvation.

By identifying John's preaching of repentance as the "how" that fulfills the "what" foreshadowed in the infancy narrative, the author partly fulfills the reader's anticipation, while at the same time modifying that anticipation.[138] The reader now anticipates repentance as the response in Luke-Acts that will secure the remission of sins and give knowledge of God's salvation. The author now foreshadows the importance of repentance within God's universal saving purpose. Repentance for the remission of sins reflects God's purpose for humanity (Luke 7:30) because it is repentance that makes the content of salvation available to all flesh. As the reader will soon find out, however, not everyone is willing to accept God's invitation to repentance.[139] Since in Luke-Acts the universal saving purpose of God is the plan of God, repentance must also be understood as part of that plan. Repentance is commanded of all people because repentance is that which secures the salvation of God in the lives of all people.[140]

Repentance can further be understood as part of the plan of God by the fact that on two occasions repentance comprises the answer to the characteristic Lukan rhetorical question, "What then shall we/I do?"[141] The question affords the author an opportunity to indicate a divine plan at work, by placing responses in the mouths of reliable characters within the story. As stated earlier, these characters are portrayed by the author as reliable in their judgments and discerning in their statements. Furthermore, they serve as spokespersons for the author in interpreting events and disclosing God's plan in the story. The first three occurrences of the question (Luke 3: 10, 12, 14) are in response to John the Baptist's command to the crowd to "Bear fruits worthy of repentance" (Luke 3:8). The questions afford the

---

[138] Regarding the role of modified expectations within narratives, see Brawley, *Centering*, 34–51.

[139] It is of course the refusal of many in Luke-Acts to repent that provides the narrative with tension and gives the narrative its sense of dynamic progression (cf. Brawley, *Centering*, 34).

[140] Paradoxically, in the author's narrative, the willingness to repent is what moves the narrative toward the fulfillment of God's plan of universal salvation, while at the same time the refusal of many of the Jewish leaders and some of the Jewish people to repent is what provides the extension of salvation to those outside of traditional Jewish acceptability. Both the acceptance and the rejection of repentance contributes to the fulfillment of God's plan of universal salvation. It is this use of repentance by the author that contributes to the suspense of Luke-Acts, because suspense is also related to tragic irony (cf. Sylvan Barnet, et. al. *A Dictionary of Literary Terms* (2d ed.; Boston: Little Brown, 1971) 83–84). The characters who refuse to repent move closer and closer to their doom, while the reader is held by the suspense generated from three facts: 1) repentance is the human response ordained by God, 2) the offer of repentance continues to remain available to the tragic characters who refuse to repent, and 3) their refusal to repent affords the extension of salvation to others, including the author's implied reader.

[141] Luke 3:10, 12, 14; Acts 2:37 (see also Luke 10:25; 18:18; Acts 16:30; 22:10).

author an opportunity, through John the Baptist, to give examples of what it means to "bear fruits worthy of repentance." In responding to the question, John the Baptist discloses that repentance is part of God's plan. Similarly, in response to the first missionary sermon delivered in Acts, the crowds ask Peter and the rest of the apostles, "Brethren, what shall we do?" Peter responds, "Repent, and be baptized every one of you in the name of Jesus Christ for the remission of sins" (2:37, 38). Peter likewise clearly discloses that repentance is definitely part of the plan of God."

Repentance is also understood as part of the plan of God by the fact that Jesus, who in Luke-Acts fulfills the plan of God, came in order to call sinners to repentance (Luke 5:32).[142] Earlier in Luke's gospel, Jesus declares that the Spirit of the Lord has anointed him "to preach good news to the poor... to proclaim release to the captives and recovery of sight to the blind, to send away the oppressed released, to proclaim the acceptable year of the Lord" (4:18–19). Shortly thereafter, Jesus declares, "I must preach the good news of the kingdom of God to the other cities also; for I was sent for this purpose" (4:43). This section (4:14–44), which serves as a general introduction to Jesus' public ministry, makes it clear that preaching the good news is the purpose of Jesus' ministry.[143] The author seeks to make it clear that Jesus was sent for the purpose of preaching.

Now, on the heels of this section that establishes the general purpose of Jesus' ministry, Jesus makes another assertion that states his purpose. As a result of a Lukan redaction, Jesus declares to the Pharisees and their scribes that he has come to call "sinners to repentance" (5:32). The literary development of Luke's gospel clearly makes this specific mission of calling sinners to repentance[144] part of Jesus' general mission of preaching good news. In other words, in Luke's gospel calling sinners to repentance is part of (if not identical with) preaching the good news.[145]

The reader is forced to conclude, through the progressive development of Luke's story[146] that it is the preaching of good news, which means the calling of

---

[142] This explicit assertion is lacking in the parallel texts found in Mark and Matthew.

[143] Although much more expanded and detailed, this section is the Lukan equivalent to Mark 1:14–15.

[144] Within the immediate context, Jesus is referring specifically to Levi and the guests Levi has invited to the feast in his house.

[145] This is confirmed first of all by the fact that immediately after the uniquely Lukan ethical preaching section of John the Baptist, where of course repentance is the focus, the author declares, "So, with many other exhortations, he [i.e. John] **preached good news** to the people" (Luke 3:18; emphasis added). The exhortations on repentance are a significant part of the preaching of good news by John the Baptist. This identification of preaching repentance with preaching the good news is further confirmed by the fact that Paul, in his defense to King Agrippa, sums up his preaching ministry as declaring "to those at Damascus, then at Jerusalem and throughout all the country of Judea, and also to the Gentiles, that they should **repent** and turn to God and **perform deeds worthy of their repentance**" (Acts 26:20). The preaching of repentance is how Paul, according to Luke, defined his ministry.

[146] See a discussion of the role of progressive development within narrative literature in Brawley, *Centering on God*, 34.

sinners to repentance, that provides the method and means for Jesus to accomplish what he declares to be his mission in his last mission statement. After the apparent repentance of Zacchaeus,[147] Jesus declares, "For the Son of man came to seek and save the lost" (Luke 19:10). Jesus seeks and saves the lost through his preaching of good news, which includes calling sinners to repentance. Finally, Jesus also declares that scripture demands that repentance be preached to all nations (Luke 24:46–47).

Repentance is further revealed by Luke to be part of the plan of God by that fact that only in Luke's gospel is there reference to the host of heaven and "the angels of God" rejoicing over "one sinner who repents" (Luke 15:7, 10).[148] Repentance is the source of joy in the heavenly realm.[149] Lastly, in Luke-Acts it is God who gives repentance. Although repentance is a human response, God is the one who gives repentance. Peter and the other apostles declared that God exalted Jesus in order "to give repentance to Israel and remission of sins" (Acts 5:31). Similarly, after Peter's report to the church at Jerusalem, all who listened "glorified God, saying, 'Then to the Gentiles also God has granted repentance unto life'" (11:18). Not only is God the one who gives repentance, but God "commands all people everywhere to repent" (Acts 17: 30b).

Without a doubt, according to Luke-Acts repentance is part of the plan of God. The extension of salvation to all flesh is the plan of God, and the human response of repentance is the method ordained by God that enables all flesh to receive the salvation of God and to live together as a community of God's people.

---

[147] The proposed repentance of Zacchaeus will be examined in more detail in Chapter Three of this work.

[148] Whether the author freely composed the second of these two parables himself (a possibility suggested but not pursued by Fitzmyer, *The Gospel*, 2:1073), or redacted a parable he inherited from an earlier source (cf. J. Lambrecht, *Once More Astonished: The Parables of Jesus* (New York: Crossroad, 1981) 28), the two parables together have clearly been built into a unit with a single theme (cf I. H. Marshall, *Luke*, p. 597), and that theme is reiterated in the two application statements (vv. 7, 10) which were most likely supplied by the author himself (contra. T. W. Manson, *The Sayings of Jesus as Recorded in the Gospels according to St. Matthew and St. Luke Arranged with Introduction and Commentary* (London: SCM, 1971) 283).

[149] In addition, as Fitzmyer points out, the joining of the two application statements to these two parables "brings out that repentance does not take place without the prevenience and initiative of the gracious shepherd" (*The Gospel*, 2:1075). God is the one who brings about repentance.

Chapter Three

The Meaning of Repentance

Although the motif of repentance has a prominence in Luke-Acts that it does not have in the rest of the New Testament, the concept of repentance did not originate with the author of Luke-Acts. The author inherited a concept that was present in Greco-Roman, Jewish, and early Christian literature. Prior to the Christian era, the occurrences of μετανοέω and μετάνοια were relatively rare. In the literature from the 8th century B.C.E. until the close of the 1st century B.C.E. the terms occur approximately 95 times. In the first two centuries of the Common Era, however, the terms occur approximately 1201 times.[1] The use of μετανοέω and μετάνοια to express the idea of repentance flourished during the Common Era in general and during the Christian literary era in particular. This does not imply, however, that the understanding of μετανοέω and μετάνοια during this time was not influenced by earlier understandings of these terms. This chapter will examine how μετανοέω and μετάνοια were used in the literary milieu inherited by the author of Luke-Acts. It will also examine the relationship between how the motif of repentance is used within the larger literary milieu and how it is used within the author's two volume work.

---

[1] These numbers are based on the citations found in the electronic version of the *Thesaurus Linguae Grecae* (*TLG*).

Μετανοέω and Μετάνοια in Classical and Hellenistic Greek Literature

Many scholars have repeatedly made the mistake of assuming that the early Christian conception of "repentance" is so special that there is nothing like it in pre-Christian Greek usage. These scholars assert that there is little or no affinity between the usage of μετανοέω and μετάνοια in non-Christian Greek literature and its usage in Christian literature. Accordingly, some writers minimize both the affective dimension of the concept and its evaluative and moral connotations prior to the Christian era. J. Behm confidently—but erroneously—declared, "Whether linguistically or materially, one searches the Greek world in vain for the origin of the NT understanding of μετανοέω and μετάνοια."[2] E. Norden went so far as to declare that μετάνοια never meant "repentance" in its pre-Christian usage.[3]

While the usage of μετανοέω and μετάνοια in early Christian writings may not have been identical with the usage found in classical and non-Christian Hellenistic Greek writings, this chapter will demonstrate that the early Christian usage was clearly influenced by the usage of the terms in classical and non-Christian Hellenistic Greek literature. Christians undoubtedly developed some special nuances in their concept of repentance; however, there are clear continuities with the way the concept was used by philosophers, orators, and popular moralists in the world around them. Moreover, whatever new things the Christians wanted to say had to be understood within the context of the way their words were commonly used in the prevailing Greek culture.

Definition of Μετανοέω and Μετάνοια

The preposition μετά can have many different meanings.[4] When used in the accusative case, the preposition is commonly translated "behind, after." Influenced by this translation of μετά, some scholars assume that during the earliest linguistic history of μετανοέω and μετάνοια a simple etymological meaning for these terms must have dominated; i.e. μετανοέω must have meant "think afterwards" and μετάνοια must have meant "afterthought."[5] While the notion of "thinking

---

[2] J. Behm, "μετανοέω, μετάνοια," *Theological Dictionary of the New Testament* (eds. G. Kittel, G. Friedrich; trns., Geoffrey Bromiley; 10 vols; Grand Rapids, MI: Eerdmans, 1964–1976) 4:980.

[3] Eduard Norden, *Agnostos Theos* (Stuttgart: B. G. Teubner, 1912) 134.

[4] See "μετά" in Liddell and Scott, *Greek-English Lexicon*; Kittel and Friedrich, *Theological Dictionary of the New Testament*; Bauer, Arndt, Gingrich and Danker, *A Greek-English Lexicon of the New Testament and Other Christian Literature*.

[5] For a discussion of the etymology of these two words, see Thompson, *Μετανοέω and Μεταμέλει in Greek Literature until 100 A.D., Including Discussion of Their Cognates and of Their Hebrew Equivalents* (Chicago: University of Chicago Press, 1908); E. Boisacq, *Dictionnaire etymologique de la Langue Grecque*; Behm and Würthwein, "μετανοέω,

afterwards" may have very well been one aspect of the earliest linguistic history of μετανοέω and μετάνοια, an examination of the literary evidence clearly indicates that more than a simple etymological sense dominated.

In the earliest literary evidence available, both terms carry some negative connotation in their ordinary use. While the terms may be rendered "think afterwards" of "afterthought," they clearly imply at least something like the phrase "to have second thoughts." This is the idea found in the fifth century B.C.E. writings of Epicharmus and Democritus. Epicharmus contrasts μετανοέω with προνοέω, "think beforehand," when he writes: οὐ μεταοεῖν ἀλλὰ προνοεῖν χρὴ τὸν ἄνδρα τὸν σοφόν ("the wise man ought not to think afterwards but rather to think beforehand").[6] Similarly, Democritus contrasts μετανοέω with προβουλεύομαι, "decide beforehand, plan in advance," when he writes: προβουλεύεσθαι κρέσσον πρὸ τῶν πράξεων ἢ μετανοεῖν ("It is better to plan in advance before one's actions, than to think afterwards").[7] Furthermore, like Epicharmus, the fifth century B.C.E. sophist/rhetorician Gorgias also places μετανοέω and προνοέω in antithesis.[8]

Undoubtedly μετανοέω and μετάνοια meant more than "think afterwards" and "afterthought." The notion of "having second thoughts" does not simply suggests "thinking afterwards;" instead it suggests a "change in thinking."[9] This becomes much clearer in succeeding centuries. The verb μετανοέω begins to commonly mean "think differently, change one's mind or view, from a different

---

μετάνοια," *TDNT* 4:975–1008.

[6] *Fragment* 280. *TLG*; cf. G. Kaibel, ed. *Comicorum Graecorum fragmenta* (Berlin: Weidmann, 1899). Unless otherwise noted, all translations of Greek and other non-English texts are my own.

[7] *Fragment* 66, *TLG*; cf. H. Diels and W. Kranz, eds., *Die Fragmente der Vorsokratiker* (2 vol.; Berlin: Weidmann, 1952) 2. #36. It should be pointed out that Dirksen, in his 1932 dissertation *The New Testament Concept of Μετάνοια*, translates the maxim from Democritus, "it is better to consider things beforehand that to **regret** them later" (emphasis added). This idea of regret will discussed later in this chapter.

[8] *Fragment* 11, *TLG* (Diels and Kranz, 2:263).

[9] The only possible exception is an occurrence of μετανοέω in one of Plato's dialogues. Socrates gives an account of a conversation he had with a man named Cleinias regarding which things in life should be identified as "good." After identifying a number of things, Socrates states that they need to consider carefully their list and make sure they haven't omitted any of the "goods." Cleinias responds that he doesn't think they have omitted any. After thinking about it, Socrates remembers one, and asserts that he and Cleinias almost forgot what he considers the greatest of the goods, "good fortune." Both men agree that they almost made a tremendous mistake by nearly omitting good fortune from their list of goods. Socrates then asserts that "after reconsidering (μετανοήσας) *the matter* once again" (αὖ πάλιν), he realizes they have made another mistake (*Euthydemus* 279.C; unless otherwise noted, English summaries or translations of Greek texts are based upon the Greek text as found in the Loeb Classical Library (LCL)). By emphatically stating that he reconsidered (μετανοήσας) *the matter* "**once again**," Socrates associates μετανοέω with his earlier process of thinking about the situation. While the use of the term here simply seems to suggest "thinking afterwards" and does not necessarily carry with it a negative connotation, Socrates does—when "thinking afterwards"—realize that a serious mistake was made.

opinion, plan or purpose." Similarly, the noun μετάνοια begins to commonly mean "a change of mind, heart, view, opinion or purpose." This notion of *changing* one's way of thinking quickly becomes the primary meaning for these two words.

The fourth century B.C.E. historian, Xenophon, uses μετανοέω to denote a change in thinking. In a historical novel which serves as a response to Plato and others who wrote on the problem of finding and educating statesmen and leaders, Xenophon presents his notions on the maintenance of authority and empire, political and military organization and moral reform. Xenophon writes:

> Thus as we meditated on this analogy, we were inclined to conclude that for man, as he is constituted, it is easier to rule over any and all other creatures than to rule over men. But when we reflected that there was one Cyrus, the Persian, who reduced to obedience a vast number of men and cities and nations, we were then compelled to change our opinion (μετανοεῖν) and decide that to rule men might be a task neither impossible nor even difficult, if one should only go about it in an intelligent manner.[10]

Xenophon's use of μετανοέω in this passage clearly denotes a change of mind or opinion. Similarly, Menander, the fourth century comic/playwright, uses μετανοέω to denote a change of mind. A character in one of Menander's plays states, "I have let you have one of my possessions. If you like it, keep it. If you don't, or if you've changed your mind (μετανοεῖς), then hand it back."[11] Another representative of the classical period who uses μετανοέω in this way seems to have been the fourth century orator Demosthenes. Writing about the unscrupulous nature of Aristogeiton and his disregard for justice, Demosthenes asks the people, "For whom has he brought into court that he succeeded in convicting on the charges that he laid against him? Or what source of revenue has he provided for you? Or what decree has he ever drafted that after being persuaded you did not later choose to change your mind (μετανοῆσαι)?"[12]

According to Stobaeus—a fifth century C.E. author of an anthology of excerpts from poets and prose writers—the third century B.C.E. Stoic, Chrysippus, asserts that the truly wise man does not change his mind (οὐδε μετανοεῖν). Instead, it is the liar and the fool who is subject to μετάνοια. The judgment of the truly wise man, i.e. the Stoic, is always correct because the Stoic perceives things in their true light;

---

[10] *Cyropaedia* 1.1.3 (English translation taken from C. L. Brownson, *et al.*, *Xenophon* LCL (7 vols.; Cambridge, MA: Harvard University Press, 1918–1968)).

[11] *Epitrepontes* 289 (Cf *The Arbitrants* 71). Other uses of μετανοέω to denote a change of mind are found in sentence fragments attributed to Menander (See *Senteniae e codicibus Byzantinis* # 147.315 and *Sententiae papyris* # 14.23 *TLG*; cf. S. Jaekel, *Menandri sententiae* (Leipzig: Teubner, 1964), as well as *Sententiae Mono*. # 1.91; 1.667 *TLG*; see also A. Meineke *Fragmenta Comicorum Graecorum* (4 vols.; Berlin: Reimer, 1841) v. 4).

[12] *Oration* 26 (*Against Aristogeiton*, II) 17.4.

therefore, the Stoic, never has a reason to change his mind.[13] The liar and the fool, on the other hand, lacks wisdom and correct judgment, and therefore constantly finds himself changing his mind. The teachings of the Stoics assert that the act of changing one's mind was indicative of the fool as opposed to the wise man. It is the fool who allows himself to be tossed back and forth under the influence of passions (πάθη), which are psychological forms of excitement which occur when reason (λόγος) falsely judges something as either a worthwhile good or an undesirable evil.[14] It is this false judgment (i.e. "ignorance") that the Stoics identify as sin.[15] As a result of this false judgment, reason surrenders its leadership to passion. When (or if) the fool recognizes his mistake, he is forced to change his mind regarding his former judgment. It is through this change of mind that the fool may become wise.[16] The truly wise man, however, would never make such a false judgment, not because passions are absent from his life, but because he is always guided by reason and never submits to passions.[17]

This Stoic sentiment that it is the fool who engages in the process of changing his mind, has led some scholars to wrongly assert that there was a Stoic polemic against μετάνοια. Eduard Norden appears to have been the first to make such an assertion. It seems that Norden based this conclusion upon his belief that the Stoics classified μετάνοια as a πάθος.[18] There is, however, no evidence to support this

---

[13] Stob. Ecl. 2.3.18.W. The quote of Chrysippus by Stobaeus can be found under Chrysippus, *Fragmenta moralia 548.23, TLG;* cf. J. von Arnim, ed., *Stoicorum Veterum Fragmenta* (4 vols.; Stuttgart: Teubner, 1966) 3.147. As in the gnome of Epicharmus, it is the "wise man" who should not engage in changing his mind.

[14] Von Arnim, *Stoicorum Vet. Frag.*, 3.142. Cf. 1.52–55; 3.164–171. Cicero identifies four types of πάθος, viz. λύπη, φόβος, ἐπιθυμία and ἡδονή. The first two arise from a false judgment regarding good, while the other two spring from a false judgment regarding evil *(Tusc.* 3.11.24). It should be pointed out that unlike the earlier Stoics, Chrysippus and the later Stoics did not condemn all πάθος as unreasonable. As a matter of fact, they introduced the teaching of the three good πάθη (εὐπαθεῖαι; see Arnold, *Roman Stoicism* (Cambridge: Cambridge University Press, 1911) 323; Diog. Laert. 7.115; Cicero, *Tusc.* 4.2). With this modification of the Stoic teaching on πάθος, came a much more relaxed attitude toward ἐπιθυμία. It became recognized among later Stoics that all desires cannot be regarded as evil, because some are aroused in the most reasonable of men (Cicero, *Tusc.* 4.12) These so-called "reasonable desires" the Stoics called βούλησις (Cicero, *Tusc.* 4.12; Diog. Laert. 7.115).

[15] Arnold, *Roman Stoicism*, 331.

[16] Cf. Arnold, *Roman Stoicism*, 294 ; E. Zeller, *The Stoics, Epicureans and Sceptics* (trans. O. J. Reichel; New York: Russell and Russell, 1962) 258.

[17] *Stoicorum Veterum Fragmenta*, 1.59, 60; 205–15; 2.65, 97; 3.377–420; Diogenes Laertius 7.117. See also J. M. Rist, *Stoic Philosophy* (Cambridge: Cambridge University Press, 1969). Although not a Stoic, Appian the historian reveals a similar view regarding wise men not needing to change their minds and fools becoming wise as a result of changing their minds. Appian writes, "Wise men are prevented from wrongdoing by their prudence, the wicked by their suffering and change of mind (μεταγνῶναι)" *(Roman History* 8.8.52).

[18] *Agnostos Theos*, 135.

belief.¹⁹ The prevailing sentiment among many Stoics concerning μετανοέω and μετάνοια was that truly wise men do not μετανοεῖν.²⁰ This sentiment, however, does not suggest a Stoic polemic against μετανοεῖν; rather it suggest a Stoic understanding that, although inappropriate for truly wise men, it is by μετανοεῖν that foolish men can become wise. For the Stoic, following reason (λόγος) is the objective of life, and it is indicative of the wise man;²¹ however, for those who go astray, i.e. the fool, μετάνοια is the means by which they get back into harmony with reason.²²

The use of μετανοέω and μετάνοια to denote a change of thinking and of purpose is of course not limited to describing the behavior of foolish and unlearned men. Polybius, the second century B.C.E. Greek historian, records that the Dardanians, after learning of the approach of Philip, disbanded and fled. When Philip heard about the "change of mind of the Dardanians (τὴν τῶν Δαρδανέων μετάνοιαν)," he also disbanded his troops and sent them home for the harvest.²³ The Dardanians, after hearing of Philip's military involvement, very wisely changed their plan of action. Polybius also gives an account of how Megaleas and Crinon, after drinking excessively at a dinner party, abused and stoned a man named Aratus. After hearing of the matter, the king reprimanded the two men. However, when they showed no regret and stated they would continue to pursue Aratus, the king fined the two men and ordered them to be imprisoned. Upon hearing what had happened to Megaleas, Leontius came to the royal tent accompanied by some soldiers, "feeling confident that he would intimidate the king, who was but a boy, and soon cause him to have a change of mind (μετάνοιαν)."²⁴

The first century B.C.E. historian Diodorus Siculus tells of an agreement made between the Athenians and the Ionians after the Greeks offered the Ionians a place

---

¹⁹ Norden may have come to this conclusion because of the often synonymous nature of μετανοέω and μεταμέλει (an issue that will be addressed later in this study). According to περὶ παθῶν, a Stoic work falsely attributed to Andronicus (cf. *Real-encyclopaedie*, I, col. 2167), μεταμέλει is a πάθος classified under λύπη (*περὶ παθῶν*, 2; cf. *Stoicorum Vet. Frag* III.100); Norden may have therefore assumed that the Stoics also considered μετάνοια to be a πάθος. There is, however, no direct evidence that the Stoics themselves considered μετανοέω and μεταμέλει to be synonymous.

²⁰ Cf. Stob. Ecl. II.3.18.W; 113.5.W. Cicero criticized certain Stoics who taught: "The philosopher surmises nothing, repents of nothing (*nullius rei paenitere*), is never wrong, and never changes his opinion" (*An Oration in Defense of Lucius Murena* 61).

²¹ Aelius Theon, a Stoic rhetorician of the second century C.E., asserted that the life of the wise man is one that is lived in harmony with nature without repentance (*Progymnasmata* 117.2; 122.9; 124.17; *TLG*; cf L. Spengel).

²² Cf. Seneca, who praises repentance as a means of moral progress by saying: "The most dependable change toward integrity comes from repentance (*ex paenitentia*)" (*Natural Questions* 3.Pref.3). As shall be seen later, this idea of repentance leading to moral progress is also reflected in the *Tabula of Cebes*.

²³ *Histories* 4.66.7.

²⁴ Ibid. 5.15–16. Other such occurrences in the writings of Polybius can be found in *Histories* 2.41.11; 5.51.8; 12.22.3; 18.33.7; 21.25.6; 33.12.6.

The Meaning of Repentance 45

of refuge from their enemies. Diodorus writes that the Greeks reminded the Ionians that:

> if they remained in Asia, they would always have the enemy on their borders, an enemy far superior in military strength, while their allies, who lived across the sea, would be unable to render them any timely assistance. When the Aeolians and Ionians had heard these promises, they resolved to take the advice of the Greeks and set about preparing to sail with them to Europe. But the Athenians changed to the opposite opinion (μετανοήσαντες εἰς τοὐναντίον) and advised them to stay where they were, saying that even if no other Greeks should come to their aid, the Athenians, as their kinsmen, would do so independently. They reasoned that, if the Ionians were given new homes by the Greeks acting in common they would no longer look upon Athens as their mother-city. It was for this reason that the Ionians changed their minds (μετανοῆσαι) and decided to remain in Asia.[25]

Diodorus also records how the Sicilian Greeks encouraged Dionysius, based on his last victory, to launch a surprise attack on Himilcon at Syracuse. According to Diodorus, Dionysius was prepared to follow their advice, "but when some of his friends told him that he ran the risk of losing the city if Magon should set out with his entire fleet against Syracuse, he quickly changed his mind (μετενόησε)."[26]

Finally, Dionysius of Halicarnassus tells of advice given to the plebeians about the need to change their behavior, and how this change of behavior would cause others to change their opinion of the plebeians. Dionysius writes:

> Then do you think it reasonable that others should endure what you yourselves refused to endure? Are these purposes of yours, plebeians, becoming to citizens and do they show moderation? By making such demands do you not yourselves confirm the truth of the charges brought against you and show that those who advise us not to permit your lawless domination to gain new strength have at heart the rights of the commonwealth? So it seems to me, at least. But if you desire to do just the opposite of what you have been charged with doing, follow my advice, moderate your behavior, and bear as fellow-citizens should, rather than with ill humour, the words which offend you. For if you do this, you will have a double advantage: you will be regarded as good men and those who are hostile to you will repent (μετανοεῖν).[27]

The use of μετανοέω and μετάνοια in the preceding passages clearly reveals that it was not simply the foolish and the unlearned who were subject to changing their minds. Armies, military leaders, kings, and entire societies were

---

[25] *Library of History* 11.37.3.
[26] Ibid. 14.61.2. Other such usages include 1.67.5; 9.25.2; 9.33.4; 11.4.6; 12.55.10; 13.53.3; 13.95.3; 14.60.1; 15.47.3; 15.79.5; 16.14.1; 16.43.4; 17.5.1; 17.45.7; 17.83.7; 18.47.2; 18.66.3; 19.48.6; 19.50.3; 19.51.4; 34/35.20.1.
[27] *Roman Antiquities* 7.31.4

subject to changing their minds. Changing one's mind was often a sign of wisdom and a cause for praise. Dio Cassius writes:

> Rufus, who, after obtaining equal authority with the dictator, had been defeated by the Carthaginians, altered his course (for disasters somehow chasten those who are not utter fools) and voluntarily resigned his command. And for this all praised him highly. He was not thought deserving of censure for his failure to recognize at first what was fitting, but was rather commended for not hesitating to change his mind (μετανοῆσαι). They deemed it really a piece of good fortune for a man to choose right at the start a proper course of conduct, whereas they were loud in their praise of the course of one, who, having learned from practical experience the better way, was not ashamed to change his course.[28]

In the quotes from both Dionysius and Dio Cassius, not only is repentance a sign of wisdom and a cause for praise, but repentance also leads to reconciliation between estranged parties. According to Dionysius, as a result of the plebeians' change of behavior, those citizens who were once hostile toward them will repent. The context clearly implies that reconciliation will take place between the plebeians and those who were once hostile toward them. Likewise, Dio Cassius records that because of the repentance of Rufus, the people did not censure him for his failure to initially do what was right; instead they commended him and praised him for his repentance. Whereas the people were initially upset with Rufus for his failure to do what was right, his repentance, brought about reconciliation between him and the people.

Other Hellenistic Greek authors who use μετανοέω and μετάνοια to denote a change in thinking, view, or purpose include Dio Chrysostom,[29] Appian,[30] Lucian,[31] Pausanias,[32] and Chariton.[33] The Hellenistic Greek author who uses μετανοέω and μετάνοια the most in his writings is the biographer/philosopher, Plutarch. These two words occur seventy-four times in the writings of Plutarch.[34] Virtually every occurrence in Plutarch conveys some aspect of a change in thinking and or purpose. Like the Stoics, Plutarch also associates the constant changing of mind with the unlearned and with those who lack the wisdom to follow reason.[35] In a discourse that discusses the nature of genuine freedom, Plutarch writes:

---

[28] *Roman History* 14.57.19–20 (English translation taken from E. Cary, *Dio Cassius* LCL (9 vols; Cambridge, MA: Harvard University Press, 1914–1927. See also 38.29.2; 46.27.4; 49.18.4; 53.11.2; 78.39.4).

[29] *Discourses* 12.45.1; 47.9.6.

[30] *Roman History* 7.6.35; 12.3.16; *Civil Wars* 1.6.50; 2.16.109; 3.13.90.

[31] *Disowned* 11.21; *Saturnalia* 15.18.

[32] *Description of Greece* 3.7.8; 3.8.7.

[33] *Chaereas and Callirhoe* 1.9.6; 2.9.3; 4.4.8.

[34] This is second only to the Jewish writer, Josephus, who uses μετανοέω and μετάνοια seventy-seven times in his writings.

[35] The use of μετανοέω and μετάνοια in general within the writings of Plutarch as a way of denoting a change of mind will be discussed later in this study.

Now the absence of control, which some of the young men, for want of education, think to be freedom, establishes the sway of a set of masters, harsher than the teachers and attendants of childhood, in the form of desires (ἐπιθυμίας), which are now, as it were, unchained. . . . But you have often heard that to follow God and to obey reason (λόγῳ) are the same thing, and so I ask you to believe that in persons of good sense the passing from childhood to manhood is not a casting off of control, but a recasting of the controlling agent, since instead of some hired person or slave purchased with money they now take as the divine guide of their life reason (τὸν λόγον), whose followers alone may deservedly be considered free. For they alone, having learned to wish for what they ought, live as they wish; but in untrained and irrational impulses and actions there is something ignoble, and changing one's mind (μετανοοῦντι) many times involves but little freedom of will.[36]

According to Plutarch, having to change one's mind several times because of an absence of self-control is not indicative of freedom, but rather is indicative of being enslaved to desires. The point being made by Plutarch and the Stoics is not that it is wrong to change one's mind, but rather that it is better to do what is right initially, which is the sign of the wise man, instead of repeatedly changing one's mind, which is the sign of the fool. Like the Stoics, Plutarch contrasts the superiority of initially doing what is right to the inferiority of having to change one's mind.[37] Plutarch further conveys this point by writing, "it is better to guard against errors by following proffered advice than to repent (μετανοεῖν) of errors."[38]

In addition, Plutarch also indicates the inappropriateness of changing one's mind after having initially done what was right. Plutarch gives an account of an accusation made by Aristogeiton against the Spartans. Plutarch writes, "Now he [Aristogeiton] cannot deny that the Spartans freed Athens from its tyrants; but he does succeed in belittling and denigrating their glorious deed by attributing a most unworthy reaction to them. He says that they soon repented (μετανοῆσαι), deciding that they had made a mistake and had been carried away by counterfeit oracles." The Spartans are then depicted as trying to bring one of the so-called tyrants back to power in Athens.[39] In this situation, Plutarch is identifying as wrong, as do the Stoics, the process of falsely judging as evil that which is good. According to Plutarch, repenting of good is "an unworthy reaction," and Aristogeiton asserts

---

[36] *Listening to Lectures* 37.C–E (English translation taken from F. C. Babbitt, *et al*, *Moralia* LCL (16 vols.; Cambridge, MA: Harvard University Press, 1927–1969).
[37] This view is also conveyed by Dionysius of Halicarnassus, who writes: "And the repentance (μετάνοια) of those who are late in beginning to be wise, though inferior to foresight, yet, when viewed in another light, is seen to be no less valuable, since it wipes out the error originally made in ignorance by preventing its consequences" (*Roman Antiquities* 7.22.4).
[38] *How to Tell a Flatterer* 74.C.
[39] *On the Malice of Herodotus* 860.F.

that the Spartans demonstrated such an error in judgment by changing their minds and trying to undo the good they achieved when they freed Athens from its tyrants.[40]

Elsewhere Plutarch tells the story of a man named Camillus, who appears to have been wrongly accused of stealing. Recognizing that his accusers were looking for any pretext for condemning him, and realizing that he had no chance of receiving a fair trial, Camillus decided to go into exile. Plutarch writes:

> Accordingly, after he had kissed his wife and son good-bye, he went from his house in silence as far as the gate of the city. There he stopped, turned himself about, and stretching his hands out towards the Capitol, prayed the gods that, if with no justice, but through the wantonness of the people and the abuse of the envious he was now being driven from his country, the Romans might speedily μετανοῆσαι, and show to all men that they needed and longed for Camillus.[41]

As in the previously cited quotes from Dionysius and Dio Cassius, the quote here from Plutarch suggests that repentance should lead to reconciliation between once alienated people.[42] After repenting, the Romans, who drove Camillus from his country, should demonstrate a need and longing for Camillus.

Clearly Plutarch used μετανοέω and μετάνοια to convey some aspect of a change in thinking, purpose, or behavior. Often associated with this change was a sense of regret. Plutarch gives an account of how Mithradates planned to execute a number of Galatians who had conspired to kill him. However, according to Plutarch, Mithradates began feeling sorry for one of the young men and therefore "changed his mind (μετενόει)."[43] Mithradates' change of mind, conveyed by μετανοέω, was preceded by a sense of sorrow.

The Emotions of Repentance

Contrary to the assertion made by E. F. Thompson at the beginning of the 20th century "that μετανοέω in the classical period is purely an intellectual term,"[44] the

---

[40] When depicting a change in thinking, μετανοέω and μετάνοια usually indicate a change from what is perceived as wrong to what is perceived as right. As is the case in this reference from Plutarch, in the few occurrences where the change in thinking is from what is perceived as right to what is perceived as wrong, μετανοέω and μετάνοια are often presented as inappropriate responses (cf. Diodorus, *History* 16.14.1; 19.48.6; 19.50.3; Plutarch, *Dinner of the Seven Wise Men* 163.F.12).

[41] *Camillus* 12.3.6 (English translation taken from B. Perrin, *The Parallel Lives* LCL (11 vols.; Cambridge, MA: Harvard University Press, 1914–1926. See also *Otho* 13.6.).

[42] The relationship between repentance and reconciliation in secular Greek literature will be examined below in the section, "Repentance: A Means of Escaping Punishment and a Source of Reconciliation."

[43] *Bravery of Women* 259.B. See also *How to Study Poetry* 26.D; *Listening to Lectures* 37.E; *Sayings of Romans* 205.D; *On Moral Virtue* 447.A; *On Brotherly Love* 484.A; *The Divine Vengeance* 563.C; *Lycurgus* 842.E.

[44] *Μετανοέω and Μεταμέλει in Greek Literature*, 10.

The Meaning of Repentance 49

verb, in both the classical and Hellenistic periods, in no way can be restricted to meaning merely an intellectual change of mind or opinion. A sense of regret and or remorse is often implied as part of the meaning of both μετανοέω and μετάνοια.[45] This presence of regret and remorse suggests that an emotional change of feeling and or will may also accompany the intellectual change of mind.[46]

Although a change of mind or opinion can be effected without any regret whatsoever, psychologically regret often accompanies or follows a change of mind. The sense of regret or remorse is in no way inherent within the etymological meanings of μετανοέω and μετάνοια, but it is often implied by the context in which these two words are found. In Xenophon's *Hellenica*, a speech is made by Euryptolemus to the Athenians supporting the innocence of six generals accused of abandoning survivors of ships wrecked in battle. Xenophon writes:

> Such being the case, are these generals to share the blame now with Theramenes and Thrasybulus, although it was those alone who blundered, and are they now, in return for the humanity they showed then, to be put in hazard of their lives through the machinations of those men and certain others? No! at least not if you take my advice and follow the just and righteous course, the course which will best enable you to learn the truth and to avoid finding out hereafter, to your sorrow (μετανοήσαντες), that it is you yourselves who have sinned most grievously, not only against the gods, but against yourselves.[47]

Xenophon clearly uses the verb μετανοέω in this passage to convey the notion of regret and remorse. It is ridiculous to think that Xenophon is using μετανοέω as an exclusively intellectual term.

Antiphon, the fifth century B.C.E. Attic orator, in an oratorical exercise designed to show in outline how speeches should be composed both for attack and defense, reproduces a fictitious speech as an example of forensic oratory. In the speech, he defends himself as the client, and concludes the defense with a plea for

---

[45] Thompson's assertion "that μετανοέω in the classical period is purely an intellectual term" seems extremely odd, especially after she reluctantly admits that the noun μετάνοια involves not only a change of mind or thought, but also a change of feeling. Thompson states, "In the noun, however, while the term itself is primarily intellectual, there is apparently implied in it a change of feeling" (p. 10). It is very unlikely, however, that a verb and noun arising from the same stem, as is the case with μετανοέω and μετάνοια, would differ so much in meaning. It is improbable that the noun would imply a change of feeling, while the verb would be devoid of any such implication (cf. Dirksen, 166). Thompson's assertion is further weakened by her conclusion that the verb alone changes its meaning in the Hellenistic period. According to Thompson, in the Hellenistic period "μετανοέω does not hold to its classical meaning, to change one's opinion.... The change is that of feeling or will" (14). It seems ridiculous, however, to think that it took the verb hundreds of years to incorporate as part of its meaning an aspect already embraced by the noun.

[46] Thompson asserts that the feeling is a nonexistent force within the verb, and that "the intellect only is operative" (11).

[47] 1.7.19.

acquittal. Antiphon writes:

> But as I am innocent of all their charges, I adjure you on my own behalf to respect the righteousness of the guiltless, just as on the dead man's behalf I remind you of his right to vengeance and urge you not to let the guilty escape by punishing the innocent; for once I am put to death, no one will continue to search for the criminal. Therefore, honoring these points, release me in a manner that is pious and just, and do not μετανοήσαντες once you've recognized your error. For μετάνοια in cases such as this is useless.[48]

Bailey, most likely following both Thompson's and Dirksen's lead, cites this passage as an example of nothing more than an intellectual "change of mind;"[49] therefore, according to Bailey, "μετανοήσαντες" should be translated as "demonstrate a change of mind," and "μετάνοια" should be translated as "a change of mind." The context of the passage, however, clearly suggests that Antiphon understands both the verb and the noun to mean more than merely an intellectual change of mind.[50] It is only natural that a sense of remorse and or regret would accompany the realization that an innocent man had been wrongfully executed. Antiphon is trying to convince the court to do what is "pious and just" rather than "demonstrating remorse" once they recognize they have executed an innocent man.[51] According to Antiphon, remorse at that point is useless.[52]

Furthermore, during the classical period the supreme oracle of Greece, presided over by Apollo, was the Delphic oracle. Questions regarding morality, which were left untouched by the city-states, deeply interested the oracle. The Delphic oracle demonstrated great firmness on moral issues. The Delphic oracle reached the high-water mark of religious and moral ethic in pagan antiquity.[53] There were commands believed to be given by Apollo carved on the front hall of the Delphic temple. The most famous is the moral precept γνῶθι σεαυτόν, "know

---

[48] *First Tetralogy*, 4.11–12.
[49] Bailey, 78; cf. Dirksen, 167; Thompson, 10.
[50] Liddell and Scott cite the passage as an example of regret.
[51] Antiphon use of "ὁσίως καὶ δικαίως" (piously and justly), indicates that Antiphon is thinking of moral and ethical conduct. Rhetorically, failure to observe such moral and ethical conduct naturally leads to a sense of remorse. This is the same language employed by Xenophon in his record of the speech given by Euryptolemus to the Athenians, arguing for the innocence of six military generals (*Hell.* 1.7.19). Euryptolemus tells the Athenians to follow "the just and righteous course" (δίκαια καὶ ὅσια). Their failure to do so also leads to a sense of remorse and regret.
[52] Antiphon makes a parallel argument in *On the Murder of Herodes* 91. Similarly, the uselessness of remorse after executing an innocent man is conveyed by Diodorus. Diodorus records how the king of Persia unjustly executed a man for ridiculing Persian manliness. Diodorus writes: "Once the king's passion had cooled he promptly regretted (μετενόησε) his act and reproached himself for having made a serious mistake, but all his royal power was unable to undo what was done" (17.30.6).
[53] See H. W. Parke and D. E. H. Wormell, *The Delphic Oracle* (2 vols.; Oxford: Blackwell, 1956) especially ch 8.

thine own self." A copy of an inscription from the Delphic temple was found at the beginning of the twentieth century in Miletupolis in Asia Minor. This inscriptional record of an earlier inscription should be dated no later than the fourth century B.C.E.[54] Among the precepts found in this inscription is one that reads, "repent after doing wrong" (ἁμαρτών μετανόει).[55] Because of the emphasis placed on morality by the Delphic oracle, it may be that "doing wrong" refers to some sort of moral or ethical wrongdoing.[56] If this is so, the fact that μετανοέω is a response that follows a perceived ethical or moral wrongdoing suggests that the term implies a sense of regret, remorse, and or guilt for that wrongdoing. The use of μετανοέω in this inscription surely represented more than an intellectual change of mind; there must have also been an emotional change of feeling and or belief arising from the regret, remorse, and or guilt associated with the wrongdoing.

In one of his many discourses, Dio Chrysostom, the Greek orator and philosopher, writes that Aristotle recorded his regret and change of feeling concerning a prior action. Dio Chrysostom writes:

> And I used to envy Aristotle at times because, being a native of Stageira—Stageira was a village in the territory of Olynthus—and having become the teacher of Alexander and an acquaintance of Philip's after the capture of Olynthus, he brought it about that Stageira was resettled, and they used to say that he alone had had the good fortune of becoming the founder of his homeland. But meanwhile, quite recently, I came upon a letter in which he exhibits a change of mind (μετανοῶν) and laments, saying that some of these settlers are trying to corrupt, not only the king, but also the satraps who came there, so as to thwart any good outcome and to prevent entirely the resettlement of the city.[57]

According to Dio Chrysostom, Aristotle displays a change of feeling regarding the resettlement of Stageira. Aristotle's change of mind is clearly more than just an intellectual change of opinion. Because of the corruption taking place in Stageira, Aristotle regrets and laments his having initiated the resettlement of Stageira. It is clear from this passage that Dio Chrysostom understands Aristotle's use of μετανοέω as conveying more than merely an intellectual change of mind.[58]

---

[54] R. Pfeiffer, "The Image of the Delian Apollo and Apolline Ethics," *Journal of the Warburg and Courtauld Institutes* 15 (1952) 31. Dittenberger dates the precepts found in the inscription to about the sixth or seventh century B.C.E. (*Sylloge Inscriptionum Graecarum* (3rd ed.; 3 vols.; Leipzig: Teubner, 1924)1268.8.

[55] Dittenberger, *Sylloge Inscriptionum Graecarum*, 1268.8 (see also θεωρῶν οὖν ὑμᾶς μετανενοηκότας τε ἐπὶ τοῖς προημαρτημένοις; 751.9).

[56] Cf. Plutarch's *The E at Delphi*; *The Oracles at Delphi*; *The Obsolence of Oracles*.

[57] *Orations* 47.9.

[58] For an examination and discussion of the Aristotelian fragment and its use of μετανοέω, see R. Hercher, *Epistolographi Graeci* (Amsterdam: Hakkert, 1965) 170. See also *Fragmenta varia* 1.1.21.8 and *Fragmenta varia* 9.56.657.7 (*TLG*).

In what appears to be the oldest extant occurrence of μετάνοια, the idea of regret also seems to be suggested. In a maxim ascribed to Bias, one of the Seven Sages, it is written: "Hate fast talking lest you make a mistake, for μετάνοια follows."[59] The moral of the proverb seems to be that quick talking inevitably leads to something being said or done that will later be regretted.[60]

Thucydides records that because of the revolt provoked by the Mytilenaeans, the leaders of Athens decided to execute all of the adult males and to enslave all of their women and children. However, "the very next day a feeling of μετάνοια came over them and they began to reflect that the design which they had formed was cruel and monstrous, to destroy a whole city instead of merely those who were guilty."[61] It is clear in this passage that a sense of regret is associated with μετάνοια. The change in thinking by the Athenian leaders was not merely an intellectual change of mind, but it was also an emotional change of feeling and will. The fact that the leaders displayed remorse is confirmed by Thucydides' continuing comment that Cleon, an Athenian politician who proposed the decree to execute all the men of Mytilene, severely criticized the Athenians for their change of mind, stating that he had often realized the inability of a Democracy to govern others, and that the Athenian's μεταμέλεια (lit. "regret/remorse")[62] concerning the Mytileneans clearly demonstrated that fact.[63] In this passage Thucydides uses μετάνοια and μεταμέλεια as synonyms.[64]

This idea of regret and remorse being associated with μετάνοια is also found in the historical writing of Timaeus of Tauromenium. Timaeus asserts that although Greece produced many great men who accomplished many great things, the lustre of their achievements was often tarnished by wicked and violent acts, which were then followed by censure and μετάνοιαν.[65] In this context μετάνοια seems to imply guilt or remorse. This sense of remorse is further depicted in *Batrachomyomachia*.[66] Here it is stated that Phusignathos, "weeping much,

---

[59] μίσει τὸ ταχὺ λαλεῖν, μὴ ἁμάρτῃις· μετάνοια γὰρ ἀκολουθεῖ. The saying is dated to the seventh century B.C.E. (Cf. Septem Sapientes, *Apophthegmata* 6.5, *TLG*; Diels, *Die Fragmenta*, 3:217).

[60] This notion of regret following fast talking is also conveyed in the Septuagint rendering of Proverbs 25:8.

[61] *History of the Peloponesian War* 3.36.3–4.

[62] For a discussion of the etymological meaning and linguistic history of μεταμέλεια, see E. F. Thompson and *TDNT*.

[63] *History of the Peloponnesian War* 3.37.1.

[64] As shall be discussed shortly, this relationship between μετάνοια and μεταμέλεια is demonstrated elsewhere, especially in the first century C.E. *Tabula of Cebes*, where we find a personified Μετάνοια who is also called Μεταμέλεια.

[65] *Fragmenta* 3b,566,F.119b.5, *TLG;* Mette, "Die 'kleinen' griechischen Historiker heute," *Lustrum* 21 (1978) 31. This sentiment of Timaeus is preserved by Plutarch in *Timoleon* 36.

[66] A. Baumeister, *Denkmäker des klassischen Altertums zur Erläuterung des Lebens der Griechen und Rome* (3 vols.; Leipzig: R. Oldenbourg, 1885) 94, identifies this as a fifth century B.C.E. work, while it is identified as a second century B.C.E. work in *TLG*.

bewailed his useless repentance" (πολλὰ δακρύων ἄχρηστον μετάνοιαν ἐμέμφετο).⁶⁷ The fact that μετάνοια is connected with weeping clearly indicates that in this passage there is a sense of sorrow and remorse associated with μετάνοια.

The Stoic philosopher, Epictetus, in a discussion concerning true friendship, identifies false opinions (δόγματα) as the greatest obstacle to true friendship. According to Epictetus these opinions must be eradicated. "When this is done, first of all, one will not be reviling himself, fighting with himself, repenting (μετανοῶν), tormenting himself; and in the second place, in relation to his comrade, he will be always straightforward."⁶⁸ In this discussion, μετανοέω is being used to express regret in the form of self-reproach.⁶⁹ Elsewhere, after highlighting the benefits of resisting the enticements of pleasures, Epictetus admonishes his readers to guard themselves against being carried away by pleasures. He instructs them to "think of the two periods of time, first, that in which you will enjoy your pleasure (ἡδονῆς), and second, that in which, after the enjoyment is over, you will later repent (μετανοήσεις) and revile your own self. Now set against these two periods of time how much joy and self-satisfaction you will get if you refrain."⁷⁰ Once again μετανοέω is being used in a context that expresses regret in the form of self-reproach.

According to Epictetus, the joy and self-satisfaction derived by refraining from wrong is far nobler than the regret and self-reproach that results from chasing after pleasures. The last two examples clearly demonstrate that Epictetus understood regret and remorse as part of the meaning of μετανοέω. According to Epictetus, the wise person is the one who does not allow himself to be carried away by pleasures and who avoids decisions and actions that will later be regretted.⁷¹ This point is also conveyed in a fragment which is ascribed to Epictetus.⁷² The fragment reads: "When you attack someone with vehemence and threatening, remember to tell yourself beforehand that you are a tame animal; and then you will never do anything fierce, and so will come to the end of your life without having to repent, (ἀμετανόητος), or to be called to account."⁷³

Another Stoic who continues this understanding of both μετανοέω and μετάνοια is Marcus Aurelius, who was a student of Epictetus. Marcus Aurelius writes, "In every action ask yourself, 'How does this affect me? Shall I regret

---

⁶⁷ *Batrachomyomachia* 70 (*TLG*; cf. Baumeister, 95).
⁶⁸ *Disc.* 2.22.35.
⁶⁹ From the fact that λοιδορούμενος "reviling himself," μαχόμενος "fighting with himself," and βασανίζων "tormenting himself" all express self-reproach, and μετανοῶν stands in juxtaposition with them, it should be concluded that μετανοῶν participates in their meaning (cf. Dirksen, p. 184).
⁷⁰ *Encheiridion* 34.1.
⁷¹ This of course is consistent with Stoic views discussed earlier.
⁷² Norden (*Agnostos Theos*, 135) denies it genuineness, while W. Oldfather, *Epictetus*. LCL (2 vols.; Cambridge, MA: Harvard University Press, 1925–1928) regards it as genuine.
⁷³ *Epictetus* 2.468.

(μετανοήσω) it?"⁷⁴ Elsewhere he writes, "'Η μετάνοια is a sort of self-reproach (ἐπίληψις τις ἑαυτοῦ) at some useful thing passed by; but the good has to be a useful thing, and always to be cultivated by the truly good man. The truly good man, however, would never regret (μετανοήσειεν) having passed a pleasure (ἡδονήν). Pleasure, therefore, is neither a useful thing nor a good."⁷⁵ This idea of self-reproach seems to suggest regret over a past decision. In addition, the regret here is not for having done evil, but for having failed to do good. In this context there can be no doubt that the author is referring to regret over one's failure to display what the author considers to be some form of virtuous and or ethical behavior. Finally, when discussing the inability of some men to win their own approval, Marcus asks, "Can he be said to win his own approval who regrets (μετανοῶν) almost everything he does?"⁷⁶

This idea of regret or remorse accompanying or following one's change of mind is also a very common feature in the writings of Plutarch.⁷⁷ The prevalence of this idea in the writings of Plutarch is what caused Thompson to mistakenly assert that in the Hellenistic period the verb μετανοέω changed in meaning, and was now used to convey the idea of regret.⁷⁸ The idea of regret was present in the verb long before Plutarch; it is just that the idea of regret is almost always present in the meaning of both μετανοέω and μετάνοια as expressed by Plutarch. Even when the terms are used simply to designate a change of mind there often seems to be an element of regret that is also suggested. At one point in the *Parallel Lives*, Plutarch writes about the strength of spirit of those individuals who are able not to be spoiled by prosperity nor humbled by adversity. In his praise of Aemilius and his criticism of Timoleon, Plutarch writes:

> The character of Aemilius, therefore, was manifestly more perfect, because in the midst of grievous misfortune and great sorrow—brought upon him by the death of his sons—he was seen to have no less greatness and no less dignity than

---

⁷⁴ Book 8.2.
⁷⁵ Book 8.10.
⁷⁶ Book 8.53. Another student of Epictetus who uses μετανοέω/μετάνοια to denote regret and remorse is Flavius Arrianus (See *Historia Indica* 14.5.1; *Fragmenta* 2b,156.F.10.23; *Fragmenta* 2b,156.F.175b.58; *TLG*).
⁷⁷ Occurrences in Plutarch's *Parallel Lives* include *Timoleon and Aemilius* 2.11; *Cato the Younger* 51.5; *Pericles* 10.2; *Alexander* 11.4; *Agis* 19.5; *Artaxerxes* 24.4; *Demetrius* 52.4; *Galba* 6.4 *Phocion* 14.4; *Eumenes* 2.6 and *Crassus* 11.2. Occurrences in his *Moralia* include *Education of Children* 10.F; *Dinner of the Seven Wise Men* 155.D; *Sayings of Romans* 205.D, 207.D; *Bravery of Women* 256.D; *On Moral Virtue* 452.D; *On the Control of Anger* 460.C; *On Tranquility of Mind* 476.F; *Can Vice Cause Unhappiness* 498.E; *Concerning Talkativeness* 515.A; *On Compliance* 533.D; 536.D; *The Divine Vengeance* 550.E–551.B; 556.D; *To an Uneducated Ruler* 781.B; *Precepts of Statecraft* 798.E, 799.A; *The Cleverness of Animals* 961.D.
⁷⁸ With the exception of two passages from Polybius and one from Diodorus Siculus, E.F. Thompson bases her conclusions regarding the meaning of μετανοέω in the Hellenistic period exclusively on material taken from Plutarch (see *Μετανοέω and Μεταμέλει*, 14–16).

in the midst of his successes. Timoleon, however, although he had behaved in a noble way with regard to his brother, could not behave with reason in the midst of his sorrow, but instead was prostrated with grief and μετάνοια.[79]

The association of μετάνοια with sorrow and grief in this passage clearly illustrates the sense of regret and remorse often associated with μετάνοια.

In the *Moralia*, Plutarch advises against hastily entering into public life without giving much thought to the decision. After pointing to the negative example of Gaius Gracchus, Plutarch writes, "And those who make themselves up for political competition or the race for glory, as actors do for the stage, must necessarily regret (μετανοεῖν) their action, since they must either serve those whom they think they should rule or offend those whom they wish to please."[80] Plutarch goes on to write, "I believe that those who, like men who fall into a well, stumble into public life by mere chance and unexpectedly must experience confusion and begin to regret (μετανοεῖν) their course, whereas those who enter into it quietly, as the result of preparation and reflection, will be sensible in their conduct of affairs and will not be discomposed by anything."[81]

Elsewhere, while discussing the manner in which human beings train animals, Plutarch explicitly identifies sorrow as μετάνοια. He writes, "They themselves punish dogs and horses that make mistakes, not idly but to discipline them; they are creating in them through pain a feeling of sorrow, which we call μετάνοιαν."[82] Finally, like Thucydides, Plutarch also demonstrates that he considers μετάνοια and μεταμέλεια to be synonymous. Plutarch writes that a dreadful deed, "like an ulcer in the flesh, leaves behind it in the soul regret (μεταμέλειαν), which ever continues to wound and prick it. For the other pangs reason (λόγος) does away with, but regret (μετάνοιαν) is caused by reason itself, since the soul, together with its feeling of shame, is stung and chastised by itself."[83]

This connection between μετάνοια and μεταμέλεια is most explicitly depicted in the philosophic work, *Κέβητος Θηβαίου Πίναξ* (*Tabula of Cebes*). The importance of the *Tabula* to this present study is that it bears witness to the existence of a system of moral philosophy in which μετάνοια plays an integral role. Cebes of Thebes was a pupil of Philolaus the Pythagorean, and later of Socrates, but the document itself makes no pretense to be by Socrates' student. The document most likely belongs to the period of the early Empire (i.e. in the period from Augustus to Domitian), rather than the fourth century B.C.E.[84] The substance

---

[79] *Timoleon and Aemilius* 2.10–11.
[80] *Precepts of Statecraft* 799.A. This passage is similar in sentiment to the previously discussed maxim ascribed to the seventh century B.C.E. sage, Bias. Both passages suggest that μετάνοια inevitably follows hasty comments and actions.
[81] Ibid.
[82] *The Cleverness of Animals* 961.D.
[83] *On the Tranquility of Mind* 476.F.
[84] See J. Fitzgerald and M. White, *The Tabula of Cebes* (Chico, CA: Scholars Press, 1983) 1–7 for a discussion of the authorship and date of the composition.

of its teaching, however, may very well be much older.⁸⁵ The document presents an eclectic doctrine, which in spite of its Pythagorean setting owes more to Plato, Aristotle, and the Stoics than to the Pythagoreans.⁸⁶

The document is cast into the form of a dialogue.⁸⁷ In metaphorical language, an old man tells a group of younger people the meaning of a painting and fable found on a tablet erected as a votive offering in the temple of Cronus. The tablet depicts life in the form of three concentric circles, each separated by walls and gates. The outer circle represents the domain of vice. The next circle is the domain of False Education (Ψευδοπαιδεία). The inner circle represents the domain of True Education (ἀληθὴς Παιδεία). The old man states that many people, as they enter into the first circle of life, are led astray by a woman named "Deceit" (Ἀπάτη), who causes them to drink of "Error" and "Ignorance." After drinking, these people are confronted and led away by women called "Opinions" (Δόξαι), "Desires" (Ἐπιθυμίαι), and "Pleasures" (Ἡδοναί).⁸⁸ Although some of these women may "lead to salvation" (εἰς τὸ σώζεσθαι), others, as a result of Deceit, "lead to destruction" (εἰς τὸ ἀπόλλυσθαι). Because of the influence of Deceit, many people wander through life aimlessly. These people are identified as "those who are without forethought" (ἀπροβούλευτοι).⁸⁹ Over the course of time many of these people submit to various vices and disgraceful acts, and are eventually handed over to women named "Retribution" (Τιμωρία), "Grief" (Λύπη), and "Sorrow" (Ὀδύνη),⁹⁰ as well as to a brother and sister named "Lamentation" (Ὀδυρμός) and "Despondency" (Ἀθυμία). After their punishment, these individuals are given over to "Unhappiness" (Κακοδαιμονίαν), where they spend the rest of their lives, unless a woman named "Repentance" (Μετάνοια) chooses to encounter them.

At this point in the dialogue the questioner asks what happens if Μετάνοια encounters someone who is sentenced to a life of unhappiness. The old man responds that the person encountered by Μετάνοια is released from his ills and introduced to another "Opinion" (Δόξαν) and "Desire" (Ἐπιθυμίαν), who leads him to "true Education," as well as through "False Education."⁹¹ If the person

---

⁸⁵ Cf. W. Jäger, "Review of Eduard Norden's *Agnostos Theos*," *Göttingische gelehrte Anzeigen* 175 (1913) 590.
⁸⁶ Fitzgerald and White, 20–27.
⁸⁷ Fitzgerald and White identify at least three genres that have contributed to the final form of the work: 1) dialogue, 2) *ekphrasis*, and 3) *erotapokriseis* (*Tabula*, 11–14).
⁸⁸ "Desires" (Ἐπιθυμίαι), and "Pleasures" (Ἡδοναί) are two of the four πάθος condemned by Cicero and the Stoics. Both of these arise as a result of false judgment regarding evil (see note 14 above).
⁸⁹ This is a very interesting identification in light of the antithesis in Classical Greek between μετανοέω with προβουλεύομαι (see earlier discussion).
⁹⁰ "Grief" (Λύπη) is another of the four πάθος condemned by Cicero and the Stoics (see note 14 above).
⁹¹ Since the domain of true Education is represented by the inner circle, all who are enroute to true Education must pass through the circle inhabited by False Education ("Those who are being saved arrive here [i.e. at False Education] first, whenever they wish to enter

encountered by Μετάνοια welcomes this Opinion, "once he is cleansed (καθαρθείς) by her he is saved (σώζεται) and becomes blessed and happy in his life."[92] However, if he does not welcome this Opinion he is led astray once again by "False Opinion (Ψευδοδοξίας)."[93] Μετάνοια provides the only hope for putting away the Opinions, Desires, and Pleasures that lead individuals astray by holding out to individuals another Opinion and Desire[94] that will lead them safely to true Education.

As the older man begins bringing his explanation of the fable to an end, he elaborates on comments made earlier. During the course of his elaboration, however, the woman that was originally identified as Μετάνοια is now identified as Μεταμέλεια.[95] In the first instance Μετάνοια is connected with deliverance from "False Opinion," while in the second instance Μεταμέλεια is connected with deliverance from False Education. It is clear, however, that both Μετάνοια and Μεταμέλεια represent the same woman. It is also clear that In this text Μετάνοια and Μεταμέλεια are synonymous. Hence, μετάνοια, as used by the author, certainly implies an element of regret.[96]

Lucian of Samosata, the second century C.E. sophist who wrote some eighty pieces, chiefly in dialogue form, clearly understood the use of Μετάνοια in the *Tabula of Cebes* as implying an element of regret. Lucian describes the fate of a writer who was once employed by a rich patron, but who now suffers miserably because his usefulness is past. Lucian writes:

> I desire, nevertheless, in imitation of Cebes, to paint you a picture of this career that we have discussed, so that you may look at it and determine whether you should enter it. . . . Imagine painted a lofty, golden gateway, not down on the level ground but above the earth on a hill; the slope is long and steep and slippery, so that many a time those who hoped soon to be at the summit have broken their necks by a slip of foot. Within, let Wealth himself be sitting, all golden, seemingly, very beautiful and fascinating; and let his lover, after ascending with great toil, draw near the door and gaze spellbound at the gold. Let Hope, herself fair of face and gaily dressed, take him in charge and conduct him within, tremendously impressed by his entrance. Then let Hope keep always in advance of him, and let other women, Deceit ('Απάτη) and Servitude,

---

into true Education." There is "no other path that leads to true education;" 12.3).

[92] As is the case with John the Baptist's "baptism of repentance," μετάνοια cleanses and prepares one for salvation (Luke 1:76–77; 3:2–6).

[93] *Tabula of Cebes* 1–11 (quote from 11.2).

[94] This distinction between evil and good Desires (Επιθυμία) echoes the distinction found among later Stoic writers (see note 14 above).

[95] *Tabula*, 35.4.

[96] This is further suggested by the fact that Μετάνοια gives the individual not only another Opinion (Δόξαν) of things but also another "Desire" (Επιθυμίαν). The change of Desire (Επιθυμία) suggests an emotional change (i.e. a change of feeling) in the individual which very well may imply an aversion from past Desires and even regret from having followed them.

receive him successively and pass him on to Toil, who, after breaking the wretch with hard labour, shall at length deliver him, now sickly and faded, to Old Age. Last of all, let Insolence lay hold of him and drag him along to Despair; let Hope then fly away and vanish, and instead of the golden portal by which he entered, let him be ejected by some remote and secret postern, naked, paunchy, pale, and old, screening his nakedness with his left hand and throttling himself with his right; and on the way out, let him be met by Repentance (Μετάνοια), weeping to no avail and helping to make an end of the poor man.[97]

It seems apparent by Lucian's reference to Cebes, his allegorical portrayal of the misery experienced in life when led astray by "Deceit," and his personification of Μετάνοια that he clearly understands Μετάνοια in the *Tabula of Cebes* to include regret and sorrow.[98] However, in Lucian's depiction, Μετάνοια is nothing more than regret and remorse; therefore, instead of offering a cleansing and salvation through the acceptance of a different opinion and desire, the guilt resulting from Μετάνοια serves to destroy the man. Similarly, Lucian tells the story of a pantomime who went to extremes imitating the insanity of Ajax. When the actor regained his composure, he intensely regretted (μετανοῆσαι) his behavior, and was stricken ill with grief as a result of his conduct, which was considered to be that of a madman.[99] Unlike the Stoic references, these examples from Lucian do indicate somewhat of a polemic against μετάνοια. In these examples, Lucian considers μετάνοια to be of no avail because for Lucian μετάνοια is nothing more than an overwhelming sense of remorse, which in these examples only leads to guilt, condemnation and the ultimate destruction of the individual.

In the few references discovered that describe μετάνοια as useless, most, if not all, depict μετάνοια as an overwhelming sense of remorse and guilt or as a possible change of opinion and or feeling that is unable to undo or correct the damage done. In a fable attributed to the famed sixth century B.C.E. fabulist, Aesop, when a caged bird becomes careful about singing, a bat tells the bird: "You do not need to be careful now when it does no good. Rather, you should have been careful before you were caught." The author then states, "the moral of the fable is that repentance (μετάνοια) because of misfortunes is useless."[100] Antiphon gives two accounts of men in court pleading for their lives, informing the court that μετάνοια after executing an innocent man is useless.[101] Diodorus gives a parallel account of

---

[97] *On Salaried Posts in Great Houses* 42 (English translation taken from Harmon, Kilburn, and Macleod, *Lucian* LCL (13 vols.; Cambridge, MA: Harvard University Press, 1913–1967).
[98] See also Lucian's personification of Μετάνοια as a woman in mourning, dressed in tattered black clothing, crying and gazing shamefully at Truth (*Slander* 5).
[99] *The Dance* 84. Other uses of μετανοέω to denote regret or remorse can be found in *A True Story* 2.35; *The Dialogues of the Dead* 20.1.6; *Gout* 309.
[100] A. Hausrath, *Corpus Fabularum Aesopicarum* (Leipzig: Teubner, 1940) Fable 48.
[101] *First Tetralogy* 4.12; *On the Murder of Herodes* 91.

the uselessness of μετανοέω that follows the unjust execution of a human being.[102] Appian depicts the uselessness of μετάνοια as he gives an account of how two men from the same nation—Caesar and Pompey—mustered troops to go to war with one another. Appian writes:

> As the danger came nearer, the ambition that had inflamed and blinded them was extinguished, and gave place to fear. Reason purged their mad passion for glory.... The leaders reflected also that they, who had recently been friends and relatives by marriage, and had co-operated with each other in many ways in order to gain rank and power; had now drawn the sword for mutual slaughter and were leading to the same impiety those serving under them—men of the same city, of the same tribe, family members, and in some cases brothers against brothers. Even these circumstances were not missing in this battle; because unnatural things must happen when thousands of the same nation come together in the clash of arms. Reflecting on these things, each of them was seized with unavailing repentance (μετανοίας τε οὐ δυνατῆς), and since this day was to decide for each whether he should be the highest or the lowest of the human race, they hesitated to begin so critical a battle. It is said that both of them even wept.[103]

The battle reluctantly commenced, with Pompey's troops eventually prevailing. In this situation, μετάνοια alone was unable to stop the wheels of war that had already been set in motion. Like Aesop, Diodorus and Antiphon, Appian does not necessarily present a polemic against μετάνοια; instead he conveys the view that μετάνοια is useless when unaccompanied by the will and or ability to change the situation.[104] Remorse alone or a mere change of opinion and or feeling is not sufficient; such sentiments must be accompanied by the will and or ability to undo the wrong or correct the situation.

As the evidence indicates, in secular Greek literature both μετανοέω and μετάνοια were used to denote an intellectual change of mind as well as an emotional sense of regret and remorse. Other Hellenistic Greek authors who use μετανοέω and μετάνοια to denote regret and or remorse include Diodorus Siculus,[105] Dionysius of Halicarnassus,[106] Dio Chrysostom,[107] Appian,[108] Chariton,[109]

---

[102] *History* 17.30.6.
[103] *Civil Wars* 2.11.77.
[104] See also *Batrachomyomachia* 70.
[105] *Library of History* 17.30.6; 17.109.3.
[106] *Roman Antiquities* 1.87.3; 10.51.4; *On Thucydides* 17.14.
[107] *Orations* 4.18; 12.45; 17.18; 32.95; 72.15; 75.2.
[108] *Roman History* 8.8.52; 8.17.116; *Civil Wars* 2.10.63–64; 2.11.77; 2.13.94; 3.6.39; 3.11.77; 4.8.58; 4.17.131; 5.2.16; 5.13.129.
[109] *Chaereas and Callirhoe* 1.14.10; 2.9.3; 3.3.11; 4.7.7; 5.7.7; 7.1.8; 7.3.11; 8.2.14; 8.5.8.

Pausanias,[110] Dio Cassius,[111] and Diogenes Laertius.[112]

Repentance as the Appropriate Response to Inappropriate Deeds

One of the reasons the change in thinking denoted by μετανοέω and μετάνοια often includes a sense of regret and or remorse is because the past action, decision or former way of thinking is often later perceived by the individual changing his or her way of thinking as having been wrong, inappropriate, or disadvantageous.[113] This point is frequently conveyed by using μετανοέω and μετάνοια with words such as ἁμαρτάνω, ἁμάρτημα, and ἁμαρτία.[114]

As we have seen in the maxim ascribed to the sage Bias, the idea of μετάνοια following ἁμαρτάνω was not unheard of during the classical period. The reader of the maxim is told to "despise fast talking lest you make a mistake (ἁμάρτηις), for μετάνοια follows."[115] Rudolph Pfeiffer points to two significant pieces of evidence that similarly support the existence during the classical period of a type of ethic in which μετάνοια follows mistakes.[116] Although it is unclear in the maxim ascribed to Bias whether μετάνοια is a desirable or undesirable response to

---

[110] *Description of Greece* 1.30.1; 7.17.12.
[111] *Roman History* 45.36.1; 53.10.8; 61.2.2.
[112] *Lives of Eminent Philosophers* 5.66; 7.179.
[113] Cf. Diodorus Siculus, *Antiquities* 13.53.3; 15.47.3; 26.17.1; Plutarch, *Numa* 10.2.6; *Timoleon* 36.2.*Lucullus* 22.4.4; *Cato the Younger* 29.1.6; *Antony* 24.6.7; *Alexander* 38.4.9; *On the Control of Anger* 459.D.5; *On Compliancy* 530.A.10; *Table-Talk* 712.C.8; *Precepts of Statecraft* 805.C.8; *On The Malice of Herodotus* 860.F.6; *On Common Conceptions* 1069.C.8; *Live Unknown* 1128.E.8; Dio Chrysostom, *Orations* 49.4.4; Dio Cassius *Roman History* 41.35.5; Diogenes Laertius 1.76.5.
[114] I disagree with Bailey's assertion that these terms do "not include the same sense of 'sin' in secular Greek as in Jewish and Christian literature" (*Repentance*, 89; cf. p. 82; this view is also found in the *TDNT* article "ἁμαρτάνω," 1:296–302). Although the use of these terms in secular Greek to denote the idea of humanity's enmity against a deity is less pervasive than in Jewish and Christian literature, it is nevertheless present (cf. Plato, *Phaedr.* 242c; *Leg.* 10.891e; Aeschylus, *Prom. Vin.* 945; Xenophon, *Hell.* 1.7.19; Dionysius of Halicarnassus, *Ant.* 8.50.3–4). The primary evidence from the Hellenistic Greek period indicating a use of these terms to denote humanity's enmity against a deity is found in the inscriptions from Asia Minor from the field of Phrygian and Lydian religion (cf. F. S. Steinleitner, *Die Beicht im Zusammenhange mit der sakralen Rechtspflege in der Antike*. München: Oldenbourg, 1913) inscription nos. 3, 6, 7, 8, 11, 12, 13, 14, 22, 23, 25, 33. In secular Greek, the terms are used predominantly to identify humanity's enmity against humanity, which is very much an aspect of the Jewish and Christian understanding of these terms as well. The evidence clearly reveals that these terms do include the same sense of 'sin' in secular Greek as in Jewish and Christian literature. The terms are, however, not confined solely to the traditional religious understanding of 'sin' as conveyed in Jewish and Christian literature. In secular Greek the terms cover a much wider range of shortcomings than in Jewish and Christian writings. These terms cover everything from harmless mistakes to heinous crimes, and include religious, moral, ethical and intellectual failings.
[115] μίσει τὸ ταχὺ λαλεῖν, μὴ ἁμάρτηις· μετάνοια γὰρ ἀκολουθεῖ (Septem Sapientes, *Apophthegmata* 6.5, *TLG*; Cf. Diels, *Vorsokratiker*, II, 217).
[116] See *Ausgewählte Schriften* (Oxford: Clarendon, 1968) 55–71; "The Image of the Delian Apollo," 26–27.

The Meaning of Repentance 61

mistakes, the evidence presented by Pfeiffer clearly presents μετάνοια as a desirable response. In addition to the precept, "repent after doing wrong" (ἁμαρτών μετανόει), believed to have been given by Apollo and found carved on the front hall of the Delphic temple,[117] Pfeiffer also presents evidence indicating that the statue of the Delian Apollo held the graces in his right hand and a bow and arrow in his left. This image of Apollo gave rise to the allegorical-ethical interpretation that the god holds the bow in his left hand because he is slower to chastise a person if that person repents of his or her misdeeds.[118] The evidence presented by Pfeiffer suggests that in the third or perhaps fourth century B.C.E., μετάνοια was considered, at least in Delphi, a required response to wrong doings.[119]

As alluded to earlier, Antiphon presents a real case of a man defending himself in court against a charge of murder.[120] The sentence for murder is death. The defendant, therefore, argues that since the evidence is inconclusive it is better to acquit him today and try him later, if future evidence warrants it, rather than to sentence him to death and find out later, when it is too late, that a mistake was made. The defendant argues:

> Indeed, supposing that you were bound to make some mistake (ἁμαρτεῖν), it would be less of an outrage to acquit me unfairly than to put me to death without just cause; for the one thing is a mistake (ἁμάρτημα) and nothing more: the other is a sin (ἀσέβημα) in addition. You must exercise great caution in what you do, because you will not be able to reconsider your action. In a matter which admits of reconsideration, a mistake (ἐξαμαρτεῖν), whether made through giving rein to the feelings or through accepting a distorted account of the facts, is not so serious; it is still possible to change one's mind (μεταγνοὺς) and

---

[117] This inscription was discussed previously on pp. 52-53. See also Dittenberger, *Sylloge Inscriptionum Graecarum*, 751.9: θεωρῶν οὖν ὑμᾶς μετανενοηκότας τε ἐπὶ τοῖς προημαρτημένοις.

[118] Pfeiffer references a fragment from *Aetia* found in his edition of *Callimachus* (fr. 114.8–17). The fragment consists of a number of short questions and answers. The answers are given by the Delian god himself. As reconstructed, one of the questions is "Why do you hold. . . the bow in your left hand, but in your right hand the comely graces?" Apollo answers: "in order to punish fools for their insolence," I have the bow—but "to good people I stretch out" my hand with the Graces. In my left hand I carry the bow, because I am "slower to chastise mortals"—but the Graces in the right hand, as I am "always disposed to distribute pleasant things." After another break, the fragment picks up with the words, "In order that it may be possible to repent of something" ἵν' ᾖ *μετὰ καί τι νοῆσαι* (Pfeiffer, *Ausgewählte Schriften*, 55–71; idem, "The Image of the Delian Apollo," 26–27; cf. P. Davies, ed., *Macrobius' Saturnalia* (New York: Columbia University Press,1969) 1.17.13, quoting from Apollodorus of Athens, *On the gods*; Philo, *On the embassy to the emperor Gaius* 95). Although lacking the words ἁμαρτάνω, ἁμάρτημα, or ἁμαρτία, the context clearly suggests that μετάνοια is a desirable response to wrong, inappropriate, or disadvantageous behavior.

[119] For some strange reason the evidence presented by Pfeiffer has long been omitted from most discussions concerning the meaning of μετάνοια in pre-Christian thought.

[120] See pp. 32, n102; 18, n51.

come to a right decision. But when reconsideration is impossible, the wrong done is only compounded by **altering one's mind** (μετανοεῖν) and acknowledging one's mistake (ἐξημαρτηκότας). Some of you yourselves have in fact demonstrated remorse (μετεμέλησεν) before now of having sent men to their death; but when you, who had been misled, felt remorse (μετεμέλησεν), most assuredly did those who had misled you deserve death.[121]

Here, μετανοέω is in response to wrongdoing, however, according to Antiphon, when the wrongdoing cannot be undone, corrected, or made right in some way μετανοέω only compounds the problem.

In the fictitious court speech cited earlier,[122] Antiphon pleads for an acquittal by saying, "release me in a manner that is pious (ὁσίως) and just (δικαίως), and do not demonstrate remorse (μετανοήσαντες) once you've recognized your error (ἁμαρτίαν). For remorse (μετάνοια) in cases such as this is useless."[123] Antiphon clearly understands μετάνοια to follow acts identified as ἁμαρτία. Furthermore, Antiphon's use of ὁσίως and δικαίως together, as well as in opposition to ἁμαρτίαν, suggests that the error in this passage violates conduct that is sanctioned by both divine and human ordinances.[124]

In another quote cited earlier,[125] Xenophon echoes this view that ἁμαρτία includes violations of both divine and human ordinances. Xenophon reproduces a speech of Euryptolemus addressed to the Athenians. According to Xenophon, Euryptolemus says, "take my advice and follow the just (δίκαια) and righteous (ὅσια) course, the course which will best enable you to learn the truth and to avoid finding out hereafter, to your sorrow (μετανοήσαντες), that it is you yourselves who have sinned (ἡμαρτηκότας) most grievously, not only against the gods, but against yourselves."[126] Once again μετανοέω is in response to ἁμαρτάνω. Furthermore, not only does the author's use of δίκαια and ὅσια together suggest that the error in this passage violates conduct that is sanctioned by both divine and human ordinances, the author's assertion that they have sinned "not only against the gods" but against themselves explicitly confirms this fact. In both this passage and the parallel passage from Antiphon, ἁμαρτάνω clearly represents a failure to observe ethical and/or moral conduct that is sanctioned by both the gods and human

---

[121] *On the Murder of Herodes* 91 [emphasis added; translation from G. Maidment, *Attic Minor Orators* LCL (2 vols; Cambridge, MA:Harvard University Press, 1941)]. Although I agree with Maidment's translation of μετανοεῖν as "altering one's mind," the author's earlier use of μεταγνοὺς to indicate a change of mind, as well as the reference to remorse (μετεμέλησεν) that immediately follows the occurrence of μετανοεῖν, indicates that the author understands μετανοεῖν as denoting more than just an intellectual change of mind. The word includes a sense of regret and or remorse for having made such a mistake.
[122] 17, n47.
[123] *First Tetralogy*, 4.11–12.
[124] See the discussion of the expression τὰ δίκαια τὰ ὅσια in Liddell-Scott, "ὅσιος."
[125] 17, n.46
[126] *Hellenica* 1.7.19.

The Meaning of Repentance 63

beings. It is this lapse in ethical and/or moral conduct that results in the need for μετανοέω.[127]

The use of μετανοέω and μετάνοια with words such as ἁμαρτάνω, ἁμάρτημα, and ἁμαρτία continued in the Hellenistic period. Diodorus records how the king of Persia, in an act of uncontrolled rage, executed a man undeserving of such punishment. Diodorus writes, "Once the king's passion had cooled he promptly regretted (μετενόησε) his act and reproached himself for having made a serious mistake (ἡμαρτηκότα)."[128] Dionysius records a speech given to Marcius in an attempt to persuade him to forgive someone who had offended him. Dionysius writes,

> For my part, I cannot commend these harsh and overbearing claims, which overstep the bounds of human nature, when I observe that a refuge for all men and the means of securing forgiveness for their offenses (ἐξαμαρτάνωσι) one against another have been devised in the form of suppliant olive branches and prayers... and when I observe also that those who act arrogantly and treat with insolence the prayers of suppliants all incur the indignation of the gods and in the end come to a miserable state. For the gods themselves, who in the first place instituted and delivered to us these customs, are disposed to forgive offenses (ἁμαρτήμασι) of men and are easily reconciled; and many have there been until now who, though greatly sinning (ἐξαμαρτάνοντες) against them, have appeased their anger by prayers and sacrifices. Unless you think it fitting, Marcius, that the anger of the gods should be mortal, but that of men immortal! You will be doing, then, what is just and becoming both to yourself and to your country if you forgive her offenses, seeing that she is repentant (μετανοούσῃ).[129]

Plutarch, while recounting Plato's depiction of God as the pattern of excellence and virtue to be emulated by all human beings, writes, "Hence it is that he is slow and leisurely in his punishment of the wicked: not because he fears for himself, that by punishing in haste, he may be involved in error (ἁμαρτίαν) or μετάνοιαν,[130] but because he wishes to remove from us all brutishness and violence in the infliction of punishment."[131] When telling of Pompey's victory over Caesar, Appian writes:

> Pompey sent letters to all the kings and cities magnifying his victory, and he

---

[127] Sophocles tells a story of a woman, who after committing adultery, is compelled by remorse to repent (μετανοοῦσα) and confront her liaison (*Fragmenta* 857.1, *TLG*).
[128] *History* 17.30.6.
[129] *Antiquities* 8.50.3–4 (English translation from E. Cary, *Dionysius of Halicarnassus* LCL (7 vols; Cambridge, MA: Harvard University Press, 1925); see also 7.22.4).
[130] The idea of God not being involved in μετάνοια was a common *topos* in Jewish and Christian literature.
[131] *The Divine Vengeance*, 550.E.6 (cf. 551.B–E; see also *Antony* 24.6; *How to Tell a Flatterer* 56.A.6; 74.C.13; *To an Uneducated Ruler* 781.B.4; *Cleverness of Animals* 961.D).

expected that Caesar's army would come over to him directly, seeing that the soldiers were oppressed by hunger and cast down by defeat, especially the officers through fear of punishment for their inappropriate conduct (ἁμάρτημα) in the battle. However, the latter, as though some god had brought them to repentance (μετάνοιαν), were ashamed of their inappropriate conduct (ἁμάρτημα), and... demanded that they should be decimated according to the traditional rule.[132]

Finally Aspasius, a second century peripatetic commentator on the works of Aristotle, when describing improvement of bad conduct, says: "it is always possible for one who is wanton to change when reason urges him on and leads him to repentance (μετάνοιαν) for wrongs (ἁμαρτήμασι).[133]

Throughout the classic and Hellenistic periods of Greek history it was common and even expected for μετανοέω and μετάνοια to follow ἁμαρτάνω, ἁμάρτημα, and ἁμαρτία. Secular Greek literature clearly reveals that both μετανοέω and μετάνοια were considered the appropriate intellectual and emotional response to inappropriate decisions and or behavior (i.e. 'sin'). The literature further reveals that the change in thinking denoted by these terms was considered the appropriate and required response not only for intentional and willful sins, but also for sins committed as a result of ignorance.[134] Aristotle writes, "give μετάνοιαν to the ones who are ignorant (ἀγνοοῦσι).[135] Dionysius asserts, "the repentance (μετάνοια) of those who later in life become wise,... wipes out the error originally made in ignorance."[136] Ignorance was frequently the source of the behavior that necessitated μετάνοια.[137]

As most of the references cited thus far have indicated, the wrongs committed that resulted in the need for μετανοέω and μετάνοια often involved inappropriate behavior toward and mistreatment of other people; however, Greek authors were not totally unfamiliar with the notion of repenting because of inappropriate behavior toward a deity. Plutarch, in his criticism of Stoic doctrine for its attempt to safeguard things that are useless and indifferent, asserts that Stoics have met with a kind of retribution for their arrogance and vainglory that is similar to the retribution experienced by "those who have meant arrogantly to insult and revile

---

[132] *Civil Wars* 2.10.63 (see also 2.13.94; 4.17.131; 5.2.16; *Roman History* 8.8.52–53; 8.17.116).

[133] *On the Nicomachean Ethics* 63 (G. Heylbut, ed. *Aspasii in ethica Nicomachea quae supersunt commentaria* (Berlin: Reimer, 1889)).

[134] Sin and vice in Greek thought were often considered to be the result of ignorance. It was believed that ignorance prevents individuals from appreciating the true worth of things. As a result, individuals often have false judgments or opinions regarding the true value of the things of life (cf. Dirksen, *New Testament Concept*, 177; "ἄγνοια" and "ἁμαρτάνω," *TDNT*, 1.116-119, 298).

[135] *Ep.* 4.21, *TLG*; cf. Hercher, 172–74.

[136] *Roman Antiquities* 7.22.4.

[137] See also Plutarch, *The Divine Vengeance* 551.E.7; *Tabula of Cebes* 5.3; 6.3; 9.3; 14.3; Lucian, *Slander* 5; *Corpus Hermeticum* 1.28; Aspasius, *Nicomachean Ethics* 63.

The Meaning of Repentance 65

shrines of certain gods or spirits" and are then forced "to repent (μετανοήσαντες) and then cower and abase themselves, extolling and exalting the divinity."[138] Furthermore, according to *Poimandres*, ignorance of God is one of the things for which men are compelled to repent. It is written, "Listen up you men born of earth, you who have given yourselves up to drunkenness and sleep in your ignorance of God; awake to soberness. . . . Repent (μετανοήσατε), you who have journeyed with error, and joined company with ignorance; rid yourself of darkness, and lay hold on the light, partaking of immortality and forsaking corruption."[139] Repentance was considered the appropriate response for inappropriate behavior toward both men and gods.

According to some Greek authors, it was the gods themselves who considered repentance to be an appropriate response to inappropriate behavior. Dio Chrysostom asserts that Zeus admires and rewards with long life kings who are brave, humane and kind toward their subjects, lending a helping hand to the weak and forcing the unrighteous (ἀδίκους) to repent (μετανοεῖν).[140] Appian, in his account of how Pompey thought the officers of Caesar's defeated army would defect because of fear of punishment for their inappropriate conduct, writes that they, "as though some god had brought them to repentance (μετάνοιαν), were ashamed of their inappropriate conduct."[141] Similarly, Plutarch explicitly states that it is God who extends to humanity the opportunity to repent. Plutarch asserts that human chastisement goes no further than repaying pain with pain; God, however,

> distinguishes whether the passions of the sick soul to which he administers his justice will in any way yield and make room for repentance (μετάνοιαν), and for those in whose nature vice is not unrelieved or intractable, he assigns a period of grace. . . to those whose sinfulness is likely to have sprung from ignorance of good rather than from preference of evil, he grants time for reform; however, if they persist in their evil, then to these he assigns suitable punishment."[142]

This idea of repentance being extended as a cure to those who are sick in soul is also found in the *Tabula of Cebes*, where it is written, "Then what happens if Repentance (Μετάνοια) encounters him? She releases him from his ills (κακῶν)."[143] Plutarch further declares, "blame which is mingled with praise and contains nothing insulting but merely frankness of speech, and arouses not anger but a pricking of the conscience and repentance (μετάνοιαν), appears both kindly and healing (θεραπευτικός)."[144]

---

[138] *On Common Conceptions* 1069.C.
[139] A. D. Nock and A. J. Festugière, eds. *Corpus Hermeticum* (4 vols.; Paris: Collection Budé, 1945–1954) I.28.
[140] *Orations* 2.77.
[141] *Civil Wars* 2.10.63.
[142] *Divine Vengeance* 551.D.
[143] 11.1
[144] *Precepts of Statecraft* 810.C; cf. *Live Unknown* 1128.E.

Plutarch expounds elsewhere on this idea of repentance being aroused by chiding, both from humans and the divine. Plutarch tells how most people experiencing good fortune become overwhelmed by pride and arrogance; however, "when the heavenly power casts them down and strips off their importance, there is in these calamities alone admonition enough to work repentance (μετάνοιαν)."[145] Furthermore, when the heavenly powers have chided, there is no need for human admonition. Plutarch writes, "Wherefore at such a time there is no use for a friend's frankness or for words charged with grave and stinging reproof; but in such reversals truly *'Tis sweet to gaze into a kind man's eyes*,' when he offers consolation and encouragement."[146] However, in the absence of divine chiding, the gentle chiding of a friend is beneficial for arousing repentance.[147] Often this chiding takes place in the form of speeches or messages of exhortations.[148]

Repentance: A Means of Escaping Punishment and a Source of Reconciliation

Plutarch was also aware that there are those who reject human chiding, and as a result fail to repent for their inappropriateness.[149] Their failure to repent prevents them from escaping judgment and punishment, since repentance serves as a means for escaping punishment. In the previous quote from Plutarch, he declared that to those who persist in their evil ways and refuse to repent, God assigns a suitable punishment. In an account of how the men of Gaul were subject to the Roman dictator, Camillus, Plutarch writes, "Now, however, they [the Gauls] must say what they wanted, for he [Camillus] came with legal authority to grant pardon to those who asked it, and to inflict punishment on the guilty, unless they showed repentance (μετανοοῦσιν)."[150]

Quite naturally, in order to avoid severe judgment and punishment some individuals would feign repentance. Dionysius tells the story of how Tarquinius feigned repentance in order to receive forgiveness from Tullius, king of Rome. Legend has it that the wife of Tarquinius advised him to seek "reconciliation with Tullius by the intercession of friends—to the end that the king, trusting him as having become his friend, might not be on his guard against him. Believing that her advice was most excellent, he [Tarquinius] pretended to repent (μετανοεῖν) of his past behavior, and through friends besought Tullius with many entreaties to forgive

---

[145] *How to Tell a Flatterer* 68.F.
[146] Ibid.
[147] See *How to Tell a Flatterer* 74.C; *On Moral Virtue* 452.C, and Appian, *Civil Wars* 2.10.63–64.
[148] Diodorus Siculus *History* 9.5.22; 9.33.4; 11.4.6; 16.43.4.
[149] *How to Tell a Flatterer* 56.A
[150] *Camillus* 29.3. See also *Pericles* 10.3; *Alexander* 11.4; Dionysius, *Ant.* 3.73.1; 7.22.4; *Cebes* 6.1–2, 11.1.

him."[151] Tarquinius feigned repentance in order to escape being punished by and to be reconciled to Tullius, king of Rome.

Recognizing that repentance could be faked, Dio Chrysostom asserted that claims alone of repentance were not sufficient: action must also accompany any and all claims of repentance. In an oration about establishing peace between rival factions, Chrysostom asserts:

> "Oh yes," you may reply, "but now we have reached an agreement and are united in our counsel." Nay, who could regard as safe and sure that sort of concord, a concord achieved in anger and of no more than three or four days' standing? . . . just because perhaps on some occasion you all have voiced the same sentiment and experienced the same impulse, you must not for that reason assume that now at last the disease has been eradicated from the city. . . . just as the act of wounding and dismembering takes place quickly and quite easily, but the process of healing and knitting together requires time and serious attention, so it is also in the case of cities: quarreling and party strife are within easy reach and frequently occur for paltry reason, whereas men may not, by Zeus, immediately arrive at a real settlement of their difficulties and acquire the mental state and the confidence of their neighbours befitting such a settlement merely by claiming to be *repentant*, nor yet by being thought to be repentant (μετανοεῖν). . . . For only by getting rid of the vices that excite and disturb men, the vices of envy, greed, contentiousness, the striving in each case to promote one's own welfare at the expense of both one's native land and the commonwealth—only so, I repeat, is it possible ever to breathe the breath of harmony in full strength and vigour.[152]

As in previously examined quotes from Dionysius, Dio Cassius, and Plutarch,[153] it is once again demonstrated how repentance in secular Greek literature often leads to some sort of reconciliation between estranged parties; however, according to Dio Chrysostom true reconciliation requires more than claims of repentance. Chrysostom asserts that such claims must be accompanied by an abandonment of envy, greed, bickering, and selfishness, and that the abandonment of such vices must be continually demonstrated over time.

Like Chrysostom, Greco-Roman writers have manifested an awareness and or belief that true repentance is demonstrated not merely by words but by a change of behavior. Affording someone the opportunity to repent, meant affording that individual an opportunity to change his or her behavior and to become a better person. In the *Sayings of the Romans*, Plutarch writes: "On gaining possession of the papers of Sertorius of Spain—among which were letters from many leading men inviting Sertorius to come to Rome for the purpose of inciting a revolution and

---

[151] *Roman Antiquities* 4.38.1.
[152] *Orations* 34.17–19 (English translation taken from J. W. Cohoon and H. L. Crosby, *Dio Chrysostom* LCL (5 vols.; Cambridge, MA: Harvard University Press, 1932–51)).
[153] See above, 11–15.

changing the government—he burned them all, thus offering an opportunity for the villains to repent (μετανοῆσαι) and become better men."¹⁵⁴

Most scholars have asserted that this change in behavior, which leads to the becoming of better men, is always in reference to individual instances of change with respect to specific acts. In other words, the change is never an overall change in life orientation. One author writes, "For the Greeks μετάνοια never suggests an alteration in the total moral attitude, a profound change in life's direction, a conversion which affects the whole of conduct."¹⁵⁵ While it may be true that for the Greeks changes in behavior were usually specific and limited alterations of attitudes and actions, it appears that at least one Greek writer was aware of μετανοέω and μετάνοια being used to suggest a complete change in behavior and life direction. Harpocration, a second century C.E. grammarian, wrote a lexicon containing words and phrases mainly from orators of the imperial age. The entries were in alphabetical order and generally assigned to their sources, with explanations of points of interest or difficulty. With regard to μετάνοια, Harpocration asserts, "to live a new life after repenting (μετανοήσαντας) of one's former life" is an impossibility.¹⁵⁶ Harpocration's remarks seem to suggest that there were Greeks who believed μετανοέω and μετάνοια could represent a profound change in life's direction—a view Harpocration adamantly opposed.¹⁵⁷

However extensive the change, it is this change in behavior that many Greek writers believed contributed to reconciliation between estranged parties.¹⁵⁸ Although the reconciliation usually took place between human beings, the notion of reconciliation taking place between human beings and the gods—because of a change in human behavior—was not alien to the Greeks.¹⁵⁹

Not only did repentance lead to reconciliation, but according to some Greco-Roman authors reconciliation was aided by the restitution that sometimes accompanied repentance. According to Dionysius, Marcius was encouraged to forgive a young woman of her offenses, "seeing that she is repentant (μετανοούσῃ) and ready to be reconciled and to restore (ἀποδιδούσῃ) to you now everything that she took away."¹⁶⁰ Plutarch, describing the naiveté of Antony, writes, "For there was simplicity in his nature, and slowness of perception, though when he did perceive his errors he showed keen repentance (μετάνοια), and made

---

¹⁵⁴ 20.4.A.7. See also *On Moral Virtue* 452.C–D; *The Divine Vengeance* 551.C–E; Dionysius, *Antiquities* 7.22.4; Dio Chrysostom, *Orations* 12.45; *Cebes* 11–14; (cf. Seneca, *Natural Questions* 3.Pref.3).
¹⁵⁵ Behm, 979 (Cf. H. Merklein, "μετάνοια," *Exegetical Dictionary of the New Testament* (3 vols.; Grand Rapids, MI: Eerdmans, 1990–93) 2:415–19; Thompson; Norden).
¹⁵⁶ W. Dindorf, ed., *Harpocrations lexicon in decem oratores Atticos* (Oxford: Oxford University Press, 1853) 31.
¹⁵⁷ Dirksen (174) concludes, especially from *Ceb. Tab.*, 10, that in secular Greek μετάνοια implies a moral and ethical change in life direction.
¹⁵⁸ Cf. Diodorus, *History* 17.109.3; Dio Cassius, *Roman History* 40.37.3.
¹⁵⁹ Cf. Dionysius, *Antiquities* 8.50.4.
¹⁶⁰ *Antiquities* 8.50.4.

full acknowledgment to the very men who had been unfairly dealt with, and there was largeness in his restitution to the wronged."[161] For some Greek writers, restitution served as one of the ways to demonstrate repentance.

Summary

After a somewhat extensive examination of the occurrences of μετανοέω and μετάνοια in Classic and Hellenistic Greek literature, our findings can be summarized as follows: 1) Even at the earliest point in their linguistic history, these two words did not merely denote the idea of thinking afterwards. Both terms carried some negative connotation in their ordinary use; implying at least something like the phrase "to have second thoughts." The notion of "having second thoughts" does not simply suggest "thinking afterwards;" instead it suggests a "change in thinking." 2) This notion of a "change in thinking" became much clearer in succeeding centuries. The verb μετανοέω began commonly meaning "to think differently, to change one's mind or view, to form a different opinion, plan or purpose." Similarly, μετάνοια began to commonly mean "a change of mind, heart, view, opinion or purpose." 3) Quite frequently, a sense of regret and or remorse is also implied as part of the meaning of these two words. This presence of regret and remorse suggests an emotional change of feeling and or belief as well as an intellectual change of mind. 4) One of the reasons the change in thinking denoted by μετανοέω and μετάνοια often includes a sense of regret and or remorse is because the past action or way of thinking is often later perceived as having been wrong, inappropriate, or disadvantageous. This point is frequently conveyed by using μετανοέω and μετάνοια with words such as ἁμαρτάνω, ἁμάρτημα, and ἁμαρτία. The change in thinking denoted by μετανοέω and μετάνοια is appropriate for "sins" committed intentionally and out of ignorance. It is also the expected response to sins committed not only against human beings but also against divine beings. According to some Greek authors, it was the gods themselves who considered μετάνοια to be an appropriate response to inappropriate behavior, and it was the gods who extended to the sin-sick soul the opportunity to repent. 5) In most, if not all, of the references in which μετανοέω and μετάνοια are described as useless, the terms are used to depict an overwhelming sense of remorse and guilt or a possible change of mind that is unable to undo or correct the damage already done. For μετανοέω and μετάνοια to be beneficial they must be accompanied by both the will and ability to either undo the wrong committed or to change the current situation. 6) The change in thinking denoted by μετανοέω and μετάνοια often occurred as a result of chiding, both divine and human. This chiding frequently took place in the form of speeches and/or messages of exhortations. 7) The change in thinking denoted by μετανοέω and μετάνοια also provided a

---

[161] *Antony* 24.6.

means for escaping judgment and punishment. 8) Some Greek authors, expressing an awareness that on occasions μετάνοια was feigned, asserted that claims of repentance alone were not sufficient. Deeds had to accompany any and all claims of repentance. Genuine repentance was manifested by a demonstrable change of behavior. 9) Ultimately, the change in behavior resulting from μετάνοια lead to forgiveness and reconciliation between estranged parties.

The evidence presented here undermines the claims of scholars who assert there is little or no affinity between the usage of μετανοέω and μετάνοια in secular Greek thought and its usage in Christian thought. While many scholars may have followed the lead of E. Norden, who denied that μετάνοια ever meant repentance in its pre-Christian Greek usage,[162] or the lead of Wilamowitz-Moellendorf, who asserted, "the Greeks had no sense for μετάνοια (and not much for pity),"[163] the evidence clearly demonstrates that while the usage of μετανοέω and μετάνοια in Christian thought may not be identical with the usage in non-Christian Greek thought, the usage in Christian thought is clearly influenced by and indebted to the usage found in non-Christian Greek thought.

Μετανοέω and Μετάνοια in Hellenistic Jewish Literature

Most scholars who assert that the early Christian conception of "repentance" is so special that there is nothing like it in pre-Christian Greek usage, maintain that μετανοέω and μετάνοια inherited their Christian meaning from the Jewish concept of "repentance" and "conversion."[164] Winston declares that repentance was "a Jewish religious ideal."[165] Wrede asserts that μετάνοια in the New Testament is not a new concept, but that it is the Old Testament concept of "conversion" taken over by the New Testament.[166] McComb states, "It is only in Judaism and Christianity that the idea of repentance is developed."[167] Montefiore declares:

> The Rabbinic doctrine of Repentance is naturally based upon the Old Testament. . . . whereas the mixture of Hellenism with Judaism sometimes improved and spiritualized a given doctrine or created interesting novelties and developments, the reverse is the case with the subject of repentance. Sirach is

---

[162] *Agnostos Theos*, 134.

[163] U. von Wilamowitz-Moellendorf, *Glaube der Hellenen* (2 vols.; Dormstadt: Wissenschaftliche Buchgesellschaft, 1952) 2:529.

[164] Many authors use the terms "repentance" and "conversion" interchangeably (cf. Dirksen, *The New Testament Concept of Metanoia*, 109–164; Behm and Würthwein, "μετανοέω, μετάνοια," *TDNT* 4:980–989). Furthermore, as discussed below, these authors never indicate how it is they determined that particular human actions, when grouped together, comprise repentance.

[165] D. Winston, "Judaism and Hellenism: Hidden Tensions in Philo's Thought," *The Studia Philonica Annual: Studies in Hellenistic Judaism* 2 (1990) 4.

[166] W. Wrede, W. "Μετάνοια—Sinnesänderung?" *Zeitschrift für neutestamentliche Wissenschaft* 1 (1900) 66–69.

[167] S. McComb, "Repentance," *Encyclopaedia of Religion and Ethics*, 10:211.

The Meaning of Repentance

better on repentance than the Wisdom of Solomon. The whole doctrine is genuinely and purely Hebraic, and Hellenism does not improve it. On the contrary, it tends to dry it up. Philo has little to say about repentance, and what he does say is of small account.[168]

Biblical scholars have gone to great lengths to preserve and perpetuate the illusion that the concept of repentance found in the Bible in general, and in the New Testament in particular, was a uniquely Jewish concept that was alien to classical and Hellenistic Greek culture.[169] However, as this section will reveal, instead of being unique, the concept of repentance reflected in much of the pre-Christian and Christian Jewish literature was very similar to the concept of repentance found in much of the classical and Hellenistic Greek literature of the time.

Furthermore, while many scholars profess that the early Christian concept of repentance is of Jewish origin, most have yet to demonstrate a direct link between the ancient Jewish concept of repentance and the early Christian concept of repentance. As a matter of fact few, if any, scholars have adequately demonstrated what the ancient Jewish concept of repentance may have been. Most scholars start with an assumption, or predefined understanding, of what comprised the ancient Jewish concept of repentance. After doing so, they then proceed to search for instances in which that predefined understanding of repentance occurs, and they use those instances as examples of the Jewish concept of repentance.

Würthwein, in his *TDNT* entry, writes, "There is in the OT no special tt. for 'repentance' or 'to repent.' But the concept is by no means absent."[170] While this statement may be true, it implies a preconceived notion as to the meaning of the concept of repentance. How does Würthwein know that the concept of repentance is by no means absent, unless he has determined beforehand what the concept of repentance is? Würthwein then proceeds to give examples of the cultic and ritual,

---

[168] C. G. Montefiore, "Rabbinic Conceptions of Repentance," *Jewish Quarterly Review* 16 (1904) 213 (As will be demonstrated later, Montefiore is drastically wrong regarding Philo's contribution to the understanding of repentance).

[169] Morgan writes that there is "nothing analogous to the biblical conception of repentance and conversion. . . known among the Greeks" ("Repent, Repentance," *Hastings Dictionary of the Bible*, 4:225). The reason most biblical scholars assert that there was no concept of repentance in secular Greek that gave rise to the concept of repentance found in the Bible is because most biblical scholars are Christians, and the concept of repentance among most Christians presupposes belief in a personal God and an awareness of sin and what sin does to the human relationship with God (cf Etzioni, *Repentance: A Comparative Perspective*, 31). It is believed by most biblical scholars that such an understanding of a personal God was alien to secular Greek culture; therefore, the concept of repentance found in the Bible must have also been alien to secular Greek culture. One of the problems, however, with the concept of repentance advanced by these biblical scholars is that it only considers the notion of repentance in the context of human/divine relationships and not in the context of human/human relationships (which is the context in which the notion of repentance was most often considered in secular Greek culture). For these biblical scholars, repentance always involves turning to God, which minimizes the importance or even the idea of repenting of human wrongs committed against other human beings.

[170] J. Behm, and E. Würthwein, "μετανοέω, μετάνοια," 4:980.

as well as the prophetic, forms of repentance without ever demonstrating how he arrives at his understanding of the Jewish concept of repentance. The readers are forced to trust that what Würthwein defines as repentance is what the ancient Jews considered to be repentance. Furthermore, without any discussion of how he comes to such a conclusion, Würthwein contends that the prophetic form of repentance is synonymous with the Jewish concept of conversion, which for Würthwein is expressed by the Hebrew verb שוב.[171]

Würthwein is following the lead of Dirksen, who in his discussion of the Jewish background of the New Testament concept of repentance writes:

> The OT has no strict term for repentance, but the idea of repentance is there, though it is variously described. It is "seeking God." It is called "directing of the heart to God." It is a return to obedience to God. It is to desire God with the whole heart and soul. Thus as sin was conceived to be a turning away from Yahweh, so repentance is a turning back to Him, a return. Hence the Hebrew word *shub* is most commonly used to convey the idea of repentance.[172]

Based on nothing more than his own preconceived notion, Dirksen defines for the reader what repentance is. Dirksen alleges that although it can be variously described, repentance represents a turning back to God. In his description of what this turning back to God consists of, Dirksen writes, "The essential thing in this return to Yahweh is that it be with the whole heart and the whole soul. This is in fact the essence of the OT repentance, the turn of the whole heart and soul to God from whom the sinner has turned away."[173]

Dirksen acknowledges that שוב cannot be regarded as a technical term for repentance because it is used to designate any kind of turn—physical, moral or religious.[174] According to Dirksen, שוב "is used by OT writers simply because it expresses so well the nature of repentance in OT religion. It gives a concrete picture of the sinner's return to God. . . . Yet if we wish to speak of a Hebrew term for repentance it can only be שוב, because there is no other term used in this sense by the OT writers."[175] Dirksen determines for himself and his readers, as well as for generations of scholars yet to come, the nature of repentance in ancient Jewish religion.[176] He declares that שוב best expresses the nature of repentance in Old

---

[171] Ibid., 984.

[172] *New Testament Concept*, 116 (for Dirksen, the Hebrew root שוב conveys the notion of repentance; for Würthwein it conveys the notion of conversion, which is synonymous to the prophetic form of repentance).

[173] Ibid.

[174] The root is more frequently used in the sense of a physical turn than as an expression of a moral or religious turn.

[175] *New Testament Concept*, 148–149.

[176] The earlier works of scholars such as C. G. Montefiore, *Rabbinic Conceptions of Repentance*, and Solomon Schechter, *Aspects of Rabbinic Theology* (1909; reprint—Woodstock, VT: JEWISH LIGHTS, 1993), undoubtedly influenced Dirksen, but these scholars focused more on the concept of repentance found in later Rabbinic literature.

Testament religion because for him the nature of repentance is a whole-hearted return of the sinner to God.[177] As a result of his examination of various Old Testament passages demonstrating what he determines to be a return to God, Dirksen also concludes that repentance requires confession of sins, contrition for sins, fulfillment of penitential works, and a willingness to amend one's life.[178]

Most scholarly analyses of the ancient Jewish understanding of repentance begin by examining the concept of repentance found in the Hebrew Bible. After all it is believed by most scholars that the basis of Jewish social, moral, and religious thought is revealed in the Hebrew Bible.[179] However, since the primary objective of this section is to discover the concept of repentance that prevailed among the Jews at the beginning of the Christian era, we will begin by examining the concept of repentance reflected in the Hellenistic writings of Greek speaking Jews. We will then work our way back to the Hebrew Scriptures in an attempt to ascertain what may have been the ancient Jewish origin for the Hellenistic Jewish understanding of repentance that prevailed among Jews at the beginning of the Christian era.

The primary advantage of this *a posteriori* method is that it discourages beginning with an assumption, or predefined understanding of what the ancient Jewish concept of repentance might have been. Instead of reading into the Hellenistic Jewish understanding of repentance preconceived notions regarding ancient Jewish understandings of repentance, this section will examine the Hellenistic Jewish use and understanding of μετανοέω and μετάνοια, and seek to determine what the Jewish basis for such an understanding might have been.

Modern scholars continue to promote the view of Dirksen, Schechter and Montefiore regarding the nature of repentance. Neusner writes with regard to the Jewish concept of repentance, "The Hebrew word is *teshuvah*, from the root for return, and the concept is generally understood to mean returning to God from a situation of estrangement" (J. Neusner, "Repentance in Judaism," *Repentance: A Comparative Perspective* (eds. Amitai Etzioni and David Carney; Lanham, MD: Rowman and Littlefield, 1997) 60–75; see also C. Nussbaum, *The Essence of Teshuvah: A Path to Repentance* (Northvale, NJ: Jason Aronson Inc., 1993)). Bailey asserts, "The idea of repentance in the Old Testament is important for the use of μετάνοια and cognate terms in the writings of Philo. In the Hebrew Bible the common term for repentance is שוב. This word has as its basic meaning 'turn back' or 'return,' and usually denotes a physical action of turning. However, it is also used in [sic] for moral, spiritual, or religious turning, and is used by the prophets to describe turning from evil and turning to God" (J. Bailey, "*Metanoia* in the Writings of Philo Judaeus," *SBL Papers 1991* (ed. E. H. Lovering, Jr. *SBLSP* 30; Atlanta: Scholars Press (1991) 136).

[177] A fundamental problem with this understanding of repentance is that it only addresses humanity's relationship with God. It fails to address a human being's relationship with another human being. According to this view, repentance is only necessary when reestablishing one's relationship with God.

[178] *New Testament Concept*, 117–125.

[179] Dirksen writes, "The basis of Jewish theological thought of course is the OT" (*New Testament Concept*, 110).

Josephus

Born in 37 C.E., Josephus was a Jewish politician, soldier, and historian, whose writings provide invaluable information for understanding both biblical history and the political history of Roman Palestine in the 1st century C.E. Josephus was born into a prominent Jewish family: his father was a priest and his mother was a descendant of the Hasmonean family. He was raised not in the diaspora, but in Jerusalem. He received an excellent education in Jerusalem, and was well acquainted with Jewish traditions, customs and religious practices. As an author, his writings were directed not only to his fellow Jews, justifying both Roman conduct during the Jewish War and his own personal conduct in switching loyalties, but they were also directed to an interested and sometimes sympathetic Roman audience, justifying Jewish culture and religious traditions.[180]

Josephus' use of μετανοέω and μετάνοια reflects a Jewish understanding of repentance. As a literary figure, he uses the terms more than any other ancient non-Christian writer.[181] Contrary to most of the scholarly assertions made regarding the Jewish concept of repentance, Josephus does not use the terms simply in the context of human/divine relationships; he also uses the terms in the context of human/human relationships. Repentance is not merely a returning back to God; it does not simply address humanity's relationship with God. It also addresses a human being's relationship with another human being.

Repentance: Regret, Remorse, and a Change in Thinking

As was the case in much of the classical and Hellenistic Greek literature previously examined, most of the occurrences of these terms in the writings of Josephus designate either some sort of remorse and regret concerning inappropriate intentions and/or actions or some sort of change in thinking and/or purpose.[182] In his account of how the Hebrew people were led out of Egypt by Moses, Josephus writes that the Egyptians "wept and regretted (μετανοούντων)" that they had treated the Hebrews so harshly.[183] Josephus continues writing that one of the reasons Moses led the Hebrews through the wilderness was so that if the Egyptians, "having changed their minds (μετανοήσαντες)," decided to pursue them they would encounter

---

[180] Louis H. Feldman and G. Hata, eds. *Josephus, the Bible, and History* (Detroit: Wayne State University Press, 1989).

[181] As stated earlier, Josephus uses μετανοέω and its cognates 77 times.

[182] As stated earlier, this change in thinking and or purpose is usually in response to former intentions that are perceived as having been inappropriate.

[183] *Antiquities* 2.315 (Translation is my own). The Greek text used in this study is from H. St. J. Thackeray, R. Marcus, A. Wikgren, and L. H. Feldman, *Josephus*, LCL, 10 vols. (Cambridge, MA: Harvard University Press, 1926–1965). Unless noted as being my own, the English translations are from W. Whiston, *The Works of Josephus: New Updated Edition*. Peabody, MA: Hendrickson, 1987.

The Meaning of Repentance   75

difficulty.¹⁸⁴ In this one passage, Josephus uses μετανοέω twice—the first time to convey the notion of remorse and regret and the second time to convey a change of mind motivated by regret.

Josephus later writes that when the Hebrew people began to reflect on what a great leader Moses had been and on how he had on several occasions risked his own life in order to preserve theirs, they became fearful that they would never have another leader like Moses, and they "repented (μετανοοῦντες) of what they had said to him in the wilderness when they were angry."¹⁸⁵ According to Josephus, the people wept so bitterly that words were unable to comfort them. They realized the inappropriateness of their behavior, and deeply regretted their actions toward Moses. Josephus also asserts that even God on occasions regrets prior acts. Josephus writes that God "told Samuel the prophet, that God regretted (μετανοεῖν) having made Saul king, since Saul had done nothing that God had commanded him, but pursued his own intentions."¹⁸⁶

Within Jewish literature, an individual's remorse is often expressed by self-inflicted acts of contrition. Josephus states that when Ahab began to be grieved by the atrocities he committed and to regret (μετάμελος) them, "he put on sackcloth, and went barefoot, and would not touch food; he also confessed his sins." In response to Ahab's contrition, God told the prophet Elijah that Ahab's actions demonstrated that he had "repented (μετανοεῖ) of those insolent crimes he had been guilty of."¹⁸⁷ Similarly, when all the other tribes of Israel began to regret having killed so many of their brothers from the tribe of Benjamin, "they expressed repentance (μετάνοια) regarding the adversity they had inflicted upon the Benjaminites, and they appointed a fast on account of it."¹⁸⁸

It was common for repentance to be associated with self-inflicted acts of contrition such as weeping, fasting, prostrating oneself before God, wearing sackcloth and covering oneself in ashes. However, Josephus also conveys that at

---

¹⁸⁴ *Ant.* 2.322.
¹⁸⁵ *Ant.* 4.195.
¹⁸⁶ *Ant.* 6.143 (my own translation). That this passage conveys the notion of regret is confirmed by the fact that the scripture Josephus is alluding to uses נחם in the Hebrew to refer to God's feelings (1 Sam 15:35) and μεταμέλομαι in the Septuagint. Furthermore, the fact that Josephus changes μεταμέλομαι to μετανοέω suggests that he understands μετανοέω to convey the notion of remorse and regret (As shall be seen throughout this section, Josephus often uses μετανοέω when it is not used in the Septuagint version of the scripture he is alluding to, paraphrasing, or even quoting).

NB: Defining what is meant by the term "Septuagint" will be discussed below. It is to the Greek texts of the editions of the Göttingen Septuaginta-Unternehmen that the term Septuagint (LXX) will refer throughout this study. For those passages for which no such critical edition is available, the Greek text found in A. Rahlfs' edition will be used.

¹⁸⁷ *Ant.* 8.362 (Again Josephus uses μετανοέω when the term is not used in the LXX version of the scripture he is alluding to (cf. 1 Kings 20:27–29)).

¹⁸⁸ *Ant.* 5.166 (my own translation). Josephus uses μετάνοια to describe Israel's feelings regarding their treatment of the Benjaminites, even though the term is not used in the LXX version of the story (cf. Judg 21:2–4, 6).

times joy and celebration can take precedence over the remorse and self-inflicted acts of contrition associated with repentance. While it was and is a common belief that repentance should always be demonstrated through acts of sorrow and contrition, on at least one occasion Josephus suggested that the sorrow and contrition associated with repentance (μετάνοια) give way to joy and celebration. Josephus describes the reading of the Law to the people by Esdras during the feast of tabernacles. When the people heard the reading of the Law, they began to experience remorse regarding their past offenses. They became displeased with themselves and started crying because of their remorse. However, when Esdras saw that the people were heavy with remorse:

> he bade them go home and not weep. . . . He exhorted them rather to proceed immediately to feasting, and to do what was suitable to a feast, and what was agreeable to a day of joy; but to let their repentance (μετάνοιαν) and sorrow for their former sins be a security and a guard to them, that they fell no more into like offenses.[189]

Josephus indicates that the sorrow and regret associated with repentance does not have to be manifested by weeping and acts of contrition, especially at a time when people should be rejoicing and celebrating.[190] According to Esdras, it was appropriate for these post-exilic Hebrews to feel regret and remorse over their past offenses, but they did not have to demonstrate their remorse through weeping and self-inflicted acts of contrition. The feast of tabernacles was a time of celebration not sorrow. When the people heard Esdras' words, "they began to feast and when they had so done for eight days, in their tabernacles, they departed to their own homes, singing hymns to God, and returning thanks to Esdras for his reformation of what corruptions had been introduced into their settlement."[191] The people celebrated not only because it was the feast of tabernacles, but also because Esdras introduced reforms addressing the sins of the people resulting from their failure to follow the Law. In this instance, repentance involved not only remorse for past offenses, but also thanksgiving for the changes wrought as a result of the people's remorse.

Conveying both the notion of regret and of changing one's mind, Josephus tells of his opposition to the practice of forcing non-Jews to be circumcised. He writes:

> At this time it was that two great men, who were under the jurisdiction of the

---

[189] *Ant.* 11.156.

[190] It should be pointed out that although Josephus is most likely relying on 1 Esdras for his depiction of this event, the Greek text of 1 Esdras does not explicitly identify the people's remorse as μετάνοια (cf. S. Tedesche, *A Critical Edition of 1 Esdras* (Ph.D. Dissertation, Yale University, 1928)).

[191] *Ant.* 11.157.

The Meaning of Repentance

king [Agrippa], came to me out of the region of Trachonitis, bringing their horses and their arms, and carrying with them their money also; and when the Jews would force them to be circumcised, if they would stay among them, I would not permit them to have any force put upon them, but said to them, "Everyone ought to worship God according to his own inclinations, and not to be constrained by force;" and that these men, who had fled to us for protection, ought not to be so treated as to repent (μετανοεῖν) of their coming.[192]

In his autobiography, Josephus tells how a number of Jews were excited by and promoted the idea of a Jewish revolt against the Romans. Josephus writes, "I therefore endeavored to discourage these riotous individuals, and tried to persuade them to change their minds (μετανοεῖν)."[193] In his account of the Roman legion's conquest of Galilee, Josephus writes

And thus did Vespasian march with his army and came to the bounds of Galilee, where he pitched his camp and restrained his soldiers, who were eager for war; he also showed his army to the enemy, in order to affright them, and to afford them a season for repentance (μετανοίας), to see whether they would change their minds (μεταβάλοιντο) before it came to a battle, and at the same time he got things ready for besieging their strongholds. And indeed this sight of the general brought many to repent (μετάνοιαν) of their revolt.[194]

These are just a few of the many examples of how Josephus uses μετανοέω and μετάνοια to designate either remorse and regret or some sort of change in thinking and/or purpose.[195] As is the case in most of these usages, the regret and remorse, as well as the change in thinking and/or purpose, are in response to perceived inappropriate acts and or intentions, many of which are identified as sins.[196]

Repentance Should be Accompanied by a Change in Behavior and Lifestyle

One of the questions raised as a result of Josephus' emphasis on remorse and a change in thinking is whether or not Josephus implies that this remorse and change in thinking leads (or at least should lead) to a change in behavior. In Bailey's discussion of Josephus' use of μετανοέω and μετάνοια, he writes:

For Josephus, this change of mind is often a change of how one feels about an error, and so it involves regret or remorse, but not necessarily any change of

---

[192] *Life* 112–113.
[193] *Life* 17 (my own translation).
[194] *War* 3.127–128.
[195] Other examples include *Ant.* 2.24, 51, 107, 163, 309, 320; 4.142, 144, 191, 313; 5.108, 151, 240; 6.38, 284, 297; 7.54, 153, 264, 320; 8.225, 301; 10.123; 11.318; 12.273; 13.314; 14.55, 391; 16.240, 392; 18.118; *War* 1.92, 278, 444, 555; 2.304; 3.139; 4.284, 350, 354, 367, 640; 5.319, 361, 572; 6.103, 123, 364; 7.379; *Life* 110; 262; *Apion* 1.274.
[196] E.g. *Ant.* 5:108; 7:153; 8:362; 11:156

action. This is evident in *Antiquities* 16.240, where he says concerning Herod: "For the king soon began to repent (ἥ τε γὰρ μετάνοια τῷ βασιλεῖ ταχύ) of having put to death persons who had not clearly committed any sin, but the terrible thing about this was that he ended not by ceasing to do this kind of thing but by punishing informers in the very same way."[197]

It seems safe to say that there is probably some truth to Bailey's assertion that for Josephus a change of mind does "not *necessarily*" involve a change of action.[198] However, Bailey's use of Josephus' reference to Herod as evidence in no way supports his assertion. If anything, the passage regarding Herod demonstrates that Josephus does believe that a change of mind should involve a change of action. For Josephus the problem with Herod's repentance is that Herod only displays remorse, but he does not change his behavior. Herod continues his inappropriate behavior by inflicting the same kind of unjust punishment upon the accusers that he had earlier inflicted upon the accused. It is clear from this passage that Josephus believed a change in behavior should have accompanied the king's repentance.

In the earlier cited passage where Josephus describes the reading of the Law to the people by Esdras, Esdras exhorts the people "to let their repentance (μετάνοιαν) and sorrow for their former sins be a security and a guard to them, that they fell no more into like offenses."[199] It seems clear from this passage that repentance should not only lead to a change in behavior, but it should guarantee a change in behavior. Repentance should keep one from committing similar offenses.

Elsewhere, Josephus tells how after Moses led the Hebrew people out of Egypt, the young men began marrying women from other nations and disregarding the laws of Moses in order to keep the laws and customs observed by their foreign wives. According to Josephus, Moses became concerned that the Hebrew people would suffer greatly because they had abandoned God and the traditions of their fathers. Moses, therefore, "sought to correct (ἐπανορθοῦν) the young men and lead them to repentance (μετάνοιαν)."[200] Repentance in this passage clearly involves a change of action. As a matter of fact, repentance seems to be associated with a profound change of lifestyle.

After the tribes of Reuben and Gad and half the tribe of Manasseh settled on the eastern side of the Jordan River—while the rest of Israel settled on the western side—they built an altar on the banks of the Jordan. However, when the other tribes heard about it they thought their countrymen had rebelled against the Lord by building for themselves an altar in order to worship other gods and to replace the

---

[197] *Repentance*, 104.
[198] It should be noted, however, that none of the references cited by Bailey in his footnote prove that for Josephus a change of mind *does not* necessarily involve a change of action. As a matter of fact many of the references suggest a change of action (cf. *War* 1.555; 3.128; 4.640; *Ant.* 5.166; 7.264).
[199] *Ant.* 11.156
[200] *Ant.* 4.141–144 (my own translation).

The Meaning of Repentance 79

altar of the Lord their God which resided in the tabernacle. Therefore, the other tribes sent a delegation to confront the tribes of Reuben and Gad and the half tribe of Manasseh, and to inquire as to why they had built the altar. The delegation rebuked their countrymen, and informed them that the matter would be considered a small offense if they repented (μετανοήσαντες) and proceeded no further in their madness; however, if they continued their current practices their fellow countrymen on the other side of the Jordan would be forced to cross the river and destroy them.[201] In this passage repentance is clearly associated with a profound change of practice and or lifestyle.

After Jehoiada, the high priest, died, king Jehoash (Joash) and the leaders of Judah stopped following after the Lord and began worshiping idols. According to Josephus, God became displeased and sent prophets to testify against them and to persuade them to cease their wickedness. However, neither the examples of how others had been severely punished for turning away from God, "nor could the fear of what the prophets now foretold bring them to repentance (μετανοῆσαι), and turn them back from their course of transgression to their former duty."[202] Once again repentance is clearly associated with a change of lifestyle. Although every occurrence of μετανοέω and μετάνοια in the writings of Josephus might not *necessarily* involve any change of action, the evidence clearly indicates that Josephus expected a change of mind to involve a chance of action.

Repentance: A Way of Avoiding Punishment

In his account of Reubel's (Reuben's) attempt to dissuade his brothers from killing their brother Joseph, Josephus tells how Reubel begged his brothers to be led by their own consciences and to consider what misfortune they would suffer from the hand of God for committing such an offense. According to Josephus, Reubel stated that God would love them if they abstained from this act "yielding to repentance and coming to their senses" (μετανοίᾳ καὶ τῷ σωφρονεῖν εἴξαντας);[203] however, if they continued to proceed with their intentions, they would suffer all sorts of punishment from the hand of God.[204] In this scenario not only does repentance involve a change of action, but that change of action serves as a way of avoiding punishment.

In the writings of Josephus, repentance frequently serves as a way of avoiding punishment.[205] As discussed previously in this chapter, this aspect of repentance is commonly found in the writings of classical and Hellenistic Greek authors. Repentance often serves as a way of avoiding both human and divine punishment.

---

[201] *Ant.* 5.108.
[202] *Ant.* 9.166–168.
[203] *Antiquities* 2.23 (Translation is my own).
[204] Josephus later records that Reuben rebukes his brothers and attributes the family's misfortunes to their failure to repent of their evil against Joseph (*Ant.* 2.107).
[205] *Ant.* 7.264; 8.362; 9.176; 20.178; *War* 1.10; 3.89; 5.361, 572; *Life* 262.

During the eighteenth year of the reign of King Josiah, the books of Moses were found in the temple. When King Josiah heard the words of the books, he tore his clothes and called for the high priest, the scribe, and others, and he sent them to Huldah the prophetess and ordered them to ask her to intercede on their behalf in order to appease God so that God would not punish them for the transgressions of their foreparents against the laws of Moses. According to Josephus:

> When the prophetess had heard this from the messengers that were sent to her by the king, she bade them go back to the king, and say that God had already given sentence against them, to destroy the people, and cast them out of their country, and deprive them of all the happiness they enjoyed; which sentence none could set aside by any prayers of theirs, since it was passed on account of their transgressions of the laws, and of their not having repented (μὴ μετανοήσαντας) in so long a time.[206]

According to Josephus, the prophetess makes it clear that the punishment the people are going to experience is partly due to their lack of repentance. For generations the prophets had warned the people of the punishment they would suffer for their impious practices, and the prophets exhorted the people to change their ways in order to avoid such punishment. The people, however, continually refused to change their ways, and as a result of their refusal to repent God was forced to execute punishment in order to fulfill the words of the prophets.[207]

In his autobiography, Josephus responds to Justus, who in his writings about the Jewish war accused Josephus and the Galileans of fomenting the revolt against the Romans and King Agrippa. Josephus not only denies such charges, he asserts that when the Galileans wanted to march against John and punish him for causing the disorder, he opposed them because he wished to defuse the matter without bloodshed. Josephus writes:

> I exhorted them to use the utmost care to learn the names of those who served under John; which when they had done so, and I was informed who the men were, I published a decree, wherein I offered security and my right hand to those serving under John who desired to choose repentance (μετάνοιαν). And I allowed twenty days' time to such as would take advantage of this offer for themselves. I also threatened, that unless they threw down their weapons, I would burn their houses, and expose their possessions to public sale.[208]

In this passage, repentance entails laying down one's weapons and changing one's

---

[206] *Ant.* 10.60.
[207] The prophetess informs Josiah's delegation that repentance at this point is unable to set aside the sentence God has passed on the people. The prophetess does inform the delegation, however, that since Josiah has been and continues to be a righteous man, that God will delay pouring out calamities on the people until after Josiah's death.
[208] *Life* 368–370 (my own translation).

mind about going to war. If the men did repent, they would not be subject to any punishment for their previous actions; furthermore, they would avoid the punishment of having their houses burned and their possessions sold for refusing to repent. Although four thousand men laid down their weapons and abandoned John, John continued in his resistance against the Romans and his opposition to Josephus. After Titus and his army surrounded John and his men, Titus sent for Josephus to exhort John and his men once again to surrender. According to Josephus, Titus was concerned about the well being of the city and the temple, as well as the cessation of daily sacrifices to the Jewish God. Josephus alleges that he begged John to spare the city and prevent the destruction of the temple. He informed John, "it is never dishonorable to repent (μετανοῆσαι), and amend what hath been done amiss, even at the last extremity."[209] By repenting John would prevent the destruction of the city and the temple, and he would spare his own life. Josephus goes so far as to promise John that if he repents, the Romans will forgive him.[210]

Repentance: Responded to with Forgiveness and Leads to Reconciliation

For Josephus, repentance served as a way of escaping punishment because Josephus believed that repentance should be responded to with forgiveness.[211] Josephus records that when Pompey marched to Jerusalem after the citizens of Jerusalem shut their gates against him, "Aristobulus repented (μετανοήσας) of what he was doing, and came to Pompey, and [promised to] give him money, and received him into Jerusalem, and desired that he would leave off the war, and do what he pleased peaceably. So Pompey, upon his entreaty forgave him."[212] Elsewhere Josephus gives an account of how when he went to Sepphoris to put an end to John's uprising, the people sent for Jesus, the captain of a band of eight hundred robbers, to fight with him. Josephus, however, outwitted Jesus, and managed to isolate him from his troops while surrounding him with armed men of his own. When the followers of Jesus heard that he had been captured, they abandoned him. Josephus writes:

> I then called Jesus to me by himself, and told him, that "I was not a stranger to that treacherous design he had against me, nor was I ignorant by whom he was sent for; that, however, I would forgive him what he had done already, if he

---

[209] *War* 6.103. Although Josephus asserts that repentance is always appropriate, even at the last hour, he makes it clear elsewhere that repentance is meaningful only if it occurs early enough to either prevent the occurrence or diminish the results of any perceived inappropriate acts (cf. *AJ* 2.51, 107; 4.191, 313; 6.38; 18.118).
[210] Ibid. 6.103–106.
[211] *Ant.* 2.162; 4.195; 8.301; *War* 2.302–304.
[212] *Ant.* 14.55.

would repent (μετανοήσειν) of it, and be faithful to me hereafter." And thus, upon his promise to do all that I desired, I let him go.[213]

Josephus also writes that when he served as general over the Galileans, John persuaded Simon, a member of a very influential family of Pharisees in Jerusalem, to work to have Josephus stripped of his authority. Simon enlisted the help of other influential figures, including a Pharisee by the name of Jonathan. Jonathan was given money and more than a thousand armed men in order to make war against Josephus and kill him. Josephus, however, marshaled eight thousand men, preventing an attack from Jonathan. Jonathan tried several times to trick Josephus to meet with him privately, at which time Josephus would be ambushed; however, each attempt failed. Jonathan then attempted to promote a revolt among the Galileans against Josephus. Josephus, however, was able to spoil Jonathan's plans and capture Jonathan as he was trying to persuade the Galileans to turn against Josephus. Josephus informed the Galileans of the lies Jonathan and his colleagues told concerning him, and he informed the Galileans how Jonathan and his colleagues were sent to kill him. Josephus writes:

> When the multitude heard these things, they were greatly provoked at Jonathan and his colleagues that were with him, and were going to attack them, and kill them; and this they had certainly done, unless I had restrained the anger of the Galileans, and said, that "I forgave Jonathan and his colleagues of what was past, if they would repent (μετανοήσειν), and go to their own country and tell those who sent them the truth as to my conduct."[214]

When David was on the run from his son Absalom, he was met in a town called Bahurim by a man named Shimei, who cursed David and threw stones at him. Shimei told David that he thanked God for stripping the kingdom from David, and that by the hand of Absalom God was punishing David for his violence against Saul and his family. However, when Absalom was killed and David regained control over the kingdom, Shimei brought his entire household, along with a thousand men from the tribe of Benjamin to greet David. According to Josephus, Shimei fell at David's feet, "and prayed him to forgive him what he had offended, and not to be too bitter against him, nor to think fit to make him the first example of severity under his new authority; but to consider that he had repented (μετανοήσας) of his failure of duty."[215] Abishai, the co-commander of David's army, suggested that Shimei be put to death; however, David informed Abishai that not only did he forgive Shimei, but to mark the first day of his reign he swore to forgive all

---

[213] *Life* 110.
[214] Ibid. 262.
[215] *Ant.* 7.207, 264 f (As is often the case, Josephus once again explicitly identifies as repentance behavior that is not so identified in either the Hebrew scriptures or the LXX (cf. 2 Sam 19:16–23)).

The Meaning of Repentance

offenders their crimes against him. As a result of his repentance, and David's forgiveness, Shimei and others were reconciled to David.

Since Josephus believed repentance should be responded to with forgiveness, repentance in the writings of Josephus often leads to reconciliation. This reconciliation takes place not only between human beings, but also between human beings and God. Josephus writes, "God is easily reconciled (διαλλάττεται) to those that confess their faults, and repent (μετανοοῦσιν) of them."[216] After David committed adultery with Bathsheba, had her husband Uriah killed in battle, and then took Bathsheba as a wife, God sent the prophet Nathan to rebuke David. Nathan revealed to David God's anger against him, and informed David that God would openly punish him for what he had done in secret. Nathan also informed David that the child born as a result of their adulterous affair would die soon after its birth. Josephus writes:

> When the king was troubled at these messages, and sufficiently confounded, and said, with tears and sorrow, that he had sinned, . . . God had compassion on him, and was reconciled (διαλλάττεται) to him, and promised that he would preserve to him both his life and his kingdom, for he said, that seeing he had repented (μετανοοῦντι) of the things he had done, he was no longer displeased with him.[217]

Josephus declares that Herod traveled to Rome to see Caesar in order to bring charges against two of his sons. Herod charged Alexander and Aristobulus, the sons of his wife, Mariamne I, with treachery and seeking to kill him in order to take over his kingdom. After weighing the evidence, and listening to the moving defense of Alexander:

> Caesar, after some delay, said, that although the young men were thoroughly innocent of that for which they were calumniated yet had they been so far to blame, that they had not demeaned themselves towards their father so as to prevent that suspicion which was spread abroad concerning them. He also exhorted Herod to lay all such suspicions aside, and to be reconciled (διαλλάττεσθαι) to his sons; for that it was not just to give any credit to such reports concerning his own children; and that this repentance (μετάνοιαν) on both sides might heal those breaches that had happened between them, and might improve that their good will to one another, whereby those on both sides, excusing the rashness of their suspicions, might resolve to bear a greater degree of affection towards each other than they had before. After Caesar had given them this admonition, he beckoned to the young men. When, therefore, they were disposed to fall down to make intercession to their father, he took them up,

---

[216] *War* 5.415.
[217] *Ant.* 7.153. According to Josephus, God declares that David has repented. There is, however, no such declaration by God in either the Hebrew scriptures or the LXX (cf. 2 Sam 12:13–25)

and embraced them, as they were in tears, and took each of them distinctly in his arms, till not one of those that were present, whether freeman or slave, but was deeply affected with what they saw. Then did they return thanks to Caesar, and went away together; and with them Antipater, with an hypocritical pretense that he rejoiced at this reconciliation.[218]

Repentance on the part of both Herod and his sons leads to reconciliation between this father and his sons.[219]

Josephus' frequent use of μετανοέω and μετάνοια with διαλλάσσω clearly indicates that Josephus is aware of a relationship between repentance and reconciliation.[220] Josephus even indicates that there may have been those who believed that estranged parties were obligated to reconcile if repentance were professed. According to Josephus, after fleeing from the Romans, John tried to pretend he departed Gischala because he was zealous to come defend the great city of Jerusalem. John convinced a number of the young men to go to war against the Romans, and he persuaded them that they could defeat the Romans. The older men of Jerusalem, however, knew better. Civil unrest arose among the Jews. Robbers and bandits (i.e. zealots) started taking over Jerusalem, unseating the high priests and appointing their own high priests.[221] After a while former high priests, especially Ananus, rallied the people together and encouraged them to oppose these young tyrants, who—according to Josephus—were more brutal and savage toward their own countrymen and more impious and sacrilegious toward the Jewish temple than the Romans had ever been. Civil war broke out between the zealots and the Jews that opposed them. The zealots defiled the temple by occupying it and using it as their fortress. Eventually the multitude entered the temple and attacked the zealots. The zealots retreated into the inner court; however, Ananus would not lead the multitude into the inner court because they were not purified. In the meantime, John, who pretended to side with Ananus and the people, was divulging every intention of Ananus and the people to the zealots. When the people became suspicious of John, they made him take an oath, affirming that he would not reveal their intentions to the zealots and that he would assist Ananus and the people in overthrowing the zealots. Ananus and the people believed John's oath, and sent him as their emissary into the inner court to negotiate with the zealots. John, however betrayed Ananus and the people, and revealed their plans to the zealots. He informed the zealots that Ananus had invited Vespasian to come and take Jerusalem, and that Ananus had appointed a fast for the next day in order that the

---

[218] *Ant.* 16.124–127.
[219] Unfortunately, however, such reconciliation was short lived (cf *Ant.* 16.229–270, 300–404).
[220] See also *Ant.* 5.151; 16.352; *War* 4.367.
[221] While I recognize there is much debate among scholars regarding the use and definition of the term "Zealots," and while I believe to use the term "Zealots" to represent a monolithic picture of revolutionaries is inaccurate, my use of the term here reflects nothing more than Josephus' use of the term.

people might enter the inner court and fight with the zealots. John advised the zealots they could not defeat Ananus and the people and that they had no choice but to send someone quickly to the Idumeans to request their assistance in overthrowing Ananus and preventing him from surrendering Jerusalem to the Romans. He also suggested that they should not even consider the idea of trying to negotiate with Ananus. According to Josephus, John told the zealots "that if they harbored for themselves the hope of pardon, in case they were subdued, they had forgotten what desperate things they had done, or supposed that as soon as the defectors repented (μετανοεῖν), those who had suffered were obligated to be reconciled (διηλλάχθαι) to them."[222] John goes on to make it clear that repentance does not automatically lead to reconciliation, especially when the repentance is disingenuous.

After an exhaustive examination of the occurrences of μετανοέω and μετάνοια in the writings of Josephus, the following conclusions can be made: 1) Josephus uses μετανοέω and μετάνοια not simply to address humanity's relationship with God, but also to address humanity's relationship with humanity. 2) As in the writings of classical and Hellenistic Greek authors, virtually all of the occurrences of these terms in the writings of Josephus designate either some sort of remorse and regret concerning inappropriate intentions and/or actions or some sort of change in thinking and/or purpose. 3) Although most of these instances of remorse and regret are associated with self-inflicted acts of contrition such as weeping, fasting, prostrating oneself before God, wearing sackcloth and covering oneself in ashes, Josephus does suggest that the remorse and contrition associated with repentance should yield to rejoicing and celebrating when the occasion permits. 4) Josephus indicates that he believed repentance leads (or at least should lead) to a change in behavior. The evidence clearly reveals that Josephus expected a change of mind to be accompanied by a chance in behavior. 5) Like classical and Hellenistic Greek authors, Josephus understood repentance to be a way of avoiding both human and divine punishment. 6) For Josephus, repentance served as a way of escaping punishment because Josephus believed that repentance should be responded to with forgiveness. 7) Since repentance should be responded to with forgiveness, repentance often leads to reconciliation. This reconciliation occurs between human beings, as well as between human beings and God.

Philo

Philo was a Hellenistic Jewish philosopher and a prominent member of the Jewish community of Alexandria. The exact dates of his birth and death are unknown; however, he is believed to have been born around 20–15 B.C.E. and to have died around 50 C.E. Although he was a Jew, Philo's writings clearly show that he received a Greek education and that he possessed a command of Greek language,

---

[222] *War* 4.221 (my own translation; 4.121–223).

literary style, and philosophy. Many scholars believe that Philo reflects more firsthand knowledge of Hellenistic culture in general and Greek philosophy in particular than any other Hellenistic Jewish writer. Many scholars also consider him a forerunner of early Christian thought.[223] With the exception of Josephus and Plutarch, Philo uses μετανοέω and μετάνοια more than any other ancient non-Christian writer.[224]

Although Josephus uses μετανοέω and μετάνοια more frequently in his writings than does Philo, Philo's usage of the terms appears to demonstrate much more development and refinement. Whereas Josephus uses the terms almost exclusively to designate either some sort of remorse and regret or some sort of change in thinking and/or purpose in general, Philo appears to be much more specific and deliberate in his usage of the terms. This is not to say that the general notions of regret, remorse, and changing one's thinking and/or purpose are absent from the writings of Philo,[225] it is just that for Philo, the terms seem to function in a much more technical sense.

Repentance: A Response to Sin

Philo uses the terms quite frequently to denote the idea of responding to sin. Philo writes that it is because of the ministry of the Levites that human beings are raised up and brought to the attention of God. According to Philo, the Levites present the human race to God as holy by means of either "whole burnt offerings, or else by saving sacrifices, or else by repentance for one's sins (μετανοίας ἁμαρτημάτων)."[226] Elsewhere Philo declares that he is extremely impressed with how the Jewish law provides a number of ways for the Jewish people to put off their sins (ἁμαρτήματα), and to demonstrate their remorse for their sins. Philo informs his readers that Jews may offer as a sacrifice for their sins a female sheep without blemish. If they cannot afford a sheep, then they can offer two turtle doves or two young pigeons. Finally, if they cannot afford the two birds, they can offer some fine flour as a sacrifice for their sins. Philo then goes on to say, "God therefore here is

---

[223] See Borgen, "Philo of Alexandria. A Critical and Synthetical Survey of Research since World War II," *ANRW* 2.21.1: 97–154; Idem., "Philo of Alexandria," *Jewish Writings of the Second Temple Period* (ed. M. Stone; Philadelphia: Fortress, 1985) 233–82; Idem., *Philo, John, Paul* (Atlanta: Scholars Press, 1986); Wolfson, *Philo: Foundations of Religious Philosophy in Judaism, Christianity, and Islam* (rev. ed.; 2 vols; Cambridge, MA: Harvard University Press, 1962); Williamson, *Jews in the Hellenistic World: Philo* (Cambridge, MA: Harvard University Press, 1989).

[224] Philo uses μετάνοια and its cognates at least 62 times. As stated earlier, Josephus uses μετάνοια and its cognates 77 times, while Plutarch uses them 74 times.

[225] Cf. *On Dreams* 1.182; 2.109; *On the Life of Moses* 1.167; *The Special Laws* 4.18, 221; *On the Virtues* 152, 208; *Flaccus* 181; *On the Embassy to Gaius* 303, 337, 339.

[226] *Sacrifices of Abel and Cain* 132. The Greek text used in this study is from F. H. Colson and G. H. Whitaker, eds., *Philo* LCL (10 vols.; Cambridge, MA: Harvard University Press, 1929–1962). Unless otherwise noted, the English translation is from C. D. Yonge, *The Works of Philo: New Updated Edition* (Peabody, MA: Hendrickson, 1993).

propitiated by three different kinds of repentance (μετανοίας), by the aforesaid beasts, or by the birds, or by the flour, according, in short, to the ability of him who is being purified and who repents (μετανοοῦντος)."[227] Philo clearly understands the various sin offerings of the Jewish people to be denoting repentance.[228]

Philo alludes to scripture to demonstrate Moses' recognition of the importance of repenting for one's sins: Philo declares, "Accordingly the scripture says that 'Moses sought and sought again' a reason for repentance for his sins (περὶ ἁμαρτημάτων μετανοίας) in mortal life."[229] In a discussion regarding the importance of hope and the need for lawgivers such as Moses to instill within the souls of human beings the virtue of hope, Philo writes, "That which is placed in the next rank after hope is repentance for sins committed (ἡ ἐπὶ τοῖς ἁμαρτανομένοις μετάνοια)."[230] Philo clearly understands repentance to be the appropriate response to sin and wrongdoing.[231]

It even appears that for Philo, the notion of repentance is contingent upon sin. When describing the erroneous thinking of the Ammonites and the Moabites, Philo writes, "even if we were to commit such an error as this, still emerging as it were out of that troubled sea, we may lay hold on repentance (μετανοίας), which is a firm and saving thing, and must never let it go till we have completely escaped from the billowy sea, the headlong violence of sin."[232] Repentance in the writings of Philo is not merely a change in thinking, but a change in thinking that involves a decisive break from sin and wrongdoing.

Repentance Includes a Change in Behavior and Conduct

Since for Philo repentance involves a break from sin, it also entails a change in behavior and conduct. In an exposition detailing what the law says regarding sins committed unintentionally and intentionally, Philo writes:

> And after having put forth these and similar enactments with reference to sins committed unintentionally, he [Moses] proceeds to lay down rules respecting intentional offences. "If any one," says the law, "shall speak falsely concerning a partnership, or about a deposit, or about a theft, or about the finding of something which another has lost, and being suspected and having had an oath proposed to him, shall swear, and when he appears to have escaped all conviction at the hands of this accusers, shall himself become his own accuser, being convicted by his own conscience residing within, and shall come and

---

[227] *On the Change of Names* 233–235 (Cf. *The Special Laws* 1.253).
[228] It is evident that Philo understands repentance to be a way of purifying oneself (Cf. *On the Unchangeableness of God* 8; *On the Change of Names* 124, 235; *On Dreams* 1.91).
[229] *On Flight and Finding* 158 (it is not clear what scripture Philo is referring to).
[230] *On Abraham* 17 (my own translation).
[231] See also *Allegorical Interpretation* 2.78; 3.106, 211; *On the Posterity of Cain* 178; *On Flight and Finding* 99; *On Dreams* 1.91; *On the Life of Moses* 2.167; *The Special Laws* 1.102; *On Rewards and Punishments* 163; *Questions and Answers on Exodus* 1.15.
[232] *The Posterity and Exile of Cain* 178.

88   The Role and Function of Repentance

openly confess the sin which he has committed, and implore pardon; then pardon shall be given to such a man, who shows the truth of his repentance (μετάνοιαν), not by promises but by works, by restoring the deposit which he has received, and by giving up the things which he has stolen or found, or of which in short he has in any way deprived his neighbour, paying also in addition one fifth of the value, as an atonement for the evil which he had done."[233]

According to Philo, true repentance is demonstrated not by words but by works and actions that reflect both remorse and a decisive break with previous sins and wrong doings.[234] Philo also suggests, by his identification of Leviticus 5:20–26 as an example of repentance, that repentance at times requires the offender to make restitution to the offended party.[235]

Praising the munificent and gracious nature of God, Philo professes that Jewish scripture reveals that "God does not visit with his vengeance even those that sin against him, immediately, but that he gives them time for repentance (μετάνοιαν), and to remedy and correct their evil conduct."[236] Philo also says that when there exists in individuals qualities that are not considered very praiseworthy, these qualities are made "to depart by arguments conducive to repentance (μετανοίας)."[237] For Philo, repentance definitely entails a change in conduct. Philo makes it clear, however, that the change denoted by repentance does not merely represent an individual instance of change. Repentance for Philo is not simply a change regarding a specific incident, it is a change in the total attitude and outlook of an individual. Repentance represents a profound change in conduct that affects an individual's entire lifestyle.[238]

In another passage where Philo ranks repentance after hope, Philo writes:

And after the victory of hope there is another contest in which repentance (μετάνοια) contends for the prize; having indeed, no share in that nature which is invincible, and which never changes its purpose, and which is always of the same character, entertaining the same disposition, but which is on a sudden seized with an admiration for and love of the better part, and which is anxious

---

[233] *The Special Laws* 1.235–236.
[234] *On Flight and Finding* 159–160; *On Rewards and Punishments* 163; *Questions and Answers on Exodus* 1.15
[235] Neither in the Hebrew scripture itself, nor in any attested Greek version of Leviticus 5:20–26, is this act of restitution explicitly identified as repentance (NB: In most English translations of Leviticus and in most LXX versions, Leviticus 5:20–26 is identified as Leviticus 6:1–7).
[236] *Allegorical Interpretation* 3.106.
[237] *On the Change of Names* 124.
[238] An interesting example of this notion is found in *The Special Laws* 1.101. Philo writes how a priest is still forbidden to marry a woman who may have once been a harlot, even though she has repented and radically changed her lifestyle. A priest is required to marry a woman pure from birth, and who descends from a pure and noble lineage. Because of her change in lifestyle, however, no one else need be forbidden to marry her.

to leave the covetousness and injustice in which it has been bred up, and to go over to moderation and justice, and the other virtues."²³⁹

For Philo, true repentance should always lead to a change in conduct and lifestyle. Furthermore, the change should be a change for the better: a change from covetousness to moderation, and from injustice to justice. Philo asserts that Enos (i.e. Enosh) is a prime example of repentance because Enos was a "man who changed from a worse system of life to a better."²⁴⁰ Elsewhere Philo writes that repentance involves a "crossing over from ignorance to a knowledge of those things to be ignorant of which is shameful; from folly to wisdom, from intemperance to temperance, from injustice to righteousness, from cowardice to confident courage."²⁴¹ Philo eloquently makes the point that repentance involves a complete change in lifestyle when he writes:

> Moreover, Moses delivers to us very beautiful exhortations to repentance (μετάνοιαν), by which he teaches us to alter our way of life, changing from an irregular and disorderly course into a better line of conduct; for he says that this task is not one of any excessive difficulty, nor one removed far out of our reach, being neither above us in the air nor on the extreme borders of the sea, so that we are unable to take hold of it; but it is near us, abiding, in fact, in three portions of us, namely, in our mouths, and our hearts, and our hands. . . . For when such as the words are, such also is the mind; and when such as the counsels are, such likewise are the actions; then life is praiseworthy and perfect.²⁴²

What Philo identifies as "exhortations to repentance" are identified in the Jewish scriptures as exhortations to "obey the Lord your God by observing his commandments and decrees that are written in this book of the law," and to "return to the Lord your God with all your heart and with all your soul."²⁴³ Clearly Philo believed that for his Jewish audience, repentance involved making a decision to return to (ἐπιστρέφειν) and to live for the Lord their God. However, for Philo returning to the Lord meant returning to virtue. According to Philo, the objective of life is to live virtuously so that one's words and one's thoughts and one's actions are in harmony with each other. Repentance is the means by which harmony is brought to a disordered life. Repentance, therefore, involves not only correcting inappropriate behavior, but altering and transforming one's way of life so that one lives a virtuous and harmonious life.²⁴⁴

---

²³⁹ *On Rewards and Punishments* 15.
²⁴⁰ *On Abraham* 17.
²⁴¹ *On the Virtues* 180.
²⁴² *On the Virtues* 183.
²⁴³ Deut 30:10 (cf. v. 2).
²⁴⁴ Elsewhere Philo writes that repentance involves returning to virtue, from which the sinner has been driven (*On the Cherubim* 2). For a discussion of the relationship between repentance and virtue in the writings of Philo, see H. Wolfson, *Philo*, 2:256; É. Bréhier, *Les*

Repentance: An Act of Improvement, Second only to Perfection

Because repentance involves transforming one's life from chaos to order and from discord to harmony, Philo considers repentance to be noble and praiseworthy,[245] and exhibited by the wisest of individuals.[246] Philo thinks so highly of repentance because he understands repentance to be second only to perfection. Philo describes repentance "as the younger brother of perfect innocence and freedom from sin."[247] Philo describes repentance as the younger brother of perfection because he understands perfection to be reserved for God.[248] Philo writes, "never to do anything wrong is the peculiar attribute of God; and to repent (μετανοεῖν) is the part of a wise man."[249] Elsewhere Philo declares:

> But we must not be ignorant that repentance (μετάνοια) occupies the second place only, next after perfection, just as the change from sickness to convalescence is inferior to perfect uninterrupted health. Therefore, that which is continuous and perfect in virtues is very near divine power, but that condition which is improvement advancing in process of time is the peculiar blessing of a well-disposed soul, which does not continue in its childish pursuits, but by more vigorous thoughts and inclinations, such as really become a man, seeks a tranquil steadiness of soul, and which attains to it by its conception of what is good.[250]

In a similar passage, Philo writes:

> Now those blessings which are of the greatest importance in the body are good health, without disease; and in a matter of navigation, a successful voyage, without danger; and in the soul, an undying recollection of all things worthy to be remembered. And the blessings of the second class are those which consist of re-establishment, such as recovery from diseases; a long wished for escape from and safety after great dangers encountered in a voyage, and a recollection

---

Idées philosophiques et religieuses de Philon d´Alexandrie (3rd ed.; Paris: Librairie philosophique J. Vrin, 1950) 304–305.

[245] *On Dreams* 2.108; *The Special Laws* 1.102.
[246] *Allegorical Interpretations* 2.60 (cf. *On the Virtues* 177).
[247] *On Dreams* 1.91.
[248] Since Philo understands perfection to be reserved for God, Philo, unlike Josephus, frequently asserts that repentance is inconsistent with the nature of God, and therefore a practice that God cannot engage in (Cf. *On the Unchangeableness of God* 33, 72; *On the Life of Moses* 1.283; *On the Eternity of the World* 40).
[249] *On Flight and Finding* 157. Similarly, Philo writes, "For absolutely never to do anything wrong at all is a peculiar attribute of God, and perhaps one may also say of a God-like man. But when one has erred, then to change so as to adopt a blameless course of life for the future is the part of a wise man, and of one who is not altogether ignorant of what is expedient" (*On the Virtues* 177). In *The Special Laws* 1.252, Philo writes, "there is no one born, however perfect he may be, who can wholly avoid the commission of sin."
[250] *On Abraham* 26.

The Meaning of Repentance 91

which ensues after forgetfulness; the brother and closest relation of which is repentance (τὸ μετανοεῖν), which is not indeed ranked in the first and highest class of blessings, but which has the principal in the class next to the first.[251]

Philo clearly understands repentance to be inferior to perfection, which is reserved for God, just as recovering from an illness is inferior to perfect uninterrupted health. Since perfection is a human impossibility, the implication is that perfect uninterrupted health is also a human impossibility. Allegorizing this health analogy, Philo writes that repentance indicates "an affliction and a disease of the soul."[252] Although recovering from an illness may be inferior to perfect uninterrupted health, when one becomes sick such recovery is ardently desired and sought after. Philo portrays repentance as the much desired and sought after recovery from that affliction and disease of the soul: he depicts it as recovering from an illness.[253] Philo writes, "for in a manner we may speak also of the man who repents (μετανοῶν) as being preserved [lit. 'saved;' σῴζεται], since he is cured of a disease of the soul, which is worse than the diseases of the body."[254] In describing the folly of Noah when he became drunk and lay naked in his tent, Philo writes, "for even if a wise man does commit folly, he still does not run to ruin like a bad man; for the evil of the one is spread abroad, but that of the other is kept within bounds, and therefore he becomes sober again, that is to say, he repents (μετανοεῖ), and as it were recovers from his disease."[255]

For Philo, repentance is what restores the sick soul to health. That is why Philo asserts that it is foolish for a man to declare he has repented while still committing iniquity. According to Philo, "It is like as if one who had a disease were to pretend that he was in good health; for he, as it seems, will only get more sick, since he does not choose to apply any of the remedies which are conducive to health."[256] Repentance may be inferior to perfection, and it may even indicate an affliction and disease of the soul, but it is a remedy conducive to good health,[257] salvation[258] and deliverance from punishment,[259] and as such is commendable and praiseworthy.

Philo further asserts that even God thinks very highly of repentance. In an exposition of the Jewish feast of trumpets, Philo writes:

---

[251] *On the Virtues* 176 (Again repentance is described as the brother of perfection).
[252] *On the Eternity of the World* 40.
[253] This is a depiction also found among Greek authors (cf *Tabula of Cebes* 10:4–11:1; Plutarch, *The Divine Vengeance* 551.D; *Precepts of Statecraft* 810.C; *Lives Unknown* 1128.E).
[254] *The Special Laws* 1.239.
[255] *Allegorical Interpretation* 2.60.
[256] *On Flight and Finding* 160.
[257] Cf. *Allegorical Interpretation* 3.211; *On Joseph* 87.4; *The Special Laws* 1.253.
[258] Philo writes, "the man who repents is saved (τὸν μετανοοῦντα σῴζεσθαι)" (*The Special Laws* 1.253; cf. *Allegorical Interpretation* 2.60.).
[259] *Allegorical Interpretation* 2.78; 3.106; *The Posterity and Exile of Cain* 178; *On Dreams* 1.91; *The Special Laws* 1.187; 253; *On Rewards and Punishments* 163; *Questions and Answers on Genesis* 2.13.

On the tenth day the fast takes place which they take seriously—not only those who are zealous about piety and holiness, but even those who do nothing religious the rest of the time. For all are astounded, overcome with the sacredness of it; in fact, at that time the worse compete with the better in self-control and virtue. The reputation of the day is due to two reasons: one that it is a feast and the other that it is purification and escape from sins for which amnesty has been given by the favors of the gracious God who has assigned the same honor to repentance (μετάνοιαν) that he has to not committing a single sin.[260]

Not only does God assign the same honor to repentance that God assigns to sinlessness, but God is the one who extends to humanity the opportunity to repent.[261] In response to the question, "Why after the entrance of Noah into the ark, did seven days elapse, after which the deluge came?," Philo writes, "The kind Saviour of the world allows a space for the repentance (μετάνοιαν) of sinners, in order that when they see the ark placed in front of them as a sort of type, . . . they might believe the predictions of the deluge which had been made to them, so that, fearing total destruction above all things, they might be speedily converted, destroying and eradicating all their iniquity and wickedness."[262] Similarly, Philo declares elsewhere that God does not immediately punish those who sin against God, but instead God "gives them time for repentance (μετάνοιαν), and to remedy and correct their evil conduct."[263] Philo also notes, however, that on occasions God withholds from individuals the ability to repent. Philo writes, "For many souls who have wished to turn to repentance (μετανοία) have not been allowed to do so by God, but, been dragged back, as it were by the ebbing tide, having returned to their original courses; in the manner in which Lot's wife did, who was turned into stone because she loved Sodom, and who reverted to the disposition and habits which had been condemned by God."[264]

Repentance and Conversion

For Philo, repentance requires abandonment of inappropriate habits and behaviors. It entails a total transformation of lifestyle: a change in thinking, speaking and living. Furthermore, this opportunity to transform one's life is extended to humanity by God. This notion of transformation is such an integral part of repentance that at one point Philo identifies as repentance what most scholars

---

[260] *The Special Laws* 1.186–187.
[261] *The Special Laws* 1.187; *On the Cherubim* 2; *On Abraham* 17; *Questions and Answers on Genesis* 1.82.
[262] *Questions and Answers on Genesis* 2.13.
[263] *Allegorical Interpretation* 3.106.
[264] *Allegorical Interpretation* 3.213 (see also *The Worse Attacks the Better* 96; *On Flight and Finding* 159; *The Special Laws* 1.58).

typically identify as conversion.²⁶⁵ Most, if not all, of the occurrences of μετανοέω and μετάνοια in the writings of Philo cited thus far have related to the repentance of Hebrew/Jewish people; however, in the tractate "On Repentance" Περὶ Μετανοίας), which is found in his work *On the Virtues*,²⁶⁶ Philo uses the terms μετανοέω and μετάνοια to describe the apparent conversion of non-Hebrews to the religious and cultural practices of the Hebrew people.

Philo begins the tractate by making it clear that repentance is for everyone. He writes, "The most holy Moses, being a lover of virtue, and of honour, and, above all things, of the human race, expects *all men everywhere* (τοὺς πανταχοῦ πάντας) to show themselves admirers of piety and of justice, proposing to them, as to conquerors, great rewards if they repent (μετανοοῦσι)."²⁶⁷ Philo goes on to write:

> when one has erred, then to change so as to adopt a blameless course of life for the future is the part of a wise man, and of one who is not altogether ignorant of what is expedient. On which account he [Moses] calls to him all persons of such a disposition as this, and initiates them in his laws, holding out to them admonitions full of reconciliation and friendship, which exhort men to practise sincerity and to reject pride, and to cling to truth and simplicity, those most necessary virtues which, above all others, contribute to happiness; forsaking all the fabulous inventions of foolish men, which their parents, nurses, and instructors, and innumerable other persons with whom they have been associated, have from their earliest infancy impressed upon their tender souls, implanting in them inextricable errors concerning the knowledge of the most excellent of all things. And what can this best of all things be except God? whose honours those men have attributed to beings which are not gods, honouring them beyond all reason and moderation, and, like empty minded people that they are, wholly forgetting him. All those men therefore who, although they did not originally choose to honour the Creator and Father of the universe, have yet changed and done so afterwards, having learnt to prefer to honour a single monarch rather than a number of rulers, we must look upon as

---

²⁶⁵ See Dirksen, *New Testament Concept*, 161; Bailey, *Repentance*, 95; A. D. Nock *Conversion: The Old and New in Religion from Alexander the Great to Augustine of Hippo* (London: Oxford University Press, 1933). The unclarity that surrounds the English word "conversion" complicates most discussions of conversion in antiquity (for a detailed analysis of the various terms used in antiquity to convey conversion, see Paul Aubin, *Le problème de la 'conversion': Étude sur un terme commun a l'hellenisme et au christianisme des trois premiers siècles* (Paris: Beauchesne, 1962)). Arthur Darby Nock defined conversion as "the reorientation of the soul of an individual, his deliberate turning from indifference or from an earlier form of piety to another, a turning which implies a consciousness that a great change is involved, that the old was wrong and the new is right" (*Conversion*, 7).

²⁶⁶ The reader should be aware that there are questions regarding whether "On Repentance" was originally a component of the actual work entitled *On the Virtues* (cf. Bailey, "*Metanoia* in the Writings of Philo Judaeus," 138–140).

²⁶⁷ *On the Virtues* 175. I emphasize the phrase *all men everywhere* (τοὺς πανταχοῦ πάντας) because of its similarity to the phrase found in Acts 17:30, God commands "*all men everywhere* (τοῖς ἀνθρώποις πάντας πανταχοῦ) to repent (μετανοεῖν)."

> our friends and kinsmen, since they display the greatest of all bonds with which to cement friendship and kindred, namely, a pious and God-loving disposition, and we ought to sympathise in joy with and to congratulate them, since even if they were blind previously they have now received their sight, beholding the most brilliant of all lights instead of the most profound darkness. We have now then described the first and most important of the considerations which belong to repentance (μετάνοιαν). And let a man repent (μετανοείτω) not only of the errors by which he was for a long time deceived, when he honoured the creature in preference to the uncreated being who was himself the Creator of all things, but also in respect of the other necessary and ordinary pursuits and affairs of life.[268]

According to Philo, Moses appealed to individuals who were seeking to correct their lives and adopt a blameless course of life. He initiated these individuals into the laws of the Hebrew people, and exhorted them to abandon their former customs, practices and beliefs—especially beliefs regarding God.[269] Moses compelled these individuals to forsake polytheism and to honor the one true Creator and Father of the universe. Philo describes this conversion process as the "first and most important of the considerations which belong to repentance (μετάνοιαν)." It is quite obvious that the individuals undergoing what Philo calls repentance are non-Hebrews, and that repentance for these non-Hebrews include not only abandoning their erroneous thinking about God, but also adopting a completely different lifestyle—abandoning their erroneous thinking regarding the necessary and ordinary pursuits and affairs of life: "forsaking as it were that very worst of all evil constitutions, the sovereignty of the mob, and adopting that best of all constitutions, a well ordered democracy. . . . For it is a very excellent and expedient thing to go over to virtue without ever looking back again, forsaking that treacherous mistress, vice."[270]

According to Philo, repentance for non-Hebrews (i.e. non-Jews) included forsaking false gods and honoring the "Creator and Father of the universe." This type of repentance, as with the repentance demanded of the Hebrew people by Moses,[271] must also result in a total transformation of lifestyle. Philo writes:

> And at the same time it is necessary that, as in the sun shadow follows the body, so also a participation in all other virtues must inevitably follow the giving due honour to the living God; for those who come over to this worship become at once prudent, and temperate, and modest, and gentle, and merciful, and humane, and venerable, and just, and magnanimous, and lovers of truth, and superior to all considerations of money or pleasure; just as, on the contrary, one may see that those who forsake the holy laws of God are intemperate, shameless, unjust,

---

[268] Ibid. 177–180.
[269] Josephus is clearly describing the process of becoming proselytes.
[270] Ibid. 180–181.
[271] *On the Virtues* 183.

disreputable, weak-minded, quarrelsome, companions of falsehood and perjury, willing to sell their liberty for luxurious eating, for strong wine, for sweet meats, and for beauty, for pleasures of the belly and of the parts below the belly; the miserable end of all which enjoyment is ruin to both body and soul.[272]

Since Philo uses the terms μετανοέω and μετάνοια to describe the apparent conversion of non-Hebrews to the religious and cultural practices of the Hebrew people, he also depicts true repentance as leading to reconciliation between once alienated people. According to Philo, when Moses called non-Hebrews to repentance, he was "holding out to them admonitions full of reconciliation and friendship."[273] Philo believed that repentance was a means by which to create community and even a sense of family among previously alienated people. Regarding those individuals who had once failed to honor the God of Israel but who had now repented, Philo writes, "we must look upon [them] as our friends and kinsmen..., and we ought to sympathise in joy with and to congratulate them, since even if they were blind previously they have now received their sight."[274] Philo believed that the repentant sinner should be received with joy and acceptance by those with whom he or she previously had been estranged. Philo further asserts that it is also through repentance that human beings are reconciled to God.[275] According to Philo, God responds to repentance with forgiveness,[276] and because of that forgiveness human beings are reconciled to God.

After an extensive examination of the occurrences of μετανοέω and μετάνοια in the writings of Philo, the following conclusions can be made: 1) Although on occasions μετανοέω and μετάνοια are used to express the general notions of regret, remorse, and changing one's thinking and/or purpose, for the most part Philo seems to use μετανοέω and μετάνοια as technical terms. 2) For Philo μετανοέω and μετάνοια represent the appropriate human response to sin and wrongdoing. Repentance is contingent upon sin because repentance is not merely a change in thinking but a change in thinking that involves a decisive break from sin and wrongdoing. 3) Since for Philo repentance involves a break from sin, Philo also affirms that repentance includes a change in behavior and conduct. True repentance is demonstrated not by words but by works and actions that reflect both remorse over and a decisive break with previous sins and wrongdoings. Furthermore, this change in behavior is not simply a change regarding a specific incident, it is a change in the total attitude and outlook of an individual: it represents a profound change in conduct that affects an individual's entire lifestyle. Repentance involves not only correcting inappropriate behavior, but altering and transforming one's way of life so that one lives a virtuous and harmonious life. 4) Philo considers

---

[272] Ibid. 181–182.
[273] Ibid. 178.
[274] Ibid. 179.
[275] *On the Unchangeableness of God* 8–9; *The Sacrifices of Abel and Cain* 132.
[276] *On Dreams* 2.292; *The Special Laws* 187.

repentance to be a noble and praiseworthy act exhibited by the wisest of individuals. It is second only to perfection and secures the healing, salvation, and deliverance of those sick in their souls. 5) Philo declares that God assigns the same honor to repentance that God assigns to sinlessness. Furthermore, Philo asserts that God not only thinks very highly of repentance but that God is the one who extends to humanity the opportunity to repent. 6) Philo makes a distinction between non-Jewish and Jewish repentance. Philo implies that repentance for non-Jews includes conversion to the religious and cultural practices of the Jewish people. 7) Philo asserts that true repentance leads to reconciliation between alienated and estranged parties. Philo believed that repentance was a means by which to create community and even a sense of family among previously alienated peoples and groups. He declared that the repentant sinner should be received with joy and acceptance by those with whom he or she previously had been estranged. Philo further asserts that it is also through repentance that human beings are reconciled to God.

The Pseudepigrapha[277]

Many, if not most, of the documents comprising the Pseudepigrapha were composed and/or compiled by Jews, while others were written by Jews but eventually expanded or rewritten by Christians.[278] The documents (or segments of documents) that reflect a Jewish pre-Christian (or early Christian) period are an invaluable source for understanding how hellenized Jews living in Palestine and the Diaspora understood their ancient traditions and concepts. There are many passages within these documents that clearly demonstrate the perceived significance, meaning and importance of repentance in the minds of hellenized Jews living in the centuries immediately preceding the Christian era. For these Jews, who were engaged in the exposition of Israel's scriptures and traditions, repentance took on a prominent role. Repentance is attributed to many of the great figures of Jewish history who were never explicitly identified in the biblical stories as having repented. The repentance of figures such as Adam and Eve, the twelve Patriarchs of Israel, King Manasseh and others is presented at length. There are at least forty

---

[277] While the term "Pseudepigrapha" is commonly used to refer to a modern collection of ancient writings considered by many scholars as essential reading for an understanding of early Judaism and of Christian origins, it is an entirely arbitrary collection of miscellaneous material having no ancient common denominator of provenance, date, or context. I am not suggesting, therefore, that the findings from the documents I have selected in this section is representative of a certain real circle of ancient Jews. Instead, each document will be examined on its own as representative of *some* ancient Jew or Jews, usually unidentifiable by either century or geography. (NB: Unless otherwise noted, the Greek used in this section is taken from the *TLG*, and English translations are from J. H. Charlesworth, ed., *The Old Testament Pseudepigrapha* (2 vols.; Garden City, NY: Doubleday, 1983–1985), hereafter cited as *OTP*).

[278] It should be remembered, however, that many (if not most) of these Christians were also Jewish.

occurrences of μετανοέω and μετάνοια in the writings examined in this section, and these occurrences prove more than worthy of examination.[279]

Several occurrences of μετανοέω and μετάνοια are found in the anonymous apocryphal Jewish romance, *Joseph and Aseneth*.[280] This midrashic elaboration of Gen 41:45, 50–52; and 46:20, which briefly mentions Joseph's marriage to Aseneth, is thought to have been written somewhere between 100 B.C.E. and 135 C.E.[281] Contrary to the patriarchal admonitions of Genesis,[282] the patriarch Joseph married a foreign woman named Aseneth, the daughter of an Egyptian priest. The story deals with this theological difficulty by describing Aseneth's conversion from idolatry to the God of Israel and by attributing to her the status of a prototypical proselyte.

Aseneth is described as a virgin of exceptional beauty who voluntarily secludes herself in order to avoid the many suitors who seek her hand in marriage. When Joseph, who is touring Egypt to gather grain, announces his intention to dine with Aseneth's father, Pentephres, priest of Heliopolis, Pentephres informs his daughter that he wishes her to marry Joseph. Aseneth, who believes she deserves to marry the king's firstborn son, vehemently and arrogantly refuses to have anything to do with Joseph, whom she considers to be nothing more than a shepherd who was once a slave and a fugitive.[283]

However, when Aseneth beholds Joseph's radiant beauty her opinion of him quickly changes, and she falls madly in love with him. She even prays to Joseph's God, saying in her heart, "But I, foolish and daring, have despised him and spoken wicked words about him, and did not know that Joseph is (a) son of God.... And now be gracious to me, Lord, God of Joseph, because I have spoken wicked words against him in ignorance."[284]

While Aseneth may have changed her opinion of Joseph, Joseph rejects the notion of taking Aseneth as a wife, declaring that it is not fitting for a man who worships God to even kiss a woman who with her mouth and life blesses and serves idols.[285] Aseneth, devastated by the words of Joseph, begins to weep. Joseph, moved with compassion, prays for God to bless Aseneth and renew her spirit and allow her

---

[279] I disagree with the disparaging remarks of Montefiore, who writes, "It may be well to state here that I shall make no reference to any passages or theories concerning repentance which may be gathered from the apocryphal, apocalyptic, or pseud-epigraphic writings. These sources are now easily accessible and fairly well known. It is, however, very noticeable, first, that nothing of great importance about repentance can be obtained from this quarter. The total amount of material is very small, and its quality on the whole is poor." ("Rabbinic Conceptions," 211).

[280] According to the *TLG*, the term occurs eight times in the document.

[281] C. Burchard, "Joseph and Aseneth," *OTP*, 2:187; see also Gideon Bohak, *Joseph and Aseneth and The Jewish Temple in Heliopolis* (Atlanta: Scholars Press, 1996).

[282] See Gen 24:3–4, 37–38; 27:46; 18:1 and the expansion of these admonitions in *Jub.* 20:4; 22:20; 30:7–16.

[283] *Jos. and Asen.* 4.9–11.

[284] Ibid. 6:3–7.

[285] Ibid. 8:5–6.

98   The Role and Function of Repentance

to be numbered among God's chosen people. Aseneth rejoices over Joseph's prayer, and returns to her room where she falls on her bed. The author writes, while on her bed "she wept with great and bitter weeping and repented (μετενόει) of her (infatuation with the) gods whom she used to worship, and spurned all the idols."[286]

The author describes at great length the intense weeping and mourning of Aseneth, as well as her fervent repudiation of the gods and idols she once worshiped. According to the author, Aseneth "took all her gods that were in her chamber, the ones of gold and silver who were without number, and ground them to pieces, and threw all the idols of the Egyptians through the window. . . . And Aseneth took. . . all the sacrifices of her gods and the vessels of their wine of libation and threw everything through the window." She then covered herself with sackcloth and ashes and wept bitterly throughout the night. She continued this intense mourning for seven days, refusing to eat or drink anything.[287] On the eighth day she rose from the floor, and declared in her heart, "All people have come to hate me, and on top of those my father and my mother, because I, too, have come to hate their gods and have destroyed them, and caused them to be trampled underfoot by men. And therefore my father and my mother and my whole family have come to hate me. . . . I have heard. . . that the God of the Hebrews is. . . a merciful God. . . , and does not count the sin of a humble person. . . . Therefore I will take courage too and turn to him. . . and confess all my sins to him. . . . Who knows, (maybe) he will see my humiliation and have mercy on me."[288]

After profuse praise and adoration, Aseneth prays, "Spare me, Lord, because I have sinned much before you, I have committed lawlessness and irreverence, and have said wicked and unspeakable [things] before you. . . . I have sinned, Lord, before you I have sinned much in ignorance, and have worshiped dead and dumb idols."[289] She declares, "all the gods whom I once used to worship in ignorance: I have now recognized that they were dumb and dead idols, and I have caused them to be trampled underfoot by men. . . . And with you I have taken refuge, O Lord my God."[290]

When she finished making confession to God, "a man came to her from heaven. . . . And the man said, 'I am the chief of the house of the Lord and commander of the whole host of the Most High. Rise and stand on your feet, and I will tell you what I have to say.'" The messenger tells Aseneth to clean herself up and take off her clothes of mourning and put on a new pure linen robe. After she does as she is instructed, the messenger informs Aseneth that her prayers and confessions have been heard, and that her humiliation has been observed. He informs her that her name has been written in the book of the living in heaven, never

---

[286] Ibid. 9:2.
[287] Ibid. 10:10–17.
[288] Ibid. 11:1–12.
[289] Ibid. 12:4–5.
[290] Ibid. 13:11–12.

The Meaning of Repentance

to be erased, and that she will be renewed and formed anew. He also informs her that she will be given to Joseph as a bride, and that Joseph will be given to her as a bridegroom.[291] The messenger further informs her:

> And your name shall no longer be called Aseneth, but your name shall be City of Refuge, because in you many nations will take refuge with the Lord God, the Most High, and under your wings many people trusting in the Lord God will be sheltered, and behind your walls will be guarded those who attach themselves to the Most High God in the name of Repentance (Μετανοίας). For Repentance (ἡ Μετάνοια) is in the heavens, an exceedingly beautiful and good daughter of the Most High. And she herself entreats the Most High God for you at all times and for all who repent (μετανοούντων) in the name of the Most High God, because he is (the) father of Repentance (Μετανοίας). And she herself is guardian of all virgins, and loves you very much, and is beseeching the Most High for you at all times, and for all who repent (μετανοούντων) she prepared a place of rest in the heavens. And she will renew them, and wait on them herself for ever (and) ever. And Repentance (ἡ Μετάνοια) is exceedingly beautiful, a virgin pure and laughing always, and she is gentle and meek. And, therefore, the Most High Father loves her, and all the angels stand in awe of her.[292]

According to this divine messenger, Aseneth has attached herself to the Most High God through her intense acts of mourning and contrition and through her passionate repudiation of the gods and idols that she once worshiped and through taking refuge with the Most High God. The messenger identifies this behavior as repentance.[293] As a result of her repentance, people of various nations and cultures will be able to attach themselves to the Most High God through similar repentance. Aseneth has opened the door that will allow non-Jews from everywhere to find refuge and shelter with the God of Israel. Repentance is the way for non-Jews to attach themselves to the Most High God. For these non-Jews repentance involves intense acts of mourning and contrition, turning away from false gods and idols and turning to the God of Israel. Repentance is also identified as a heavenly figure who appeals to the Most High God on behalf of those who turn away from idols and false gods and turn to the Most High God.[294]

Like Philo, this author uses the term μετανοέω to identify the turning away by non-Hebrews from false gods and idols and their acceptance of the God of the Hebrews as Father and creator of the universe. Repentance for this author is clearly a religious transformation. Unlike Philo, however, this author uses μετανοέω only to describe a fundamental change in the life of non-Hebrews. This author is in no

---

[291] Ibid. 14:3–15:6.
[292] Ibid. 15:7–8.
[293] See also *Jos. and Asen.* 16:14.
[294] This type of personification of repentance as an angelic figure is also found in *1 Enoch* 39:9.

way concerned with identifying what repentance among Hebrew (i.e. Jewish) people might entail. The author only seeks to make explicit that repentance for non-Jews entails a radical and thorough religious transformation, marked by an utter repudiation of idols and false gods, a transformation that is traditionally identified as conversion.

When Joseph returns to the house of Pentephres, Aseneth meets him at the entrance, and he is amazed at her beauty. She informs Joseph that she has forsaken her gods and idols and has turned to the God of Israel. She also tells Joseph of her encounter with the heavenly messenger, and shares with Joseph all that the messenger said to her. After her testimony, Joseph embraces Aseneth, gives her an extended kiss, and accepts her as his future bride.

Like Philo, and a number of the classical and Hellenistic Greek authors previously discussed, this author suggests that true repentance leads to reconciliation between once alienated and estranged parties. The marriage of the patriarch Joseph and the Egyptian virgin Aseneth marks the greatest type of reconciliation, and clearly demonstrates that repentance is a means by which to establish a sense of community and family among previously alienated people. The author suggests that those who have repented of idolatrous practices and the worship of false gods, and have embraced the religious practices of Judaism, are beneficiaries of all the privileges and blessings of the Jewish people and that as such they should be fully and joyfully received into the community of God's people.[295]

The notion of repentance also plays a prominent role in the *Sibylline Oracles* of Jewish origin.[296] According to Greek legend, the sibyl was an ecstatic prophetess who uttered generally gloomy oracles about future events. It was the eschatology of these oracles that usually provided a framework for moral exhortation. Destruction was viewed as punishment for wrongdoings, but it could be avoided by observing certain righteous actions—repentance being one such action.[297] Over the course of approximately thirteen centuries, pagans, Jews, and Christians generated an immense amount of oracular literature—most of which has been lost—attributed to several sibyls.[298] It is believed that the genre of the Sibylline Oracles was first adapted by Jews for their own propagandistic purposes in the second century B.C.E.[299]

The standard collection of *Sibylline Oracles* contains fourteen books of Jewish and or Christian origin that range in date from the mid–second century B.C.E. to the

---

[295] For a discussion of how the author seeks to establish the place of converts within the Jewish community, see Chestnut, "The Social Setting and Purpose of Joseph and Aseneth," *Journal for the Study of the Pseudepigrapha* 2 (1988) 37–43.

[296] According to the *TLG*, the term μετάνοια occurs five times within these writings.

[297] J. J. Collins, "The Sibylline Oracles," *OTP*, 1:323.

[298] J. J. Collins, "The Development of the Sibylline Tradition," *ANRW* 2.20.1: 421–59.

[299] Collins, *The Sibylline Oracles of Egyptian Judaism* (Missoula, MT: Scholars Press, 1974) 28–32.

seventh century C.E.³⁰⁰ The references to μετάνοια occur in Books 1–2,³⁰¹ 4 and 8. Book 1–2 and Book 8 represent original Jewish oracles that were later adapted for Christian apologetic purposes.³⁰² It is believed that the Jewish stage of Book 1–2 was composed after 30 B.C.E. and before 70 C.E. The Christian redaction probably took place between 70–150 C.E. Book 8, which demonstrates Christian composition as well as redaction, is believed to have been composed around 175 C.E.³⁰³ The first two occurrences of μετάνοια found in Book 1–2 are in a section of the book that displays no sign of Christian redaction. The oracle depicts the division of world history into ten generations. According to the sibyl, in the fifth generation there was no human being who was righteous except Noah. To Noah God spoke from heaven, "Noah, embolden yourself, and proclaim repentance (μετάνοιαν) to all the peoples, so that all may be saved (σωθῶσιν). But if they do not heed. . . I will destroy the entire race with great floods of waters."³⁰⁴ Noah then goes out and preaches to the people declaring that God has commanded him to announce to the people, "Be sober, cut off evils, and stop fighting violently with each other, having a bloodthirsty heart, drenching much earth with human blood. . . . It will truly come to pass that the immortal savior will cast forth upon men. . . unless you propitiate God and repent (μετάνοιαν) as from now, and no longer anyone do anything ill-tempered or evil, lawlessly against one another."³⁰⁵

In this eschatological context, repentance provides for salvation and deliverance from judgment and destruction. Repentance is to be preached to "all the peoples," in order that "all may be saved." Through the preaching of Noah, the author reveals that he understands repentance to involve turning away from evil and violence—changing one's behavior and conduct toward one's fellow human being. It means no longer engaging in ill-tempered, evil, violent, lawless deeds against one's fellow human being. Repentance for this author involves a moral and ethical transformation.³⁰⁶

Although the next occurrence of μετάνοια in this book is found in a section that shows clear signs of Christian redaction, its usage is based on a Jewish tradition. The sibyl prophesies concerning the punishment of the wicked: she declares, "Often they will request God, who rules on high in vain, and then he will manifestly turn away his face from them. For he gave seven days of ages to erring

---

³⁰⁰ See J. J. Collins, "The Sibylline Oracles," *OTP*, 1:317–472.
³⁰¹ The first two books in the standard collection are not separated in the manuscripts and should be read as a single book (Collins, "The Sibylline Oracles," *OTP* 1:330).
³⁰² Collins, "The Sibylline Oracles," *OTP*, 1:330.
³⁰³ Ibid. 331; 416.
³⁰⁴ *Sib. Or.* 1:128–131.
³⁰⁵ Ibid. 1:154–169.
³⁰⁶ Once again we see that another Jewish author understood repentance as entailing more than simply turning to God with one's whole heart. The preaching of Noah has moral and ethical similarities to the preaching of John the Baptist found in Luke's gospel.

men for repentance (μετανοίας) through the intercession of the holy virgin."³⁰⁷ It is clearly conveyed in this passage that the opportunity for repentance is granted to erring (i.e. sinful) human beings by God, however, if human beings fail to take advantage of the opportunity for repentance, they will be forced to suffer the consequences of their wicked ways. The occurrence of μετάνοια in Book 8 is identical to this Christian redaction found in Book 1–2.³⁰⁸

There is one more occurrence of μετάνοια, which is found in Book 4. Although there is no evidence of Christian redaction in Book 4, the book is considered to be a composite nonetheless. *Sibylline Oracles* 4 "consists of a political oracle from the Hellenistic Age updated by a Jew in the late first century A.D., and adapted for specifically religious purposes."³⁰⁹ The original oracle is thought to have been written not long after the time of Alexander, and the Jewish redaction is believed to have occurred around 80 C.E. The use of μετάνοια occurs in the second stage, and it reflects the moral, ethical and religious teachings of the Jewish redactor.³¹⁰ In a context of eschatological urgency, the sibyl warns of the wrath of God that will be poured out on the entire race of humanity because of the evil and wicked deeds perpetrated by humanity against humanity. The sibyl declares:

> Ah, wretched mortals, change these things, and do not lead the great God to all sorts of anger, but abandon daggers and groanings, murders and outrages, and wash your whole bodies in perennial rivers. Stretch out your hands to heaven and ask forgiveness for your previous deeds and make propitiation for bitter impiety with words of praise; God will grant repentance (μετάνοιαν) and will not destroy. He will stop his wrath again if you all practice honorable piety in your hearts.³¹¹

It is revealed once again that repentance is what is necessary in order to avert disaster. It is also conveyed once again that the behavior which needs to be changed is the violence committed by human beings against other human beings. If these wretched individuals agree to abandon their wicked and sinful ways—their brutal mistreatment of other human beings—and if they submit themselves to baptism,³¹²

---

³⁰⁷ *Sib. Or.* 2:309–312. Although repentance here is granted because of the intercession of the Virgin Mary, 4 Ezra 7:101 gives an account of the souls of the dead having seven days of freedom after separating from their bodies, in order to observe the eschatological consequences that await them. The author makes it clear to these souls, however, that there will be no intercession made or honored at the judgment.
³⁰⁸ 8.357.
³⁰⁹ Collins, "The Sibylline Oracles," *OTP* 1:381.
³¹⁰ Ibid.
³¹¹ *Sib. Or.* 4:162–170.
³¹² Although most scholars agree that the second stage of *Sibylline Oracles* 4 reflects Jewish redaction, the role of baptism here and its relation to judgment bears strong similarities to John's baptism. Baptism here is also quite different from the ritual washings of *Sib. Or.* 3:592.

ask God to forgive them for their previous wrongdoings, and offer words of praise to God, then God will honor their request for forgiveness by granting them an opportunity to repent and by withholding destruction, if indeed they manifest a changed lifestyle. As was the case in Books 1–2 and 8, the author clearly conveys that the opportunity for repentance is granted to human beings by God.

In the *Letter of Aristeas*, which is possibly the oldest of the documents comprising the Pseudepigrapha, the author conveys that it is mercy and forgiveness that causes the wicked to repent. This document was composed somewhere between 250 B.C.E. and 100 C.E.[313] It claims to describe how the Torah was translated from Hebrew to Greek in the third century B.C.E. by seventy-two Palestinian Jews sent to Alexandria at the request of Ptolemy II Philadelphus. The author, Aristeas, who writes this letter to his brother Philocrates, is believed to have been a Jew from Alexandria who served as an influential courtier of king Ptolemy. The longest and major section of the writing details king Ptolemy's reception of the Jewish translators. The translators dine with the king at daily banquets that last for seven consecutive days. During these banquets the king addresses questions to these translators concerning the theory and practice of kingship. The crux of every answer is that God inspires the human heart and guides kings who seek guidance from God. The answers stress the point that the wise king should seek to imitate God's characteristics and virtues. One question asked by the king is, "How can one keep his kingdom without offense to the end?" The answer given is, "You would administer it best by imitating the eternal goodness of God. By using longsuffering and treatment of those who merit *punishment* more leniently than they deserve, you will convert them from evil and bring them to repentance (εἰς μετάνοιαν)."[314] Mercy and forgiveness extended to those who deserve punishment will often lead the wicked to repentance.

An example of the mercy and forgiveness of God leading to repentance and of a king seeking the guidance of God, can be found in the *Prayer of Manasseh*. It is believed by many scholars that this document was written by a Jew in either the second or first century B.C.E.[315] King Manasseh (687–642 B.C.E.) is considered to have been one of the most wicked kings of Judah. According to 2 Kings 21, Manasseh died unrepentant; however, according to 2 Chronicles 33:11–13, Manasseh repented and prayed to God for forgiveness. The author of the *Prayer of Manasseh* attempts to supply this prayer of the king mentioned by the Chronicler.

The central focus of this document is repentance, and the two main themes that permeate the words of Manasseh's prayer are: the assurance of God's infinite mercy

---

[313] For a summary of the dating see S. Jellicoe, *The Septuagint and Modern Study* (Cambridge: Cambridge University Press, 1968) 48–50; cf. R. J. H. Shutt, "Letter of Aristeas," *OTP* 2:7–34.

[314] *Let. Aris.* 187–188 (The Greek text used is from H. St. J. Thackeray, "The Letter of Aristeas," *An Introduction to the Old Testament in Greek* (ed. H. B. Swete; Cambridge: Cambridge University Press, 1902)).

[315] See J. H. Charlesworth, "Prayer of Manasseh," *OTP*, 2:627.

104   The Role and Function of Repentance

and grace, and the conviction that authentic repentance does indeed lead to deliverance and forgiveness.[316] Manasseh begins his prayer by offering profuse praise unto God. Manasseh declares:

> But unending and immeasurable are your mercies; because you are the Lord, long-suffering, and merciful, and greatly compassionate; feeling sorry (μετανοῶν) over the evils of men. You, O Lord, according to the abundance of your goodness, have promised repentance (μετανοίας) and forgiveness to those who have sinned against you, and in the multitude of your compassion you have appointed repentance (μετάνοιαν) toward salvation (σωτηρίαν) for sinners."[317]

Repentance for this author clearly entails a sense of sorrow and remorse over sin. Even God experiences feelings of sorrow regarding human sin. The author understands repentance to be granted to human beings by God. It is God's unending grace, mercy, goodness and compassion that leads sinners to repentance and that makes repentance available to them, and it is repentance that secures salvation for sinners.

Not only has God promised repentance to sinners, but God has also promised forgiveness. Forgiveness is the only appropriate and acceptable response to repentance, and it is this promise of forgiveness that leads Manasseh to repentance. This is conveyed by the king when he prays:

> I make my supplications before you: forgive me, O Lord, forgive me; and do not destroy me with my transgressions. Do not forever be angry with me, nor lay up evil for me; and do not condemn me to the depths of the earth! For you are Lord, God of those who repent (τῶν μετανοούντων); and in me you will manifest all of your goodness. Since I am unworthy you will save me according to your great mercy."[318]

The author of this document makes it clear that repentance is contingent upon sin, because repentance is promised by God only to those who have sinned against God. Repentance is not for the righteous but for sinners only. Manasseh declares, "Therefore you, O Lord, God of the righteous, have not appointed repentance (μετάνοιαν) for the righteous, for Abraham and Isaac and Jacob, who have not sinned against you; but you have appointed repentance (μετάνοιαν) for me a sinner.[319]

What Manasseh's repentance entailed is not made explicit, but it seems clear from the context of the prayer that the author understands repentance to include

---

[316] Ibid. 2:629.
[317] *Pr. Man.* 6–7. My English translations are based on the Greek from O. F. Fritzsche, *Libri apocryphi veteris testamenti graece* (Leipzig: Teubner, 1871), 90.
[318] *Pr. Man.* 13.
[319] *Pr. Man.* 8 (cf Lk 5:32).

contrition and remorse regarding sin.[320] This notion that repentance should include contrition and remorse regarding one's sin is also conveyed by the author of the *Apocalypse of Moses*.[321]

Although there is no extant Hebrew text, it is believed by many scholars that the *Apocalypse of Moses* was originally composed in Hebrew between 100 B.C.E. and 100 C.E., with the Greek and Latin translations being made between that time and 400 C.E.[322] While on his deathbed, Adam asks Eve to tell their children the story of how he and she were expelled from Paradise. Eve tells the story at great length (*Apoc. Mos.* 15–30). She tells the children that immediately after they had been cast out of Paradise, Adam and she mourned for seven days. After fulfilling their days of mourning they began looking for food; however, they were unsuccessful in finding any. Eve then proposed to Adam that he kill her in order that God and the angels would no longer be angry with him on account of her sin. Adam rejected Eve's proposal and told her, "let us repent (μετανοήσωμεν) and offer prayers for forty days." The repentance of Adam and Eve entailed Eve fasting for thirty-four days and standing in the Tigris River with water up to her neck crying silently to God. Adam fasted for forty days and stood in the Jordan River praying and crying aloud to God that God might forgive him and Eve and have mercy upon them.[323]

After Eve finishes telling the story to her children, she mourns for her husband who is dying. Adam instructs Eve what she is to do after he has died. He tells her to pray to God until he has given back his spirit to the one who has given it, because

---

[320] Although the author does not describe what repentance for Manasseh entailed, the author clearly composed the *Prayer of Manasseh* with 2 Chronicles 33:12-17. in mind. That being the case, the author must have understood Manasseh's repentance to have entailed taking away the foreign gods and idols from the house of the Lord, and destroying the profane altars that had been built on the mountain of the house of the Lord and in Jerusalem, and restoring the altar of the Lord and offering sacrifices on it (2 Chr 33:15–16). Repentance for Manasseh entailed a radical change in his religious allegiance and devotion.

[321] The Latin text is entitled *Vita Adae et Evae* (Life of Adam and Eve). The title of the Greek text is based on a much later appended preface that reads, "The narrative and life of Adam and Eve the first made, revealed by God to Moses his servant when he received the tablets of the law of the covenant from the hand of the Lord, after he had been taught by the archangel Michael." Other than the preface, the Greek text has nothing to do with Moses (See, M. D. Johnson, "Life of Adam and Eve," *OTP* 2:249–295).

[322] *OTP*, 2:251 ff (cf. Michael E. Stone, ed. *Armenian Apocrypha Relating to Adam and Eve* (Leiden: E. J. Brill, 1996); idem, *History of the Literature of Adam and Eve* (Atlanta: Scholars Press, 1992)). While Greek translations were made sometime between 100 and 400 C.E., making this document of minimal service here, the parallels with other Jewish documents indicate that the traditions embodied in the document fit well into the 1st and early 2d centuries C.E. (e.g. *Apoc. Mos.* 33–37 ≈ *4 Ezra* 8:44–45; *Apoc. Mos.* 27–29 ≈ *2 Bar.* 4:3–7; *Apoc. Mos.* 14, 28, 30 ≈ *4 Ezra* 3:20–27; 4:26–32; 7:11–14, 116–31; *2 Bar.* 17:1–18:2; 23:4–5; 48:42–47; 54:13–19; *Vita* 49:1–50:2 ≈ Josephus' *Ant* 1.2.3; *Vita* 9 ≈ *2 Cor* 11:14; *Apoc. Mos.* 37:5 ≈ 2 Cor 12:2–3).

[323] *Apoc. Mos.* 29:11–14 (The account of the repentance of Adam and Eve is found only in MSS F and H).

he does not know whether God will be angry or have mercy. The author writes:

> Then Eve rose and went out and fell on the ground and said, "I have sinned, O God; I have sinned, O Father of all; I have sinned against you, I have sinned against your chosen angels, I have sinned against the cherubim, I have sinned against your steadfast throne; I have sinned, Lord, I have sinned much; I have sinned before you, and all sin in creation has come about through me." While Eve was still on her knees praying, behold, the angel of mankind came to her and lifted her up, saying, "Rise Eve, from your repentance (μετανοίας), for behold, Adam your husband has gone out of his body. Rise and see his spirit borne up to meet its maker."[324]

Adam was taken up into the presence of God, where God forgave Adam and commanded the archangel Michael to escort Adam into Paradise.[325]

For this author, repentance clearly entails penitential acts of remorse and contrition. Repentance is also understood as a way of obtaining deliverance from the wrath and punishment of God because human repentance elicits divine mercy and forgiveness. God has ordained repentance as a way for sinful human beings to escape punishment and divine retribution because God cares for sinners.

In the *Testament of Abraham*, which is thought by many scholars to be an unmistakably Jewish document written in Greek around 75–125 C.E.,[326] the archangel Michael takes Abraham on a tour of the inhabited world. Abraham, witnessing people engaged in various sins, calls down death upon them. The author writes:

> And when Abraham looked down upon the earth, he saw a man committing adultery with a married woman. And Abraham turned and said to Michael, "Do you see this sin? But, lord, send fire from heaven, that it may consume them." And immediately fire came down from heaven and consumed them. For the Lord (had) said to Michael, "Whatever Abraham asks you to do for him, do." And again Abraham looked up and saw other men slandering (their) fellows, and he said, "Let the earth open and swallow them up." And while he was speaking, the earth swallowed them up alive. And again the cloud brought him to another place. And Abraham saw some people leaving for a desert place to commit murder. And he said to Michael, "Do you see this sin? But let wild beasts come out of the desert and rend them in two." And in that very hour wild beasts came out of the desert and devoured them. Then the Lord God spoke to

---

[324] *Apoc. Mos.* 32.
[325] Ibid. 33–37.
[326] E. P. Sanders, "Testament of Abraham," *OTP* 1:873–5. (For opposing views see M. R. James, *The Testament of Abraham: The Greek text now first edited with an introduction and notes*. Texts and Studies 2:2 (Cambridge: Cambridge University Press, 1892), who asserts the document was written in the second century C.E. and received its present form perhaps in the ninth or tenth century (29); N. Turner, "The 'Testament of Abraham': Problems in Biblical Greek," *NTS* 1 (1954/55) 219–23) proposes a much earlier Hebrew original that was first translated into Greek around 200–165 B.C.E.

Michael saying, "Turn Abraham away to his house, and do not let him go round all the creation which I have made, because his heart is not moved for sinners, but my heart is moved for sinners, so that they may convert (ἐπιστρέψουσιν) and live and repent (μετανοήσωσιν) of their sins and be saved (σωθήσονται).[327]

As seen in the *Prayer of Manasseh*, God has ordained repentance for sinners as a means of salvation because God's heart is moved for sinners.

The most occurrences of μετανοέω and μετάνοια appear to be found in the *Testament of the Twelve Patriarchs*.[328] There are, however, disagreements regarding the dating of this document, which leads to questions concerning its usefulness as a representative of pre-Christian Judaism. H. C. Kee asserts that apart from the Christian interpolations, this work was most likely written by a Hellenist Jew sometime during the second century B.C.E.[329] M. de Jonge, however, who regards any Jewish substrate as entirely hypothetical, argues that the document we have is a 9th century Christian work, and that the form of the earlier version known to both Origen and Jerome is irrecoverable.[330] Since the references in Origen indicate that *T. 12 Patr.* existed as early as the second century C.E., the occurrences of μετανοέω and μετάνοια in *T. 12 Patr.* will be considered here.[331]

The work allegedly gives the parting words of each of the twelve sons of Jacob, spoken immediately before their deaths to all of their assembled offspring. Each of the dying patriarchs is depicted as reflecting on aspects of his own life: exhorting his offsprings to imitate his virtues and avoid his vices. For the most part the exhortations are concerned with ethical matters. The ethical appeal, however,

---

[327] *T. Abr.* 12:1–13 (Recension B). Cf. Luke 9:51–56.

[328] There appear to be at least sixteen occurrences of μετανοέω and μετάνοια in this work. The Greek citations are based on M. de Jonge's *The Testaments of The Twelve Patriarchs. A Critical Edition of the Greek Text* (Leiden: E. J. Brill, 1978), and the English translations are from H. W. Hollander and M. de Jonge, *The Testament of the Twelve Patriarchs: A Commentary* (Leiden: E. J. Brill, 1985).

[329] The Christian interpolations are said to have been added around the second century C.E. (H. C. Kee, "Testaments of the Twelve Patriarchs," *OTP* 1:775–778). R. H. Charles asserted that there was a second century B.C.E. pro-Hasmonean original (written in Hebrew) to which extensive anti-Hasmonean passages were added in the first century B.C.E. The earliest Greek translation was then made sometime before 50 C.E. (R. H. Charles, *The Greek Versions of the Testaments of the Twelve Patriarchs* (Oxford: Clarendon Press, 1908) xxiii–xliv).

[330] H. W. Hollander and M. de Jonge, *A Commentary*, 10–17, 23–25; M. de Jonge, *A Critical Edition*, XI–XLI (for various articles regarding the text of the Testaments see M. de Jonge, ed. *Jewish Eschatology, Early Christian Christology and the Testament of the Twelve Patriarchs: Collected Essays* (Leiden: E. J. Brill, 1991); idem., *Studies on the Testaments of the Twelve Patriarchs. Text and Interpretation* (Leiden: E. J. Brill, 1975)).

[331] The reader should be aware, however, that how long before Origen the document was written, and whether it underwent any substantial changes before reaching him remains uncertain.

rarely refers to specific legal statutes of the Torah, but rather to universal virtues reminiscent of Stoicism.[332]

Virtually every use of μετανοέω and μετάνοια in this document demonstrates that the author understands repentance to be an appropriate response to sin and evil deeds.[333] Asher tells his sons, "Thus, if the soul has pleasure in the good, every action of it is in righteousness, and if he sins, he repents (μετανοεῖ) immediately."[334] Zebulon, prophesying about the dividing of the kingdom of Israel, declares to his offspring:

> I have learnt in the writing of the fathers, that in the last days you will depart from the Lord, and you will be divided in Israel and will follow two kings, and you will commit every abomination and worship every idol. And your enemies will lead you captive and you will be afflicted among the Gentiles with all infirmities and tribulations and anguish of soul. And after these things you will remember the Lord and repent (μετανοήσετε), and he will bring you back, because he is merciful and compassionate.[335]

After turning away from the Lord and committing every imaginable kind of sin and wickedness—including idolatry—Israel's only appropriate response is to repent. As a result of such repentance, God reconciles Israel back to Godself.

This type of reconciliation reveals the forgiveness of God. Judah, in his final words to his children, warns them to avoid a love of money, testifying, "For the sake of money I lost my children, and without *the repentance of my flesh* (τῆς μετάνοιά σαρκός μου). . . . I would have died childless. But the God of my fathers, the compassionate and merciful, forgave me."[336] Gad tells his children, "if somebody becomes rich also by evil means, as Esau the brother of my father, do not be jealous, for wait for the decision of the Lord: for either he takes them (the riches) away by misfortune, or he forgives them when they repent (μετανοήσαντι), or for the unrepentant (ἀμετανόητος) he reserves the punishment. for ever."[337] Telling his children about the importance of love and forgiveness, Gad exhorts them to "love one another from the heart, and if a man sins against you, speak to him in peace. . . . And if he confesses and repents (μετανοήσῃ), forgive him."[338]

---

[332] See Hollander, *Joseph as an Ethical Model in the Testaments of the Twelve Patriarchs* (Leiden: E. J. Brill, 1981); Kee, "The Ethical Dimensions of the Testament of the XII as a Clue to Provenance, *NTS* 24 (1978) 259–70.

[333] *T. Reu.* 1:9–2:1; *T. Sim.* 2:13; *T. Jud.* 15:4; *T. Gad* 5:6; *T. Jos.* 6:6. *T. Ben.* 5:4.

[334] *T. Ash.* 1:6

[335] *T. Zeb.* 9:5–7.

[336] *T. Jud.* 19:2–3.

[337] *T. Gad* 7:5. This passage also indicates that the author understands repentance as providing deliverance from punishment. On at least four occasions repentance is associated with deliverance from physical maladies (*T. Reu.* 1:8; *T. Sim.* 2:12; *T. Zeb.* 9:6; *T. Gad* 5:6–9).

[338] *T. Gad* 6:3. This exhortation sounds and looks very much like Luke. 17:3, ἐὰν μετανοήσῃ, ἄφες αὐτῷ.

Repentance is responded to with both divine and human forgiveness.[339] As a matter of fact, it is often mercy and forgiveness that causes the wicked to repent.[340]

As a result of repentance, God effects a total transformation of one's way of thinking and living. Gad claims:

> For he who is righteous and humble is ashamed to do what is wrong. . . . He does not speak evil of any man, since the fear of the Most High overcomes hatred. For fearing that he should offend the Lord, he does not want to do anything wrong to a man, even in thought. I learned these things at the last after I had repented (μετανοῆσαι) concerning Joseph. For godly and true repentance (μετάνοια) destroys **ignorance** and drives away darkness, and it enlightens the eyes and gives knowledge to the soul, and it leads the disposition to salvation (σωτήριαν). And the things it has not learned from men, it knows through repentance (μετανοίας).[341]

It was only after repenting of the sin committed against Joseph that Gad's way of thinking and living changed. As a result of repentance, the power of sin is broken because ignorance is destroyed, darkness driven away, vision illumined, knowledge gained and salvation obtained.[342] A radical transformation in one's way of thinking and living takes place as a result of repentance, and the author suggests that the transformation is divinely initiated. What could not be accomplished and understood as a result of human agency is accomplished through godly repentance.[343]

Finally, the author reveals that he understands repentance to be associated with mourning and penitential acts of contrition. Reuben states that he repented for seven years—mourning over his sin, and refusing to drink wine and liquor or to eat meat and pleasurable food.[344] Judah likewise declares that during his time of repentance, "I did not take wine or meat until my old age nor did I see any joy."[345] Simeon, after describing the suffering he experienced as a result of the wickedness he committed against his brother Joseph, tells his children, "And I knew, children, that because

---

[339] The term μεταμέλομαι occurs once in the *T. 12 Patr.*, and it likewise is responded to with divine forgiveness (*T. Jud.* 23:5).

[340] Cf. *T. Ben.* 5:3–4; *T. Gad* 6:4–7.

[341] *T. Gad* 5:3–8 (see also 6:5–6). While the variant ἀπείθειαν ("disobedience") is present in two MSS, the context seems to require ἄγνοιαν ("ignorance") rather than ἀπείθειαν (cf *T. Reu 1:6*; *T. Jud.* 19:3).

[342] In a variant reading of *T. Reu.* 4:4, Reuben declares, "From then, repenting (μετανοῶν), I have been on my guard and I did not sin." (for an explanation why μετανοῶν should be considered original, see Hollander and de Jonge, *A Commentary*, 97–98). Repentance causes one's lifestyle to change because repentance destroys the hold of sin over one's life.

[343] This notion of gaining new found understanding and spiritual insight as a result of repentance is also conveyed elsewhere (e.g. *T. Jud.* 15:4–6; *T. Reu.* 1:8–2:1.

[344] *T. Reu.* 1:8–2:1.

[345] *T. Jud.* 15:4 (cf. *Jub.* 41:23–24).

of Joseph this had happened to me; and I repented (μετανοήσας) and wept, and I prayed to the Lord that I might be restored."[346]

The passages from the various pseudepigraphical documents examined clearly demonstrate that μετανοέω and μετάνοια were understood by many hellenized Jews in the centuries preceding the Christian era as denoting moral, ethical, and religious transformations in the lives of idolatrous and sinful human beings. Often such transformations were indicated by penitential acts of remorse, mourning and contrition over sin. Repentance was considered the only appropriate human response to sin, and it was appointed solely for sinners: repentance was not for the righteous. For non-Jews, repentance entailed an abandonment of idols and false gods and a turning to the God of the Jewish people. For Jews, repentance entailed a return to God after going astray, but more frequently it entailed an abandonment of wicked and sinful behavior, especially behavior that involved mistreating other human beings. Repentance for Jews frequently entailed a moral and ethical transformation.[347]

These pseudepigraphical writings also indicate that repentance elicits forgiveness, both divine and human. Therefore, since repentance elicits forgiveness, repentance often leads to reconciliation between alienated and estranged parties. Repentance serves as a means by which to establish a sense of community and family. Since God responds to repentance with forgiveness, wayward Jews are restored to fellowship with God, and non-Jews who repent of their idolatrous practices and the worship of false gods, and who embrace the religious practices of Judaism, are received by God into the family of God. Furthermore, since human beings are required to forgive those who repent, once alienated people are now reconciled to one another as a result of repentance. Repentance requires individuals to abandon their evil and unfair treatment of others and to embrace and care for those whom they once treated harshly. Non-Jews who repent of their former practices and who embrace the practices of Judaism, are to be recognized by Jews as beneficiaries of all the privileges and blessings of the Jewish people, and as such are to be fully and joyfully received into the community of God's people.

Finally, repentance is also understood as a way for human beings to escape the wrath and punishment of God. The passages examined make it clear that although repentance is accomplished by human effort, it is extended to humanity as a gift from God. God desires to see all humanity saved and delivered from the wrath and punishment that accompanies sins. Because of God's grace, mercy and compassion,

---

[346] *T. Sim.* 2:13 (see also *T. Jos.* 6:6–8).

[347] This point is of inestimable significance for the study of repentance in Luke-Acts because it reveals the notion of repentance current among the Jewish people to whom John the Baptist preached at the Jordan River. The various writings examined indicate that the emphasis placed by the author of Luke-Acts on the moral and ethical preaching of John the Baptist, associating moral and ethical transformation with the repentance, was not a Lukan invention. Moral and ethical transformation was considered an integral part of repentance in the centuries immediately preceding the Christian era.

God extends repentance to all humanity in order that humanity might be reconciled to God and to one another, and in order that humanity might receive salvation and avoid the wrath and punishment of God.[348]

The Septuagint[349]

The Hebrew scriptures were translated into Greek in several stages. It is believed that the translation process began in the third century B.C.E. and was completed early in the first century B.C.E. The Septuagint is an invaluable source for understanding how hellenized Jews living in Palestine and the Diaspora during the third century B.C.E., and for quite some time thereafter, understood their ancient traditions and concepts; more specifically, it explains the way Hebrew scriptures were understood and interpreted by these hellenized Jews. The Septuagint also reveals how hellenized Jews interpreted and understood traditional Greek concepts and terms: the Septuagint provides a crucial link in helping to understand what Hebrew concepts and terms underlie the Jewish usage of traditional Greek concepts and terms. The Septuagint is also important to this present study because it represents the Jewish Bible read and cited by the author of Luke-Acts, as well as by the other New Testament authors.

As previously mentioned, many, if not most, scholars assert that the Hebrew term that best expresses the idea of repentance is שוב. In Rabbinic Judaism, the noun תשובה is used as a technical term for repentance.[350] The evidence presented thus far clearly reveals that as early as the second century B.C.E. (and possibly as early as the third century) Greek speaking Jews often used μετανοέω and μετάνοια to express the idea of repentance. One would expect, therefore, that if

---

[348] This idea is also conveyed in the Latin versions of *4 Ezra* 7:82; 9:9–12; *Testament of Moses* (aka. *Assumption of Moses*) 1:18 and the Ethiopic version of *1 Enoch* 50:2–5.

[349] Although there is some dispute in modern discussions regarding the precise referent of the term "Septuagint," I use the term to designate a collection of Greek literature encompassing: 1) translations of the contents of the Hebrew Bible; 2) additions to some of its books; and 3) works written originally in Greek or Hebrew but not included in the Hebrew Bible (for a discussion of the problem of terminology, see Melvin K. H. Peters, "Septuagint," *ABD* 5:1093–1104; cf. Emanuel Tov, *The Text-Critical Use of the Septuagint in Biblical Research* (Jerusalem: Simor Ltd., 1981) 29–50).

[350] C. G. Montefiore, "Rabbinic Conceptions," 209–257; Solomon Schechter, *Rabbinic Theology*, 313–343; Chaim Nussbaum, *The Essence of Teshuvah*; Jacob Neusner, "Repentance in Judaism." Montefiore asserts that "The Rabbinic doctrine of Repentance is naturally based upon the Old Testament" (211), but interestingly enough, the noun *teshubah* is never used in the Hebrew Bible to convey what Rabbinic Judaism identifies as repentance (cf. 2 Sam 11:1; 2 Kgs 20:22, 26; Job 21:34; 34:36; 1 Chr 20:1; 2 Chr 36:10, *et. al.*). Because of the difficulty, if not impossibility, of establishing a link between the concept of repentance in the writings of rabbinic Judaism and the concept of repentance in Luke-Acts, and because the documents of rabbinic Judaism were composed much later than Luke-Acts and cannot be used to determine specific Jewish attitudes about repentance in the first century C.E. or the centuries immediately preceding the Christian era, the documents of rabbinic Judaism will not be examined in this study.

in the minds of ancient Jews the Hebrew root שוב best expressed repentance, then the Jewish translators of the Hebrew Bible would have translated the root שוב with the Greek verb μετανοέω. However, of the twenty two occurrences of μετανοέω and the five occurrences of μετάνοια in the Septuagint, there are no instances where either of the words is used to translate an occurrence in the Hebrew Bible of the root שוב.[351] The Hebrew root שוב is most often translated by one of the many Greek compounds of στρέφω (e.g. ἐπιστρέφω, ἀναστρέφω, ἀποστρέφω, et. al.),[352] which according to most scholars, commonly conveys the idea of conversion.[353] Like שוב, στρέφω and its compounds have a wide range of meaning: designating turns of any kind— physical, moral or religious.[354]

Clearly, if שוב was the term that best expressed the idea of repentance within the Hebrew Bible, the Jewish translators were either unaware of it or had a different understanding of repentance. The translators rarely used μετανοέω and μετάνοια to express the ideas conveyed by שוב.[355] Instead of using μετανοέω to represent

---

[351] According to E. Hatch and H. Redpath, *Concordance to the Septuagint and Other Greek Versions of the Old Testament* (3 vols.; Oxford: Oxford University Press, 1897; reprinted., Grand Rapids: Baker, 1983) 916, some have suggested that μετανοέω in Isaiah 46:8 might have been used by the translators to render the root שוב, which is found in the Hebrew text. However, an examination of the Hebrew (E. Elliger and W. Rudolph, *Biblia Hebraica Stuttgartensia* (Stuttgart: Deutsche Bibelgesellschaft, 1977)) and the LXX version of Isa 46:8 reveals that the translators used ἐπιστρέφω to translate the root שוב. There is no word in the Hebrew text that corresponds to the LXX μετανοέω (Isa 46:8 will be discussed in more detail below). The only time μετανοέω is used in the Septuagint to translate the Hebrew root שוב is Sirach 48:15 (cf. Z. Ben-Hayyim, *The Book of Ben Sira: Text, Concordance and an Analysis of the Vocabulary* (Jerusalem: Academy of the Hebrew Language, 1973)). The much later Greek version of the Hebrew Bible attributed to Symmachus uses μετανοέω and μετάνοια several times to translate שוב; e.g. Job 36:10; Isa 30:15; 31:6; 55:7; Jer 18:8; Ezek 33:12.

[352] Of the 1056 occurrences of שוב in the Hebrew Bible, the term is translated ἐπιστρέφω 408 times and ἀποστρέφω 310 times.

[353] G. Bertram, "στρέφω," *TDNT* 7:714–729; W. L. Holladay, *The Root of "Shub" in the Old Testament* (Leiden: E. J. Brill, 1958). It is clear, however, that when used to refer to Jews returning to a relationship with the God of Israel, στρέφω and its compounds do not convey the sociological aspects often associated with conversion (for a discussion of the sociological aspects of conversion, see J. A. Beckford, "Accounting for Conversion," *British Journal of Sociology* 29 (1978) 249–262; J. T. Richardson, *Conversion Careers: In and Out of the New Religions* (Beverly Hills, CA: Sage, 1978)). When Jews return to the worship of the God of Israel, there is not a change of primary reference groups or a resocialization into an alternative community. This is not to say that a transformation of some sort does not occur, but every religious transformation is not a conversion.

[354] That the words have such a wide range of meaning is demonstrated by the fact that although the Greek translators usually use some compound of στρέφω when translating שוב, they also use more than ninety other Greek words for the root שוב. Furthermore, some fifty other Hebrew words serve as the original for στρέφω and its various compounds.

[355] There are, however, a small number of instances in the Septuagint where the Jewish use of ἐπιστρέφω and ἀποστρέφω appears to be synonymous with the Jewish use of μετανοέω and μετάνοια (e.g. 1 Kgs 8:35, 47; 2 Kgs 17:13; 2 Chr 6:26; 7:14; Jer 3:14; 18:8a; 25:5; 33:3 (26:3); 51:5 (44:5); Ezek 3:19; 14:6; 18:21, 30; 33:9, 11, 14, 19; Dan 9:13; Jonah 3:8; Zech 1:4). Because these terms do at times seem to be synonymous, some scholars falsely suggest that in Jewish and Christian writings στρέφω and μετανοέω should

the root שוב, the translators used μετανοέω to represent the root נחם, "be sorry, moved to pity, have compassion, have regret, console oneself,"[356] for which μεταμέλομαι is also frequently used.[357] The choice of μετανοέω to translate the root נחם, suggests that the translators wanted to convey the notion of a change in thinking, action or behavior that is motivated by regret, remorse, pity or compassion.[358] The fact that some compound of στρέφω frequently accompanies the use μετανοέω, however, does suggest that this change in thinking often includes a "turning away" from something (usually evil) or a "turning to" something (usually God).[359]

Unlike most of the Jewish literature examined thus far, the Septuagint frequently uses μετανοέω to refer to a change in the thinking, intent, action or behavior of God. At times God is depicted as unwilling to change. It is recorded that after King Saul sinned before the Lord, the prophet Samuel declared to Saul, "The Lord has torn the kingdom of Israel out of your hand this day, and will give it to your neighbor who is better than you. And Israel shall be divided in two; and

---

be thought of as synonyms (see Thomas M. Finn, *From Death to Rebirth: Ritual and Conversion in Antiquity* (New York: Paulist Press, 1977) 23–32). However, the number of instances in Jewish and Christian literature where both words are used together to convey related but differing concepts seem to suggest that there is in the minds of many Jewish and Christian authors a distinction between these terms, even though at times a symbiotic relationship may exist between the concepts represented by them (i.e. repentance, as conveyed by μετανοέω, very well may include the idea of "turning away" from sin or "returning" to God, which may be conveyed by the use of ἐπιστρέφω or ἀποστρέφω). Furthermore, the fact that over fifty Hebrew words serve as the original for στρέφω and its various compounds indicates that the wide range of meanings for στρέφω prevents it from always functioning as a synonym for μετανοέω.

[356] Francis Brown, S. R. Driver, and Charles A. Briggs, *The New Brown-Driver-Brings-Gesenius Hebrew and English Lexicon* (Peabody, MA: Hendrickson Publishers, 1979) 636–637 [hereafter cited as *BDBG Lexicon*]). The only passages from the Hebrew Bible where something other than the root נחם is represent by μετανοέω or μετάνοια are Prov 14:15; 20:25; 24:32 (47); Isa 46:8.

[357] E.g. Exod 13:17; 1 Sam 15:35; 1 Chr 21:15; Pss 105(106):45; 109(110):4; Prov 5:11; 25:8; Sir 30:28 (33:20); 35:19 (32:24); Jer 20:16; Hos 11:8. In the Septuagint, μετανοέω and μεταμέλομαι often function synonymously (this synonymous relationship was discussed above in "Μετανοέω and Μετάνοια in Classical and Hellenistic Greek Literature"). Dirksen wrongly asserts that μεταμέλομαι "is never used by the LXX when there is a question of regret for morally wrong action or *contrition*" (*The New Testament Concept*, 153–4). This is exactly how the term is used in Prov 5:11–12. Dirksen then goes on to incorrectly assert, "The LXX therefore makes a sharp distinction between μετανοεῖν and μεταμέλεσθαι." (154).

[358] As already demonstrated, μετανοέω was used in classical and Hellenistic Greek to convey the idea of a change in thinking and/or behavior; the translators of the Hebrew Bible, therefore, knowingly employed the term to convey the idea of a change in thinking and/or behavior. The term was fully prepared in Greek literature to serve the usage which these Greek speaking Jews made of it. The translators used the term to translate the root נחם because they wanted to make sure the notion of regret and remorse was associated with the idea of a change in thinking and/or behavior.

[359] 1 Sam 15:29; Sir 27:24–29; Joel 2:12–14; Jonah 3:8–10; Isa 46:8; Jer 4:28; 18:8; 38:18–19.

God will not turn (ἀποστρέψει) nor change his mind (μετανοήσει), for God is not like a human being who changes his mind (μετανοῆσαι)."[360] The prophet Jeremiah declares, "Thus says the Lord: the whole land shall be desolate; but I will not make a full end. Because of these things let the earth mourn, and let the sky be dark above; for I have spoken and I will not change my mind (μετανοήσω), I have purposed, and I will not turn back (ἀποστρέψω) from it."[361] At other times, however, God displays a willingness to change. The prophet Joel declares:

> Now therefore, says the Lord your God, return (ἐπιστράφητε) to me with all your heart, and with fasting, and with weeping, and with mourning; and rend your hearts, and not your clothing; and return (ἐπιστράφητε) to the Lord your God, for he is merciful and compassionate, longsuffering and abundant in mercy, and changes his mind (μετανοῶν) regarding evil. Who knows if he will return (ἐπιστρέψει) and change his mind (μετανοήσει), and leave a blessing behind him?[362]

The prophet Jeremiah declares that the word of the Lord came to him saying:

> In the end I might speak concerning a nation, or concerning a kingdom, to cut them off, and to destroy them, and that nation might turn (ἐπιστραφῇ) from all their sins, and I will change my mind (μετανοήσω) regarding the evils which I purposed to do to them. And in the end I might speak concerning a nation and kingdom, to rebuild and plant them, and they do evil before me, so as not to listen to my voice, and I change my mind (μετανοήσω) regarding the good which I spoke of, to do to them.[363]

From examining these few references, it appears that the Hellenistic Jewish translators inherited from the Hebrew Bible an image of God that reveals both the certainty of God's punishment of sin and the assurance of God's mercy to those who genuinely turn away from their sins. However, in an effort to select a Greek verb that expresses both these aspects of God's nature, the translators, unlike most hellenized Jewish authors to follow, often use μετανοέω to convey the idea of God changing God's intentions. Because of God's compassion, God often changes God's mind regarding the punishment of sinners who turn away from their sin.[364]

Of course μετανοέω and μετάνοια are also used to depict a change in the thinking, action and behavior of human beings as well. The Wisdom of Solomon speaks of how the righteous shall condemn the ungodly at the time of judgement.[365]

---

[360] 1 Sam 15:29. All English translations of the LXX in this section are my own.
[361] Jer 4:28; cf. Zech 8:14 (see also Ps 109[110]:4; Jer 20:16; Num 23:19).
[362] Joel 2:12–14 (cf. Amos 3:3, 6; Jonah 4:2; see also 1 Chr 21:15; Ps 105[106]: 45).
[363] Jer 18:7–10 (cf. Jonah 3:8–10).
[364] As we have seen, God may also change God's mind regarding the rewarding of those who once followed God, but have now turned to evil and have stopped following God.
[365] The work is not a translation of a Hebrew original, but a Greek composition by a Hellenistic Jewish author. There appears to be no consensus regarding the date of this work. While many scholars place it anywhere between 220 B.C.E. and 50 C.E., the apocalyptic vision

The Meaning of Repentance 115

The author declares:

> Then shall the righteous person stand in great boldness before the face of those having afflicted him, and having made no account of his labors. When they behold him, they shall be troubled with terrible fear, and shall be amazed at the marvelous nature of his salvation. And they repenting (μετανοοῦντες), and groaning for anguish of spirit shall say to themselves, "This is he, whom we sometimes made a subject of laughter and a parable of reproach. We fools considered his life madness, and his destiny without honor.... Therefore, we have erred from the way of truth.... What has pride profited us? and what good have riches with our boasting brought us?"³⁶⁶

When the ungodly behold the marvelous salvation of the righteous, they will experience terrible regret and anguish, which will cause them to change both their thinking regarding those whom they used to ridicule and reproach and their thinking regarding the lifestyle of the ungodly.

Deutero-Isaiah declares that God warns Israel to change their thinking regarding idols and the God of Israel. According to the prophet, God says:

> To whom have you compared me? Behold, shrewdly consider *these things*, you who have gone astray. The ones who furnish gold out of a purse, and silver by weight, will weigh it in a scale, and after hiring a goldsmith they make idols, and bow down, and worship them. They bear it upon their shoulders, and go; and when they put it upon its place, it remains, it cannot move: and whosoever shall cry to it, it cannot hear; it cannot save that person from trouble. Recognize these things, and groan, repent (μετανοήσατε), you who have gone astray, return (ἐπιστρέψατε) in your heart, and remember the former things that were of old: for I am God, and there is none other besides me.³⁶⁷

Deutero-Isaiah presents to the children of Israel the folly of idolatry. Those who have turned to idolatry are exhorted to recognize the foolishness of their practices and to groan with remorse—remorse which will cause them to repent, forsaking their idolatrous practices and returning to their former religious practices.³⁶⁸ Again,

---

seems to point to the reign of Gaius "Caligula" (37–41 C.E.) (see David Winston, "Solomon, Wisdom of," *Anchor Bible Dictionary* (6 vols.; New York: Doubleday, 1992) 6:120–27; cf. J. M. Reese, *Hellenistic Influences on the Book of Wisdom and its Consequences* (Rome: Biblical Institute Press, 1983).

³⁶⁶ Wis 5:1–6a, 8.
³⁶⁷ Isa 46:8.
³⁶⁸ The translators of the Hebrew Bible go out of their way to convey the notion that remorse lies at the heart of repentance. The Hebrew word that the translators render as "groan" (στενάξατε) is a *hapax legomenon* in the Hebrew Bible. Its meaning is uncertain and disputed. It is possible that the word is derived from the noun אִישׁ, "man" (cf. KJV "show yourself men"). The translators, however, render it στενάξατε, conveying the notion of deep regret and or remorse. Next, there is no Hebrew antecedent for the Greek μετανοήσατε, "repent." The root שוב is found in the Hebrew, but it is rendered

repentance represents a change in thinking, action and behavior that is motivated by a sense of regret and remorse.[369] It involves a (re)consideration of one's ways.

The translator of Proverbs 24:47(32) declares, "A foolish man is like a farm, and a senseless man is like a vineyard. If you leave him alone, he will altogether remain barren and covered with weeds; and he becomes destitute, and his stone walls are broken down. Afterwards I reflected (μετενόησα); I looked that I might receive instruction." The Hebrew states that the author considered in his heart the conduct of the sinful man and took instruction from it. The translator renders the phrase "consider in the heart" (שׁיר לב) with the verb μετανοέω. Similarly, in Proverbs 20:25 the author talks about reconsidering a matter. But in this case the translator clearly has the notion of regret in mind. The author speaks of the pitfall of hastily making a vow, an action which will lead to reconsideration and cause the one making the vow to have regret (μετανοεῖν γίνεται). It is also written, "There is a way which seems to be right with humanity, but its ends go to the depth of Hades. . . . The simple person believes every word, but the prudent person comes to repentance (μετάνοια)."[370]

As has been the case in all of the Jewish (and a large amount of the Greek) literature examined thus far, repentance denotes the appropriate human response to sin and wickedness. It entails a turning away from evil and ungodly behavior.[371] Jesus Ben-Sira writes that God created humanity in the image of the Divine, and gave humanity dominion over all creation. God created an everlasting covenant with humanity and instructed everyone to avoid unrighteousness. God set rulers over every nation, but Israel belonged to God. Their works were forever before God, and none of their unrighteous deeds went unseen. The deeds of the upright served as the apple of God's eye, and God continually rewarded them. God also extended mercy to those who went astray and repented. According to Ben-Sira, "unto those who repent (μετανοοῦσιν), he gave an opportunity to return, and he comforted those who failed in patience." Ben-Sira exhorts these repentant sinners to "Return unto the Lord, and forsake your sins, make your prayers before his face, and offend less. Turn again to the most High, and turn away from iniquity. . . and vehemently hate abomination."[372] The idea of returning to the Lord is not enough; there must be a

---

ἐπιστρέψατε, "return," not μετανοήσατε, "repent." There is no command to repent in the Hebrew. A literal translation of v. 8 from the Hebrew might be, "Remember this and consider it, take it to heart, you who have gone astray." The translators, however, want to convey the notion that remorse at the heart of repentance and that a change in behavior results from such remorse, so they give the command, "στενάξατε," add the command "μετανοήσατε," and render the root שׁוב "ἐπιστρέψατε."

[369] Cf. Prov 20:25; Sir 17:24; 48:15; Jer 38[31]:19 (see also Ex. 13:17).

[370] Prov 14:15. The notion is that the prudent person comes to reconsideration (possibly motivated by regret or remorse).

[371] Prov 24:24 (29:27); Wis 11:23; 12:10–11, 19; Sir 48:15; Isa 46:8; Jer 8:6; 38(31):19 (cf. Prov 5:11).

[372] Sir 17:1–26 (quotes from vv. 24, 25–26).

The Meaning of Repentance   117

sense of regret and a vehement hatred of sin and wickedness which causes the sinner to turn from sin and turn to God.

As the writing of Ben-Sira implies, God is the one who makes repentance available to humanity. Allegedly Solomon says of God, "But you have mercy on all, because you are able to do all things, and you look past the sins of humanity in order to bring about repentance (εἰς μετάνοιαν)."[373] Solomon further declares that God spared the ungodly who inhabited the holy land before the children of Israel. Solomon writes, "Not that you were unable to bring the ungodly under the hand of the righteous in battle, or to destroy them at once with cruel beasts, or with one rough word: but executing your judgments upon them little by little, you gave them an opportunity for repentance (μετανοίας)."[374] Finally, for Solomon, the fact that God gives repentance serves as an example of mercy and a source of hope for the children of Israel. Solomon states:

> But you have taught your people through these works that it is necessary for the righteous person to be merciful; and you have made your children to be of good hope, because you give repentance (μετάνοιαν) for sins. For if you aided with so much consideration the enemies of your children and the ones condemned to death, having given them time and opportunity whereby they might be delivered from their wickedness, with how great precision you must have judged your own children, unto whose foreparents you have sworn and given covenants of good promises?[375]

Because God is merciful, God gives repentance for sins, and God's mercy serves as an example to the righteous that they should likewise be merciful and extend an opportunity for repentance to the ungodly.[376] As always, those who do repent are delivered from punishment and destruction.[377]

The earliest translators of the Hebrew Bible emphasized the aspects of remorse, regret and compassion associated with the concept of repentance. For them, the Hebrew word that served as the basis for μετανοέω and μετάνοια, and therefore best conveyed the notion of repentance, was נחם. The idea conveyed by שוב was indeed a part of repentance, but for the Jewish translators שוב was not the term that conveyed the notion of repentance.[378] For these hellenized Jews, the most

---

[373] Wis 11:23.
[374] Wis 12:9–10a.
[375] Wis 12:19–21.
[376] Although the point is somewhat unclear to the contemporary reader, Enoch likewise serves as "an example of repentance (μετανοίας) to all generations" (Sir 44:16).
[377] Prov 24:24 (29:27); Wis 11:23.
[378] Unless the contemporary reader, like Bailey, wishes to assert that the translators of the Hebrew Bible, unlike all of the Hellenistic Jewish authors to follow—including the Jewish authors of the New Testament—expressed the concept of repentance with the Greek term ἐπιστρέφω rather than with μετανοέω, which seems highly unlikely since in the Septuagint the verb ἐπιστρέφω is used to translate thirty one Hebrew roots or modifications of these roots. Furthermore, the verb ἐπιστρέφω is not used consistently in any one sense.

118   The Role and Function of Repentance

important aspect of repentance was a genuine sense of remorse and or regret regarding sin and wrongdoing. By using μετανοέω to represent the root נחם, the translators of the Hebrew Bible are stressing the idea of a genuine sense of remorse, regret and compassion underlying repentance.[379] It is this genuine sense of remorse and regret that compels the ungodly to change their way of thinking and behaving. Furthermore, it is this genuine sense of compassion that causes God at times to engage in repentance. God does not repent of sins committed by God, but instead, since God is merciful and compassionate, God repents of the punishment initially planned for those who once walked in sin but who have since turned away from their sin.

The translators of the Hebrew Bible make it clear that repentance involves a change in thinking and behavior, but these translators are not particularly concerned with emphasizing what repentance entails or how it is manifested. The translators of the Hebrew Bible are more concerned with emphasizing the aspects of remorse, regret and compassion underlying repentance, because the change associated with repentance is the result of a genuine sense of remorse, regret and compassion. Over the course of the next few centuries, however, Jewish authors began placing less emphasis upon the aspects of remorse, regret and compassion, and more emphasis upon the idea of a change in thinking and behaving.[380] These later Jewish authors also began placing more emphasis on specifying what exactly repentance entails, how it is manifested, and how it should be responded to.

Nevertheless, Bailey adamantly asserts, in the section of his dissertation examining repentance in the Septuagint, "the most significant Greek terms for repentance in Luke-Acts are of minor importance in the Septuagint. For the authors of the New Testament, and especially Luke, the most important words for repentance are μετανοέω and μετάνοια. In the Septuagint, these words denote repentance only rarely. . . . As noted above, the most important term associated with repentance in the Hebrew Bible is the word שוב. In the Septuagint, the Hebrew root שוב is usually translated by the Greek verbs στρέφω, "turn" and ἐπιστρέφω, "turn around" (*Repentance*, 32–33). Bailey has difficulty recognizing the actual Jewish concept of repentance conveyed in the Septuagint because Bailey, like most scholars, refuses to question the assumption that שוב is the Hebrew term that best conveys the ancient Jewish notion of repentance.

[379] This may be because the Hebrew Bible was translated during the post-exilic period of Israel's history: the period after Israel had come out of captivity for refusing to adhere to the admonitions of the prophets, who continually rebuked and condemned Israel for the empty ritualistic practices that had crept into the religious activity and thought of the people. The prophets frequently stressed the internal rather than the external aspects of turning to God (cf. Zech 7:2–12; 12:11–13:1; Amos 5:15, 21–24; Joel 2:12–13; Hos 6:1–6; 14:2; Ezek 6:9; 16:61–63; 18:31; 36:31; Jer 3:25–4:1; Is 58). Yet the people rejected the words of the prophets, and were carried away into captivity. The translators of the Hebrew Bible may have wanted to convey the notion that sinners had to be genuinely sorry for their sins; the external ritualistic acts often associated with turning to God were not enough.

[380] This can be readily confirmed by comparing later Greek versions of the Hebrew Bible with the Septuagint. In these later translations μετανοέω is repeatedly used to translate the Hebrew root שוב (or as a variant for ἐπιστρέφω; cf F. Field, *Origenis Hexaplorum Fragmenta* (2 vols.; Oxford: Oxford University Press, 1875) Lev 5:5; 26:40; Isa 30:15; 31:6; Hos 7:10).

Μετανοέω and Μετάνοια in the New Testament and Other Early Christian Literature

Unfortunately, most—if not all—of the studies that attempt to examine the notion of repentance that existed during the earlier Christian period are significantly flawed from the outset. Most scholars of early Christianity begin their studies of repentance with the same false assumption made by those who study the Jewish concept of repentance. The assumption that שוב is the Hebrew term that best conveys the notion of repentance has been handed down to countless generations of New Testament and Early Christianity scholars, and now serves as the starting point for virtually every study of repentance during the early Christian period.

Bailey, who has written the most recent work on repentance in the New Testament, repeatedly asserts, "The most common term for repentance is the word שוב."[381] Dunn asserts that μετάνοια usually means "change of mind" or "remorse" in secular Greek literature. He goes on to write, "In the earliest Christian tradition, however, it is the more pregnant sense of 'conversion' which dominates, the verb μετανοέω, 'repent, convert,' being used as the equivalent of the Hebrew שוב, 'turn back, return.'"[382] Without question, the assertion made in Kittel's *Theological Dictionary of the New Testament* has given validity to this inaccurate assumption. Innumerable scholars have accepted as truth the statement, "What the religious language of the OT expresses by שוב, and the theological terminology of the Rabbis by תשובה . . . the NT, like the Jewish Hellenistic writings, expresses by μετανοέω and μετάνοια."[383]

This study has demonstrated, however, that the evidence clearly cannot sustain the assumptions that שוב is the Hebrew term that best conveyed the notion of repentance for ancient Jews and that μετανοέω and μετάνοια should be recognized in early Christian literature as the Greek equivalent of the Hebrew שוב.[384] By abandoning such an assumption, this study will afford μετανοέω and μετάνοια the rare opportunity of being examined in a different light. It will allow these two terms to step out from behind the shadow of שוב and make their own impression upon the reader.

Dating the various writings of the New Testament is a somewhat difficult, and often controversial endeavor, because there is very little hard evidence upon which to date most of the writings. This applies to the two-volume work of Luke-Acts as well. Since the story of Acts comes to a somewhat abrupt ending with the house-arrest of Paul, making no mention of his death, many scholars have concluded that

---

[381] *Repentance*, 31 (cf 30–35; 41–44; 50–51; 54–58).
[382] J. G. Dunn, *Romans*, Word Biblical Commentary (2 vols.; Waco: Texas, 1988) 82.
[383] *TDNT* 4:999 (see also *NIDNNT* 1:354–357).
[384] I fail to understand how scholars can repeatedly assert that μετανοέω was used by the earliest Jewish Christians as the equivalent of the שוב, when the Jewish translators of the Hebrew scriptures never once used μετανοέω to translate שוב.

Luke-Acts was composed prior to the death of Paul.³⁸⁵ Other scholars, however, have chosen to date Luke-Acts in the second century.³⁸⁶ Despite these varying opinions, there is an overwhelming consensus among most scholars that Luke-Acts should be dated prior to the formation or circulation of the Pauline corpus and after the composition of the Markan Gospel, which would place the two-volume work in the latter half of the first century C.E.—roughly between 75 and 90.

Since Luke-Acts was most likely produced within the Christian movement of the late first century, the writings of the New Testament and of early Christianity serve as important sources for revealing how the notion of repentance might have been understood by the intended readers of Luke-Acts. These documents also provide a window into the historical, social, and literary context in which the author developed his own ideas about repentance.

As stated at the beginning of this chapter, the use of μετανοέω and μετάνοια to express the idea of repentance drastically increased during the Christian literary era. Most of the increase, however, occurs in the works of non-Jewish (and even anti-Jewish) Christian authors writing after the composition of Luke-Acts.³⁸⁷ These later Christian writings, which reflect the beginnings of the development of a Christian theology of repentance (i.e Penance) as well as a penitential discipline in the Church, cannot and should not be used to determine Jewish/Gentile-Christian attitudes regarding repentance during the first century C.E. This section, therefore, will examine ideas regarding repentance found in the New Testament and in Christian writings dating no later than the opening years of the second century C.E.

*The New Testament*³⁸⁸

The terms μετανοέω and μετάνοια occur fifty-six times in the New Testament.³⁸⁹ Outside of the twenty-five occurrences in Luke-Acts, the terms occur

---

³⁸⁵ Among the most notable scholars arguing for this early date are A. von Harnack, *The Date of the Acts and of the Synoptic Gospels* (NTS IV; London: William and Norgate, 1911); J. A. T. Robinson, *Redating the New Testament* (Philadelphia: Westminster, 1976) 57–60. For a list of other scholars see W. G. Kümmel, *Introduction to the New Testament* (trans. H. C. Kee; 17th ed.; Nashville: Abingdon Press, 1975) 150 n. 90, 186 n. 118.

³⁸⁶ Most notably J. C. O'Neill, *The Theology of Acts in its Historical Setting* (London: SPCK, 1961) 1–53 (The weaknesses of O'Neill's arguments are presented in a review of his book by H. F. D. Sparks, *JTS* 14 (1963) 454–466). For a list of other scholars who choose a late date for Luke-Acts, see W. G. Kümmel, *Introduction to the New Testament*, 186.

³⁸⁷ The terms occur over 335 times in the writings of Origen, over 125 times in the writings of Clement of Alexandria, and over 135 times in the so-called *Shepherd of Hermas*.

³⁸⁸ All Greek citations are from B. Aland, K. Aland, J. Karavidopoulos, C. M. Martini, and B. M. Metzger, eds. *The Greek New Testament* (4th ed., United Bible Societies; Stuttgart: Deutsche Bibelgesellschaft, 1993). Unless otherwise noted, English translations are from the New Revised Standard Version.

³⁸⁹ There is also one occurrence of the *alpha privative*—ἀμετανόητος (Rom 2:5). All references to the numerical occurrences of Greek terms in the New Testament are based on W. F. Moulton, A. S. Geden and H. K. Moulton, *A Concordance to the Greek Testament*

ten times in the Synoptics (seven times in Matthew and three times in Mark), with no occurrences in John's gospel. There are four occurrences in the Pauline epistles,[390] one occurrence in 2 Timothy, three occurrences in Hebrews, one occurrence in 2 Peter, and twelve occurrences in Revelation. Although never used by the author of Luke-Acts, there are also six occurrences of the verb μεταμέλομαι,[391] and two occurrences of the adjective ἀμεταμέλητος.[392]

Pauline Literature

The earliest attested Christian usage of μετανοέω and μετάνοια is found in Paul's second letter to the Christians at Corinth. At one point Paul was compelled to write a very difficult letter to the Christians at Corinth. Paul declares, "For I wrote you out of much distress and anguish of heart with many tears." (2 Cor 2:4). After receiving the good news brought by Titus of the effects of this letter, Paul writes:

> For even if I made you sorry (ἐλύπησα) with my letter, I do not regret (οὐ μεταμέλομαι) it (though I did regret (μετεμελόμην) it, for I see that I grieved (ἐλύπησεν) you with that letter, though only briefly). Now I rejoice, not because you were grieved, but because your grief led to repentance (εἰς μετάνοιαν); for you felt a godly grief, so that you were not harmed in any way by us. For godly grief produces a repentance that leads to salvation (μετάνοιαν εἰς σωτηρίαν) and brings no regret (ἀμεταμέλητον), but worldly grief produces death. For see what earnestness this godly grief has produced in you, what eagerness to clear yourselves, what indignation, what alarm, what longing, what zeal, what punishment![393]

Like the translators of the Hebrew Bible, Paul conveys the idea that sorrow lies at the heart of repentance. The noun λύπη, "sorrow, grief," and the verb λυπέω, "grieve, make sorrowful"[394] occur eight times in these three verses.[395] It was

---

(5th ed.; Edinburgh: T&T Clark, 1978).

[390] This does not include the *alpha privative*—ἀμετανόητος (Rom 2:5).

[391] Matt 21:29, 32; 27:3; 2 Cor 7:8 (x2); Heb 7:21. It has been previously demonstrated in this study that μεταμέλομαι and μετανοέω often function synonymously in the Septuagint, and in much of the non-Jewish/Christian Greek literature of the Hellenistic period.

[392] Rom 11:29; 2 Cor 7:10. The adjective is best translated, "without regret" in 2 Cor 7:10 and "irrevocable" in Rom 11:29.

[393] 2 Cor 7:8–11b.

[394] W. Gingrich and F. Danker, eds. *A Greek-English Lexicon of the New Testament and Other Early Christian Literature* (2nd ed.; Chicago: University of Chicago Press, 1958) 481–482.

[395] The verb occurs six other times in 2 Corinthians and the noun occurs four other times. Paul only uses the verb and the noun a total of four times outside of 2 Corinthians. Clearly the notion of sorrow and grief plays a prominent role in Paul's second letter to the Corinthians. This may be why three of the four Pauline occurrences of μετανοέω and

the grief and sorrow experienced by the Corinthians that led them to repentance. It was their grief that compelled them to change their situation eagerly and zealously, to clear themselves, and with indignation put away the sin and wrongdoing from among them.[396] Paul suggests that it is a genuine sense of sorrow and grief that compels the ungodly to change their way of thinking and behaving. Paul identifies this genuine sense of sorrow as "κατὰ θεὸν λύπη."[397] According to Paul, there is another type of sorrow, "τοῦ κόσμου λύπη"; however, this type of sorrow produces death rather than repentance. Only "godly sorrow" produces repentance that leads to salvation. Only "godly sorrow" leads to actions for which there is no regret.

Paul also seems to make a distinction here between μετάνοια and μεταμέλομαι.[398] It appears that for Paul, μεταμέλομαι represents nothing more than regret. It is simply an emotional feeling that one experiences. Initially Paul regretted having sent such a harsh letter, but after seeing the results he no longer had any regrets. He realized that the pain was necessary in order to bring the Corinthians to a change (ἐλυπήθητε εἰς μετάνοιαν). Unlike his use of μεταμέλομαι, Paul's use of μετάνοια clearly represents more than regret; it represents a change in perspective and behavior. Μετάνοια is the result of godly sorrow, which is different from regret or even worldly sorrow; godly sorrow compels one to eagerly and zealously put away sin and wrongdoing. Godly sorrow produces repentance (μετάνοιαν) not regret (ἀμεταμέλητον).[399] Furthermore, repentance leads to salvation; therefore, according to Paul, it should be received with joy not regret. Paul declares, "Now I rejoice (χαίρω). . . because your grief led to repentance."[400]

In 2 Cor 12:20–21, Paul informs the Corinthians that he is afraid that when he comes to visit them he might find them engaged in "quarreling, jealousy, anger, selfishness, slander, gossip, conceit, and disorder." He continues, "I fear that when

---

μετάνοια are found in 2 Corinthians.

[396] Bailey misses the meaning of the passage when he writes, "Here Paul clearly contrasts repentance (μετάνοια) with grief (λύπη), indicating that repentance which leads to salvation is more than remorse or contrition" (*Repentance*, 58). Paul is not contrasting repentance with grief, but instead he is conveying the idea that "godly grief," not "worldly grief" is the source of repentance.

[397] Based on Paul's use of κατὰ θεὸν elsewhere (Ro 8:27), as well as his use of κατὰ σάρκα/πνεῦμα (e.g. 2 Cor 1:17; 5:16; 10:2–3; 1 Cor 1:26; Rom 8:4–5, 12–13;), Paul's use of κατὰ θεὸν λύπη most likely suggests sorrow according to God's standard and or will; however, the phrase may also suggest sorrow produced by God (cf. 1 Cor 12:8; Rom 1:3–4; Gal 4:29).

[398] Paul uses μεταμέλομαι twice in all of his writings, and both occurrences are found here—where two of his three usages of μετάνοια are also found.

[399] Paul's only other use of ἀμεταμέλητος conveys the notion of regret as well. In Rom 11:29 Paul writes, "For the gifts and calling of God are irrevocable" (i.e. "without regret"; ἀμεταμέλητα).

[400] As shall be demonstrated below, the notion of repentance leading to salvation and the notion of rejoicing over repentance are both prominent themes in Luke-Acts.

I come again, my God may humble me before you, and that I may have to mourn over many who previously sinned and have not repented (μὴ μετανοησάντων) of the impurity, sexual immorality, and licentiousness that they have practiced." Paul's use of μετανοέω here is consistent with the notion of a change in perspective and behavior conveyed by Paul's earlier use of μετάνοια. As was the case with μετάνοια in 2 Cor 7:8–10, the Corinthian readers and listeners should understand the use of μετανοέω here as representing an eager and zealous putting away of sin and wrongdoing.

As has been the case in most of the literature examined in this study, repentance is depicted by Paul as an appropriate human response to sin and wickedness. The only other occurrence of either μετάνοια or μετανοέω in the genuine letters of Paul is found in Rom 2:4–5, and once again Paul presents μετάνοια as the only appropriate human response to sin and wickedness. Rom 2:4–5 is a part of Paul's universal indictment against humanity (1:18–3:20).[401] In 1:18–32, Paul presents what he considers to be the sinful nature of humanity. He also makes it clear to his audience that the wrath of God is directed against all the ungodliness and wickedness of humanity—to "the Jew first and also the Greek" (2:9).[402] Throughout 1:18–3:20, Paul continually suggests that because of the universality of sin, the Jews, as much as the Greeks, are in need of God's eschatological grace.

After concluding 1:18–32 with a typical Hellenistic vice list, Paul engages in a personal address to an imagined interlocutor. Paul addresses the inexcusability of the interlocutor's behavior. Paul rebukes this imagined interlocutor for judging and condemning those engaged in the same sins the interlocutor is engaged in. Paul then declares, "Or do you despise the riches of God's kindness and forbearance and patience? Do you not realize that God's kindness is meant to lead you to repentance (εἰς μετάνοιάν σε ἄγει)? But by your hard and impenitent (ἀμετανόητον) heart you are storing up wrath for yourself on the day of wrath, when God's righteous judgment will be revealed" (2:4–5). Paul's words here are part of the diatribe style Paul frequently employs.[403] In antiquity, diatribe did not function as a polemic against opponents but rather as a critical questioning of individuals designed to lead those individuals to the truth.[404] Paul uses diatribe here not to condemn the interlocutor but to lead this imagined interlocutor to the truth about repentance: God has been kind and patient with the interlocutor because God desires to lead the

---

[401] For a detailed structural analysis of the book of Romans, see: Dunn, *Romans*.
[402] The "Jew first and also Greek" is a common theme throughout Paul's letter to the Romans (cf. 1:16; 2:10; 3:9, 29; 9:24; 10:12; note also 3:1–4; 11:18, 28–29).
[403] Regarding Paul's use of diatribe, see: S. Stowers, *The Diatribe and Paul's Letter to the Romans*, SBLDS 57 (Chico, CA: Scholars Press, 1981); D. E. Aune, *The New Testament in its Literary Environment*, LEC (Philadelphia: Westminster, 1987) 200–201, 219.
[404] Stowers, *Diatribe*, 75–78.

interlocutor to repentance.[405] For Paul, repentance is the means by which the interlocutor is afforded an opportunity by God to avoid the wrath of God on the day of God's righteous judgment. As Paul asserted in 2 Cor 7:10, repentance leads to salvation. Failure to repent,[406] however, will result in the interlocutor experiencing the wrath of God on the day of judgment. Repentance is the only source of hope in the midst of this universal indictment against sinful humanity.

Although Paul does not make explicit what repentance entails, the context makes it clear that repentance involves a change in perspective and behavior. It involves a fundamental change in lifestyle: a turning away from the wicked and sinful deeds and the unrighteous lifestyle described in Rom 1:18–32. As in 2 Corinthians, it involves an eager and zealous putting away of sin and wrongdoing. Furthermore, reminiscent of much of the Jewish literature already examined, Paul emphasizes that it is the kindness and mercy of God that should lead sinners to repentance.[407]

While the concept of repentance, may not play a prominent literary role in the extensive corpus of Pauline literature, Paul is consistent in his usage of μετανοέω and μετάνοια, and clear in his understanding of repentance. For Paul, repentance is a change in thinking—precipitated by a genuine sense of sorrow and remorse—that is manifested by a fundamental change in lifestyle. Repentance always involves putting away sin and wrongdoing from one's life.[408] Furthermore, Paul understands repentance as providing an escape from the wrath of God—it leads the sinner to salvation.

---

[405] The notion of a divine being dealing patiently with sinners in order to afford them an opportunity to repent is a theme that has been witnessed in pagan Greek literature (As mention earlier, the image of the Delian Apollo holding the graces in his right hand and a bow and arrow in his left gave rise to the allegorical-ethical interpretation that the god holds the bow in his left hand because he is slow to chastise sinners and the graces in his right hand because he is desirous to grant repentance. Plutarch also speaks of God granting "a period of grace" in order that sinners might have an opportunity to repent (*The Divine Vengeance* 551 C–D)), Hellenistic Jewish scriptures (Wis 11:23; 12:9–10) and other Hellenistic Jewish writings (*T. Abr.* 12:1–13 (Recension B); *Pr. Man* 6–7; *Let. Aris.* 187–188; *Sib Or.* 2.309–312; 8.357; Philo, *Allegorical Interpretation* 3.106; *The Special Laws* 1.186–187; *Questions and Answers on Genesis* 2.13).

[406] Paul's use of ἀμετανόητος, "impenitent," is the only occurrence in the New Testament. The only other Jewish occurrence is found in *T. Gad.* 7:5.

[407] (Cf. *T. Ben.* 5:3–4; *T. Gad.* 6:47; *Let. Aris.* 187–188; *Pr. Man* 6–7; Wis 11:23; 12:9–10, 19–21). This possibly sheds some light on what Paul may have meant by the phrase κατὰ θεόν λύπη, "godly sorrow." Since it is God's kindness and forbearance and patience, as well as "godly sorrow," that leads the sinner to repentance, "godly sorrow" may represent the sorrow that arises within the sinner when the sinner recognizes that he or she has despised "the riches of God's kindness and forbearance and patience" by continually engaging in sin.

[408] It should be pointed out that Paul never uses στρέφω nor any of its compounds to convey the idea of turning away from sin.

Pauline Tradition

Written in the Pauline tradition, 2 Timothy also employs the noun μετάνοια.[409] 2 Timothy assumes the form of an epistolary testament in the name of Paul on the eve of his death. The apostle becomes a dying patriarch, leaving "sound teaching" and words of instruction to one of the heirs of his ministry—Timothy. Paul informs Timothy that "the Lord's servant must not be quarrelsome but kindly to everyone, an apt teacher, patient, correcting opponents with gentleness, *in order that perhaps God might grant them repentance (μήποτε δῷη αὐτοῖς ὁ θεὸς μετάνοιαν) unto knowledge of the truth, and that they might escape from the snare of the devil.*"[410] Just as Paul asserts that the patient kindness of God is intended to lead the sinner to repentance, the author of 2 Timothy asserts that the patient gentleness of the Lord's servant is intended to lead the sinner to repentance. As implied by Paul, and explicitly expressed by other Jewish and Greek authors, the author of 2 Timothy also makes it clear that repentance is granted to human beings by God.[411] It is provided as a means of deliverance from the snares of the devil. It entails a change of thinking that involves abandoning false doctrine and embracing a knowledge of the truth. For the author, such a change in thinking leads to a change in behavior because false doctrine results in ungodly behavior, while a knowledge of the truth results in good works.[412]

The General Letters

The noun μετάνοια occurs three times in the Letter to the Hebrews.[413] Two occurrences are found in Heb 6:1–6. In the first five chapters, the author develops his unique Christological insights; however, because of what he perceives as spiritual dullness among his readers, the author shifts from Christology and makes

---

[409] While the "Pastoral Epistles" (i.e. Titus; 1–2 Timothy) are widely considered to be non-Pauline, most scholars see them as the production of a "Pauline school," written in the Pauline tradition (cf. A. E. Barnett, *Paul Becomes a Literary Influence*, (Chicago: University of Chicago Press, 1941) 251–253). Unlike many of the so-called Pauline compositions (e.g. *3 Corinthians, Letter to the Laodiceans, Letters of Paul and Seneca, Acts of Paul and Thecla*), the Pastorals were universally accepted as genuine by the early church. Furthermore, 2 Timothy displays the closest affinities to the genuine letters of Paul. Luke T. Johnson asserts, "It may well be. . . that 2 Timothy can lay a far better claim to authenticity on every count than 1 Timothy" (*The Writings of the New Testament* (Philadelphia: Fortress, 1986) 389).
[410] 2 Timothy 2:24–26 (italics represent my own translation).
[411] Cf. *Sib. Or.* 2:309–312; 4:162–170; 8.357; *Pr. Man.* 6–7; Wis 11:23; 12:9–10a, 19–21; Philo *The Special Laws* 1.187; *On the Cherubim* 2; *On Abraham* 17f.; *Questions and Answers on Genesis* 1.82; 2.13; Plutarch, *The Divine Vengeance* 551.D.
[412] 2 Tim 3:1–17.
[413] Because of the later superscription "to the Hebrews," this document had been previously identified as a letter written in the Pauline tradition to a specific Christian community (cf. P[46]). The document, however, which is not a letter, nowhere claims Pauline authorship, and it is now universally agreed among scholars that it did not originate with Paul nor was it the production of a "Pauline school."

a parenetic insertion.[414] This parenetic insertion serves as both an exhortation and a rebuke. The author makes it clear that while his intended readers have been Christians for quite some time, they do not display spiritual maturity and they still need to be taught the beginning principles of God's word.[415] However, rather than going over these basic rudimentary principles again, the author exhorts his readers, "Therefore let us go on toward perfection, leaving behind the basic teachings about Christ, and not laying again the foundation: repentance (μετανοίας) from dead works and faith toward God, instruction about baptisms, laying on of hands, resurrection of the dead, and eternal judgment."[416]

There appears to have been some form of initial catechesis given to new members of the Christian sect.[417] The concept of repentance was obviously part of these foundational instructions. It seems that repentance entailed a change in thinking and or behavior regarding what the author calls "dead works" (νεκρὰ ἔργα). Although it is not clear what the author means by νεκρὰ ἔργα, the use of the phrase again in Heb 9:14 suggests that the author understands the phrase to represent sins that defile a person and that lead to death.[418] One of the first things those joining the Christian community are taught is the importance of changing their thinking and behavior regarding sin.

The author desires for his Christian readers to move on toward maturity instead of constantly having to be taught the basic principles of Christianity. The author informs his readers that it is still possible for them to move on if God permits it. He also warns them, however, that at some point God will not allow Christians who fail to adhere to the basic principles of Christianity, and in so doing fall away from Christianity, to move on toward maturity. The author declares:

> For it is impossible—those once having been enlightened, having tasted the heavenly gift and having become participators in the Holy Spirit and having tasted the goodness of the word of God and the powers of the age to come, and having fallen away—to renew *them* again unto repentance (μετάνοιαν), since they are crucifying for themselves the son of God and exposing him to public scorn.[419]

---

[414] Heb 5:11–6:20.
[415] Heb 5:12–14.
[416] Heb 6:1–2.
[417] Harold W. Attridge, *The Epistle to the Hebrews*, Hermeneia (Philadelphia: Fortress, 1989) 163.
[418] A similar expression is found in 4 Ezra 7:49, "deeds that bring death." Heb 9:14, which reads, "how much more will the blood of Christ... purify our conscience *from dead works to worship the living God*" (emphasis added), also suggests that "repentance from dead works and faith toward God" in Heb 6:1 should be understood as going hand in hand. Here we see the idea of turning from sin and turning toward God.
[419] Heb 6:4–6 (my own translation).

The author of Hebrews appears to be one of the first Christian rigorists among early Christians leaders who does not believe in the possibility of repentance for apostasy.[420] For this author, repentance represents a renewing (ἀνακαινίζειν): those who repent from "dead works" are renewed. However, if after being renewed they continue to produce dead works, and in so doing mock the son of God, then they are incapable of being restored to a renewed state. These individuals are like a garden that, after receiving rain and being cultivated, produces thorns and thistles instead of a useful crop. According to the author, such a garden is useless; it is not re-cultivated but instead is destined to be burned over.[421] The author is exhorting his readers to move on to maturity while God still allows them, in order that they not end up falling away from Christianity and finding themselves unable to be renewed again unto repentance.[422]

Elsewhere the author gives an example of someone not being afforded an opportunity to repent. The author begins his final parenetic section (12:14–13:19) with an exhortation to his readers to watch over one another in order to avert the dangers of apostasy. The author has already stated that those who commit apostasy are unable to repent again. Here the author encourages his readers to "See to it no one becomes like Esau, an immoral and godless person, who sold his birthright for a single meal. You know that later, when he wanted to inherit the blessing, he was rejected, for he *did not find an opportunity for repentance* (μετανοίας), even though he sought *it* with tears."[423] For the author, Esau serves not only as an example of apostasy but also as an example of the impossibility of repentance after apostasy.

In Hebrews, repentance represents a change in thinking and behavior with regard to sin. It marks a renewing of the individual, and as such it is part of the foundational teaching given to all new Christians. The author also uses μεταμέλομαι once, but the word means nothing more than to change one's mind or to regret one's decision.[424]

The noun μετένοια occurs once in the pseudepigraphic letter of 2 Peter. Since Peter regards his death as imminent (1:13–15), 2 Peter is written as a testament to provide a permanent reminder of Peter's teaching. The author

---

[420] cf. Heb 10:26–31 (see also Hermas, *Man.* 4.3.1–3; 4.3.4–5; 12.6.1–2; *Vis.* 2.2.3–5; 3.3.1–2; 3.5.4–6; 4.1.1–3; Tertullian, *On Repentance* 7–12; *On Modesty*).
[421] Heb 6:7–8.
[422] As mentioned earlier, Philo refers to the inability of some sinners to repent: "For many souls who have wished to turn to repentance have not been allowed to do so." (*Allegorical Interpretation* 3:213; cf. *On the Cherubim* 2; *That the Worse attacks the Better* 96; *The Special Laws* 1:58). See also Josephus, *Ant.* 9:168.
[423] Heb 12:16–17 (italics represents my own translation). Although it is grammatically unclear whether the "it" Esau sought after was "the blessing" or "repentance," the story of Esau in Genesis 27:30–38 makes it clear that it was the blessing that Esau sought after with tears. Even though Esau desired the blessing, he never took the opportunity to repent of selling his birthright to Jacob.
[424] Heb 7:21.

expresses moral outrage at the deviance and defiance manifested in the community of his readers.[425] The author seeks to defend the common Christian heritage against distortion and corruption. He unleashes moral condemnation against false teachers who propagate destructive doctrines of eschatological skepticism and moral libertinism.[426] In chapter three, the author warns his readers to remember the promises and commandments of the Lord and to resist the false teachers, who question not only the return of the Lord but also whether or not God renders judgment. Because of their skepticism, these false teachers pursue their own passions, and encourage others to do likewise. The author assures his readers, however, "The Lord is not slow about his promise, as some think of slowness, but is patient with you, not wanting any to perish, but all to come to repentance (μετένοιαν)."[427]

The Lord's delay in returning and punishing the wicked should not be seen as proof that the promises are false, but rather as a sign of God's grace and mercy. The patience (μακροθυμία) of God is actually a gift, given to afford sinners an opportunity to repent.[428] The reference to the Lord's patience sounds remarkably similar to Paul's statement in Rom 2:4. The author reveals that he is aware that he is indebted to Paul for his understanding of the Lord's patience: he writes, "Therefore, beloved, . . . regard the patience of our Lord as salvation. So also our beloved brother Paul wrote to you according to the wisdom given him, speaking of this as he does in all his letters."[429] The author of 2 Peter, like Paul, asserts that the Lord is patient in rendering judgment because the Lord wishes to afford those engaged in sin an opportunity to repent.

Once again repentance is portrayed as the appropriate human response to sin, as well as a means of escaping punishment. Sinners can avoid perishing at the day of judgment if they repent of their sins; and because of God's patience, sinners are afforded an opportunity to do just that. The false teachers, however, mock and despise the riches of the Lord's patience, and encourage others to do likewise.

For the author, repentance involves not only a change regarding specific behavior, it involves a change regarding one's entire way of life. The false teachers encourage an immoral and ungodly lifestyle by denying the Lord's return and the accompanying eschatological judgment. Repentance, therefore, requires not simply

---

[425] According to testament conventions, the author is responding to predicted immoralities and false teachings (2:1–3).

[426] J. H. Neyrey, "The Form and Background of the Polemic in 2 Peter," *JBL* 99 (1980) 407–31; Richard J. Bauckham, *Jude, 2 Peter*, WBC (Waco Texas: Word, 1983).

[427] 2 Pet 3:9.

[428] The scriptural roots of this notion can be found in Exod 34:6–7, where it is asserted that God is "slow to anger." The phrase gets translated in the LXX as God's patience (μακροθυμία; cf. Num 14:18; Neh 9:17; Ps 85[86]:15).

[429] 2 Pet 3:14–16a. The false teachers, however, because they do no understand Paul's teachings regarding the patience of the Lord, twist them to their own destruction (16b). Besides the reference found in Rom 2:4, it is not clear what other references and letters the author might have in mind.

changing a specific behavior; it requires changing one's entire way of life. Repentance addresses what type of person an individual should be with regard to living lives of holiness and godliness.[430] The author is seeking to convey to his readers that Christians must live a holy and godly lifestyle if they are to inherit the promises of eschatological salvation, because "the day of the Lord will come like a thief," and God will definitely judge and destroy the ungodly.[431] However, for those not living a godly lifestyle, God has provided, through divine patience, an opportunity for them to repent—changing the way they live—whereby escaping the wrath of God's promised judgment.

The Revelation to John

There are no occurrences of μετάνοια in any of the Johannine literature, and μετανοέω only occurs in the Revelation to John. The verb μετανοέω occurs twelve times in Revelation. Such frequency is second only to Luke-Acts. The bulk of the occurrence are found in the declarations from Christ to the seven churches.[432] Christian communities, not sinners nor simply individuals, are exhorted to repent. The declarations have a strong emphasis on the behavior expected of the members of these Christians communities. The communities are first commended for their praiseworthy behavior and works, which usually involve opposing the teachings of false prophets and teachers, as well as correcting or removing from the community those embracing the teachings of these false leaders. The communities are also commended for adhering to what they were initially taught and for remaining faithful and steadfast in the face of persecution, imprisonment and even death. After being commended, the communities are then chastised for inappropriate behavior and works, and are exhorted to repent (μετανοῆσαι) before an imminent coming of Christ to render judgment.[433]

The condemned behavior and works include abandoning one's first love, tolerating false teachers and those who embrace the idolatrous and sexually immoral practices associated with libertine false teachings. Repentance does not just entail a change in thinking, but it entails a change in behavior. It entails forsaking inappropriate behavior and works, and doing works (ἔργα ποίησον) consistent with a change in thinking.[434] For the Christian communities at Ephesus and Sardis

---

[430] 2 Pet 3:11.
[431] 2 Pet 3:10a, 5–7; 2:4–10a.
[432] Eight occurrences of the verb are found in the messages delivered to five of the seven churches (Ephesus, Rev 2:5 [x2]; Pergamum, Rev 2:16; Thyatira, Rev 2:21–22 [x3]; Sardis, Rev 3:3; Laodicea, Rev 3:19). Only the churches in Smyrna and Philadelphia are not called to repentance.
[433] Rev 2:5, 16, 21–23; 3:3, 19. It is unclear whether the references to the coming of Christ in the declaration to the churches refer to the promised return of the Messiah on the day of judgment (Rev 16:15) or to a particular act of temporal judgment.
[434] Rev 2:5a.

repentance specifically entails returning to the works they were initially involved in.[435]

As has been the case in much of the literature examined throughout this study, time has been granted by a divine figure to those engaged in inappropriate behavior, in order to give them an opportunity to repent. In a statement regarding a prophetess identified as "Jezebel," Christ declares, "I gave her time to repent (μετανοήσῃ), but she refuses to repent (μετανοῆσαι) of her fornication."[436] Just like Paul and the author of 2 Peter, the author of Revelation stresses that those who have been given time to repent should not presume on God's patience, because failure to repent will result in Christ coming "like a thief," rendering swift and severe punishment.[437]

After addressing the seven churches, the emphasis of John's vision shifts away from the Christian communities to the eschatological tribulations that must be poured out on the world immediately before the promised return of Christ and the final judgment and destruction of the world (4:1–22:5). In the four verses where μετανοέω occurs, the phrase is repeated οὐ[δὲ] μετενόησαν ("they did not repent").[438] Even after the terrible plagues and judgments poured out upon the world—destroying at one point over a fourth of the earth and at another point one-third of all creation and severely afflicting the remaining two-thirds—those engaged in idolatrous and immoral practices still refused to repent "of the works (ἐκ τῶν ἔργων)" of their hands.[439] Many of them even cursed God, but they still refused to repent.[440]

Unlike the Christian communities that were earlier exhorted to repent, the ones here who refuse to repent are non-Christians, engaged in idolatry, murders, sorceries, immorality and thefts. However, as with the Christian communities who were exhorted to repent, repentance for these non-Christians also entails a change in behavior. It entails abandoning idolatry, murders, sorceries, immorality, thefts, and all other inappropriate behavior and works. The author makes it clear that repentance applies to Christians and non-Christians alike. It entails not just a change in thinking, but also a change in behavior. It entails forsaking inappropriate

---

[435] Rev 2:5; 3:3.

[436] Rev 2:21. The declaration to the church in Thyatira is the only one of the seven declarations where individual repentance is alluded to rather than communal repentance. Jezebel, and those who commit adultery with her, are specifically identified as the ones needing to repent (vv. 21–22), and if they fail to repent, they will experience severe punishment. The declaration makes it clear that those rejecting the idolatrous and immoral teachings of Jezebel have nothing to repent of, they are simply exhorted to remain steadfast until Christ returns (vv. 24–25), because Christ searches minds and hearts, and punishes and rewards everyone according to their works (v. 23). This individual emphasis is also found in the declaration to the church in Sardis. The community, rather than individuals, is still exhorted to repent, however, the few "who have not soiled their clothes" have nothing to repent of and will walk with Christ, "dressed in white, for they are worthy" (Rev 3:3–4).

[437] Rev 3:3 (cf. 2:5, 22; 16:15).

[438] Rev 9:20, 21; 16:9, 11.

[439] Rev 9:20; 16:11 (cf. 6:8; 8:7–9:15).

[440] Rev 16:9, 11.

behavior and works, and doing works consistent with a change in thinking. For Christians repentance entails returning to the lifestyle and works they were involved in during the initial stages of their Christian experience. Repentance prevents Christ from visiting Christian communities with swift and severe punishment. For non-Christians repentance entails a forsaking of idolatry, immorality and various other inappropriate works.

Although the author portrays repentance being extended to non-Christians, he gives no indication whether or not the non-Christians would have been delivered from the wrath of God had they repented of their sins. This is because the author is actually not concerned about the repentance of the non-Christians. The message of Revelation is for the churches. The author wants to assure his Christian audience both of the blessings in store for them if they repent of their inappropriate deeds and remain faithful in the face of persecution and of the punishment in store for their persecutors. Such assurance is meant to encourage the Christians to remain faithful and not to be like their persecutors who refuse to repent of their sins, because in the end Christ rewards everyone according to their works. At the end of the revelation, a loud voice from the throne of God tells John to write, "See, I am coming soon; my reward is with me, to repay according to everyone's work. . . . Blessed are those who wash their robes, so that they will have the right to the tree of life and may enter the city by the gates. It is I, Jesus, who sent my angel to you with this testimony for the churches."[441] Repentance delivers those who have fallen into sin from the judgment of Christ.

The Synoptic Gospels

Both μετανοέω and μετάνοια are found in the Gospel according to Mark and the Gospel according to Matthew, which indicates the theme of repentance was present in the Gospel tradition shared with Luke.[442] In the Synoptic Gospel tradition, John the Baptist bursts onto the scene "preaching a baptism of repentance (μετανοίας) for the forgiveness of sins."[443] From the outset, the Gospel tradition makes it clear that repentance is the appropriate human response to sin. If the sinner addresses his or her sins by repenting of those sins, then God will grant forgiveness to the sinner.[444]

Although the Gospel tradition makes it clear that repentance is in response to sin, sin in and of itself is not the catalyst for repentance. The sinner is not compelled to repent simply because repentance is the appropriate response to sin; instead, the

---

[441] Rev 22:12–16a.
[442] As mentioned earlier, neither term is found in the Gospel according to John.
[443] Mark 1:4; Luke 3:3 (cf Matt 3:2).
[444] Matthew never makes an explicit connection between repentance and sin. Furthermore, Matthew postpones the notion of forgiveness of sins until 26:28, where he attributes the power to forgive sins to the death of Jesus.

sinner is compelled to repent because a new period in history has begun. There is an eschatological motivation for repentance. In Mark's gospel, Jesus declares, "The time is fulfilled, and the kingdom of God has come near; repent (μετανοεῖτε), and believe in the good news."[445] The reference to "the time (ὁ καιρός)" being fulfilled suggests the arrival of the "kingdom of God" was appointed by God and anticipated by the people.[446] The "kingdom of God" refers primarily to the establishment of God's rule over all creation.[447] The people are compelled to repent because the inauguration of God's reign is upon them. Matthew stresses this point not only by having Jesus declare the inauguration of God's reign, but also by omitting the reference to John "preaching a baptism of repentance for the forgiveness of sins," and writing, "In those days John the Baptist appeared in the wilderness of Judea, proclaiming, 'Repent (μετανοεῖτε), for the kingdom of heaven has come near.'"[448]

Because of the inauguration of God's reign, individuals are compelled to repent. They are compelled to "Bear fruit worthy of repentance."[449] The Gospel tradition makes it clear that repentance is the first and apparently most important requirement for human beings as the reign of God on earth begins. John the Baptist prepares the people for the coming of God's reign with a baptism of repentance, and the first command given to the people by Jesus is "repent (μετανοεῖτε)." According to the Gospel tradition, the inauguration of the reign of God—in the person of Jesus—marks the decisive intervention of God into human history, and has created a situation that demands repentance.[450]

In describing the preaching of John the Baptist and Jesus, Mark and Matthew make no effort to elaborate on what repentance entails. Exhortations to repent and discussions regarding repentance in Mark and Matthew suggest that within the Gospel tradition the meaning of repentance was understood without explanation. It is an undisputed fact that the earliest Christians were Jews. It has also been demonstrated in this study that repentance among Jews entailed a change in thinking and behavior with regard to sin. Since there is no attempt in either Mark or Matthew

---

[445] 1:15 (cf. Matt 4:17). This reference has been omitted from Luke's gospel. As predominant as the theme of repentance is in Luke-Acts, it is significant when the author omits from the gospel tradition a reference to repentance. Possible reasons for this Lukan omission will be discussed below when we examine repentance in Luke's gospel.

[446] Cf. Daniel 7:13–14. The problem with the terminology the "kingdom of God/heaven" in the gospels is the absence of comparative evidence in other Jewish sources (see Norman Perrin, *The Kingdom of God in the Teaching of Jesus* (Philadelphia: Westminster, 1963)).

[447] See A. Ambrozic, *The Hidden Kingdom: A Redactional-Critical Study of the References to the Kingdom of God in Mark's Gospel* (*CBQ* Monograph Series 2, 1975).

[448] 3:1–2. Because Matthew alters the reference regarding John "preaching a baptism of repentance for the forgiveness of sins," Matthew later adds the clause, "for repentance" to John's declaration, "I baptize you with water." (3:11; cf Mark 1:8; Luke 3:16).

[449] Matt 3:8 (cf Luke 3:8).

[450] According to *Q*, John the Baptist declares that the situation demands repentance because the wrath of God is imminent (Matt 3:7; Luke 3:7). Mark, however, omits the aspect of judgment from John's preaching of repentance.

The Meaning of Repentance

to elaborate on the meaning of repentance, it should be concluded that the meaning of μετανοέω and μετάνοια in Mark and Matthew is consistent with the meaning found in other Hellenistic Jewish writings. Therefore, the inauguration of the reign of God requires individuals to change the way they think about sin and the way they live: it demands a reorientation of life.

The notion that repentance in the Gospel tradition entails a reorientation of life is also suggested by the other occurrences of μετανοέω. The only other occurrence in Mark is found in the sixth chapter. After ministering throughout Galilee and its surrounding regions, Jesus returns to Nazareth where he is not well received. The author even asserts that Jesus himself is amazed at the people's unbelief.[451] Jesus, therefore, goes throughout the villages teaching; he also sends the twelve out as well. The author writes, "So they went out and proclaimed that all should repent (μετανοῶσιν)."[452] The literary context suggests that repentance entails a change of thinking, especially with regard to the ministry of Jesus. Furthermore, the fact that Mark describes the ministry of the twelve with a summary statement similar to the summary statements used for John the Baptist and Jesus suggests that the apostle's preaching of repentance is consistent with the preaching of repentance by John the Baptist and Jesus.[453] The author is stressing the continuity of the apostle's message with that of both John and Jesus.

The three other occurrences in Matthew also suggest that repentance entails a reorientation of life. In the eleventh chapter of Matthew, John the Baptist, who is in prison, sends messengers to Jesus to ask him if he is the one who is to come. Jesus sends the messengers back to John and informs them to tell John what they hear and see. After the messengers leave, Jesus speaks to the crowd about John and clarifies the false expectations and misperceptions they might have had regarding John. Jesus praises John and informs the crowd that John is indeed Elijah who is to come and prepare the way of the Lord. He then criticizes the crowd for their faulty thinking and lack of wisdom. Jesus says to them:

> But to what will I compare this generation? It is like children sitting in the marketplaces and calling to one another, "We played the flute for you, and you did not dance; we wailed and you did not mourn." For John came neither eating nor drinking, and they say, "He has a demon"; the Son of Man came eating and drinking, and they say, "Look, a glutton and a drunkard, a friend of tax collectors and sinners!" Yet wisdom is vindicated by her deeds.[454]

---

[451] Mark 6:6.
[452] Mark 6:12.
[453] The three explicit references to repentance in Mark are contained in summary statements regarding the ministry of John the Baptist (1:4), Jesus (1:15), and the twelve (6:12).
[454] Matt 11:16–19.

The author then immediately writes:

> Then he [Jesus] began to reproach the cities in which most of his deeds of power had been done, because they did not repent (οὐ μετενόησαν). "Woe to you, Chorazin! Woe to you, Bethsaida! For if the deeds of power done in you had been done in Tyre and Sidon, they would have repented (μετενόησαν) long ago in sackcloth and ashes. But I tell you, on the day of judgment it will be more tolerable for Tyre and Sidon than for you."[455]

The literary context clearly suggests that for the author repentance entails both a change in thinking regarding the ministry of Jesus and a reorientation of life. Similarly, in the author's final usage of μετανοέω, Jesus rebukes the Pharisees for their hypocrisy. Jesus tells the Pharisees, "Either make the tree good, and its fruit good; or make the tree bad, and its fruit bad; for the tree is known by its fruit. You brood of vipers! How can you speak good things when you are evil?"[456] The author continues:

> Then some of the scribes and Pharisees said to him, "Teacher, we wish to see a sign from you." But he answered them, "An evil and adulterous generation asks for a sign, but no sign will be given to it except the sign of the prophet Jonah. For just as Jonah was three days and three nights in the belly of the sea monster, so for three days and three nights the Son of Man will be in the heart of the earth. The people of Nineveh will rise up at the judgment with this generation and condemn it, because they repented (μετενόησαν) at the proclamation of Jonah, and see, something greater than Jonah is here!"[457]

Once again the literary context clearly suggests that repentance entails both a change in thinking regarding the ministry of Jesus and a reorientation of life. The exhortation to the Pharisees to "make the tree good and its fruit good" is of course an exhortation to change their way of living; it also paves the way for the discussion of the Ninevite's repentance. The implication is that the reorientation of life resulting from repentance should be similar to the reorientation manifested in the lives of the Ninevites when they repented at the preaching of Jonah,[458] but in order for such a reorientation of life to take place the Pharisees are going to have to change their thinking regarding the life and ministry of Jesus.

---

[455] Matt 11:20–22.
[456] Matt 12:33–34a (the reference to "fruit (καρπόν)" and the designation "You brood of vipers (γεννήματα ἐχιδνῶν)" is clearly meant to echo the earlier call to repentance extended to the Pharisees by John the Baptist (cf. 3:7–8)).
[457] Matt 12:38–41.
[458] Jonah 3:4–10. In the LXX, the response of the Ninevites is not identified as μετανοέω or μετάνοια. The men of Nineveh are depicted as believing God, proclaiming a fast, putting on sackcloth, sitting in ashes, and turning (ἀπέστρεψαν) from their evil. The response of God, however is identified as μετανοέω: 'And God saw their works, . . . and repented (μετενόησεν) of the evil which he had said he would do to them." (Jonah 3:10).

Matthew is the only one of the canonical gospels which also employs the term μεταμέλομαι.[459] In the parable of the two sons, which is found only in Matthew, the author uses μεταμέλομαι twice. The author writes, "What do you think? A man had two sons; he went to the first and said, 'Son, go and work in the vineyard today.' He answered, 'I will not'; but later he changed his mind (μεταμεληθείς) and went. The father went to the second and said the same; and he answered, 'I go, sir'; but he did not go." After telling the parable, Jesus asked the chief priest and elders of the people, "Which of the two did the will of his father?" They replied, "The first." Jesus then said to them, "Truly I tell you, the tax collectors and the prostitutes are going into the kingdom of God ahead of you. For John came to you in the way of righteousness and you did not believe him, but the tax collectors and the prostitutes believed him, and even after you saw it, you did not change your minds (οὐδὲ μετεμελήθητε) and believe him."[460] While μεταμέλομαι does not entail a change in thinking regarding the ministry of Jesus, it does entail a change in thinking and a reorientation of life.

The author also uses μεταμέλομαι in his discussion of Judas. The author writes, "When Judas, his betrayer, saw that Jesus was condemned, he *changed his mind* (μεταμεληθείς) and brought back the thirty pieces of silver to the chief priests and the elders."[461] In this passage, μεταμέλομαι clearly denotes a change in thinking regarding the ministry of Jesus; it does not, however, seem to denote a reorientation of life. Judas merely changes his mind regarding a specific decision he previously made.[462]

As demonstrated throughout this study, there have been instances in other literature when μετανοέω and or μετάνοια have been used to denote the type of change of mind depicted by Judas, as well as the type of change of mind depicted in the parable of the two sons, but in Matthew the terms are not used simply to depict a change of mind regarding a specific decision. In Matthew, as well as in the Gospel tradition, the change in thinking denoted by μετανοέω/μετάνοια results in a reorientation of life.[463]

Summary

Outside of Luke-Acts, and with the possible exception of Revelation, the motif of repentance does not have a dominant literary role and presence within the New

---

[459] As mentioned earlier, μεταμέλομαι and μετανοέω are often used synonymously.
[460] Matt 21:28–32.
[461] Matt 27:3 (italics represents my translation).
[462] The fact that Judas immediately went out and hanged himself after he realized that the chief priests and elders were not going to free Jesus suggests that Judas experienced a change of mind and regret rather than a reorientation of life.
[463] While not necessarily using the language of repentance, Matthew and Mark do convey the urgency of changing one's way of life as well as the cost and reward associated with making such changes (e.g. Matt 5:20–24, 27–30; 6:1–8, 16–18; 13:44–46; 18:8–9 [Mark 9:43–47]).

Testament. Nevertheless, the few explicit references to repentance present in the New Testament do suggest that repentance had a foundational role within early Christianity. With the use of summary statements, Mark stresses the fact that repentance comprised the content of the preaching of John the Baptist, Jesus, and the apostles. The message of repentance was at the center of early Christian preaching. Furthermore, Hebrews identifies repentance as part of the foundational teachings of early Christianity.

In the writings of the New Testament, the motivation for repentance is varied. Paul asserts that it is a genuine sense of sorrow that compels people to repent. In Revelation, and elsewhere, it is the threat of divine judgment and punishment that compels repentance; and in the Gospel tradition reflected in Mark and Matthew, people are compelled to repent because the inauguration of God's reign is upon them. Whatever the motivation, however, repentance entails a change in thinking and behavior by people who realize that their present way of think and behaving is displeasing to God. The change in thinking involves both a change in thinking with regard to sin and a change in thinking with regard to the life and ministry of Jesus of Nazareth. The change in behavior involves a fundamental change in the way one lives: it entails a reorientation of life that requires putting away sin and wrongdoing. In the New Testament, repentance represents the only appropriate human response to sin and wrongdoing.

Although repentance is a human response, the opportunity to repent is extended to human beings by God. Because of God's patience, kindness and mercy, those involved in sin are given time to change their behavior. It is not merely non-Christians, however, who are given the opportunity to repent, but more commonly it is Christians who are afforded opportunities to repent of sins and wrongdoings. According to Hebrews, however, Christians who fall into apostasy are either no longer allowed to repent or are incapable of repenting.

Finally, there is also a slight distinction between μετανοέω and μεταμέλομαι in the New Testament. In the New Testament, μεταμέλομαι represents nothing more than regret or a change of mind regarding a specific decision. Μετανοέω and μετάνοια, however, represent a change in thinking that results in a reorientation of life. The New Testament makes it clear that repentance entails more than regret or a simple change of mind.

Early Christian Literature Outside of the New Testament

After the writing of the New Testament, the subject of repentance became increasingly important in the development of early Christianity;[464] however, since the objective of this chapter is to examine how μετανοέω and μετάνοια were used in the literary milieu inherited by the author of Luke-Acts, this section will be

---

[464] O. D. Watkins, *History of Penance* (2 vols.; London: Longmans and Green, 1920).

limited to those works that are thought to have been composed roughly around the same time as Luke-Acts.[465] There are no extant Christian writings outside of the New Testament that are thought to have been written before Luke-Acts, and there are very few writings thought to have been composed around the same time as Luke-Acts. One of the most important Christian documents thought to have been written around the time of Luke-Acts in which μετανοέω/μετάνοια plays a role is the so-called *First Epistle of Clement to the Corinthians*.

While *1 Clement* was one of the most widely known and authoritative writings in the early church—cited by several early church patriarchs, translated into three languages and attributed canonical status in the churches of Egypt and Syria[466]—there is no way of identifying the author of *1 Clement*. The letter represents itself as a writing of the Roman church, and gives no indication of the author's identity. That the author's name was Clement appears to have been the unanimous opinion of the ancient church.[467] While both Irenaeus and Eusebius claim that the author was Clement, the third successor of Peter as Bishop of Rome,[468] the most that can be said about the author's identity is that he was a leading personality in the church at Rome.

The letter is commonly dated to the end of the reign of Domitian (95 or 96 C.E.).[469] In the opening sentence of the letter, Clement writes, "Owing to the sudden and repeated misfortunes and calamities which have befallen us, we consider that our attention has been somewhat delayed in turning to the questions disputed among you."[470] Since in chapter five the author presents the persecution of Nero as something long past, the present persecution alluded to in the opening sentence of this letter most likely refers to the sporadic assaults that took place under Domitian.[471]

---

[465] All of the Greek texts and English translations found in this section are taken from Kirsopp Lake, *The Apostolic Fathers* (vol 1; Cambridge, MA: Harvard University Press, 1917).

[466] Johanness Quasten, *Patrology* (4 vols.; Westminster, MD: Christian Classics, 1992 [1950]) 1:42–53.

[467] Cf. Eusebius, *Eccl. Hist.* 4.22.1; 4.23.11; Hermas, *Vis.* 2.4.3

[468] *Adv. Haer.* 3.3.3; *Eccl. Hist.* 3.15.

[469] Laurence Welborn, "On the Date of First Clement," *Biblical Research* 29 (1985) 35–54. Eusebius claims that Clement began his reign as Bishop during the twelfth year of Domitian's reign, and concluded his bishopric during the third year of Trajan's reign (*Eccl. Hist.* 3.15, 34). This means Clement would have reigned as Bishop from 92 to 101 C.E.

[470] *1 Clem.* 1.1.

[471] Although some authors question whether or not 1.1 refers to persecution at all (E. T. Merrill, *Essays in Early Christian History* (London: Macmillan, 1924) 160), that it does refer to persecution seems to be supported by the fact the author follows the accounts of the persecution and suffering experienced by Peter, Paul and other Christian martyrs with the statement, "We are not only writing these things to you, beloved, for your admonition, but also to remind ourselves; for we are in the same arena, and the same struggle is before us" (7.1.). Because of how little is actually known about Christian persecution in general, and the alleged persecution that occurred during the reign of Domitian in particular, it is best to date the document between 75 and 100 C.E.

1 Clement addresses an outbreak of disputes within the church at Corinth. It appears that factions, severely reprimanded on occasions by Paul, were once again causing discord in the community. An ecclesiastical coup was taking place in the church as jealousy, envy and strife arose, and older leaders were deposed by young arrogant rebels seeking to gain control and leadership of the church in Corinth. Clement condemns jealousy and envy, and cites examples of the injustice, suffering and persecution resulting from these vices.[472] Clement then exhorts the Corinthians to repent and put away such vice from among them. He writes:

> Wherefore let us put aside empty and vain cares, and let us come to the glorious and venerable rule of our tradition, and let us see what is good and pleasing and acceptable in the sight of our Maker. Let us fix our gaze on the Blood of Christ, and let us know that it is precious to his Father, because it was poured out for our salvation, and brought the grace of repentance (μετανοίας) to all the world. Let us review all the generations, and let us learn that in generation after generation the Master has given a place of repentance (μετανοίας τόπον) to those who will turn to him. Noah preached repentance (μετάνοιαν) and those who obeyed were saved. Jonah foretold destruction to the men of Nineveh, but when they repented (μετανοήσαντες) they received forgiveness of their sins from God in answer to their prayers, and gained salvation, though they were aliens to God. The ministers of the grace of God spoke through the Holy Spirit concerning repentance (μετανοίας), even the Master of the universe himself spoke with an oath concerning repentance (μετανοίας); "For as I live, said the Lord, I do not desire the death of the sinner so much as his repentance (μετάνοιαν)," and he added a gracious declaration, "Repent (Μετανοήσατε), O house of Israel, from your iniquity. Say to the sons of my people, If your sins reach from the earth to Heaven, and if they be redder than scarlet, and blacker than sackcloth, and ye turn to me with all your hearts and say 'Father,' I will listen to you as a holy people." And in another place he speaks thus, "Wash you, and make you clean, put away your wickedness from your souls before my eyes, cease from your wickedness, learn to do good, seek out judgment, rescue the wronged, give judgment for the orphan, do justice to the widow, and come and let us reason together, saith the Lord; and if your sins be as crimson, I will make them white as snow, and if they be as scarlet, I will make them white as wool, and if ye be willing and hearken to me, ye shall eat the good things of the land, but if ye be not willing, and hearken not to me, a sword shall devour you, for the mouth of the Lord has spoken these things." Thus desiring to give to all his beloved a share in repentance (μετανοίας), he established it by his Almighty will.[473]

In this one exhortation the author uses μετανοέω and μετάνοια nine times. Repentance is without question the thrust of this exhortation. In the first reference

---

[472] *1 Clem.* 1–6.
[473] *1 Clem.* 7.2–8.5.

to repentance the author makes it clear that μετανοίας is for all the world, and the author closes the exhortation by stating that μετανοίας is for all of God's beloved. Within the exhortation itself the author declares that throughout history God has extended repentance to anyone willing to turn to God. The men of Nineveh were afforded an opportunity to repent, whereby gaining forgiveness of their sins and salvation, even "though they were aliens to God." The author clearly seeks to convey that repentance is for all people, and that all sins will be forgiven as a result of repentance.

The author also makes it clear that although repentance is a human response, it is made available to humanity by God. Through the blood of Jesus, God has made repentance available to everyone. It is God who provides the opportunity for repentance because God desires to see sinners repent rather than perish. God provides repentance as a means of avoiding destruction. Repentance secures for the sinner forgiveness of sins and salvation.

In language reminiscent of the ancient Jewish Scriptures, Clement conveys the idea that repentance entails a turning away from sin and a (re)turning to God.[474] However, repentance is not merely an act that addresses and corrects the relationship between God and the repentant sinner, repentance also addresses and corrects human relationships. In what appears to be a quotation from Ezekiel 33:11–27, Clement demonstrates that he understands repentance to entail both putting away wickedness and doing good. Repentance involves forsaking the wicked and unjust treatment of others. It involves learning to practice just and ethical behavior: delivering the wronged from injustice and defending the defenseless. Repentance corrects inappropriate relationships between alienated human beings, as well as between human beings and God.

This notion of repentance addressing and correcting inappropriate relationships between human beings, as well as between human beings and God, is also emphasized in the author's last two usages of μετάνοια. After chastising and rebuking the instigators of the discord in Corinth, Clement writes, "You therefore, who laid the foundation of the sedition, submit to the presbyters, and receive the correction of repentance (παιδεύθητε εἰς μετάνοιαν), bending the knees of your hearts. Learn to be submissive, putting aside the boastful and the haughty self-confidence of your tongue."[475] For the troublemakers in Corinth, repentance entailed their reinstating and correcting their relationship with the church leaders they had earlier deposed. It entailed their forsaking arrogance and pride, humbling and submitting themselves to the authority of the presbyters. Finally, as Clement begins closing his letter, the first point he makes by way of summary is how repentance addresses and corrects inappropriate relationships between human beings, as well

---

[474] In this exhortation, the author uses ἐπιστρέφω twice (7:5; 8:3).
[475] *1 Clem* 57.1–2.

as between human beings and God. Clement begins his summation:

> We have now written to you, brethren, sufficiently touching the things which befit our worship, and are most helpful for a virtuous life to those who wish to guide their steps in piety and righteousness. For we have touched on every aspect of faith and repentance (μετανοίας)..., and reminded you that you are bound to please almighty God with holiness in righteousness and truth and long-suffering, and to live in concord, bearing no malice, in love and peace with eager gentleness, even as our fathers, whose example we quoted, were well-pleasing in their humility towards God, the Father and Creator, and towards all men.[476]

Repentance is one of those things Clement considers most helpful for those who wish to live a virtuous and righteous life. Repentance enables one to have a righteous, patient, peaceful, pleasing and humble relationship with God and with other human beings.[477]

A few years after Clement's epistle to the Corinthians, Ignatius, Bishop of Antioch, composed seven epistles as a prisoner on his way to Rome—where he would experience martyrdom. Eusebius, in his *Chronicon*, fixes the date of Ignatius' martyrdom in 108 C.E. There is much debate, however, regarding this date. The commonly accepted dating for the letters is 100–118 C.E., with most scholars selecting a date around 110 C.E.[478]

---

[476] *1 Clem.* 65:1–2.

[477] Repentance plays an even more significant role in the so-called *Second Epistle of Clement to the Corinthians* and the *Pseudo-Clementines*.
2 *Clement* is not a letter but a sermon on self-control, repentance, and judgment. It is the earliest surviving Christian sermon. The author uses μετανοέω and μετάνοια twelve times in this sermon. However, it is universally recognized that 2 *Clement* was not written by the author of *1 Clement*. Furthermore, the author demonstrates dependence upon the canonical gospels, especially the Gospel of John (cf. *2 Clem* 9:5–6). Since *2 Clement* is thought to have been composed around 150 C.E., the use of μετανοέω and μετάνοια in it will not be considered in this study (for a discussion of *2 Clement* see K. Donfried, *The Setting of Second Clement* (NovTSup 38; Leiden: Brill, 1974)). The *Pseudo-Clementines*, with over forty occurrences of μετανοέω and μετάνοια, are thought to have been composed in the 3rd or 4th century (F. S. Jones "The Pseudo-Clementines: A History of Research," *SecCent* 2 (1982) 1–33, 63–96).

[478] W. Schoedel, *Ignatius of Antioch* (Hermenia; Philadelphia: Fortress, 1985). If written in the beginning years of the second century, the letters of Ignatius reflect the transitional period in Christianity when the diverse achievements of first century Christianity were just beginning to be secured and when organizational and doctrinal issues of the second century were beginning to be faced. However, the astonishing presence in so early a document of fully developed theological and ecclesiological themes such as theological reflection on the unity of God and the incarnation, the tensions caused by docetic christologies, the rise of gnosticism, the eucharist as the medicine of immortality, the emergence of the three-fold ministry, the vivid depiction of the hierarchical dignity and prestige accorded a bishop, and the use of the term 'Catholic Church' to denote the faithful collectively has caused some scholars to question the authenticity of these letters (R. Jolly, *Le dossier d'Ignace d'Antioche* (Brussels: Éditions de l'université, 1979); J. Rius-Camps, *The Four Authentic Letters of Ignatius, the Martyr* (Christianismos 2; Rome: Pontificium

The Meaning of Repentance   141

Six of the letters are addressed to Christian communities, while one is addressed to Bishop Polycarp of Smyrna. There are seven occurrences of μετανοέω and μετάνοια in what are generally believed to be the genuine epistles of Ignatius.[479] The letters of Ignatius suggest that he understands repentance to entail a change in thinking with regard to Jesus and Church doctrine. In the first three chapters of his letter to the Smyrnaeans, Ignatius opposes docetic teachings that are being circulated. Ignatius tells his readers to avoid those individuals spreading what he considers to be false doctrines about Jesus, and to "pray for them, if perchance they might repent (μετανοήσωσιν), difficult though that be,—but Jesus Christ who is our true life has the power over this."[480] He goes on to write, "There are some who ignorantly deny him. . . . Now I have not thought right to put into writing their unbelieving names; but would that I might not even remember them, until they repent (μετανοήσωσιν) concerning the Passion, which is our resurrection."[481]

For those spreading false views about Jesus, repentance entails changing those views and accepting the traditional Christological doctrines of the Church. The author also indicates that he understands repentance to entail changing one's views when those views oppose other accepted doctrines of the Church, as well as when they challenge established Church leadership. In his letter to the Smyrnaeans, Ignatius writes:

> See that you all follow the bishop, as Jesus Christ follows the Father, and the presbytery as if it were the Apostles. And reverence the deacons as the command of God. Let no one do any of the things appertaining to the Church without the bishop. . . . Moreover it is reasonable for us to return to soberness, while we still have time to repent (μετανοεῖν) towards God. It is good to know God and the bishop. He who honours the bishop has been honoured by God; he who does anything without the knowledge of the bishop is serving the devil.[482]

The context clearly conveys that repentance is a necessary human act directed toward God when one has disobeyed the will and commandment of God by dishonoring the Church and it's leadership. For the author, repentance entails

---

Institutum Orientalium Studiorum, 1979); For a negative critique of these views, see Schoedel, "Are the Letters of Ignatius of Antioch Authentic?" *RelSRev* 2 (1980) 195–201).

[479] These occurrences are found in *Eph.* 10:1; *Phld.* 3:2; 8:1 (x2); *Smyrn.* 4:1; 5:3; 9:1. There are also eight additional occurrences of μετανοέω and μετάνοια found in a later recension of these epistles. The textual history of the seven letters of Ignatius is extremely complicated (cf. Schoedel, *Ignatius*; V. Corwin *St. Ignatius and Christianity in Antioch* (New Haven: Yale University Press, 1960)). The authenticity of what is commonly called the "middle recension" is generally accepted by scholars; while the so-called "long recension" is usually regarded as a 4th century revision of the letters. Since the "long recension" represents a much later revision, the eight occurrences of μετανοέω and μετάνοια found in the long recension will not be considered in this study.
[480] *Smyrn.* 4:1
[481] *Smyrn.* 5:1–3.
[482] *Smyrn.* 8:1–9:1.

changing one's views regarding Church leadership. Those who have not submitted to the established Church leadership, and who have been involved in conducting Church affairs without the approval of the bishop need to repent, because their dishonoring of the Church's leaders represents a dishonoring of God. This view is also conveyed by Ignatius in his letter to the Philadelphians. He tells the Christians in Philadelphia, "For as many as belong to God and Jesus Christ,—these are with the bishop. And as many as repent (μετανοήσαντες) and come to the unity of the Church,—these also shall be of God, to be living according to Jesus Christ."[483]

The author encourages adherence to the doctrines of the Church and allegiance to the Church leaders because the author is concerned with maintaining the unity of the Church. The author explicitly makes this point when he writes, "I then did my best as a man who was set on unity. But where there is division and anger God does not dwell. The lord then forgives all who repent (μετανοοῦσιν), if their repentance (μετανοήσωσιν) leads to the unity of God and the council of the bishop."[484] Once again repentance involves changing one's mind regarding any views which threaten the unity of the Church and challenge the leadership of the bishop.

For this early second century bishop, repentance represents the necessary change of mind in response to heterodoxy. Ultimately, repentance seeks to establish unity in the Church and allegiance to the established Church leadership. Unlike much of the earlier Christian and Jewish literature, there is no eschatological aspect to repentance found in the letters of Ignatius. The author is far less concerned with any impending judgment than he is with the present disunity, which threatens the future survival of the Church.

There is also one occurrence of μετάνοια in the *Epistle of Barnabas*. The document is an anonymous Christian tractate composed after 70 C.E. and before 135 C.E.[485] The author's purpose is to disseminate traditional material, in order that the readers' knowledge and faith may be perfected.[486] In a section dealing with the correct understanding of the temple, the author distinguishes between the physical temple built with hands and the true temple of God. The author asserts that the Jews "erred by putting their hope on the building, and not on the God who made them."[487] The author asserts that although the Jewish temple has been destroyed, a temple of God does exist, and this temple "shall be built gloriously in the name of the Lord."[488] The author further writes to his apparently Gentile audience, "Before we

---

[483] *Phld.* 3:2.
[484] *Phld.* 8:1.
[485] The reference to the destruction of the temple by the enemy places the composition after 70 C.E., and the expectation that the temple would be rebuilt by the servants of the enemy (16:3–4) most likely places the composition after Hadrian's founding in 130 C.E. of *Colonia Aelia Capitolina*, as Jerusalem was to be called, and before the completion the Roman temple to the Capitoline Triad (Jupiter, Minerva, and Juno) in 135 C.E. The Roman temple was built on the cite of the former Jewish temple.
[486] *Barn.* 1:5 (cf. 4:9; 19:1; 21:1).
[487] *Barn.* 16:1.
[488] *Barn.* 16:6.

believed in God the habitation of our heart was corrupt and weak, like a temple really built with hands, because it was full of idolatry, and was the house of demons through doing things which were contrary to God."[489] He continues:

> When we received the remission of sins, and put our hope on the Name, we became new, being created again from the beginning; wherefore God truly dwells in us, in the habitation which we are. How? His word of faith, the calling of his promise, the wisdom of the ordinances, the commands of the teaching, himself prophesying in us, himself dwelling in us, by opening the door of the temple (that is the mouth) to us, giving repentance (μετάνοιαν) to us, and thus he leads us, who have been enslaved to death into the incorruptible temple....This is a spiritual temple being built for the Lord.[490]

The author makes it clear to his Gentile audience that God now dwells in them. After placing their hope on the Name—which most likely denotes the name of Jesus—they became new, being rebuilt. Spiritual (re)construction began taking place in their lives. There is now a spiritual temple being built for the Lord within them. This spiritual renewing is the result of repentance (μετάνοιαν) being granted to them by God. Although the Jewish temple has been destroyed, repentance has led these believers into the true temple of God and has delivered them from the bondage of death.

The author does not explicitly state what repentance entails. However, by contrasting the time before they believed in God with the time after they put their hope on the Name, the context clearly suggests that repentance for these non-Jews entailed changing their opinion about God. It entailed going from unbelief to belief, and placing their hopes on the name of Jesus.

Finally, there are two occurrences of μετανοέω found in the *Didache*. The *Didache* is a compact handbook of Christian ethical and liturgical community instructions. It represents the earliest of a series of Church Orders. There is much dispute regarding the date of the *Didache*: scholars have dated the work as early as the middle of the first century and as late as the beginning of the third century.[491]

---

[489] *Barn.* 16:7. Although the traditions passed on by the author reflect the teachings of Judaism, this passage seems clearly to suggest that the author and his readers were Gentiles, who were most likely familiar with Jewish traditions (This is also conveyed in 15:8 where the author stresses the celebration of the eighth day of the week, i.e. Sunday, instead of the Sabbath of the Jews because Sunday is the day of the resurrection).

[490] *Barn.* 16:7–10.

[491] Although most scholars date the *Didache* around the middle of the second century, there are a few scholars who assign the *Didache* to the first century (J. A. Kleist, *The Didache* (Ancient Christian Writers 6; Westminster, MD: The Newman Press, 1948); Rordorf and Tuilier, *La doctrine des douze apôtres (Didache): Introduction, Texte, Tradition. Notes, Appendice et Index* (SC 248; Paris: Editions du Cerf, 1978); J. P. Audet, *La Didachè. Instructions des apôtres* (Paris: J. Gabalde, 1958), dates it as early as 60 C.E.). Other scholars, however, assign it to the late second or early third century (cf. F. E. Vokes, "The Didache—Still Debated," *CQ* 3 (1970) 57–62.).

In a section dealing with the final prayer to be given after celebrating the Eucharist, the author exhorts Christians to conclude the prayer by saying, "Let grace come and let this world pass away. Hosannah to the God of David. If any man be holy, let him come! if any man be not, let him repent (μετανοείτω): Maran atha, Amen."[492] Although the author does not explicitly state what repentance entails, the author does make it clear that repentance is required of those who are living an unholy life. The context suggests that repentance involves some type of change in thinking and or behavior whereby someone living an unholy life begins living a holy life. Since the exhortation to repent immediately precedes the request for the Lord to come (i.e. μαρὰν ἀθά), the context also suggests that repentance provides a means of escape from the judgment of the Lord.

The only other occurrence of μετανοέω indicates that repentance is the appropriate response from someone who has mistreated a fellow human being. The author instructs Christians to "reprove one another not in wrath but in peace as you find in the Gospel, and let none speak with any who has done a wrong to his neighbour, nor let him hear a word from you until he repents."[493] Once again that author does not explicitly state what repentance entails, but the context clearly conveys that repentance involves correcting injustices done against one's neighbor.

Since the *Didache* functions as an instructional handbook for Christian communities, the fact that the author does not explicitly state what μετανοέω entails indicates that he felt his Christian audience fully understood what it meant to repent. The author's use of μετανοέω is most likely consistent with that found in the Christian literature of the time. Repentance involved a change in thinking and behavior. It entailed turning away from sin and inappropriate behavior. The use of μετανοέω in the *Didache* also indicates that repentance was something expected and required of Christians as well as non-Christians.

1 Clement, the letters of Ignatius, the *Epistle of Barnabas* and the *Didache* all reflect the Christian understanding of μετανοέω and μετάνοια current around the time of the writing of Luke-Acts. These early Christian writings indicate that most Christians believed that God made repentance available to all people, even those who may have at one time been aliens to God. Repentance was the means by which sins were forgiven and salvation obtained. Repentance represented the appropriate human response to sin and wrong doing. It entailed a change in thinking and behavior that sought to address and correct one's relationship with God and Jesus, one's relationship with other human beings, and—as was the case in the late first and early second century—one's relationship with the Church. In these early Christian writings, repentance reconciled previously alienated parties, because it entailed turning away from inappropriate treatment of and inappropriate relationships with others.

---

[492] *Did.* 10:6.
[493] *Did.* 15:3.

Chapter Four

The Role and Function of Repentance in Luke-Acts

As evidenced by their usage in the larger literary milieu, μετανοέω and μετάνοια essentially mean a change in thinking that usually leads to a change in behavior and or way of life. This is also the meaning that is found in the two-volume work of Luke-Acts. Although there is a degree of truth to Bailey's assertion "that Luke's understanding of repentance is unique in its religio-historical context,"[1] the author of Luke-Acts does not ascribe some novel or unique meaning to μετανοέω and μετάνοια. Instead, he employs the meaning he inherited from Greco-Roman, Jewish, and early Christian literature. That which may be considered unique is not the meaning of repentance in Luke-Acts, but rather the role and function of repentance within the author's narrative.

Unlike in most literary narratives, in Luke-Acts the motif of repentance plays a central role in the development and meaning of the author's story. In Luke-Acts repentance is not only a change in thinking that represents an appropriate response to inappropriate thoughts and/or actions, repentance is also a necessary change in thinking and behavior required of individuals in order to help fulfill God's plan of universal salvation and to help establish a community embracing all people.[2]

Countless scholars have written about the centrality of the theme of universal salvation in Luke-Acts;[3] however, the author of Luke-Acts is not merely concerned

---

[1] *Repentance in Luke-Acts*, 5.

[2] As discussed in Chapter Two, the outworking of God's plan of universal salvation is the principle theme of Luke-Acts, and within that theme the motif of repentance forms an important subtheme.

[3] K. N. Giles, "Salvation in Lukan Theology," *RTR* 42 (1983) 10–16; K. P. Donfried, "Attempt at Understanding the Purpose of Luke-Acts. Christology and the Salvation of the Gentiles," *Christological Perspectives* (eds. R. F. Berkey and S. A. Edwards; New York: Pilgrim, 1982) 112–122; N. A. Dahl, "The Story of Abraham in Luke-Acts," *Studies in*

with emphasizing the universality of salvation, he is also concerned with emphasizing the required change in thinking and living that will enable diverse individuals to receive the salvation of God and to live together as a community of God's people. For the author, the plan of God involves making salvation accessible—through Jesus—to all flesh. Everyone, therefore, is now eligible for membership in the community of God's people. Such inclusivity, however, requires a fundamental change in thinking on the part of many in the emerging religious community of Luke-Acts, a community with which the author's audience surely could have identified.[4] Repentance in Luke-Acts represents a fundamental change in thinking that enables diverse individuals to receive the salvation of God and to live together as a community of God's people, and, according to the author, it is an essential element in the preaching of John the Baptist, Jesus, and the apostles.

Repentance in the Preaching of John the Baptist

As stated earlier, chapter three marks the beginning of what the author considers to be the gospel tradition.[5] At the very outset the author suggests that he understands repentance to represent a fundamental change in thinking that permanently and radically alters the way things use to be. In the author's narration

---

Luke-Acts (eds. L. Keck and J. Martyn; Philadelphia: Fortress, 1980) 139–158; N. M. Flanagan, "The What and How of Salvation in Luke-Acts," *Sin, Salvation, and the Spirit* (ed. D. Durken; Collegeville, MN: Liturgical Press, 1979) 203–213; R. P. Martin, "Salvation and Discipleship in Luke's Gospel," *Int* 30 (1976) 366–380; Wilson, S. G. *The Gentiles and the Gentile Mission in Luke-Acts* (London: Cambridge University, 1973); N. Q. King, "The 'Universalism' of the Third Gospel," *SE I* (TU 73, 1959) 199–205;

[4] There has been much debate concerning the composition of Luke's audience. Most scholars maintain that the author's audience is entirely or predominately Gentile (e.g. J. Fitzmyer, *The Gospel*, 1:57–59; J. T. Sanders, *The Jews in Luke-Acts* (Philadelphia: Fortress, 1987) passim), while a few suggest a Jewish-Christian audience (e.g. J. Jervell, *Luke and the People of God: A New Look at Luke-Acts* (Minneapolis: Augsburg, 1972) 41–74; 153–183; idem, "The Church of Jews and Godfearers," *Luke-Acts and the Jewish People: Eight Critical Perspectives* (ed. J. B. Tyson; Minneapolis, MN: Augsburg, 1988) 11–20; M. Salmon, "Insider or Outsider? Luke's Relationship with Judaism," *Luke-Acts and the Jewish People* 76–82). However, as suggested by the Lukan canticle of Simeon—in which Jesus is declared to be a "light for revelation to the Gentiles and for glory to... Israel" (Luke 2:32)—as well as by the Lukan emphasis on universal salvation and universal inclusion within the community of God's people, Luke's audience was most likely a socially diverse group, composed of individuals of different ethnic, religious and socio-economic backgrounds (for a discussion of the various opinions regarding the Lukan audience, see Mary Moscato, "Current Theories Regarding the Audience of Luke-Acts," *CurTM* 3 (1976) 355–361).

[5] This is attested by a number of factors: 1) the account now begins to correspond to Mark 1; 2) the author explicitly regards the information conveyed in chapter three as the beginning of the Gospel tradition (cf. Acts 10:37; see also 1:22; 13:24; Luke 16:16); 3) the author begins the chapter with a long periodic sentence resembling (although not as carefully constructed) that of the prologue (the sentence clearly marks a fresh start in the story); 4) John the Baptist is introduced anew, as if the reader had not been introduced to him in the first two chapters.

of the appearance of John the Baptist, he extends the prophetic reference from Second Isaiah found in Mark and Matthew. Although most scholars point to Luke's emphasis on universal salvation as the reason for and outcome of extending the quote from Second Isaiah, universal salvation is not the only implication of Luke's redactional activity. By extending the quote from Second Isaiah, the author implies that repentance is analogous to the filling in of valleys, the leveling of hills and mountains, the straightening (εὐθύς) of crooked places (σκολιά) and the smoothing out of rough places.[6] Tannehill writes, "this drastic transformation of a terrain that obstructs travel becomes a symbol of the repentance that the Lord's coming requires."[7]

In Luke's gospel, the preaching of John the Baptist explicitly identifies repentance as a radical and fundamental change in the way people think about and interact with others. As the previously examined literary evidence has indicated, changes in thinking may be demonstrated in a number of ways. In Luke-Acts, when the change involves a change in the way people think about and interact with others, such a change is commonly demonstrated by ethical social behavior.[8] As a result of the preaching of John the Baptist, the author immediately establishes that he wants his implied reader to associate repentance with ethical social behavior that enables once alienated people to live together as a community of God's people.

Repentance as a Responsibility and a Possibility

The ethical preaching activity of John the Baptist (Lk 3:10–14), which serves as an exposition of what it means to "Bear fruits worthy of repentance," is unique to Luke's gospel.[9] The presentation of John the Baptist as a prophetic preacher calling for repentance (3:1–6) is shared by all three of the synoptic gospel writers, as is the initial portion of the messianic preaching activity of John (3:16a). Furthermore, the eschatological preaching activity of John (3:7b–9), as well as the latter portion of John's messianic preaching activity (3:16b–17) is shared by

---

[6] As discussed above in Chapter Two, it is specifically the preaching of "repentance for the remission of sins" that was foretold "in the book of the words of the prophet Isaiah." Furthermore, the images of crooked and straight both appear in other contexts where repentance is important. In the preaching of Peter a connection is made between repentance and saving oneself from the crooked (σκολιᾶς) generation of which one is a part (Acts 2:38–40), and after being told that his heart is not right (εὐθεῖα; lit. "straight") before God, Simon, the former magician, is told to repent in order that the intent of his heart might be forgiven (Acts 8:21–22). In another passage clearly meant to echo Luke 3:4–5, Paul rebukes the magician Elymas for distorting "the straight paths of the Lord (τὰς ὁδοὺς [τοῦ] κυρίου τὰς εὐθείας)" (Acts 13:10).

[7] *Narrative Unity*, v.1, p. 48.

[8] Fitzmyer states that repentance in the gospel of Luke "connotes a new beginning in moral conduct" (*The Gospel*, 1:237).

[9] Similar ethical concerns do occur, however, in Jewish literature from the Old Testament to Rabbinic Judaism (see J. Sahlin, "Die Früchte der Umkehr: Die ethische Verkündigung Johannes des Taüfers nach Lk 3:10–14," *ST* 1 (1948) 54–68).

Matthew and Luke, and is attributed to Q. It is only the ethical preaching activity of John that is limited to Luke's gospel.[10] The author seeks to emphasize the ethical social dimensions associated with John's preaching of repentance.[11]

In the ancient Jewish scriptures, bearing (good) fruit is usually not something that is commanded of people but something that results from being in relationship with God. God produces fruit in the lives of those in relationship with God.[12] Although such fruit is sometimes associated with human behavior, this human behavior is not the result of human resolve or human power, but rather the result of fellowship with God. Fruit in such a context is contingent upon the power of God at work in one's life.[13] In the preaching of John the Baptist, however, bearing fruit is something that people have to do on their own.[14] It is a human responsibility, not a divine obligation.[15]

---

[10] Although a few scholars (e.g. A. Plummer, *A Critical and Exegetical Commentary on the Gospel According to St. Luke* (Edinburgh: T&T Clark, 1922) 90; H. Schürmann, *Das Lukasevangelium* (Freiburg: Herder, 1982) 169) believe the ethical preaching activity of John the Baptist (Luke 3:10–14) comes from Q, being omitted by Matthew, most scholars attribute the verses to either Lukan source material or Lukan composition.

[11] Josephus describes John's preaching and baptism in ethical terms. He writes, "Herod had him [John] put to death, though he was a good man and had exhorted the Jews to lead righteous lives, to practice justice towards their fellows and piety toward God, and so doing to join in baptism. In his view this was a necessary preliminary if baptism was to be acceptable to God. They must not employ it [i.e. baptism] to gain pardon for whatever sins they committed, but as a consecration of the body implying that the soul was already thoroughly cleansed by right behavior" (*Ant.* 18.5.2).

[12] Cf 2 Kgs 19:30–31; Ps 1:1–3, Jer 17:7–8; Hos 14:5–8. This holds true except in the cases in which fruit represents offspring. In such cases individuals are frequently commanded to bear fruit.

[13] This is also the notion conveyed in New Testament passages such as Gal 5:22–25, Phil 1:9–11, and John 15:4–5. After studying the theories of W. Bauer and R. Bultmann, who attribute the notion of fruitfulness in the Gospel of John to Gnostic and Mandean sources, Borig finds the Jewish background for this notion of fruitfulness far more plausible (see R. Borig *Der wahre Weinstock* (Munich: Kösel, 1967) 135–187).

[14] Contra Tannehill and others who seem to eliminate any sense of human moral culpability or responsibility with assertions such as "People do not turn in a new direction of their own power" (*Luke*; p. 78). Why would John the Baptist command people to repent and to bear fruit worthy of repentance if it were impossible for them to do it on their own? Repentance as a means of securing forgiveness and salvation is a gift to humanity from God (Lk 5:32; Acts 5:31; 11:18; 17:30), but it is still humanity's responsibility to repent.

[15] The author of Luke-Acts further stresses this idea in the Lukan composition, 13:1–9, and in his presentation of Jesus' explanation of the Parable of the Sower (Luke 8:11–15; par. Mark 4:13–20, Matt 13:18–23). In Luke 13:1–9 the author follows a pronouncement story (vv. 1–5) that stresses the necessity of repentance with an interpretive parable (vv. 6–9) that emphasizes the human responsibility to bear fruit. In Luke's account of Jesus' explanation of the Parable of the Sower, Jesus explicitly states that it is the person's responsibility to "believe and be saved" (8:12c). More importantly, the author also eliminates from the explanation of Jesus any expression regarding the degree of fruitfulness (cf Mark 4:20; Matt 13:23); stressing instead the human responsibility to hold fast to the word of God with "an honest and good heart" and to "bear fruit with patient endurance" (Luke 8:15). As a result of this latter redactional activity, Luke's explanation emphasizes only the human responsibility aspect of the parable.

The command "Bear fruit(s) worthy of repentance" suggests that John the Baptist believed that those who choose to repent are obligated to bear fruits that attested to their repentance.[16] Although the crowds came out to participate in a "baptism of repentance," the baptism by itself is meaningless unless the people bear fruits that attest to their repentance. Bearing fruits authenticates and renders visible the change in thinking involved in repentance. According to the preaching of John, as recorded in the *Q* tradition, repentance is a change in thinking that must be accompanied by a change in behavior.

The *Q* material clearly indicates that repentance requires fruit, but *Q* fails to make explicit what that fruit looks like. *Q* gives no indication of what exactly is expected. It neglects to state for the reader how life should be lived, even though "the ax is lying at the root of the trees" (Luke 3:9; Matt 3:10). The "fruit worthy of repentance" is not the focus of the *Q* passage, nor is it the focus of Matthew's usage of the *Q* passage. Instead, the eschatological preaching of doom is the focus of the preaching of John the Baptist preserved in *Q* and conveyed in Matthew (3:7–12).[17] The addition of the ethical preaching activity of John the Baptist in Luke, however, clearly makes the "fruits worthy of repentance" the focus of the Lukan baptist preaching unit (Luke 3:7–18).[18]

The author shifts the emphases away from the imminent judgment and impending wrath of God and onto the "fruits worthy of repentance," which provide escape from the wrath of God.[19] Matthew does not give examples of fruit worthy of repentance because in Matthew the Pharisees and Sadducees are incapable of bearing "fruit worthy of repentance," and therefore unable to escape the wrath to come. In Matthew, John's eschatological and messianic preaching does not hold out hope, but instead announces the wrath to come and stresses the doom of the

---

[16] As discussed above in Chapter Two, the importance to the author of the motif of "bearing fruit" that attest to one's repentance is demonstrated by the author's placing of a similar phrase in the mouth of the apostle Paul. The first command given with regard to repentance is John's command to "Bear fruits worthy of repentance," and the last reference to repentance in the author's two volume work is Paul's description of his declaration to the Gentiles to "perform deeds worthy of repentance" (Acts 26:20).

[17] One theme that is universally recognized as characterizing much of the *Q* material is that of eschatological warning and imminent judgment (cf. C. M. Tuckett, "Q (Gospel Source)," *Anchor Bible Dictionary* 6 vols (New York: Doubleday, 1992) 5:569; R. A. Edwards, *A Theology of Q: Eschatology, Prophecy, and Wisdom* (Philadelphia: Fortress, 1976) 55, 81).

[18] In an examination of the structure and genre of Luke 3:10–14, E. Scheffler, "The Social Ethics of the Lukan Baptist," *Neot* 24, 1 (1990) 26, demonstrates how the passage "actually forms the center of John's preaching, although 3:15–17 can be regarded as its climax."

[19] Several passages in Luke-Acts indicate that the author understood repentance as providing a means of escape from the wrath of God (cf. Lk 10:13–14; 11:32; 13:1–5; 16:27–30; Acts 8:22–24; 17:30–31).

religious leaders.[20] In Luke, however, the insertion of the ethical preaching of John the Baptist between his eschatological and messianic preaching, as well as the redaction made to both the eschatological and messianic preaching of John the Baptist, clearly places the emphasis of John's preaching on the fact that repentance is a possibility, and that deliverance is indeed available to everyone who bears "fruits worthy of repentance."[21]

Those who respond to the preaching of John the Baptist demonstrate recognition of their responsibility to bear fruit by asking the question, "What then shall we do?"[22] Identifying exactly what repentance entails is very important to the author of Luke-Acts. This is indicated by the author's inclusion of the ethical preaching activity of John the Baptist, which identifies various fruits the author considers to be indicative of repentance.[23] In the Lukan account, John the Baptist identifies fruits required of specific groups of people as well as fruits required of people in general.

Luke's use of the plural, "fruits worthy," represents one of only three differences in wording between Luke's and Matthew's eschatological preaching section.[24] The changing of καρπὸν ἄξιον to καρποὺς ἀξίους helps to establish

---

[20] Matthew gives an extremely negative portrayal of the Pharisees, Sadducees and other religious leaders. They are commonly portrayed as "blind." They are incapable of seeing the truth (15:14; 23:16, 17, 19, 24, 26), and incapable of receiving revelation from God (2:1–12; 9:6–8; 11:25–27; 28:11–15). They are incapable, therefore, of repenting of their sins. Not only are they blind, they are also "evil" (9:4; 12:34, 39, 45; 16:4; 22:18). The concept of evil (πονηρός) plays a prominent role in the narrative world of Matthew. To be evil implies a relentless opposition to God and a fundamental association with the devil, who in Matthew is known as "the evil one" (13:19, 38). Throughout Matthew, judgment has already been pronounced on the religious leaders. On three occasions they are described with the epithet "brood of vipers" (3:7; 12:34; 23:32). They are also identified as "a child of hell" (23:15). Matthew even suggests that because of their unrighteousness, they will never enter the kingdom of heaven (5:20).

[21] The use of προσδοκῶντος in 3:15, as well as παρακαλῶν and εὐηγγελίζετο in the summary and generalizing statement of 3:18, clearly indicates that the author considered John's preaching to represent hope, encouragement, and good news rather than gloom and doom. Both παρακαλέω and εὐαγελλίζω are used throughout Luke-Acts for exhorting, teaching and preaching, but never for announcing doom. Furthermore, with Q material preceding and following it, the social ethical teaching of 3:10–14 serves to soften the harsh and severe judgment preaching of the Q tradition.

[22] Luke 3:10, 12, 14. This is a characteristic Lukan literary device employed by the author throughout his two-volume narrative as a way of introducing what the author believes to be required human behavior (cf Luke 10:25; 18:18; Acts 2:37; 16:30; 22:10; in Acts 2:37, Peter responds to the question, "What shall we do?" with the command, "Repent"). The questions enable the readers to identify more closely with the characters in the narrative as they hear questions and answers that most likely apply to their own situation.

[23] Since these fruits are associated with the earliest occurrence of the motif of repentance, they influence the reader's understanding of repentance throughout the remainder of Luke-Acts. From this point forward the reader will expect this type of social-ethical behavior to be associated with repentance.

[24] Sixty out of sixty-three (Matthew) / sixty-four (Luke) words in the Greek text of these verses are identical (Although a couple of manuscripts retain the singular spelling for

a link between the pericope taken from *Q* and the ethical preaching activity of John found in Luke. The question τί ποιήσωμεν, "what shall we do" (3:10, 12, 14), is in direct response to the command, "Bear fruits worthy of repentance" (3:8), as well as to the warning for the people not to trust in their ancestral connection to Abraham as a way of escaping the impending wrath of God.[25] Since those being addressed by John can no longer trust in their ancestral heritage, they ask John what type of behavior will attest to their repentance and protect them "from the wrath to come." The use of καρποὺς ἀξίους rather than καρπὸν ἄξιον allows the author to identify a number of specific changes in behavior as "fruits worthy of repentance." The changing of καρπὸν ἄξιον to καρποὺς ἀξίους sets the stage for the ethical preaching of John that follows.

Unlike Matthew, Luke introduces John's preaching activity by indicating that John addresses "the crowds (ὄχλοι)" rather than simply "the Pharisees and Sadducees."[26] This is the first of many instances of the uniquely Lukan use of ὄχλος.[27] The author frequently uses ὄχλος to designate an anonymous audience that witnesses the ministry of John the Baptist or Jesus.[28] Such a use of the term alludes to the universal scope of their ministries (especially that of Jesus) and emphasizes the universal aspect of the author's gospel.

---

fruit, e.g. *Codex Bezae* [D] and *Washington Codex* [W], the plural is attested by most manuscripts).

[25] This notion of Israel's physical descent from Abraham serving as protection from God's wrath is depicted in rabbinic literature (cf. H. Strack and P. Billerbeck, *Kommentar zum Neun Testament* (6 vols.; Munich: Beck, 1922–1961) 1:116–121). Later in the Luke, the author demonstrates that Abrahamic descent is not enough to protect one from God's wrath when a rich man's appeal to "father Abraham" is of no avail (16:24, 27, 30). The passage is linked to the Lukan preaching of John the Baptist by the fact that the rich man did not share his substance with a poor man named Lazarus. If Abrahamic descent is to have any importance at all, it must be accompanied by a concern for those who have been wronged (Luke 19:8–10).

[26] Luke makes no direct reference to Pharisees and Sadducees as does Matthew, because in Luke the preaching of John the Baptist is not meant to function as a condemnation of the religious leaders. Although the Pharisees rejected God's plan of repentance for themselves (Lk 7:30), the religious leaders are not portrayed by the author as unworthy of repentance simply on the basis of who they are. According to the author, there were some believers in the early Christian community who belonged—or at least at one time had belonged—to the party of the Pharisees (Acts 15:5). The author also notes that Paul was a Pharisee (Acts 23:6; 26:5). The invitation to repentance is repeatedly extended to the religious leaders throughout Luke-Acts, but their own self-righteousness prevents most of them from recognizing their need for repentance (cf. Lk 5:31–32; 7:41; 10:29; 15:7; 16:15; 18:9–12; *et. al.*). One of the things that makes Luke-Acts so tragic is not that the religious leaders were rejected because of who they were, but that because of who they were they rejected the repeated invitations of God.

[27] While there are uses of ὄχλος that the author has in common with Mark (cf 5:19; 8:4, 19, 40, 42, 45; 9:37, 38; 22:47) and Matthew (6:17; 7:24; 8:4, 19; 9:11, 12, 16, 37; 11:14; 22:47), most of the uses are uniquely Lukan (3:7, 10; 4:42; 5:1, 3, 15, 29; 6:17, 19; 7:9, 11, 12; 9:18; 11:27, 29; 12:1, 13, 54; 13:14, 17; 14:25; 18:36; 19:3, 39; 22:6; 23:4, 48)

[28] Luke 3:7, 10; 4:42; 5:1, 3, 15; 7:9, 11, 12; 9:18; 11:27, 29; 12:1, 13, 54; 13:14, 17; 14:25; 18:36; 19:3, 39; 22:6; 23:4, 48.

The use of ὄχλοι in 3:7 and 3:10 helps the author link his unique ethical preaching section (3:10–14) to the eschatological preaching section taken from Q.[29] It also gives way to the use of λαός, "people," in 3:15, 18. In Luke, everyone—not merely the Pharisees and Sadducees—needs to "Bear fruits worthy of repentance."

The Fruits Worthy of Repentance

The answer that John the Baptist gives to the question asked by the ὄχλοι reflects what people in general are expected to do in response to the command "Bear fruits worthy of repentance."[30] John tells the ὄχλοι—everyone gathered who has food and clothing in excess of what is needed in order to survive—to share their excess with those who have nothing. John is not simply addressing the wealthy; he is addressing everyone—the ὄχλοι.[31] By means of the ethical preaching of John the Baptist, the author indicates that everyone has a responsibility to share their substance with those who have nothing.[32]

---

[29] It is difficult to say whether "the Pharisees and Sadducees" belonged originally to Q, or whether Matthew has introduced the designation for his own theological purposes; however, given the address, "Brood of vipers," it is easier to imagine John the Baptist addressing a specific segment of people (e.g. Pharisees and Sadducees) rather than an entire crowd. Furthermore, given the uniquely Lukan use of ὄχλος, it is also easy to imagine the author having substituted ὄχλοι for "the Pharisees and Sadducees."

[30] Unlike Matthew's use of Pharisees and Sadducees, Luke's use of ὄχλοι allows John's preaching to speak to people in general.

[31] A tunic (χιτών; 3:11) was an undergarment worn either against the bare skin or over a linen shirt (W. Rebell, "χιτών" EDNT, 3:468). It was worn by both rich and poor, and together with a ἱμάτιον constituted one's clothing (Luke 6:29). Even though the rich are frequently rebuked by the author of Luke-Acts for their failure to share with the poor (Luke 6:24; 12:16–21; 16:19–26; 18:22–25), the modern interpreter should not assume that the wealthy are the only ones being exhorted to share food and clothing (the view of Bailey, Luke 149; P. Hollenbach, "Social Aspects of John the Baptizer's Preaching Mission in the Context of Palestinian Judaism," ANRW II.19.1 (1979) 870). Possessing two tunics does not in any way indicate wealth. Virtually all people, with the exception of the poorest of the poor (i.e. beggars—e.g. Lazarus) possessed a change of underclothing. According to Josephus two tunics were usually taken on journeys, even by slaves (Ant. 17.136; cf Luke 9:3). John the Baptist commands all those with food and two tunics to share with those who have none. The words of John the Baptist foreshadow Jesus' teachings about love and sharing (cf. 6:30–36). As will be demonstrated later, the teachings of Jesus in Luke's gospel often reflect "fruits worthy of repentance."

[32] The verb μεταδίδωμι, "share," not only conveys the notion of sharing in the sense of jointly possessing, it also conveys the notion of relinquishing by giving or imparting to others (cf. Rom 1:11; 12:8; Eph 4:28). This is also conveyed in the Hellenistic notion of charitable giving (cf. Seneca Epistles 81.15–20; Plutarch Moralia [Philosophers and Men in Power] 778C). The notion of jointly possessing (i.e. communal sharing) is also emphasized in the book of Acts, where it is recorded that the first believers "had all things in common; they would sell their possessions and goods and distributed the proceeds to all, as any had need" (2:44b–45; cf 4:34–35). For an examination of this practice in the early church, see M. Hengel, Property and Riches in the Early Church: Aspects of a Social History of Early Christianity (trans. J. Bowden; Philadelphia: Fortress, 1974) 3–8, 54–59. This is also consistent with Hellenistic practice of sharing possessions (see Plato The Republic 3.416C–E; 4.424A; 5.449C; Aristotle Nicomachean Ethics 8.9.1159B; Strabo

This is most likely a principle that the author is trying to convey to his readers. Although John Donahue is correct when he asserts that recent scholarship has made a valuable contribution to Lukan studies by demonstrating that the author of Luke-Acts was primarily addressing the more prosperous and powerful members of his community,[33] for the author of Luke-Acts, it is not simply a matter of the prosperous and powerful learning to share with the poor; it is a matter of all people learning to share with and treat others fairly, justly and equitably.[34] This type of communal concern is part of what the author considers to be "fruits worthy of repentance."

What John requires of the crowd is not simply some internalized sense of guilt or remorse[35] nor is it merely some introspective philosophical spiritualized exercise of piety. Instead, what John requires are concrete acts of selfless concern for the well-being of others. Such acts reflect compassion and mercy toward all people, and help enable diverse individuals to live together as a caring community of people.

After addressing how repentance should be manifested by people in general, the author turns his attention to two specific classes of people: tax collectors and soldiers. The tax collectors and soldiers serve at least two functions in the author's narrative. On the one hand they serve as examples for the tax collectors and soldiers who were most likely part of the author's community.[36] On the other hand they demonstrate that repentance is accessible to everyone. By having both tax

---

Geography 7.3.9; Diodorus Siculus *Library of History* 10.3.5; Iamblichus *On the Pythagorean Life* 30.168).

[33] J. R. Donahue, "Two Decades of Research on the Rich and the Poor in Luke-Acts," *Justice and the Holy: Essays in Honor of Walter Harrelson* (eds. D. Knight and P. Paris; Atlanta: Scholars Press, 1989) 142–143.

[34] No other New Testament writer speaks out as emphatically as does Luke about proper use of material possessions, wealth, and money (See L. T. Johnson, *The Literary Function of Possessions in Luke-Acts* (Missoula MT: Scholars Press, 1977); idem, *Sharing Possessions: Mandate and Symbol of Faith* (Philadelphia: Fortress, 1981); D. P. Seccombe, *Possessions and the Poor in Luke-Acts* (Linz: Fuchs, 1982); W. E. Pilgrim, *Good News to the Poor: Wealth and Poverty in Luke-Acts* (Minneapolis, MN: Augsburg, 1986); W. Stegemann, "The Following of Christ as Solidarity between Rich, Respected Christians and Poor Despised Christians (Gospel of Luke)," *Jesus and the Hope of the Poor* (ed. L. Schottroff and W. Stegemann; Maryknoll, NY: Orbis Books, 1986); J. González, *Faith and Wealth: A History of Early Christian Ideas on the Origin, Significance, and Use of Money* (San Francisco: Harper and Row, 1990) 78–86.

[35] Repentance in Luke-Acts often begins with a sense of guilt over past conduct—guilt over the fact that sin has set one in opposition to God (cf. Luke 5:8; Acts 2:37–38)—but guilt itself is not repentance, nor is it the fruit that testifies to repentance. Guilt must be accompanied by a change in the way one lives one's life.

[36] Although the tax collectors and soldiers are placed within the historical setting of John the Baptist, the favorable portrayal of tax collectors in Luke (cf. 3:12; 7:29; 15:1; 18:9–14; 19:1–10) and soldiers in Acts (cf. 10:7; 21:30–36; 23:10, 23–31; 28:16; see also "centurions;" Luke 23:47; Acts 10:1 ff; 23:17; 27:43) suggests that the author has most likely chosen people of special significance to his community. Furthermore, while τελώνης occurs more often in Luke than in Matthew and Mark, there is no mention in Luke of Jesus' pejorative references to tax collectors (cf. Matt 5:46; 18:17). There were most likely tax collectors and soldiers (or at least former tax collectors and soldiers) within the author's own community.

collectors, who comprised one of the most socially despised segments of the population at that time,[37] and soldiers approach John and ask what they must do in order to bear fruits consistent with repentance, the author demonstrates to his audience that repentance is available to everyone—even tax collectors and soldiers.[38] No one is doomed merely on the basis of who they are, but everyone is capable of receiving forgiveness and escaping the wrath to come.[39]

This reality demands a change in thinking on the part of many in the Lukan community. The dual function served by the tax collectors and soldiers is typical of the dual function served by other repentant characters within the narrative. The repentance of tax collectors, soldiers, sinners, and Gentiles not only serves as examples to the members of the Lukan community who identify with these groups, it also serves to challenge the thinking of others in the Lukan community. Those who may have treated tax collectors, soldiers, sinners, Gentiles, and other socially unacceptable people with contempt, and considered them unworthy of fair treatment and participation in the community of God's people, are being forced to change their way of thinking if they wish to be a part of the community of all people established by Jesus.[40]

---

[37] Contrary to Bailey's unfounded (and unnecessary) assertion that tax collectors "were people of relatively high social status and not outcasts" (*Repentance*, 170), the gospel's presentation of human sentiments about tax collectors (τελῶναι) is uniformly negative (cf. Mark 2:15; Matt 5:46; 9:10; 11:19; 18:17; 21:31; Luke 5:30; 7:34: 15:1–2; 18:11–13; 19:7). Negative views of tax collectors can also be found in the secular literature of the time (Cicero, *De offic.* 15–51; Diogenes Cynicus, *Ep.* 36.2; Lucian *Pseudolog.* 30; *Menippus* 11; Herodas *The Private Conversation* 64; Dio Chrysostom, *Orat.* 14.14), as well as in rabbinic writings (cf John R. Donahue, "Tax Collectors and Sinners: An Attempt at Identification," *CBQ* 33 (1971) 39–71; Michel, "τελώνης," *TDNT*, 8:88–105). N. Perrin, *Rediscovering the Teachings of Jesus* (New York: Harper & Row, 1967) 93–94, claims that Jewish tax collectors were considered "Jews who made themselves as Gentiles," and were scorned as political figures who had betrayed their country because they collected taxes from their fellow Jew on behalf of the hated gentiles. Bailey apparently considers financial status and social status to be synonymous (which is not the case). For a general overview of the economic and social status of tax collectors at that time, see T. Frank, ed., *An Economic Survey of Ancient Rome* (6 vols.; Baltimore, MD: Johns Hopkins Press, 1933–1959) 4.231–245, 453–460; M. Rostovtzeff, *The Social and Economic History of the Roman Empire*, 2nd ed., rev. P. M. Fraser (2 vols.; Oxford: Oxford University Press, 1957) 137, 339–342; A. Jones, *The Roman Economy: Studies in Ancient Economic and Administrative History* (ed. P. A. Brunt; Oxford: Basil Blackwell, 1974) 151–185.

[38] Although it was commonly believed by many Jews during the first century that it was virtually impossible for tax collectors to repent (Donahue, "Tax Collectors," 41; J. Jeremias, *Jerusalem in the Time of Jesus* (trans. F. H. and C. H. Cave; London: SCM, 1969) 310–311), tax collectors in Luke's gospel are often characterized by repentance and faith (cf. 5:27–32; 7:29; 15:1; 18:13; 19:1–10).

[39] The author further stresses the availability of repentance to all people, including the most despised, through his redaction of Jesus' statement, "I have not come to call the righteous, but sinners **to repentance**" (Luke 5:32). This availability of repentance to all people is also stressed in the post-resurrection declaration of Jesus: "Thus it is written, that Christ should suffer and... that repentance for forgiveness of sins should be preached in his name to all nations." (Luke 24:46–47).

[40] This point is climactically emphasized in the Peter-Cornelius episode of Acts 10.

As with his reply to the ὄχλοι, John's reply to both the tax collectors and soldiers requires concrete acts of selfless concern that alter the way human beings interact with each other. The tax collectors and the soldiers are given specific commands that address practices common to their respective vocations, and these practices concern the way they interact with other people.

During the Roman Republic, taxes were collected by groups of individuals, the *societas publicanorum*, composed mainly of Romans of the equestrian order.[41] The publicans often exploited their provinces; therefore, attempts were made by both Julius Caesar and Augustus to rehabilitate the system.[42] When Judaea came under the Roman prefects, direct taxes (i.e. tribute) were collected by officials of the Roman government, while indirect taxes (e.g. tolls, tariffs, customs on transported goods, taxes on business transactions, contracts, legacies, inheritances, and the use of municipal real estate) were collected by contracted tax collectors. Jews were also assessed religious taxes such as the temple tax, creating an extra burden of taxation.[43]

The opportunity to collect indirect taxes were farmed out to local residents by the Roman government. Someone of financial means and prominence would usually purchase from the government the right to collect taxes within a geographical region. That person would then sell to other intermediaries the right to collect taxes within a segment of the region he had purchased from the government. Those intermediaries would then employ local toll booth collectors or tax office agents to physically collect the taxes. There quickly developed a hierarchy of tax collectors, all of whom were identified as τελῶναι.[44]

Collectors at each level paid for the privilege of collecting taxes. These collectors would then seek to earn their livelihood, and usually gain relative wealth, by collecting more than they paid for the privilege of collecting taxes.[45] As can be seen in the case of Zacchaeus, a chief tax collector (Luke 19:1–8), and Levi, a local toll booth collector or tax office agent, who "gave a great banquet" in his house for Jesus (Luke 5:29), tax collectors often grew rich. The bulk of their wealth usually resulted from collecting more than they had contracted with and paid their superiors.[46]

---

[41] E. Badian *Publicans and Sinners: Private Enterprise in the Service of the Roman Republic* (Ithaca, NY: Cornell University Press, 1976) 48–66.

[42] P. Garnsey and R. Smaller, *The Roman Empire: Economy, Society, and Culture* (London: Duckworth, 1987) 87.

[43] P. Perkins, "Taxes in the New Testament," *JRE* 12 (1984) 185–186.

[44] For an examination of how the term τελῶναι could be used of three distinct groups, see F. Herrenbrück, "Wer waren die 'Zöllner'?" *ZNW* 72 (1981) 178–194.

[45] S. Safrai, *The Jewish People in the First Century: Historical Geography, Political History, Social, Cultural and Religious Life and Institutions* (Philadelphia: Fortress, 1974) 330–336. For discussions of the greed and corruption practiced by tax collectors, see J. R. Donahue, "Tax Collectors" and O. Michel, *TDNT* 8:88–105.

[46] In Josephus' account of a man named Joseph who won the rights for collecting taxes in Syria, Phoenicia, Judaea and Samaria (*Ant.* 12, 160–186), Joseph used violence—arresting and even killing leading citizens—in order to collect taxes. Josephus

John's command that the tax collectors "Collect no more than the amount prescribed" was a radical command. As Paul Hollenbach has asserted, "For such persons to heed John's call for repentance with its accompanying demand would entail a total rejection of their former way of life. . . . For when he demanded that they should not collect funds beyond what they had contracted for, he was striking at the root of a large part of the tax system."[47] For the author, repentance among the tax collectors required them to be willing to reject and abandon their unjust practices.[48] In Luke, John the Baptist expected tax collectors to treat others fairly and justly, instead of taking advantage of others for their own personal gain. It would have been impossible for tax collectors and tax-paying Jews to live together as a community of God's people without a fundamental change occurring in the unjust practices of tax collectors that permanently and radically altered the way things used to be.

After John addressed the tax collectors, a group of soldiers asked what they should do. Some scholars argue that it is not clear whether these are Gentile or Jewish soldiers;[49] however, John's earlier warning to the people not to think they will escape the consequences of their actions simply because they "have Abraham" as their "ancestor," suggests that John was addressing a Jewish listening audience.[50] Furthermore, because of the gradually progressive development of a ministry to the Gentiles in Luke-Acts, the literary design of the work suggests that at this point in

---

states that "By this means he [Joseph] gathered great wealth together, and made vast gains by this farming of the taxes; and he made use of what estate he had thus gotten, in order to support his authority. . . . This good fortune he enjoyed for twenty-two years" (184–186).

[47] "Social Aspects," p. 871. In support of this view, Hollenbach cites a statement made by W. R. Farmer that "sums up this point very well. 'The requirement that tax collectors refrain from collecting more than was appointed to them would have set them at odds with the social and economic structures of which they were a part. It would have resulted in a radical reduction in their standard of living and necessitated serious economic and social readjustments on the part of their families. Furthermore, it would have required a complete reorientation of their motivation in accepting the responsibilities of their office. Because, once the prospect of becoming rich has been removed, few would want to continue the onerous duties of collecting unpopular taxes from a resentful people. Especially so when the money directly or indirectly supported the (Roman) occupation forces and the concomitant collaborating (Jewish) bureaucracy' (*IDB*, II, p. 960)" [n75]. See also Donahue, 41.

[48] The total abandonment of these practices is emphasized by the author of Luke's gospel, who is the only one among the synoptic authors who states that when Levi—a tax collector—was confronted by Jesus "he left everything" (5:29).

[49] Bailey, *Repentance*, 173.

[50] Although the tax collectors and soldiers are depicted separately from "the crowds" and not necessarily as stepping forward from "the crowds," the brevity of space used to describe their coming to John (for a discussion of the ways in which the duration of "discourse time" may be related to that of "story time," see Genette, *Narrative Discourse*, 86–112), as well as the fact that they ask the same question of John as the crowds, causes the reader to understand them as part of John's listening audience. As stated above, the questions "what shall we do?" appear to be in direct response to the command "bear fruits worthy of repentance" and to the warning for the people not to trust in their ancestral connection to Abraham.

the narrative these soldiers should probably be recognized as Jewish soldiers.[51] The angel of God declared that John would "turn many of the **sons of Israel** to the Lord their God (1:16); it was Jesus, not John who was prophesied as being "a light for revelation to the Gentiles" (2:32). John's ministry was to the Jewish people; therefore, these soldiers were most likely Jewish soldiers. The fact that John's dialogue with the crowds, the tax collectors and the soldiers is immediately followed by a Lukan construction that serves as a conclusion to John's ethical preaching and an introduction to John's messianic preaching in which the author declares that "the people (λαός) were filled" with messianic expectations (3:15), suggests that the author seeks to convey that all the people previously addressed by John were expecting the arrival of the Messiah, and were, therefore, most likely Jewish.[52]

The association of the soldiers with tax collectors suggests that the author felt that these soldiers would be viewed by his readers the same way the tax collectors were viewed. Josephus records that the tax collector Joseph, "took with him two thousand foot soldiers from the king, for he desired that he might have some assistance, in order to force such as were refractory in the cities to pay."[53] This reference from Josephus, combined with the close association of the soldiers and tax collectors in the Lukan passage, suggests that the soldiers addressed by John the Baptist were most likely Jewish soldiers assigned by a Roman sanctioned Jewish leader such as Herod Antipas to assist tax collectors in the gathering of taxes.[54] These soldiers, therefore, belong in the same corrupt social system as the tax collectors.[55]

The soldiers, like the tax collectors, are also commanded not to exploit their positions in order to obtain money by violence or false pretenses.[56] This may have

---

[51] The first explicitly identified Gentile soldier in the Lukan narrative is the centurion with the sick servant (Luke 7:1–10). This story was clearly part of the gospel tradition inherited by the author (cf. Matt 8:5–13). Unlike the account in Matthew, however, the centurion in Luke is not the one who approaches Jesus; the author employs the testimony of Jewish elders to defend the soldier's worthiness for a visit from Jesus. Even when Jesus approaches the house, it is not the centurion who physically addresses Jesus. The centurion himself never speaks to Jesus. In light of this, and in light of the fact that this scene is intended to be the first scene in a progressively developing ministry to the Gentiles, it is highly unlikely that the soldiers addressing John the Baptist were Gentile soldiers.

[52] That the author's use of "people (λαός)" in 3:15 is most likely intended to include the crowds, the tax collectors and the soldiers of 3:10–14 seems to be further supported by the emphatic phrase "John answered **them all** (πᾶσιν)." (3:16a).

[53] *Ant.* 12, 180.

[54] See I. H. Marshall, *The Gospel of Luke*, 143; J. Fitzmyer, *The Gospel*, 1:470; J. Nolland, *Luke 1–9:20*. Word Biblical Commentary (Dallas: Word, 1989) 150.

[55] Like the tax collectors, however, these soldiers—as well as other classes of soldiers—are depicted favorably by the author throughout Luke-Acts (cf. Luke 7:1–10; 23:44–47; Acts 10:1–48; 21:31–38; 22:22–29; 23:10, 17–32; 27:1–6, 42–44; 28:16.)

[56] The verb διασείω, "take money by force or intimidation," occurs only here in the New Testament. It does, however, have a similar usage in 3 Macc 7:21, Philo's *Alleg. Interp.* 2.99, and *Oxyrhynchus Papyri* 240.5; 284.5; *Tebtunis Papyri* 43.26. The verb συκοφαντέω,

been even harder for the soldiers because unlike tax collectors, soldiers were not in business as independent contractors. They had not purchased the rights to be soldiers, whereby being free to conduct their business as they deemed appropriate. The soldiers directly served the needs of those who commanded them. Even if the soldiers became content with their wages and chose not to rob others in order to further their own self-interest, if they were serving the needs of tax collectors or other corrupt forces who demanded violence be used in order to receive monies, these soldiers would have to disobey those who ruled them in order to obey John's command, "Do not extort money from anyone by threats or false accusations." By commanding them not to extort money, John is telling these soldiers to challenge the very foundations of the social order and to treat others fairly, justly and equitably even when those whom they serve command them to do otherwise.[57] By commanding them, "be satisfied with your wages," John is also telling them not to allow greed to cause them to be like the tax collectors, who use their power and authority for their own personal gain.[58]

By having John the Baptist address the crowds in general, and the tax collectors and soldiers in particular, the author conveys the point that social and ethical acts of selfless concern for others, which represent "fruits worthy of repentance," should be reflected in the personal and professional lives of his readers. At this point in the narrative, repentance represents the adoption of a new set of social standards that guides human behavior in every aspect of life: it represents a complete reorientation of one's beliefs with a corresponding change in one's behavior. It is this fundamental change in thinking and living that radically alters the way things are, and creates an environment where diverse and once alienated people can live together as a community of God's people.

From the outset, one of the first things the author wants his audience to recognize about repentance is that the fruits of repentance are often manifested in the context of human social interactions. Repentance may represent an individual decision, but it often transforms social relationships. Throughout Luke-Acts, the author presents his readers with an idealized depiction of the earliest Christian community in order to challenge his readers to make proper use of their own possessions. For the author, when repentance depicts a change in the way one thinks

---

"accuse falsely; defraud," is found here and in Zacchaeus' declaration that if he had "defrauded (συκοφαντέω) any one of anything" he would restore it fourfold (19:8b). This represents another effort by the author to place these soldiers in the same corrupt social context as tax collectors. The verb is also used in the LXX for oppression of the poor (Gen 43:18; Lev 19:11; Job 35:9; Ps 118 [119]:122; Prov 14:31; 22:16; 28:3; Eccl 4:1) The nouns συκοφάντης and συκοφαντία also denote oppression of the poor (Ps 71 [72]:4; 118 [119]:134; Prov 28:16; Eccl 4:1; 5:7; 7:8; Amos 2:8). The verbs διασείω and συκοφαντέω occur together in the second century B.C.E. *Tebtunis Papyri* 43.26, 36.

[57] Hollenbach, "Social Aspects," 873.
[58] On the power and authority of soldiers—Jewish and Gentile—during this time, see R. Evans, *Soldiers of Rome: Praetorians and Legionnaries* (Cabin John, MD: Seven Locks, 1986); R. Davis, *Service in the Roman Army* (New York: Columbia University Press, 1989).

about and interacts with others, it most often represents a voluntary human response ordained by God as a method of correcting economic and social disparity among people. However, if people fail to repent, thereby correcting the situation themselves, God will eventually set things in order and bring about a reversal of the present social and economic situation.[59]

The author, by way of the dialogical scheme of Luke 3:10–14, depicts John the Baptist not as a preacher of gloom and doom but as a preacher of hope and encouragement, even to the most despised segments of the population at that time. Part of the hope and encouragement that John brings is that repentance, which delivers people from the wrath to come, is available to all people and that repentance requires the just, merciful and equitable treatment of all people by all people, enabling diverse individuals to receive the salvation of God and to live together as a community of God's people.

Repentance in the Preaching of Jesus

In Luke, μετανοέω and μετάνοια occur quite frequently in the preaching and teaching of Jesus.[60] Jesus is clearly depicted by the author as a preacher of repentance. Although the author associates μετανοέω and μετάνοια with the preaching and teaching of Jesus far more than the other synoptic authors do, there is an obvious omission of μετανοέω from the preaching of Jesus in Luke.

The Obvious Omission

In both Mark and Matthew, Jesus begins his public ministry in Galilee by exhorting the people to repent (μετανοεῖτε) because the kingdom of God has drawn near.[61] However, rather than identifying what it was Jesus said to the people when he began his ministry in Galilee, the author of Luke opens his account of the beginnings of Jesus' public ministry with a summary statement that concludes, "He began to teach in their synagogues and was praised by everyone."[62]

As predominant as μετανοέω and μετάνοια are in Luke-Acts, clearly the omission of μετανοέω here reflects a conscious and deliberate decision on the part of the author. While it is not clear why the author omits Jesus' command to repent,

---

[59] Cf. Lk 1:53; 6:20, 24; 14:15–24; 16:19–26. For an analysis of the Lukan use of reversals, and a discussion of how this literary technique may have been used by the author in order to shape the values and responses of his first–century audience, see J. O. York, *The Last Shall be First: The Rhetoric of Reversal in Luke* (Sheffield: JSOT, 1991).

[60] In Luke's Gospel the terms occur twelve times in the preaching and teaching of Jesus (Luke 5:32; 10:13; 11:32; 13:3, 5; 15:7[x2];, 10; 16:30; 17:3, 4; 24:47) however, only once is μετανοέω associated with the preaching of Jesus in Mark's Gospel (Mark 6:12), and the term is used only twice by Jesus in Matthew's Gospel (Matt 11:21; 12:41).

[61] Mark 1:14–15; Matt 4:12–17.

[62] Luke 4:14–15.

it may be that the author does not want to give the impression that the inauguration of the reign of God should serve as the motivation for repentance.⁶³ As a result of the ethical teachings of John the Baptist, the author has shifted the focus away from the eschatological motivation for repentance and unto the social implications of repentance. The omission from Luke of Jesus' eschatological reference to repentance is consistent with such a shift of emphasis.⁶⁴ Furthermore, since the theme of repentance forms an important subtheme within the one principal theme of the entire narrative of Luke-Acts, which is the outworking of God's plan of universal salvation,⁶⁵ and since Jesus is the bringer of that salvation, the author very likely has omitted Jesus' preaching of repentance so that the first words of Jesus' public ministry within the Lukan narrative depict him as the bringer of salvation.⁶⁶ Jesus is first and foremost the one who brings salvation, and as such he teaches the people that repentance is the appropriate human response to the divine offer of salvation.

The author replaces the repentance preaching of Jesus found in Mark and Matthew with a summary statement that serves as a transitional introduction. The statement concludes the previous section and introducing the teaching of Jesus that immediately follows.⁶⁷ When Jesus came to Nazareth, he entered the synagogue and began teaching the people.⁶⁸ According to the author, Jesus stood up in the synagogue and read from the scroll of the prophet Isaiah.⁶⁹ Throughout Luke's narrative, literary prophecies often serve programmatic functions. These prophecies are typically spoken by characters at critical junctures within the narrative, and they usually provide an interpretive framework for the narrative that follows (i.e. the plot

---

⁶³ For a discussion of the inauguration of the reign of God serving as the motivation for repentance in Mark and Matthew, see the section, Μετανοέω and Μετάνοια in the New Testament and Other Early Christian Literature, in chapter three above.

⁶⁴ Regarding Luke 4:14–15, H. Conzelmann, *The Theology of St. Luke* (Philadelphia: Fortress, 1961) 114, has rightly noted, "Compared with Mark i, 15 there is a shift of emphasis in Luke."

⁶⁵ See chapter two, "Repentance Within the Narrative Structure of Luke-Acts."

⁶⁶ Before this scene, Jesus is introduced to the shepherds (and to the author's audience) by the angel of the Lord as a Savior (σωτήρ; Luke 2:11). Likewise, in the temple Simeon takes the baby Jesus in his arms and blesses God, saying, "my eyes have seen your salvation" (σωτήριόν σου; 2:30).

⁶⁷ The reference to the Spirit (πνεῦμα) in v. 14 forms an inclusio with a similar reference in 4:1, bringing that section to an end, and the reference to teaching in the synagogues introduces the synagogue teaching that takes place in 4:16–30 (cf. Nolland, *Luke*, 185–186, 191).

⁶⁸ The phrase "as was his custom" (κατὰ τὸ εἰωθὸς αὐτῷ) is clearly a reference back to v. 15, confirming the notion that the summary statement of Luke 4:14–15 functions as a transitional introduction, introducing the teaching of Jesus that takes place in the synagogue at Nazareth. The kerygmatic announcement of 4:18–21 serves as a substitute for the proclamation of repentance found in Mark and Matthew.

⁶⁹ There is no mention of this reading in the parallel passages found in Mark and Matthew.

development fulfills the prophecy).[70] Luke 4:18–19 is one of many such programmatic prophecies within the author's narrative. The prophecy defines Jesus' mission as the bringer of salvation, and functions as a guide for better understanding the life and ministry of Jesus presented in Luke.

The author has clearly moved this reference regarding Jesus coming to his hometown and teaching in the synagogue from later on in the gospel tradition to the beginning of Jesus' public ministry.[71] Placing this scene first is an important interpretive move by the author because the scene serves as a paradigm for defining both the purpose and objective of Jesus' ministry and the reaction of many of his fellow countrymen to his ministry.[72]

The author's adding of the programmatic prophecy to this scene, his moving of the scene from later on in the gospel tradition to the beginning of Jesus' public ministry, and the appearance of themes within this pericope that will be important elsewhere in the author's two-volume work,[73] sufficiently indicate the importance of this scene to the author's narrative development. The scene also helps link the ministry of Jesus with important themes that have already been introduced and with incidents that have already occurred within the narrative.

The rejection of Jesus by those in the synagogue at Nazareth links this pericope to the prophecy of Simeon in the temple: "This child is destined for the falling and the rising of many in Israel, and to be a sign that will be opposed" (2:34). The pericope demonstrates the type of opposition foreshadowed by Simeon's prophecy, and it prepares the reader for the continued opposition that will be directed against Jesus throughout the entirety of this two-volume narrative. The phrase "The Spirit of the Lord is upon me" continues a thread that runs back through 4:14 and 4:1 to 3:22, where the Spirit descended upon Jesus in bodily form. Luke 4:18–19 makes it clear that the Spirit's descent upon Jesus after his baptism was God's anointing of him for a specific purpose.[74] Finally, John is depicted as having preached a "baptism of repentance for the forgiveness (ἄφεσιν) of sins,"

---

[70] Luke Johnson, *The Writings of the New Testament* (Philadelphia: Fortress, 1986) 206.

[71] There is a partial parallel to this scene in Mark 6:1–6a and Matthew 13:54–58, but it much shorter and occurs later in the public ministry of Jesus.

[72] Fitzmyer asserts that the author has deliberately placed 4:16–30 at the beginning of the public ministry of Jesus in order to "encapsulate the entire ministry of Jesus and the reaction to it" (*The Gospel*, 1:529).

[73] Jesus is anointed to "preach good news to the poor." Preaching has a significant place within Luke's two-volume work. The verb εὐαγγελίζομαι occurs only once in Matthew and not at all in Mark, while it occurs ten times in Luke and fifteen times in Acts. The verb is used quite frequently to refer to the preaching of Jesus (Luke 4:43; 7:22; 8:1; 9:6; 16:16; 20:1). That it is the "poor" to whom the good news is preached also corresponds to a Lukan emphasis (cf. Luke 6:20; 7:22; 14:13, 21; 16:20, 22; 18:22; 19:8; 21:3). The special concern of Jesus for the outcasts and poor is rooted in the gospel tradition, but Luke gives special emphasis to this and to the corresponding condemnation of the proud and rich (Cadbury, *The Making of Luke-Acts*, 258–263).

[74] This is later confirmed by the author through the preaching of Peter in Acts 10:38.

and Jesus is depicted here as having been sent by the Spirit of the Lord to proclaim release (ἄφεσις) to the captives and to the oppressed.

In Luke-Acts, salvation refers to the "release" or "setting free" of God's people. This is conveyed by the author's use of the noun ἄφεσις with the nouns σωτηρία and σωτήρ.[75] Like σωτήρ, σωτηρία and σωτήριον, which occur a combined total of seventeen times in Luke-Acts but never in Mark or Matthew, ἄφεσις is also a Lukan term. The word occurs only twice in Mark and once in Matthew. It occurs ten times, however, in Luke-Acts.[76] The word is used by the author in two contexts. First, the word is used to refer to a physical setting free, such as a release from captivity, blindness, and oppression. This is of course how the term is used by the author in Jesus' self-identification of his own ministry with the prophet Isaiah: "The Spirit of the Lord is upon me for he anointed me; he has sent me to preach good news to the poor: to proclaim release (ἄφεσιν) to the prisoners and recovery of sight to the blind, to send away the oppressed released (ἐν ἀφέσει), to proclaim the acceptable year of the Lord."[77] Second, the word is used in the construction "release from sins (ἄφεσις ἁμαρτιῶν)," which is commonly translated "forgiveness of sins."[78] This of course is how it is employed in connection with the John's preaching of a baptistism of repentance.[79]

The author immediately establishes a connection between the preaching of Jesus and the preaching of John the Baptist through his use of the noun ἄφεσις. The author achieves this connection through his deliberate and conscious literary reworking of his source material. Luke 4:18–19 represents a patchwork of materials that has been brought together by the author. The verses are a conflation of Isa 61:1a,b,d; 58:6d; 61:2a as found in the Septuagint. This conflation emphasizes the idea of "release" (ἄφεσις).[80] Furthermore, not only does this pericope connect the preaching of Jesus to the earlier preaching of John the Baptist by its use of the term ἄφεσις, the pericope is also connected to that earlier scene by the fact that both

---

[75] Luke 1:77; 3:3–6; Acts 5:31; 13:38–47.

[76] Luke 1:77; 3:3; 4:18 [x2]; 24:47; Acts 2:38; 5:31; 10:43; 13:38; 26:18.

[77] Luke 4:18–19 (my own translation). Although it is not clear in the Greek text whether εὐαγγελίσασθαι ("to preach good news") is to be taken with the preceding verb, ἔχρισέν με ("he anointed me"), or with the following, ἀπέσταλκέν με ("he sent me"), the Hebrew seems to suggest that "to preach good news" should be taken with "he sent me." This also seems to the be the sense conveyed in the LXX. I have also interpreted the phrase "to preach good news to the poor" as an encompassing and defining designation of Jesus' entire ministry, which is then expanded upon in the remainder of the prophecy. Both of these interpretive choices seem to be supported by the Lukan statement of Jesus found in 4:43.

[78] Luke 1:77; 3:3; 24:47; Acts 2:38; 5:31; 10:43; 13:38; 26:18.

[79] Luke 1:77; 3:3. The use of "repentance" and "release from sins" together reflects a technique which Robert Alter has called the "type-scene" (*Art of Biblical Narrative*, 47–62). Type-scene is a technique of forming episodes from a set of motifs which can be repeated with variations. This leads to connections being made by the implied reader between various scenes (see also Luke 24:47; Acts 2:38; 5:31; 26:18–20).

[80] On the significance of this conflation, see further Robert C. Tannehill, "The Mission of Jesus according to Luke IV 16–30," *Jesus in Nazareth* (ed. Walther Eltester; Berlin: Walter de Gruyter, 1972) 66, 70–71

John's and Jesus' public ministry are introduced as fulfillment of Isaian prophecies.[81]

The ministry of Jesus as presented in the rest of the Lukan narrative should be understood through the lens of Luke 4:16–30. Jesus has been anointed by the Spirit of the Lord, and has been sent to minister to those on the margins of society: the poor, the captives, the blind and the oppressed. As my earlier translation of Luke 4:18–19 suggests, the phrase "to preach good news to the poor" is an encompassing and defining designation of Jesus' entire ministry, which is then expanded upon in the remainder of the prophecy. This is why the captives most likely represent those who have been imprisoned for debt. This is further supported by the fact that in the context of Third Isaiah, "the acceptable year of the Lord" refers to the Jubilee year, when, according to Mosaic law, family property that may have been lost or taken is returned to its original owners, indentured servants are released, and debts are cancelled.[82] According to the Septuagint this Jubilee year is also called the "year of release."[83]

In Luke when the Holy Spirit descended upon Jesus at his baptism, Jesus was anointed and commissioned by God to bring salvation, i.e. "release." The author's construction of the quotation from Third Isaiah indicates that he is seeking to emphasize that salvation has been inaugurated in the person and ministry of Jesus. Not only has the author inserted a line from Isa 58:6 into the quotation, thereby emphasizing the idea of "release" (ἄφεσις), the author has also terminated the quotation immediately before the mention in Isa 61:2b of the "day of vengeance" (ἡμέραν ἀνταποδόσεως), making salvation the climax of the prophecy.[84] Jesus does not simply announce the time of salvation, instead, he inaugurates the time of salvation. This is why he declares, "Today this scripture has been fulfilled in your hearing."[85]

---

[81] The author also makes a connection between Jesus and John the Baptist when he records that Jesus, in one of his post-resurrection appearances, told his disciples, "Thus it is written that the Christ should suffer and. . . that repentance for the forgiveness of sins (μετάνοιαν εἰς ἄφεσιν ἁμαρτιῶν)" should be preached in his name to all nations (Luke 4:46–47).

[82] The Jubilee year language (Lev 25:8–55) is clearly being picked up in Isa 61:1–2.

[83] Lev 25:10 (the noun ἄφεσις occurs fourteen times in Lev 25:10–55). While it cannot be stated with certainty that the author recognized and was intentionally evoking the Jubilee year imagery that is being picked up in Isa 61:1–2, the insertion of the line from Isa 58:6, with the additional reference to ἄφεσις, suggests that the author does recognize and is intentionally evoking the Jubilee year imagery. Furthermore, the social concern for the poor that motivated the Jubilee year legislation clearly permeates the entire narrative of Luke-Acts (cf R. Sloan, *The Favorable Year of the Lord. A Study of Jubilary Theology in the Gospel of Luke* (Austin, TX: Schola Press, 1977); Sharon H. Ringe *Jesus, Liberation, and the Biblical Jubilee* (Philadelphia: Fortress, 1985) 16–90).

[84] In the first Isaian quotation (Luke 3:4–6), the author extends the quote in order to include a direct reference to the "salvation of God." Here, the author ends the quotation in the middle of a sentence in order to make salvation the focus of the quotation.

[85] Luke 4:21. That salvation is realized in the person and ministry of Jesus is confirmed by the praise of Simeon, "for my eyes have seen your salvation" (Luke 2:30), and by the declaration of Peter, "There is salvation in no one else, for there is no other name under

The author wants his reader to understand that Jesus has been anointed and sent by God in order to inaugurate the time of salvation and to extend salvation to those who are normally overlooked by society and/or considered by so-called insiders as unworthy of salvation.[86] As previously stated, this is most likely the reason why the author replaces the kerygmatic announcement found in Mark and Matthew, in which Jesus demands repentance, with the kerygmatic announcement found in Luke 4:18–21. However, as the reader of the narrative will soon discover, one of the ways Jesus accomplishes his mission of extending salvation to those who are normally overlooked by society and/or considered by others as unworthy of salvation is by calling on people to change their ways of thinking and living, i.e. by calling on them to repent. Through repentance, salvation is made available to all people, and all people are enabled to live together as a community of God's people.

Sent to Call Sinners to Repentance

In Luke, Jesus concludes his ministry in Capernaum the same way he began it in Nazareth—with a programmatic declaration that he "has been sent to preach the good news" (εὐαγγελίσασθαι... ἀπεστάλην).[87] Immediately after this declaration, Jesus is portrayed as proclaiming the word of God, performing miracles, healing the sick, forgiving sins (ἀφιέναι ἁμαρτίας), and calling

---

heaven given among mortals by which we must be saved" (Acts 4:12).

[86] This notion of being overlooked and considered unworthy of salvation is further conveyed in vv. 23–28 (cf. B. Malina, *Windows on the World of Jesus: Time Travel to Ancient Judea* (Louisville: Westminster/John Knox, 1993) 47–70. Initially the analogies employed in these verses seem somewhat out of place since the emphasis seems to be on the fact that the widow and Naaman are Gentiles and Jesus himself never develops a ministry to the Gentiles. However, in addition to their ethnic identity, the social status of the widow (i.e. a very poor woman) and of Naaman (i.e. a wealthy man of high rank in the Syrian army) emphasizes the inclusivity of Jesus' ministry. At this point in the narrative, the widow and Naaman most likely serve two purposes: 1) they represent the social, economic, and gender diversity of the Lukan community (Esler, *Community and Gospel in Luke-Acts: The Social and Political Motivations of Lukan Theology* (Cambridge: Cambridge University Press, 1987) 179–180), and 2) they provide a historical and scriptural precedent for the Gentile mission that develops later in Acts (Tannehill, "The Mission of Jesus according to Luke iv 16–30," *Jesus in Nazareth* (ed. W. Eltester; Berlin: de Gruyer, 1972) 60). It may also be that within the immediate narrative context the point is not that others are recipients of salvation, but rather that the people of Nazareth—those with Abraham as their ancestor—are not recipients.

[87] Cf. Luke 4:18, 43. In a sense Luke 4:42–44 brings to a close the account of the beginnings of Jesus' Galilean ministry (4:14–44). Verse 44 ends the section by forming an inclusio with v. 15. Since 4:14–43 takes the place of Mark 1:14–15, Jesus is depicted at the close of this section as a preacher of "the kingdom of God;" however, the kingdom is not depicted as an imminent eschatological moment demanding repentance (cf. Mark 1:15; Matt 4:17), instead "the good news of the kingdom of God," which Jesus has been sent to preach, is the "good news to the poor" (Luke 6:20), which he has also been sent to preach, and the good news to the poor is the proclamation of "release" (i.e. salvation).

disciples.[88] In a small but significant redaction to one of the sayings of Jesus, Luke records Jesus making another programmatic declaration. Jesus informs the Pharisees and their scribes that he has "not come to call the righteous, but sinners to repentance (εἰς μετάνοιαν)."[89]

This is the first reference to repentance since the ethical preaching section of John the Baptist, and it is the third of four programmatic statements made by Jesus regarding his own ministry.[90] As a result of this Lukan redaction, Jesus himself further describes the objective of his ministry as calling sinners to repentance.[91] One of the ways in which Jesus fulfills his ministry of bringing salvation to all people, for which he has been anointed and sent by the Spirit of the Lord, is by calling sinners to repentance.[92]

---

[88] Luke 5:1–32. Jesus earlier declared that he was anointed by the Spirit of the Lord both to preach release (ἄφεσις) to the captives and to send the oppressed away released (4:18). Jesus fulfills this declaration by pronouncing release (ἀφίημι) from sins to a paralytic (5:20) and sending him away released. Jesus' declaration that the "Son of Man has authority on earth to release (ἀφιέναι) sins" (5:24) suggests that the release which Jesus was sent to proclaim according to 4:18 includes release from sins.

[89] Luke 5:32. The reader should not conclude that Jesus' statement, "I have not come to call the righteous. . . to repentance," indicates that he has not come to call everyone to repentance. To ask whether there are, or who are the righteous whom Jesus does not call to repentance is to miss the point of the passage (cf. 15:7). The passage is not about the righteous but rather about sinners. The thrust of the passage should be determined by the imagery of v. 31: "Those who are well have no need of a physician, but those who are sick." It is sinners not the righteous who are the focus of the passage, because they are the ones in need of repentance. Furthermore, the previous scene regarding the healing of the paralytic man suggests that healing sickness and forgiving sins are synonymous. As a result of his redactional activity, the author suggests that there is a connection between sickness and sin. The author also suggests that releasing people from their sins, thereby healing them of their sickness, is analogous to calling them to repentance. Susan Garrett writes, "In Luke's schema, this bringing of persons to repentance is essential for their healing. . . . Sinners who have not yet repented—or those who suppose themselves to be righteous and who therefore refuse to repent—constitute the *sick*" (Susan R. Garrett, "Beloved Physician of the Soul? Luke as Advocate for Ascetic Practice," *Asceticism in the New Testament* (eds. Leif Vaage and Vincent Wimbush; New York: Routledge, 1999) 75).

[90] Luke 4:18–19, 43; 5:32; 19:10. The relationship between these four statements is discussed above in Chapter Two.

[91] As in the case of John the Baptist (cf. Luke 1:77; 3:3), the author progressively establishes in the ministry of Jesus a connection between **release** from sins (4:18, 39; 5:20–25) and **repentance** (5:31–32). This connection becomes explicit when Jesus declares to his disciples immediately before his ascension, "Thus it is written, that the Christ should suffer. . . and that **repentance for the release of sins** [The preferred reading here is μετάνοιαν εἰς ἄφεσιν (cf 3:3b); the variant καὶ instead of εἰς is found in mss. A, C, D, L, W, Θ, Ψ, 063, $f^{1,13}$, the Koine text-tradition (i.e. Majority Text), and in many ancient versions.] should be preached in his name." (Luke 24:46–47a). After the resurrection and ascension of Jesus, Peter declares before the high priest, the Sadducees, the council, and the senate of Israel that God has exalted Jesus as Savior in order to give "**repentance** to Israel and **release of sins** (ἄφεσιν ἁμαρτιῶν)" (Acts 5:31). Both John the Baptist and Jesus have come to offer sinners **release** from their sins through a call to **repentance**.

[92] As demonstrated in Chapter Two, the extension of salvation to and the inclusion of all people within the family of God represents the plan of God in Luke-Acts, and the human response of repentance to the offer of salvation comprises a vital part of that plan.

Because of the Lukan addition of the ethical preaching of John the Baptist, at this point in the narrative the reader understands repentance to be associated with bearing fruits of ethical social behavior. The reader understands repentance to address the manner in which human beings interact with each other. It entails the rejection and abandonment of one's former ways of thinking and living and the adoption of new ways of thinking and living that result in the just, merciful and equitable treatment of all people by all people. Therefore, since Jesus defines what he is calling sinners to as repentance, the reader expects this type of abandonment of one's former ways of thinking and living and the adoption of new ways of thinking and living to be what Jesus is calling sinners to.

In both Mark and Matthew, Jesus declares that he has come to call sinners, but he does not state that it is repentance that he has come to call them to. The Lukan addition of the words "to repentance" to Jesus' declaration, "I have not come to call the righteous but sinners," must not be considered merely a stylistic change. The Lukan addition of the words "to repentance" helps to further define the objective of Jesus' ministry.[93] The redaction also clarifies the nature of the call made by Jesus, as well as the meaning of the action of those who respond to the call from Jesus. The Lukan redaction clearly indicates that the author wants the manner of life to which Jesus is calling sinners to be recognized as fruits worthy of repentance. It must be concluded, therefore, that the teachings of Jesus—most of which address the ways in which human beings live in relationship with one another—are indicative of the repentance to which Jesus is calling sinners. The teachings of Jesus indicate the kinds of changes in thinking and living that Jesus demands of those whom he is calling. Therefore, both the teachings of Jesus and the actions of the characters who respond favorably to the call and teachings of Jesus further demonstrate what the author considers to be fruits worthy of repentance.[94]

The redaction of Luke 5:32 must not be examined in isolation, but in conjunction with the other redactional activity surrounding it.[95] This programmatic declaration not only provides an interpretive framework for the material that follows, it also provides an interpretive framework for the material that has

---

[93] Since Jesus has come to call sinners to repentance, all the teaching, healing, and associating with people by Jesus should be understood as directed toward this objective. This is expressed in the rebukes of Jesus: "Woe to you, Chorazin! Woe to you, Bethsaida! For if the deeds of power done in you had been done in Tyre and Sidon, they would have repented (μετενόησαν) long ago" (Luke 10:13); "The people of Nineveh will rise up at the judgment with this generation and condemn it, because they repented (μετενόησαν) at the proclamation of Jonah, and see, something greater than Jonah is here!" (Luke 11:32).

[94] The author implies that to follow and obey the teachings of Jesus is in fact to repent: "The people of Nineveh will rise up and at the judgment with this generation and condemn it, because they repented (μετενόησαν) at the proclamation of Jonah, and see, something greater than Jonah is here!" (11:32). Repentance is the proper response to the teachings of Jesus.

[95] Nolland very persuasively demonstrates how 5:32, 38–39 function as the key verses from the central episode in a sevenfold structure (i.e. 5:1–11, 12–16, 17–26, 27–39, 6:1–5, 6–11, 12–16) (*Luke,* 218–272; especially 241–251).

preceded it. The current scene, the immediately preceding scenes and the scenes that immediately follow, all demonstrate that the author is consciously concerned with presenting in a particular way the actions of those who respond to the call of Jesus. The author is not merely recounting for his reader events that are part of a tradition he has received. In these scenes, as well as in future scenes, the identified individuals who respond to the call and teachings of Jesus play an important role in the development of the narrative,[96] and the way in which they respond plays an important role as well, because the way in which they respond to the call and teachings of Jesus partly reveals what it means to repent.[97]

In Jesus' encounter with a tax collector named Levi, Jesus tells Levi to follow him.[98] In describing Levi's response to the call of Jesus, Luke alone among the Synoptics states that Levi "**after leaving everything**, got up and followed him" (5:28). Mark and Matthew simply state that Levi "got up and followed him" (Mk 2:14c; Mt 9:9c). In the Lukan account, Levi's response to the call of Jesus involves a complete break with his occupation and an abandonment of his former ways of thinking and living. Levi abandons his occupation as a tax collector, as well as the practices associated with that occupation, in order to follow Jesus.[99] That the author seeks to emphasize the fact that Levi left everything is demonstrated by the author's addition of καταλιπὼν πάντα, "after leaving everything," which echoes 5:11, where the author alone among the Synoptic writers states that Peter, James and John "**after leaving everything** (ἀφέντες πάντα)" followed Jesus.[100] The author

---

[96] In 5:1–6:16, elements of personal response to Jesus feature prominently. Nolland states, "The sharp Christological focus of 4:14–44 now broadens; in this section [i.e. 5:1–6:16] the individual people who personally respond to Jesus become important. Sinners find a new life; apostles are called to join Jesus in his task; Pharisees prefer to stay with their old but false righteousness" (*Luke,* 218).

[97] Since Jesus has come to call sinners to repentance, the response of those who follow Jesus, and who react favorably to the ministry and call of Jesus, is implicitly associated with repentance.

[98] The author's redundant use of τελώνης to identify Levi, who is "sitting at the tax booth," emphasizes Levi's status as a tax collector. Since there has been no other mention of tax collectors since the ethical preaching section of John the Baptist, this identification of Levi as a tax collector immediately causes the reader to remember the tax collectors who asked John the Baptist what they must do in order to bear fruits worthy of repentance. The implied reader is therefore paying attention to see whether or not Levi will bear fruits worthy of repentance.

[99] The reader quite naturally interprets Levi's behavior in light of the commands given to tax collectors by John the Baptist. Levi's behavior reflects one way tax collectors can fulfill the ethical demands placed on them by John the Baptist; however, as seen in the case of Zacchaeus, tax collectors did not have to give up their occupation, just their unjust practices (Luke 19:1–10). The author is not saying that repentance requires the abandonment of certain occupations, instead repentance requires the abandonment of ways of thinking and living that focus exclusively or primarily on one's own well being at the expense of others.

[100] Mark and Matthew are not unaware of the notion of Peter having left everything in order to follow Jesus, because later in the gospel tradition Peter tells Jesus, "Look, we have left everything (ἀφήκαμεν πάντα) and followed you" (Mark 10:28; Matt 19:27). Luke, however, moves this reference about leaving everything to the disciples' initial response to the call of Jesus in order that it might serve a paradigmatic function. The author seeks to

appears to be intentional in his efforts to emphasize the notion of a totally new beginning. Leaving everything entailed more than simply leaving material goods behind. The author conveys to his readers that before following Jesus, Peter, James, John and Levi left everything associated with their previous ways of thinking and living.[101]

In both of these scenes, Luke heightens the sense of a new beginning. According to Luke, Jesus has not only called Levi, but has also called Peter, James and John to repentance,[102] and it is their abandonment of their former ways of thinking and living—their willingness to leave "everything" and to follow Jesus in a new way of living that Jesus will prescribe for them—that serves as a paradigm for repentance.[103] By adding the words "to repentance" at the end of 5:32, Luke creates a situation where Jesus himself identifies this break with the past and its accompanying willingness to follow the lifestyle and teachings prescribed by Jesus as repentance.

The author seeks to make it clear that responding to the call of Jesus is not simply about following Jesus or having some sort of physical affiliation with Jesus.[104] In Luke, Jesus is not simply calling sinners to follow him; he is calling them to repentance. Responding to the call of Jesus is not about following Jesus while trying to maintain one's present way of thinking and living. Responding to the call of Jesus includes following Jesus, but it also includes forsaking everything.[105]

---

make it known at the outset that responding to the call of Jesus involves leaving everything. That this shift is intentional is indicated by the fact that regarding Peter's later statement to Jesus, Luke writes that Peter tells Jesus, "Look we have left our own things (ἀφέντες τὰ ἴδια) and followed you" (Luke 18:28) instead of "Look, we have left everything (ἀφήκαμεν πάντα) and followed you" (in an attempt to harmonize Luke 18:28 with Mark and Matthew, some manuscripts have ἀφήκαμεν πάντα, while others have ἀφέντες πάντα τὰ ἴδια).

[101] The author does not suggest that there was something wrong with being a fisherman. It was not Simon's vocation that indicated a need for a change in his way of thinking and living, instead it was Simon's confession, "I am a sinful (ἁμαρτωλός) man, O Lord" (5:8c). In response to that confession, Jesus told Simon that from that day forward he would be catching people rather than catching fish. After that pronouncement, Simon, James and John left everything and followed Jesus.

[102] Jesus declares that he has come to call "sinners" (ἁμαρτωλούς) to repentance (5:32). As a tax collector, Levi is automatically identified with sinners (5:30; cf, 7:34; 15:1; 18:13), and in the account of the calling of Peter, James and John, Peter confesses, "I am a sinful (ἁμαρτωλός) man, O Lord" (5:8c).

[103] The expectation that one will abandon "everything" associated with one's former way of living is an important component of Jesus' call in Luke. Only the Lukan Jesus states, "whoever of you does not renounce **all** that he has cannot be my disciple" (14:33). Only the Lukan Jesus responds to the rich ruler with the command, "Sell **all** that you have" (18:22b). In the Lukan parable of the prodigal son, the younger son started down the road of transgression by selfishly desiring what he felt belonged to him. He "gathered **all** he had" (15:13) rather than abandoning all that he had.

[104] Cf. Lk 9:49.

[105] Later Jesus calls a would-be follower with the same words that he used to call Levi: ἀκολούθει μοι, "follow me" (9:59). However, when the man expresses a desire to return home first in order to bury his father, Jesus denies the request by saying, 'leave the dead to

Simply following Jesus is not enough; there must also be a willingness to abandon one's present way of thinking and living.[106] The author is aware that many people desire to follow Jesus, but not all are willing to abandon their current ways of living.[107] The multitudes "followed" Jesus,[108] but only a few were willing to forsake everything while following him.[109] Repentance in Luke entails changing one's way of thinking and living and adopting a new way of thinking and living consistent with the lifestyle prescribed in the teachings of Jesus.[110] By adopting this new way of thinking and living, an environment is created in which diverse individuals are able to live together as a community of God's people.

Like John the Baptist, Jesus considers repentance to mean an abandonment of former ways of thinking and living. Peter, James, John, and Levi leave everything in order to follow Jesus. Repentance clearly entails abandoning "old" ways of thinking and living and adopting "new" ways of thinking and living. John the Baptist, who was sent to prepare the way for Jesus, depicted these new ways of thinking and living in terms of ethical social behavior that treats others fairly, justly and equitably, enabling diverse individuals to live together as a community of God's people. At this point in the narrative the author creates a sense of anticipation and even suspense by not having Jesus give examples, as did John the Baptist, of what he understands the new ways of thinking and living to look like. Instead of having Jesus give examples, the author presents three scenes, or pronouncement

---

bury their own dead" (v. 60). Like Levi, this man is being called to leave everything.

[106] Cf. Lk 18:22–30.

[107] Luke alone records Jesus as telling a would-be follower who asks to return home to tell his family good-bye that "No one who puts a hand to the plow and looks back is fit for the kingdom of God" (9:62). The call of Jesus demands a break with the past.

[108] Cf. Lk 7:9; 9:11; 23:27–30.

[109] Cf. Lk 18:28–30.

[110] My emphasis on following the lifestyle prescribed in the teachings of Jesus is based upon the Lukan use of the term μαθητής, "disciple." This pericope contains Luke's first use of the term μαθητής (v. 30). An association is made between Levi and the disciples. The disciples spend time with Levi and other tax collectors in one of the most intimate forms of socialization (i.e. table-fellowship; cf D. E. Smith, *Social Obligation in the Context of Communal Meals* (Ph.D. Dissertation, Harvard University, 1980); *idem*. "Table Fellowship as a Literary Motif in the Gospel of Luke," *Journal of Biblical Literature* 106 (1987) 613–38). The disciples, like Levi, are those who have been called to follow Jesus (as a matter of fact, since Levi was called to follow Jesus before the table-fellowship controversy, and since he is recorded as "having left everything" to follow Jesus before the banquet was given, Levi should most likely be considered one of the disciples at this point). In the Lukan section outlining the cost of discipleship (Luke 14:25–33), the author reveals that following Jesus is about adopting a particular lifestyle. Jesus says unto the crowds following after him, "If any one comes to me and does not hate his own father and mother and wife and children and brothers and sisters, yes, even his own life, he cannot be my **disciple** (μαθητής). Whoever does not bear his own cross and come after me, cannot be my **disciple**. . . . So therefore, whoever of you does not **renounce all that he has** cannot by my **disciple**" (emphasis added). In Luke's gospel, responding to the call from Jesus (i.e. the call to repentance) is about following the lifestyle prescribed by Jesus, and that lifestyle entails renouncing everything associated with one's former way of living and adopting new guidelines for living.

stories (5:33–39; 6:1–5, 6–11), in which Jesus challenges old ways of thinking and living with new ways of thinking and living. Jesus stresses in these three pronouncement stories the necessity of being able to change one's ways of thinking and living.[111]

In the first scene, the Lukan Jesus indicates his recognition of how difficult it is for most people to change their ways of thinking and living by ending the Lukan pericope on repentance (5:27–39) with the statement, "And no one after drinking old wine desires new; for he says, 'The old is good.'" Although some scholars consider Luke 5:33–39 to be separate from 5:27–32,[112] that the unit for Luke is in fact 5:27–39 can clearly be seen from the author's redactional activity.[113] In Mark the fasting question is presented as a separate episode (2:18–22). Luke, however, drops Mark's introduction (v. 18a), creating a situation where the issue about fasting (Luke 5:33) is read as a continuation of the exchange between Jesus and the Pharisees and their scribes at the banquet (δοχή) given by Levi.[114] The banquet provides the setting for the Pharisees' murmuring against and questioning of the disciples' behavior. At the banquet the Pharisees and their scribes raise two concerns. The first is raised as a question directed at Jesus' disciples. The Pharisees and their scribes ask Jesus' disciples why they "eat and drink" with tax collectors and sinners (5:30). After Jesus responds to the question, the Pharisees and their scribes raise their second concern. They inform Jesus that while the disciples of John the Baptist and the disciples of the Pharisees fast and pray, his disciples "eat and drink" (5:33). In both of the concerns raised by the Pharisees and their scribes, Luke employs the construction "eat and drink" (ἐσθίω καὶ πίνω), creating a literary connection between the question asked of Jesus' disciples and the statement made to Jesus.[115] The author has redacted his source material in order to make this

---

[111] These pronouncement stories, like most other pronouncement stories, are composed for the purpose of changing attitudes among its readers and hearers (see Robert C. Tannehill, "Attitudinal Shift in Synoptic Pronouncement Stories," *Orientation by Disorientation: Studies in Literary Criticism and Biblical Literary Criticism Presented in Honor of William A. Beardslee* (ed. Richard A. Spencer; Pittsburgh: Pickwick Publications, 1980) 183–197).

[112] See Fitzmyer, *The Gospel*, 1:587–603.

[113] For a discussion of Lk 5:27–39 as one unit, see Nolland, *Luke*, 241–51; Tannehill, *Luke*, 107–109.

[114] It is worth noting that Luke not only clarifies the ambiguity of Mark's text concerning whether the dinner was at Levi's house or Jesus' house, Luke alone identifies the dinner as a banquet (δοχή). The term is used again in Luke by Jesus when he tells a ruler of the Pharisees, "when you give a banquet (δοχή), invite the poor, the maimed, the lame, the blind, and you will be blessed, because they cannot repay you" (14:13–14a). Since the author changes the Markan tradition, and specifically identifies Levi's gathering as a banquet (δοχή), it is very possible that the author wants the reader to understand the "others" (v. 29b) who are gathered at the meal as being comprised of the poor, maimed, lame, and blind. This way the banquet (δοχή) not only honors Jesus, but it also serves as a concrete expression of Levi's repentance.

[115] It is interesting to note that the objections against mingling with tax collectors and sinners, as well as feasting instead of fasting, also appear together in 7:34, where Jesus declares that he "has come" (ἐλήλυθεν; cf. 5:32) "eating and drinking " (cf. 5:30, 33), and

connection. Mark 2:18 simply reads, "your disciples do not fast." The Lukan redaction, however, provides a link between 5:30 and 5:33. The redactional activity by the author throughout this unit clearly suggests that the author wants 5:27–39 to be read as a single unit.

Because Fitzmyer separates vv. 33–39 from vv. 27–32, he understands the controversy in vv. 33–39 as intended to give a different perspective on the Jewish custom of fasting. As Fitzmyer himself acknowledges, however, such an interpretation creates a Lukan "emphasis on the difference between (Pharisaic) Judaism and Christianity," which contradicts the author's tendency throughout Luke-Acts where "he is otherwise at pains to stress the continuity between them."[116] When the sections are recognized as one unit, however, it becomes clear that the controversy is not about a different perspective on fasting but rather a different perspective on repentance, a perspective arising from the new era in the history of salvation inaugurated by the coming of Jesus.[117] When read as one unit, the Pharisees' concern about fasting is understood as a response to Jesus' assertion that he has come to call sinners to repentance.

The author's redactional activity causes the reader to clearly recognize that the Pharisees and their scribes are questioning Jesus' assertion that he has come to call sinners to repentance. If Jesus has in fact come to call sinners to repentance, then why are Levi, the large company of tax collectors, the others who have gathered, and Jesus' disciples engaged in "eating and drinking" instead of mourning and fasting? The appropriate expression of and response to one's acceptance of a call to repentance was believed to be prayer, fasting, and mourning—not eating, drinking and celebrating.[118] However, the author suggests that as a result of this new era in the history of salvation, an era which has been inaugurated by the coming of Jesus, rejoicing and celebrating are now appropriate expressions of and responses to one's acceptance of a call to repentance.[119] The offer of repentance is part of the

---

is accused of being a "friend of tax collectors and sinners" (cf. 5:30) as well as a "glutton and a drunkard." The association of these motifs is another example of what Robert Alter has called the "type-scene."

[116] *The Gospel*, 1:596–97 (cf p. 178). Most traditional interpreters have mistakenly asserted that 5:33–39 teaches that Judaism (i.e. the old) and Christianity (i.e. the new) are incompatible (see Alistair Kee, "The Old Coat and the New Wine: A Parable of Repentance," *NovT* 12 (1970) 13–21, for a critique of this traditional interpretation).

[117] This difference in perspective, however, in no way suggests that the Lukan Jesus is trying to demonstrate the incompatibility between Judaism and Christianity. It would be extremely anachronistic to project such a distinction back into the ministry of Jesus. It would also be inconsistent with the prevailing Lukan tendency to demonstrate a continuity between Judaism and Christianity (cf. Jervell, *People of God*; Brawley, *Luke-Acts*; Fitzmyer, *The Gospel*, 1:178). The Lukan Jesus is simply calling for a change in thinking regarding the appropriate expression of and response to repentance (cf. Luke 15:7, 10).

[118] Cf. Luke 10:13; 11:32 (cf Jonah 3:5–8); see also Joel 1:13–16.

[119] This point is also conveyed by the author in Luke 15:1–32. The author clearly seeks to make connections between 5:27–39 and 15:1–32. The setting for the latter is also the murmuring of the Pharisees and the scribes because of Jesus' eating with tax collectors and sinners. Jesus then presents two parables and declares that "there will be more joy in

good news preached by both John the Baptist and Jesus,[120] and as good news it should be responded to with rejoicing. Eventually, the sadness resulting from Jesus' being taken away will lead to a time of mourning and fasting,[121] but for now the disciples and those experiencing the gift of repentance have reason to celebrate.[122] For Luke, Jesus' presence, his interaction with sinners and his call for repentance should be marked by celebrating not fasting.

Unlike Mark and Matthew, Luke provides an introduction to the sayings of Jesus by adding the phrase, "And he also told them a parable" (5:36a). In this parable, which has two parts (vv. 36; 37–38), Jesus suggests that it is impossible and destructive to mix new ways of thinking and living with old ways of thinking and living. The two explicit references to 'tearing' a new garment (v 36), both of which are absent in Mark and Matthew, stress the damage done to the new when it is used as nothing more than a means for trying to preserve the old.[123] According to Luke, the new era in the history of salvation, which has been inaugurated by the coming of Jesus, cannot be used simply as a means of preserving the old era.[124] The new ways of thinking and living, reflected in repentance and ushered in as a result of this new era in salvation history, are not meant to preserve old ways of thinking and living, instead they are meant to replace old ways of thinking and living.[125] The response of fasting and mourning may have been the appropriate response to repentance during the old era, but in the new era eating, drinking, and celebrating have now become appropriate responses to repentance.

Furthermore, the old era of salvation history is unable to accommodate the new ways of thinking and living associated with the new era of salvation history. In

---

heaven/there is joy before the angels of God over one sinner who repents" (vv. 7, 10). Even in heaven, joy is the appropriate response toward repentance. Finally, the parable of the prodigal son revolves around feasting and celebrating when the younger brother returns home (vv. 22–24, 32).

[120] Luke 3:18; 4:43.

[121] 5:35; Luke's emphasis here is not on fasting, but rather on the time of sadness that will lead to mourning and fasting (cf. Luke 17:22; 19:43–44; 21:6; 23:27–31; 24:17–21).

[122] The time of mourning and fasting alluded to will not mark a permanent end to the time of joy and celebration, but rather a brief interruption or transition (cf. Luke 24:41, 52–53; Acts 2:46–47; 13:52; 15:3).

[123] Both Mark and Matthew seem to suggest that even though the old is damaged it is still worth preserving, even at the expense of the new.

[124] Cf. A. Kee, "The Old Coat...," *NovT* 12 (1970) 13–21.

[125] As already mentioned above, this section is not meant to be an allegorical depiction of the superiority of Christianity over Judaism nor of the discontinuity between Christianity and Judaism. This is demonstrated in the very next scene where Jesus challenges the Pharisees' accusation that he and his disciples have violated the law regarding the Sabbath-rest by going through the grainfield plucking and eating some of the heads of grain. Jesus responds to the accusation and justifies the behavior of both himself and his disciples by appealing to the actions of one of Israel's greatest kings, David (Luke 6:1–5). By doing so, the author demonstrates not a discontinuity but rather a continuity between Judaism and Christianity. The author is not challenging Judaism with Christianity, but rather challenging traditional ways of thinking and living with new ways of thinking and living (even though the "new" ways of thinking and living have historical antecedents).

the analogy, when new wine is placed in old wineskins the skins burst, ruining the skins and spilling the wine. The old wineskins burst because the weakened and aged fibers of the old wineskins are unable to expand to accommodate the pressure created by the fermenting new wine, causing the skins to burst and the wine to be spilled. New wine must therefore be put into new wineskins. In the words of one scholar, "The two brief parables in 5:36–38 stress the radically new day brought by Jesus which cannot be accommodated to the existing structures and old patterns. This is a day for celebration," not fasting and mourning.[126] New ways of thinking and living can only be accommodated by a new era in the history of salvation. The Lukan Jesus, however, recognizing the difficulty most people have with accepting new ways of doing things, ends this section with a proverb: "And no one after drinking old wine desires new; for he says, 'The old is good.'" The author is most likely alluding to the difficulties those who cling to old ways of thinking and living have with accepting new ways of thinking and living.[127]

This scene is immediately followed in the Lukan gospel with two Sabbath controversies, in which Jesus challenges the thinking of the *some* of the Pharisees and scribes regarding the Sabbath-rest (6:1–5, 6–11).[128] The theme of the old and the new from 5:27–39 provides the perspective from which to approach these two controversies. In both scenes the author illustrates how difficult it can be accepting new ways of thinking and living.[129] The Lukan Jesus demonstrates in these two scenes that even traditions as sacred as the Sabbath-rest must give way to social concerns such as hunger and physical well-being.[130] Providing for and doing good to others takes precedence over the observation of religious rules and traditions, even traditions as sacred as the Sabbath-rest.[131]

---

[126] Cousar, "Luke 5:29–35," p. 62.

[127] The proverb explains the negative reactions of Jesus' opponents depicted not only in the violent response of those in Nazareth to Jesus' interpretation of his ministry (Luke 4:16–30), but also in the responses of those throughout Luke-Acts reacting to the teachings of Jesus and the apostolic teachings about Jesus.

[128] Rather than condemning the Pharisees as a whole, the author has modified the mention of the Pharisees in v. 2, using the indefinite pronoun τινὲς and the partitive genitive ("some of the Pharisees").

[129] In addition to the conspiring done by the scribes and Pharisees, against Jesus, Luke records that "they were filled with fury (ἀνοίας; 6:11)." In contrast to the "change of thinking (μετανοία)" desired, the scribes and Pharisees are described as being in a state of unthinking (ἀνοία), i.e. madness.

[130] According to later rabbinical writings, Pharisaic traditions apparently provided for exceptions to the Sabbath-rest: "Whenever there is doubt whether life is in danger, this overrides the Sabbath" (*m. Yoma* 8:6; Strack and Billerbeck, *Kommentar zum Neuen Testament* 1:622–629).

[131] Cf. Luke 13:10–17; 14:1–6. In the Lukan parable of the good Samaritan (Luke 10:25–37), the author further demonstrates how providing for and doing good to others should take precedence over the observation of religious rules and traditions. Both the priest and the levite, who were more concerned with avoiding ritual defilement, passed by the apparently dead man (cf. Num 5:2; 19:11–16; Ezek 44:25), the Samaritan, however, disregarded both the historical animosity between Samaritans and Jews (cf. Luke 9:51–54; John 4:7–9), as well as the regulations on defilement from contact with a dead body, in order

Bear the Fruits of Repentance or Perish

After the two Sabbath controversies, Jesus retired to the mountain, where he spent the entire night in prayer to God.[132] In the morning he selected twelve from among his disciples, whom he called apostles. He came down the mountain with them, and was confronted by a great crowd (ὄχλος) and a multitude of people (ὁ λαός) who came to hear and to be healed.[133] After healing many of their diseases, Jesus began teaching the people. It is at this point that the author finally has Jesus give a depiction of what the new ways of thinking and living reflected by repentance looks like (6:20–49).[134]

In the first detailed preaching section of Jesus, Jesus is depicted as preaching good news to the poor (οἱ πτωχοί; v. 20)—those to whom he has been sent to preach good news (4:18).[135] The good news is an eschatological promise to the poor (6:20–21; cf. 14:21), that is accompanied—as indicated in the preaching of John the Baptist—by an ethical challenge to those with resources to share those resources with the poor in order to help meet their need and/or relieve their poverty (6:24–25; cf. 14:12–14). Throughout this extensive sermon, the author portrays Jesus presenting ethical social teachings that parallel the teachings of John the Baptist.[136]

---

to care for the wounded man. The thrust of parable is that providing for and doing good to others should take precedence over the observation of religious rules and traditions; this is summed up in Jesus' command to go and show mercy (v. 37; cf. 6:36).

[132] In Luke-Acts, prayer is an important aspect in the life and ministry of Jesus and the disciples. In the gospel, the author depicts Jesus in prayer more often than any of the other gospel writers. Many of the major episodes in his ministry are explicitly linked with prayer (3:21; 5:16; 6:12; 9:18, 28–29; 11:1; 18:1; 22:32, 41–45; 23:46). Prayer also continues to be a vital part of lives of the early Christians depicted in Acts (Acts 1:14, 24; 2:42; 3:1; 6:4, 6; 8:15; 9:11, 40; 10:4, 9, 30, 31; 11:5; 12:5, 12; 13:3; 14:23; 16:13, 16, 25; 20:36; 21:5; 22:17; 28:8). This Lukan emphasis on prayer suggests that the author may be trying to stress the notion of God's guidance regarding, blessings upon, and sanctioning of what is said and done by Jesus and his disciples in Luke-Acts.

[133] This is reminiscent of the crowds (ὄχλοι) and people (λαοί) who confronted John the Baptist (3:7–15).

[134] Since the most recent programmatic statement of Jesus is that he has come to call sinners to repentance, the lifestyle and behavior prescribed here by Jesus should be understood as describing what a repentant lifestyle looks like.

[135] The "poor" here, and throughout Luke represent not only the economically deprived but also the socially marginalized (see Joel Green, "Good News to Whom? Jesus and the 'Poor' in the Gospel of Luke," *Jesus of Nazareth: Lord and Christ. Essays on the Historical Jesus and New Testament Christology* (eds. Joel Green and Max Turner; Grand Rapids, MI: Eerdmans, 1994) 59–74).

[136] See the author's use of χιτών in 3:11 and 6:29. In contrast to the parallel section in Matthew, i.e. 5:40, χιτών here is in the emphatic position. In the Lukan Beatitudes, Jesus emphasizes physical poverty and hunger as opposed to spiritual poverty and hunger implied by Matthew. The Lukan version of Jesus' teaching has several references to sharing and giving that echo the ethical teachings of John the Baptist and that are not part of Matthew's version of Jesus' teaching (e.g. 6:30b, 34–35b, 37c–38b). Lastly, the Lukan Jesus stresses mercy rather than perfection when he says, "Be **merciful**, even as your Father is merciful" (6:36), instead of "Be **perfect**. . ." as is recorded in Matthew (5:48). The Lukan Jesus presents a radical ethic of love and acceptance that challenges old ways of thinking and

As a matter of fact throughout Luke, most of the teachings of Jesus, like those of John the Baptist, emphasize ethical social behavior that focuses on abandoning greed and treating all people fairly, justly and equitably.[137] The sermon closes with exhortations—reminiscent of John the Baptist's—to bear fruits indicative of the teachings presented by Jesus throughout the sermon. What Jesus requires is not simply people coming out to hear him (6:18), he requires them to act upon what they have heard (6:43–49).[138] Like John the Baptist, the Lukan Jesus suggests that the fruits worthy of repentance are those that are manifested in the context of human interpersonal relationships and that demonstrate ethical social concern for the well being of others. It is the fruits worthy of repentance that enable diverse individuals to accept and care for each other and to live together as a community of God's people. Such fruits represent the "good fruit" produced by the "good tree." This kind of fruit results from following both the preaching of John the Baptist and the lifestyle and preaching of Jesus presented here and throughout Luke.[139]

In Luke 13:1–9, the importance of repentance and of bearing fruit that attest to repentance is once again alluded to by Jesus. Some members of the crowd tell Jesus about what happened to some Galileans whom Pilate put to death. Jesus, recognizing that the people think (or at least want to think) that the Galileans have

---

living with new ways of thinking and living, and that makes possible the formation of a community comprised of all people, where everyone is welcomed and treated mercifully. For those who accept and demonstrate this new way of thinking and living, "your reward will be great" (ὁ μισθὸς ὑμῶν πολύς, 6:35b; reward in this context is not payment, but a concrete form of God's approval; cf. v. 23), but for those who refuse to accept this new way of thinking and living, they will experience great suffering (cf. 16:19–23).

[137] Cf. Luke 9:51–56; 10:29–37; 12:13–21, 33; 13:10–17; 14:12–14; 15:11–32; 16:14–15, 19–31; 18:22; 19:1–10; 23:39–43.

[138] Throughout Luke-Acts, it is not simply hearing that is required but also acting upon what has been heard (Luke 3:10–14; 5:5–6; 6:27, 35; 7:3, 29–30; 8:12; 21; 9:15; 10:25, 28, 37; 11:28; 12:47–48; 16:29–31; 17:9–10; 18:18, 22–24; 23:34; Acts 2:37; 3:22–23; 4:4, 20; 5:19–21; 8:6; 9:6, 36; 10:2; 11:30; 13:22, 48; 15:7; 16:14–15, 30; 18:8; 19:5; 22:10; 28:28).

[139] That the lifestyle, ministry, and preaching of Jesus should lead to repentance is suggested by Jesus himself on two occasions: 1) when Jesus rebukes the unrepentant cities of Chorazin and Bethsaida, saying, "if the deeds of power done in you had been done in Tyre and Sidon, they would have repented (μετενόησαν) long ago" (Luke 10:13), and 2) when Jesus rebuked the crowds encountered on his way to Jerusalem, saying, "The people of Nineveh will rise up at the judgment with this generation and condemn it, because they repented (μετενόησαν) at the preaching of Jonah, and see, something greater than Jonah is here!" (11:32). These two passages also demonstrate that repentance is a change in thinking and living that entails turning away from the unfair treatment of others. Much of the ancient condemnation of Tyre and Sidon was directed against their confidence in their wealth and against their greed at the expense of others (Isa 23:1–9; Ezek 26:2, 12; 27:3–27, 33; 28:4–5, 16, 18; Zech 9:3). Repentance for them would have entailed turning away from the ways of thinking and living that focused exclusively or primarily on their own well being at the expense of others. Similarly, the repentance of the Ninevites, who were considered the greatest enemies of the kingdoms of Israel and Judah (cf. Nahum 2:8–9; 3:1, 7, 16, 19), entailed all of them abandoning their evil and violent treatment of others (Jonah 3:8b, 10).

suffered because of their sins, responds:

> Do you think that because these Galileans suffered in this way they were worse sinners than all other Galileans? No, I tell you; but unless you repent, you will all perish (ἀπολεῖσθε) as they did. Or those eighteen who were killed when the tower of Siloam fell on them—do you think that they were worse offenders than all the others living in Jerusalem? No, I tell you; but unless you repent, you will all perish (ἀπολεῖσθε) just as they did.[140]

The fact that the admonition to repent is given twice clearly makes repentance the thrust of this unit. Jesus then tells a parable about a barren fig tree. The man who planted the fig tree sought fruit on the tree for three years, but the tree never produced any fruit. Finally the man told the gardener to cut the tree down. The gardener, however, pleaded for the tree, asking for one more year to care for it. If after being nurtured and provided one more opportunity to bear fruit the tree still had not produced any fruit, then the owner of the vineyard could cut it down.[141]

The placement of Luke 13:1–9 is significant in the development of the author's narrative. An important shift takes place in the Lukan narrative at 9:21. The Galilean ministry of Jesus begins at Luke 4:14. After an extensive ministry of teaching, preaching, healing and other miracles, Jesus asks his disciples, "Who do the crowds say that I am?" After a number of answers, Jesus then asks his disciples, "But who do you say that I am?" Peter responds, "The Christ of God" (9:19–20). This confession serves as the crowning climax of Jesus' Galilean ministry, and it confirms the earlier prophecies concerning Jesus' identity.[142] After Peter's confession, however, the tone of the gospel becomes severe.[143] Jesus turns his attention to the suffering that awaits him in Jerusalem. The disciples are prohibited from telling anyone that Jesus is the Christ of God (9:21). For the first time in the Lukan narrative Jesus clearly and explicitly speaks of the suffering, rejection, death, and resurrection that he must experience (9:22). He then addresses everyone regarding the costs and conditions of discipleship, emphasizing the importance of

---

[140] Luke 13:2–5.

[141] The threat that unproductive trees will be cut down and destroyed was already part of the preaching of John the Baptist (3:9). The parable shared here by Jesus, therefore, resonates with the notion of bearing "fruit worthy of repentance (3:8).

[142] See Luke 2:11, 26 (cf. 1:32–33, 69; 3:15–16; 4:41). Peter's confession is also an explicit christological answer to Herod's earlier question regarding Jesus' identity (9:9). By omitting the material in Mark 6:45–8:26 from the Lukan gospel, the author not only limits Jesus' ministry to Galilee in this part of the gospel, he also brings Peter's confession into close proximity with Herod's question. The rumors heard by Herod regarding Jesus' identity (9:7–8) are clearly echoed by the disciples in their report to Jesus regarding who the crowds say that he is (9:19). Peter's answer, however settles the matter.

[143] Luke 9:21–50 functions as a transitional section preparing the reader for the so-called Lukan travel account that begins at 9:51. As Nolland writes, "In 9:51 Jesus sets his face to go to Jerusalem; 9:21–22 is the beginning point for the explanation of what that involves" (*Luke,* 448).

self-denial over selfish gain (9:23-27). That which awaits Jesus in Jerusalem is further revealed in his transfiguration (9:30-31). The inability of the disciples and the faithlessness of the crowd (ὄχλος) comes to the forefront (9:37-42).[144] Jesus announces for the second time the suffering that awaits him in Jerusalem; the disciples, however are prevented from understanding what Jesus means (9:43-45). The disciples display pride, arrogance, and lack of understanding regarding the meaning of greatness (9:46-48). Jesus rebukes John twice and James once for their lack of understanding, tolerance and mercy toward those thought of as outsiders or enemies (9:49-50, 54-55).[145] The willingness to leave everything and follow Jesus as demonstrated earlier in the gospel is now absent (9:57-61). The cost involved in following Jesus is stressed (9:62). Jesus now tells those whom he sends out that he is sending them out as "lambs in the midst of wolves" (10:3). He pronounces condemnation on those who reject the ones sent out by him (10:12). He rebukes the Galilean towns of Chorazin and Bethsaida for their refusal to repent, and foretells the destruction of Capernaum (10:13-16). He warns against pride (10:17-20), and illustrates through the telling of a parable the importance of not allowing rules and traditions to prevent one from showing mercy to all people (10:25-37). He stresses to Martha and Mary the importance of taking time to listen to and to follow his teachings (10:38-42). He teaches his disciples about prayer (11:1-13), and warns that those who are not with him are against him (11:14-23). He emphasizes the importance of not only hearing the word of God but also keeping it (11:28). He rebukes the crowds (ὄχλων) for their failure to repent at his preaching and teaching, especially in light of the fact that the people of Nineveh repented at the preaching of Jonah (11:29-32). He then makes a series of admonitions, denouncements, and rebukes against Pharisees, lawyers, crowds, rich people, and even his own disciples. He warns them all of the punishment they will receive from God if they fail to fear and acknowledge God, and turn from their hypocritical and selfish ways (11:37-12:34). He tells them of the importance of always being ready for the return of the Son of man, since he is coming at an unexpected hour (12:35-48). He tells them how he has come to bring division and not peace, and he criticizes them for not being able to discern the time nor settle conflicts with their adversaries (12:49-59). Then, after all these stern and solemn warnings, criticisms,

---

[144] Unlike in Mark (9:23-24) and Matthew (17:19-20), the healing of the spirit-possessed boy in the Luke is not a story about the power of faith, but a story about the inability of the disciples and the faithlessness of the crowd.

[145] James and John clearly display a lack of understanding regarding what it means to "Love your enemies" (Luke 6:27-29) and to be merciful (Luke 6:36). Not only does Jesus rebuke James and John for their eagerness to destroy the Samaritans with fire (9:54-55), in the two Samaritan episodes that come later in the Lukan travel account Jesus portrays the Samaritans more favorably than the Jews (Luke 10:29-37; 17:15-19). The author of Luke is the only Synoptic writer who depicts the Samaritans favorably, or shows Jesus having any interaction with the Samaritans. In Matthew 10:5 Jesus forbids the disciples to enter a Samaritan town (see also the favorable depiction of the Samaritans in Acts 8:4-8, 14-17, 25; 9:31).

admonitions and rebukes—immediately after Jesus' remarks about making an effort to settle a dispute with one's accuser—the author places a unit in which Jesus warns the people that unless they repent they will all perish.

In his rebuke of those who asked the question regarding the Galileans, the Lukan Jesus stresses that it is actually not sin itself but rather the lack of repentance that leads to destruction.[146] To the story about the Galileans, who were apparently murdered by Pilate, Jesus adds the story about the eighteen in Siloam, who were accidentally killed when a tower fell on them. Jesus' remarks seem to imply that neither the Galileans nor those in Siloam were destroyed because of the severity of their sin; instead, they were destroyed because of their failure to repent.[147] Their cruel and sudden deaths are meant to challenge those who are still alive to repent.[148]

Many of the scenes in Luke 9:21–12:59 demonstrate that sin is part of the human condition. Chorazin and Bethsaida, however, were not condemned because of their sin, but because of their failure to repent (10:13–14). The crowds following and listening to Jesus were not condemned because of their sin, but because of their failure to repent at the preaching of Jesus (11:32). The Galileans whose blood Pilate had mingled with their sacrifices and the eighteen who were killed when the tower of Siloam fell on them did not perish because of their sin, but because of their failure to repent; likewise, those addressing Jesus in Luke 13:1 are being condemned, and will perish—like the Galileans and those at Siloam—if they do not repent.[149]

Jesus illustrates this point in the parable of the barren fig tree. Like the gardener, Jesus seeks to provide sinners with an opportunity to repent and bear fruit (after all he has come in order to call sinners to repentance—5:32). If, however, they fail to repent and bear fruit, they also—like the fig tree—will be destroyed.[150]

---

[146] As conveyed throughout the Lukan narrative, repentance provides forgiveness of sins and deliverance from destruction (Luke 3:3, 7–14; 10:13–14; 11:32; 16:27–30; 17:3–4; 24:47; Acts 2:38; 3:17–23; 5:31; 8:20–24; 17:30–31; 26:16–20).

[147] The author suggests that ultimately this type of destruction comes from God, not man. The comment regarding the suffering inflicted by Pilate, reveals the people's failure to understand Jesus' earlier warning, "I tell you, my friends, do not fear those who kill the body, and after that can do nothing more. But I will warn you whom to fear: fear him who, after he has killed, has authority to cast into hell. Yes, I tell you, fear him!" (Luke 12:4). Jesus had also told them a parable about a rich man whose soul was suddenly required of him by God because of his greed (12:13–21; however, as the author will soon illustrate in the so-called "Parable of the Prodigal Son" (15:11–32), greed can be forgiven if one changes his way of thinking and living).

[148] The Lukan Jesus had just warned the people about the necessity of being watchful and ready since destruction can come unexpectedly (12:35–48).

[149] Jesus makes it clear, however, that his suffering is not the result of sin or a failure to repent, but part of the plan of God (cf. Luke 9:22, 30–31, 43b–44, 58).

[150] Since the "fruit" of repentance has been depicted in the gospel as ethical social behavior that seeks the well being of all people, including one's enemies (Luke 3:8–14; 6:27–45), and since this passage echoes from the preaching of John the Baptist the notion of cutting down an unfruitful tree, "fruit" here is naturally associated with ethical social behavior.

The author is clearly trying to convey in Luke 13:1–9 that sinners who repent and bear fruit do not have to perish (ἀπόλλυμι) like the Galileans or the eighteen in Siloam. The author further conveys this point in his next depiction of repentance. While it is commonly recognized that Luke 15:1–10 has several points of contact with Luke 5:27–32, the passage also has points of contact with 13:1–9.[151] One major point of contact concerns the relationship between repentance and perishing (ἀπόλλυμι). In Luke 13:1–9, those who fail to repent are the ones who end up perishing (ἀπόλλυμι); throughout Luke 15, however, repentance serves as a corrective for ἀπόλλυμι.[152] Since ἀπόλλυμι is commonly translated "perish" in Luke 13:3, 5 but "lost" throughout most of Luke 15, the English reader often fails to make the connection between Luke 13:1–9 and Luke 15:1–32.[153] Through his use of ἀπόλλυμι in Luke 13:3, 5, the Lukan Jesus makes it clear that only repentance can deliver sinners from perishing. In response to the criticism of the Pharisees and scribes in Luke 15:1–2 regarding Jesus keeping company with tax collectors and sinners, the Lukan Jesus makes an explicit comparison between the recovery (εὑρίσκω) of that which was lost (ἀπόλλυμι) and the repentance of one sinner (15:6–7, 9–10).[154] In Luke 13:1–9 repentance serves as the means by which sinners are delivered from perishing (ἀπόλλυμι), and in 15:1–32 it serves as the means by which that which was once lost (i.e. perishing; ἀπόλλυμι) is now found and restored. In both passages, repentance serves as a preventive and as a corrective to ἀπόλλυμι.[155]

As previously mentioned, there are several points of contact between Luke 15:1–10 and Luke 5:27–32. Just as the Pharisees and scribes criticized Jesus and his disciples for eating with tax collectors and sinners at the feast given by Levi (5:30), in Luke 15:1–2 they once again criticize Jesus for interacting and eating with tax collectors and sinners.[156] Furthermore, just as the earlier criticisms of eating with tax collectors and sinners elicited a response from the Lukan Jesus that he had not "come to call the righteous (δικαίους) but sinners (ἁμαρτωλοὺς) to repentance (μετάνοιαν)," so also the later criticisms of eating with tax collectors and sinners elicited a response from Jesus that "there will be more joy in heaven over one sinner

---

[151] For a discussion of the similarity in content and structure between Luke 15:1–32 and Luke 13:1–9, see Bailey, *Repentance* 188–190.
[152] ἀπόλλυμι occurs eight times in chapter 15.
[153] ἀπόλλυμι is commonly translated as "perish" in 15:17.
[154] Εὑρίσκω is also part of the vocabulary of 13:1–9 (vv. 6, 7).
[155] In support of my earlier remarks regarding the author's use of the parable of new wine and old wineskins as a way of demonstrating that Jesus has ushered in a new era of salvation history with new ways of thinking and living—attested by repentance—that are no longer compatible with the old era of salvation history, it should be pointed out that the parable states that if someone places new wine into old wineskins, the old wineskins will be destroyed (ἀπολοῦνται). In the new era of salvation history, however, new ways of thinking and living serve as a preventive and/or corrective to ἀπόλλυμι, not as a source of it.
[156] The scenario of Pharisees and scribes grumbling at Jesus' association with tax collectors and sinners functions as a "type-scene" in Luke that serves as a setting for challenging ways of thinking that need to be changed (see also Luke 7:34–35).

(ἁμαρτωλῷ) who repents (μετανοοῦντι) than over ninety-nine righteous persons (δικαίοις)[157] who have no need of repentance (μετανοίας)."[158] Finally, just as repentance previously resulted in rejoicing, eating and drinking, repentance throughout Luke 15 is explicitly identified with rejoicing, eating and drinking (15:5–7, 9–10, 22–23, 32).[159]

In the parable of the lost sheep (15:3–7) and the parable of the lost coin (15:8–10), Jesus compares the discovery of those items which were lost (ἀπολωλός) to the repentance of one sinner. While the parable of the lost sheep has a parallel in Matt 18:12–14, only in Luke is it associated with repentance.[160] The discovery of the lost sheep serves as a source of joy not only for the owner of the sheep but also for his friends and neighbors.[161] The joy expressed over the discovery of one lost sheep is analogous to the joy expressed in heaven over one sinner who repents. Similarly, in the parable of the lost coin, Jesus declares that the discovery of the coin serves as a source of joy for its owner, her friends and her neighbors. The joy expressed over the discovery of the lost coin is analogous to the "joy in the presence of the angels of God over one sinner who repents (μετανοοῦντι)" (15:10). Both the parable of the lost sheep and the parable of the lost coin teach that the repentance of sinners is a source of joy in heaven, and it should be responded to with joy on earth as well (as was the case in Luke 5:27–29).[162]

---

[157] This explicit contrast between the many (i.e. the ninety-nine) and the one is a contrast that is somewhat ambiguous and that is not carried over to the parable of the lost coin. This is most likely because the contrast was inherited by the author and is not an essential part of the author's message. The use of the parable of the lost sheep in Matthew suggests that in it's original context the parable of the lost sheep was not designed to make the point that there should be joy over the repentance of one sinner; instead, it was designed to make the point that God desires none to be lost (cf. Matt 18:14), that is why the shepherd will leave the ninety-nine sheep who are safe in order to search for the one that has gone astray. While this emphasis on none being lost may still be inferred by the parable in its Lukan context (cf. the uniquely Lukan phrase ἕως εὕρῃ αὐτό: "until he finds it" (15:4; cf. v. 8); see also Luke 19:10), Lukan redaction has clearly altered the previous intent of the parable.

[158] The ninety-nine "have no need (οὐ χρείαν ἔχουσιν) of repentance" (15:7), just like those who are well "have no need (οὐ χρείαν ἔχουσιν) of a physician" (5:31).

[159] Each time Jesus addresses the Pharisees and scribes about the nature of repentance, he emphasizes the fact that repentance should be responded to with joy and celebrating.

[160] Parallels to Luke 15:3–7 are also found in *The Gospel of Thomas* 107 and in *The Gospel of Truth* 31:35–32:17. As in Matt 18:12–14, these two versions of the parable make no mention of repentance.

[161] In the Lukan account of the parable, the shepherd calls together his friends and neighbors to celebrate with him. This detail is missing in Matthew 18:13, which simply states, "And if he finds it, truly I tell you, he rejoices over it more than over the ninety-nine that never went astray." *The Gospel of Thomas* 107 and *The Gospel of Truth* 31:35–32:17 make no mention at all of rejoicing over the discovery of the lost sheep.

[162] The stress on joy is made obvious throughout chapter 15 by the use of such terms as χαρά (15:7, 10), χαίρω (15:5, 32), συγχαίρω (15:6, 9), and εὐφραίνω (15:23, 24, 29, 32). These terms occur thirty times in the gospel of Luke and thirteen times in Acts, while only occurring twelve times in Matthew and three times in Mark.

While 15:11–32 does not explicitly mention repentance nor does it share the same structural design as the parable of the lost sheep and the parable of the lost coin, the fact that it retains the themes of the lost being found and of public rejoicing indicates that it is indeed—like the parable of the lost sheep and the parable of the lost coin—a parable about repentance. The rejoicing in all three parables stands in contrast to the grumbling of the Pharisees and scribes. Since the grumbling of the Pharisees and scribes is being contrasted to the rejoicing that occurs when one sinner repents, the parables of the lost sheep, the lost coin, and the lost son, suggest that the tax collectors and sinners in 15:1 were not simply coming out to listen to Jesus; they were also engaging in repentance.[163]

In the parable of the lost son, rather than sharing his wealth and possessions with others, which is an ethical principle promoted throughout the gospel, the younger of the two sons demanded his father give him his portion of his inheritance. The younger son then gathered together for himself all that belonged to him. The reader, having recently encountered both the story of the greedy man who approached Jesus and told him to tell his brother to give him his portion of the family inheritance and the parable that Jesus told in response to the incident, easily recognizes the inappropriateness of the younger son's request.[164] Not only does the younger son demonstrate greed and selfishness, he compounds his sinful behavior by wasting (διασκορπίζω) his possessions.[165]

---

[163] This is further suggested by the fact that in the section immediately preceding Luke 15:1 (i.e. 14:25–35), Jesus expounds on the extreme cost of discipleship. Much of this section is unique to the Lukan Jesus (i.e. vv 28–33, 35c), and in it Jesus declares that only those willing to renounce their possessions are able to become his disciples (as discussed earlier, this notion of leaving everything in order to follow Jesus is associated with repentance). The Lukan Jesus concludes the section by stating, "Let anyone with ears to hear listen (ὁ ἔχων ὦτα ἀκούειν ἀκουέτω)!" The author then immediately states that "the tax collectors and sinners were coming near to listen (ἀκούειν) to him [i.e. Jesus]" (15:1). It is the tax collectors and sinners rather than the Pharisees and the scribes who, because they have ears to hear, are listening and repenting and renouncing all that they have (cf 5:27–28). The tax collectors were also among those addressed by John the Baptist concerning repentance in 3:10–14.

[164] See Luke 12:13–21. In the earlier account, Jesus warned the man demanding his portion of the family inheritance be given to him to "Take care! Be on your guard against all kinds of greed; for one's life does not consist in the abundance of possessions" (12:15). The reader would most likely now apply this same warning to the younger son. The reader would also most likely notice that in both the parable of the rich fool and the parable of the lost son, instead of sharing their possessions with others, both the rich man and the younger son gathered together (συνάγω) for themselves what belonged to them (Luke 12:17, 18; 15:13). Lastly, the son's request for his father to give him the portion of the family inheritance that will belong to him, stands in sharp contrast to admonition of Jesus that immediately precedes chapter 15: "So therefore, whoever of you who does not renounce all those things belonging to him, he is unable to be my disciple" (14:33).

[165] 15:13; cf. 16:1.

When the younger son recognizes that he is perishing (ἀπόλλυμαι) needlessly, he changes his way of thinking and makes plans to return to his father.[166] He expresses a willingness to live as a hired servant rather than as the son of a wealthy father.[167] However, before the younger son can even confess his sin to his father and declare that he is no longer worthy to be called his son, the father joyfully receives his son. After the son confesses, the father, like the shepherd with the lost sheep and the woman with the lost coin, calls others to celebrate with him because his son who had once been lost (ἀπολωλώς) is now found.[168] The embrace, the kiss, the robe, the ring, and the sandals together symbolize the love, forgiveness, reconciliation and honor bestowed upon the younger son by the father, and the slaughter of a calf would have easily provided enough meat for a large celebration, perhaps one involving the entire community.[169]

The elder son, however, becomes angry at the father and refuses to participate in the celebration. As suggested by 15:1–10, the purpose of the parable of the lost son is to emphasize the appropriateness of rejoicing over a sinner who repents. The parable's introduction, "There was a man who had two sons" (15:11), clearly indicates that a contrast will be made between these two sons. The introduction even

---

[166] Although this change in thinking is indicated by the phrase εἰς ἑαυτὸν δὲ ἐλθών ("But when he came to himself") rather than by the verb μετανοέω, the literary context clearly suggests that the parable is about the repentance of the younger son. Some scholars have suggested that the phrase εἰς ἑαυτὸν δὲ ἐλθών represents a Hebrew or Aramaic expression for repentance (see Strack and Billerbeck, *Kommentar zum neuen Testament*, 2:215; Jeremias, *The Parables of Jesus*, 130. For a rejection of this view, see K. E. Bailey, *Poet and Peasant. A Literary Cultural Approach to the Parables in Luke* (Grand Rapids, MI: Eerdmans, 1976) 173–180). While this may or may not be true, the phrase is used interchangeably with the noun μετάνοια by Diodorus Siculus, who gives an account of how citizens, after giving dictatorial power to a general, came to themselves (εἰς ἑαυτοῖς ἐρχόμενοι) and wanted to reverse their actions. The general, however, attempted to overcome this change of mind (τὴν μετάνοιαν) by the people (*Library of History* 13.95.2–3). Clearly the phrase "to come to oneself" was understood as another way of depicting repentance.

[167] While some scholars and interpreters are troubled by the fact that the younger son seems to be motivated by self-interest and preservation rather than by remorse (see George W. Ramsey, "Plots, Gaps, Repetitions, and Ambiguity in Luke 15," *Perspectives in Religious Studies* 17 (1989) 37–41), within this passage (as within much of Luke-Acts) the author only seeks to demonstrate that repentance involves recognition of the inappropriateness of previous ways of thinking and living, and a willingness to change those ways of thinking and living. The declaration that he had sinned against heaven and before his father indicates that the son recognizes the inappropriateness of his actions. The author is more concerned with depicting a change in thinking and behavior than he is with depicting the emotional feelings (e.g. remorse) that accompany that change. Here—as in Luke 5:27–39—the author's primary objective is to demonstrate that repentant sinners should be received with joy and celebration. The author is concerned with the emotional feelings of those responding (i.e. the father and the elder son) to the repentant sinner (i.e. the younger son) rather than with the emotional feelings of the repentant sinner. To question the motivation for and the authenticity of the younger son's repentance is to miss the point of the parable.

[168] Luke 15:22–24, 32.

[169] Bailey, *Poet and Peasant*, 185–186; Jeremias, *The Parables of Jesus*, 130; Fitzmyer, *The Gospel*, 2:1090.

suggests that the parable will be built upon a contrast between these two sons. However, as the story unfolds, the parable actually ends up being built upon a contrast between the response of the father and the response of the elder son toward the younger son's repentance.[170] The thrust of this parable is not about contrasting the behavior of a prodigal son and a faithful son; the thrust of the parable is about contrasting responses toward repentance. The response of the elder son (vv. 25–30) mirrors the negative responses of the Pharisees and scribes toward tax collectors and sinners, while the response of the father mirrors the rejoicing of the shepherd and the woman over their lost sheep and lost coin—which of course mirrors the rejoicing in heaven over one sinner who repents.[171] Furthermore, just as Jesus addresses the grumbling of the Pharisees and the scribes by trying to teach them the importance of rejoicing over the discovery of that which was once lost, the father addresses the grumbling of the elder son by trying to teach him the importance of rejoicing over the discovery of that which was once lost.[172]

Through the parables of the lost sheep, the lost coin, and the lost son, the author clearly conveys that repentance should be responded to with joy and celebration because repentance delivers sinners who were once lost and perishing (ἀπόλλυμι). The parables are in response to the criticisms of the Pharisees and the scribes against Jesus for welcoming and eating with tax collectors and sinners. Jesus did not simply have a casual relationship with tax collectors and sinners; by eating with them he was engaging in one of the most solemn and intimate of social relationships. Meals, as social institutions, define social boundaries in terms of who is included and who is excluded.[173] By eating with tax collectors and sinners, Jesus

---

[170] This is highlighted by the author's literary artistry when the elder son responds, "But when **this son of yours** (ὁ υἱός σου οὗτος) came back, who has devoured your property with prostitutes, you killed the fatted calf for him!" and the father replies, "It was necessary to make merry and be glad, for **this brother of yours** (ὁ ἀδελφός σου οὗτος) was dead and has come to life; he was lost and has been found" (15:30, 32). The elder son rejects his brother by referring to him as his father's son (cf. 12:24), but the father here refers to his younger son as his elder son's brother. The rejection of the younger son by the elder suggests that there were most likely those in the Lukan community who had difficulty accepting repentant sinners (just as Jonah had difficulty accepting the repentance of the Ninevites).

[171] Repeating almost word for word the earlier declaration of 15:24, the father's declaration in 15:32 clearly parallels the declarations made by the man and the woman in the first two parables after the man had found his sheep and the woman had found her coin. There is most likely no explicit mention of repentance in the father's declaration because much more than the recovery of a lost sheep or of a lost coin, the restoration of the lost son can easily be understood by the reader as corresponding to the repentance of a sinner. The two references to the joy over one sinner who repents (vv 7. 10) has prepared the reader to understand the father's joy as representing joy over the repentance of his son.

[172] Charles H. Giblin, "Structural and Theological Consideration on Luke 15," *CBQ* 24 (1962) 25. Giblin asserts that 15:25–32 is "exegetically normative for the whole chapter insofar as it forms a sort of inclusio with the opening verses" (22).

[173] Mary Douglas, "Deciphering a Meal," *Daedalus* 101 (1972) 61; J. Goody, *Cooking, Cuisine and Class: A Study in Comparative Sociology* (Cambridge: Cambridge University Press, 1982), 191.

was including them in the family of God, which according to Luke offended the Pharisees and the scribes.[174]

Chapter 15 reveals at least two important things about repentance. The first is that sinners need to repent, because it is repentance that delivers those who are lost and perishing (ἀπόλλυμι). The second is that no matter who they are, where they are from or what they have done, repentant sinners should be welcomed and joyfully received by others into the community of God's people (this often requires those already within the community to change their way of thinking as well) because it is through repentance that sinners receive the salvation of God and are joyfully welcomed and accepted by God.[175] As L. Ramaroson has suggested, chapter 15

---

[174] In the story of Zacchaeus, Jesus is once again criticized for associating with a tax collector, who is identified by the crowd as a sinner (Luke 19:7). While repentance is not explicitly mentioned in the story of Zacchaeus, as it is not in the parable of the lost son, the story of Zacchaeus clearly depicts the repentance of Zacchaeus. Just as the sheep, the coin, and the younger son were all lost (ἀπολωλός; 15:4, 6, 24, 32), so Zacchaeus was also once lost (19:10) before welcoming Jesus into his home and declaring to Jesus, "Look, half of my possessions, Lord, I give to the poor; and if I have defrauded anyone of anything, I pay it back fourfold" (19:8) While there is much debate among scholars as to whether this declaration expresses a customary action of Zacchaeus or a repentant resolve, it seems to me that the context suggests a repentant resolve. If Zacchaeus had customarily engaged in giving half his possession to the poor and restoring fourfold that which he had cheated from people, why was he responded to by the crowd with such hostility, and why would Jesus speak of saving "the lost," especially in light of the fact that the lost represented sinners in Luke 15 (for a discussion of this issue and an opposing opinion, see Fitzmyer, *The Gospel*, 2:1220–21, 1225)? The declaration of Zacchaeus clearly echoes what John the Baptist had told the tax collectors and soldiers they needed to do in order to bear fruit worthy of repentance (3:12–14). Furthermore, the story of Zacchaeus is clearly related to the call of Levi and his banquet in 5:27–32. Both the story of Zacchaeus and the banquet of Levi deal with the motif of "grumbling" at Jesus for associating with tax collectors, and both conclude with a declaration by Jesus regarding what he has come to do (19:10; 5:32) As Tannehill suggests, Jesus' interaction with Levi and Zacchaeus in both these scenes is meant to function as an illustration of a his mission to call sinners to repentance and to seek and save the lost (*Narrative Unity* 1:107). Early in his ministry Jesus proclaimed that he had come to call sinners to repentance (ἁμαρτωλοὺς εἰς μετάνοιαν; 5:32), now, after being a guest in the home of a man identified as a sinner (ἁμαρτωλῷ; v. 7), Jesus proclaims that he has come to seek (ζητῆσαι; v. 10; cf. 15:8) and to save the lost (ἀπολωλός; v. 10). The implication is that Jesus seeks and saves the lost by calling them to repentance (it is very possible that 5:32 and 19:10 form an inclusio, interpreting the ministry of Jesus). Just as Luke 13:1–9 and Luke 15 demonstrate that repentance delivers those who are lost and perishing (ἀπόλλυμι), so Luke 19:1–10 demonstrates that repentance delivered Zacchaeus, who was once lost and perishing.

[175] The use of the imperfect of δεῖ in the father's declaration, "It was necessary (ἔδει) to celebrate and rejoice" (v. 32), echoes the Lukan use of δεῖ throughout Luke-Acts as an indicator of a divine plan at work (see Chapter Two above). In the Lukan narrative, rejoicing over the repentance of a lost sinner is part of the plan of God (cf. vv. 7, 10). As demonstrated earlier, this notion of repentant sinners being welcomed and joyfully received into the community of God's people is also found in the writings of Philo. Regarding the repentance of Gentiles, Philo writes to his Jewish readers, "we ought to sympathize in joy with and to congratulate them, since even if they were blind previously they have now received their sight (*On the Virtues* 179). Philo also informs his Jewish readers, "we must look upon [these men] as our friends and kinsmen." This idea of repentance leading to acceptance within a

serves as a double invitation for sinners to repent of their sins, and for God's people to share in God's joy by welcoming all who repent into the community of God's people.[176]

As I have suggested several times throughout this chapter, in the Lukan community the ability to welcome **ALL** who repented into the community of God's people often required a fundamental change in thinking on the part of some who considered themselves to already belong to the community of God's people. Repentance in Luke-Acts, therefore, represents a fundamental change in thinking that enables every sinner to receive the salvation of God and that should enable diverse and even once alienated people to live together as a community of God's people.[177]

While repentance delivers sinners who are perishing (ἀπόλλυμι), as the warnings in Luke 13:1-9 and the parable of the lost son indicate, sinners must repent while they still have time. In a parable that follows very closely on the heels of the parable of the lost son and that examines inappropriate attitudes toward and use of material possessions—and that is most likely intended to remind the reader of the ethical preaching and teachings of John the Baptist—the author depicts the nature and certainty of the destruction one can expect when one misuses material possessions and fails to repent.[178]

John the Baptist previously informed the crowds that one of the fruits of repentance requires everyone who has food and clothing in excess of what is needed for survival to share their excess with those who have nothing. In another exclusively Lukan parable, the author demonstrates what happens to someone who refuses to share their food and clothing with someone who has nothing. In the parable of the rich man and Lazarus (16:19-31), Jesus tells a story about an unnamed rich man who dressed himself in the finest of clothing and who feasted

---

community also has parallels in Greek philosophical and religious writings. People responding to the call of philosophy would often turn from their old life and begin a new life, becoming part of a philosophical school or community (cf. Plutarch *On Listening to Lectures* 46D; Lucian *Thes Wisdom of Nigrinus* 5; *The Double Indictment* 17; Diogenes Laertius *Lives of Eminent Philosophers* 2:29, 31, 48, 113, 114, 125; 6:26, 27, 82, 87; Seneca *Epistles* 14:10; 16:3; 39:12; 44:3; 89:13; 90:1, 34; 94:50; 108:4-23). In Greek conversion stories, those who turned from old ways of thinking and living and adopted new ways of thinking and living are welcomed into religious communities as they demonstrate continued adherence to the religious and social mores of those communities (cf. Plutarch *Superstition* 166E-168D; Apuleius *The Golden Ass (Metamorphoses)* 11; Ovid *Epistles from Pontus* 1:51-64; Juvenal *Satires* 6).

[176] L. Ramaroson, "Le coeur du troisième évangile: Lc 15," *Biblica* 60 (1979) 348-360.

[177] As Bailey has stated, "For Luke's Christian readers, among whom were Jews and Gentiles, rich and poor, free persons and slaves, men and women, repentance was thus foundational for the continued existence of their community" (*Repentance*, 228).

[178] While the parable of the lost son dealt mainly with the joy that should be expressed over a sinner who repents, the notion of inappropriate attitudes toward and use of material possessions was foreshadowed in the example given by the younger son who squandered (διασκορπίζω) his possessions (15:13; cf. 16:1).

sumptuously everyday.[179] However, lying at the rich man's gate was a poor destitute man named Lazarus who failed to possess clothing to cover his sore infested body and who would have *gladly been satisfied* (ἐπιθυμῶν χορτασθῆναι)[180] with eating the scraps that fell from the rich man's table.[181]

The author places this parable after a series of confrontations with the Pharisees.[182] Immediately prior to this parable, Jesus had criticized the Pharisees for their attitudes toward worldly possessions, and toward God and God's word.[183] The author emphasizes the rich man's lack of concern for Lazarus by bringing attention to the dogs licking on Lazarus' sores.[184] Lazarus was in need of someone to care for him and to share with him the necessities of life, but the rich man refused to do so. By placing Lazarus at the gate of the rich man, the author implies that the rich man consciously refused to help Lazarus. As one scholar has written, "Lazarus was not lying in some dark corner of town or in the street or in some alley nor in the middle of the marketplace but is lying at the very gate of the rich man where the rich man, his servants and guests passed him by each day, perhaps several times."[185] The author wants the reader to recognize that the rich man was clearly aware of Lazarus' plight and chose to do nothing about it.[186]

After both Lazarus and the rich man died, Lazarus was carried by the angels to Abraham's bosom, while the rich man, after he was buried, found himself

---

[179] This man's possession of clothes and food went well beyond the δύο χιτῶνας and βρώματα mentioned by John the Baptist as the basis for sharing with others. That the rich man is so extravagantly arrayed and that his garments are of the color of purple suggests that he is not only exceedingly rich but is also very likely of some sort of royalty ("Those who are gorgeously appareled and live in luxury are in the kings' courts"— Luke 7:25; see Fitzmyer's discussion of purple as the raiment of royalty, *The Gospel*, 2:1130).

[180] The verbal construction ἐπιθυμῶν χορτασθῆναι (16:21), which literally means "longing to be fed," is virtually identical to the verbal construction the author uses in the parable of the lost son, where the author writes that the son was "*desiring to be fed* (ἐπεθύμει χορτασθῆναι) with the pods that the pigs were eating" (15:16a). It is interesting to note that the two most extreme references to people desiring food to eat are found in contexts where repentance is the overarching theme (and even though the lost son is the one who repents in Luke 15, the author explicitly notes that while the son desired to eat the pods that the pigs were eating, "no one gave him anything;" 15:16b).

[181] J. Jeremias (*The Parables of Jesus*; 184) points out that the Aramaic expression translated as "scraps that fell from the table" does not refer to crumbs that might accidentally fall from the table, but rather small pieces of bread that individuals dipped into water and used as a towel to wash their fingers. After cleaning their fingers, they would discard the bread onto the floor.

[182] Luke 11:37–54; 13:10–17; 14:1–24; 15:1–32.

[183] Luke 16:1–18.

[184] As Fitzmyer notes, "The attention of the dogs has only added to his [Lazarus'] miseries. The description of the beggar is vivid and detailed to bring out the lack of concern for him on the part of the rich man" (*The Gospel*, 2:1132).

[185] Edward Matthews, Jr. "The Rich Man and Lazarus," p. 93.

[186] The rich man's mentioning of Lazarus by name (v. 24) indicates that he knew who Lazarus was. The author makes it clear that while the rich man was alive, he and his family knew Lazarus well enough to know his name, yet they chose to ignore his condition.

tormented in Hades.[187] The rich man appealed to Abraham as a son appeals to his father—crying out, "Father Abraham, have mercy on me."[188] The reader, quite naturally, is reminded that John the Baptist had previously warned the crowds not to assume they would escape the wrath to come simply because they had Abraham as their ancestor. The rich man addressed Abraham three times as "father" (vv. 24, 27, 30), and Abraham even addressed him as "son" (v. 25); however, the rich man's status as a descendant of Abraham could not keep him from having to pay the consequences of failing to bear fruit worthy of repentance. Like an unfruitful tree, the rich man was cut down and thrown into the fire, while Lazarus, as John the Baptist promised, was raised up from the stones by God to become a child of Abraham.

While Abraham reminds the rich man how during his lifetime he received good things and how Lazarus received bad things (v. 25), the rich man is not perishing in Hades simply because he was rich.[189] Instead, he is perishing because he failed to repent of his greed and selfishness by sharing his resources with Lazarus.[190] Because the rich man failed to take advantage of a lifetime of

---

[187] Unlike with the rich man, no reference is even made to Lazarus being buried.

[188] In Luke mercy (ἔλεος) is what God demonstrates toward those who fear God (1:50, 54, 58, 72, 78), and what Jesus shows toward those who are despised by other (17:13 ff; 18:38 ff), and what God requires human beings to show toward each other (10:37; cf 6:36). In this parable, he who showed no mercy toward Lazarus on earth is now denied mercy from Abraham in Hades.

[189] While there was an Egyptian folktale written on the back of a Greek document dated 46–47 C.E. depicting the retribution of a rich man in the afterlife, that story does not state that the rich man is being punished simply because he was rich. It also makes no explicit references to the mistreatment of the poor by the rich man nor of the rich man's failure to repent. The story simply asserts that whoever is good on earth will receive good things in the underworld and whoever is evil on earth will receive evil things in the underworld (H Gressmann, "Vom reichen Mann und armen Lazarus: Eine literargeschichtliche Studie," *AbhKPAW* phil.-hist. Kl. 7 (1918) 63–68; see also F. L. Griffith, *Stories of the High Priests of Memphis* (Oxford: Clarendon, 1900) 42–43). For a criticism of the scholarly consensus that an Egyptian folktale lay behind vv. 19–26 and a proposal that the rich man's wealth is the reason for his condemnation (and Lazarus' poverty the reason for his reversal of fortune) see Ronald F. Hock, "Lazarus and Micyllus: Greco-Roman Backgrounds to Luke 16:19–31," *JBL* 106, 3 (1987) 447–463.

[190] As vv. 8–9, 14–15 suggest, it is not the rich man's possession of wealth that is being condemned in this parable; instead, it is his attitude toward wealth and his failure to use his wealth appropriately. Following the parable of the steward (16:1–8), Jesus says, "Make friends for yourselves by means of unrighteous mammon" (v. 9), which in the context of the parable means making friends by cancelling debts (cf. Luke 7:41; 11:4; 16:5, 7). As a result of the steward's shrewdness (v. 8), he abandons his own greed by forsaking his commissions, whereby reducing the debts of his master's debtors and securing for himself "the eternal habitations (τὰς αἰωνίους σκηνάς)" when his wealth is gone (v. 9; "the eternal habitations" clearly has an eschatological connotation and is illustrated in vv. 22–24; cf. the author's use of αἰώνιος elsewhere: Luke 10:25; 18:18, 30; Acts 13:46, 48). By abandoning his own greed, the steward becomes an example of one who is "faithful with the unrighteous mammon" and who is no longer a slave of it (vv. 10–13). The "unrighteous" mammon is not necessarily wealth acquired by unrighteous means, but rather wealth that leads to unrighteous behavior. Those enslaved by the pursuit of wealth are unable to serve God and

opportunities to ameliorate the economic and social disparity between Lazarus and himself by sharing his wealth with Lazarus, God now sets things in order by bringing about a reversal of the situation.[191] Lazarus is now comforted (παρακαλεῖται) while the rich man now suffers.[192]

In order to now make it clear that repentance is the focus of this parable[193] and that the behavior of sharing food and clothing with those in need is recognized as one of the fruits of repentance, the author depicts the rich man as begging Abraham to send Lazarus to his father's house so that Lazarus might warn his brothers, whereby they might repent (μετανοήσουσιν) and avoid the torment of Hades.[194] The context of the parable clearly suggests that repentance for the rich man's brothers entails changing the way they interact with the poor.[195] Apparently, not only had the rich man refused to share food and clothing with Lazarus, but his five

---

to attend to the needs of others. The Pharisees, who are "lovers of money," ridicule Jesus' teaching about money (v. 14). In the narrative, the parable of the rich man and Lazarus serves as a warning to the Pharisees—it also serves as a warning to those in the Lukan community who are enslaved by selfishness and the pursuit of wealth—by showing what happens to people who do not use their wealth to benefit those in need. The rich man is punished not simply because he is rich, but because during his life he became a slave to his wealth and refused to repent of his greed and selfishness by using his wealth to respond to the needs of a beggar such as Lazarus.

[191] Cf. Bultmann, *History of the Synoptic Tradition*, p. 178.

[192] The comfort now given to Lazarus and denied to the rich man (16:25) was also denied to the rich in the Lukan version of the beatitudes. In the Lukan beatitudes the rich are rebuked and informed that they have received all the comfort (παράκλησιν) they are going to receive (6:24). This does not, however, mean there is no hope for the rich. The rich who share food with the poor (14:12–14), and in so doing bear fruit worthy of repentance, will be "blessed" (μακάριος; 14:14; cf. 6:20–22) and repaid at the resurrection of the righteous. Those who are unwilling, however, to share their wealth with the poor will never enter the kingdom of God (Luke 18:18–25; cf., T. D'Sa "The Salvation of the Rich in the Gospel of Luke"). In addition, that which Lazarus desired (i.e. "to be fed," χορτασθῆναι; 16:21) was promised to the hungry in the Lukan beatitudes (6:21). The parable of the rich man and Lazarus not only echoes the blessings and woes pronounced in the Lukan version of the beatitudes, but that which Lazarus and the rich man receive fulfills the prophecy spoken by Mary: "He has cast down the mighty from their thrones and has raised up the lowly. He has filled the hungry with good things and the rich he has sent away empty" (Luke 1:52–53).

[193] J. Jeremias, *Parables*, 186, and T. W. Manson, *Sayings*, 301 are two among many who rightly assert that the main stress in the parable lies in the section focusing on repentance.

[194] Bultmann (*History of the Synoptic Tradition*, 197) tells of a Jewish legend about a rich married couple who misused their wealth and power. After the wife died, a boy journeyed to Hades where he saw the woman in fiery torment. The boy returned from his journey with a message for the rich man from his wife, "Tell my husband to turn over a new leaf, for the power of repentance is great." Since it is hard for Bultmann to imagine that the Jewish story is dependent upon the gospel story, he asserts that the Jewish story must lie behind Luke 16:19–31 (ibid.). Fitzmyer, however, sees no basis for such a conclusion (*The Gospel*, 2:1127).

[195] Introducing the brothers at this point in the parable shifts the attention to people—like the author's readers—who still have time to repent and to escape the torment of Hades. The parable is clearly meant to function as a warning to those in the Lukan community who ignore the plight of those in need in order to enjoy their own possessions.

brothers had also refused to share their wealth with Lazarus. The fact that the rich man wants Abraham to send Lazarus indicates that the rich man was confident that his brothers would recognize Lazarus as the beggar who use to lay outside their gate. The rich man also must have believed that an encounter with Lazarus would force his five brothers to recognize their own unrighteous treatment of Lazarus and cause them to repent of their unrighteous treatment of others who might be in need.

Through his request for Lazarus to be allowed to go warn his brothers, the rich man is acknowledging that his own failure, as well as the failure of his brothers, to share food and clothing with Lazarus and to attend to the physical malady of Lazarus demonstrated a failure to repent, and that it is this failure to repent that is the source of his present suffering and will be the source of his brothers' future suffering. The rich man also confirms, through his dialogue with Abraham, the warning of John the Baptist that repentance, not ancestry, is what keeps one from perishing.

In this parable repentance is identified, as it is in Luke 3:7–14, as a change in thinking that focuses on sharing with and treating others fairly, justly and equitably. Once again, repentance requires people to abandon selfishness and to demonstrate concrete acts of selfless concern for the well-being of others. Such acts reflect compassion and mercy toward all people, especially those who are normally despised, and help enable diverse individuals to live together as a caring community of God's people.[196]

Repentance Requires Forgiveness

While the author of Luke-Acts promotes the notion of an ideal community where everyone lives together and cares for each other as a community of God's people, the author also acknowledges that obstacles to such a community are inevitable. Immediately after rebuking the Pharisees and sharing with them the parable of the rich man and Lazarus, Jesus informs his disciples that it is impossible for stumbling blocks not to come (17:1). Unfortunately, there will always be members of the community who sin against others in the community and who may even cause some in the community to stumble because of their sins. Jesus pronounces judgment on such people, and instructs his disciples not to allow the sins of their brothers committed against them and against others to cause them to stumble.

---

[196] Manson has identified the unit beginning at Luke 15:1 and running to the end of the Lukan travel account (at least 18:14, but possibly 19:27) as "the Gospel of the Outcast" (*Sayings* 282). Manson asserts that Luke's use of his material in this unit reveals an attempt by the author to show God's concern for those human beings whom people tend to despise. According to Manson the parable of the rich man and Lazarus—and therefore the theme of repentance itself—plays an important role within Luke's "Gospel of the Outcast" (301).

Since these words of warning immediately follow the parable of the rich man and Lazarus, the sins committed by members of the community against other members of the community, causing some in the community to stumble, are easily identified with the sins committed by the rich man and his brothers against Lazarus.[197] The type of moral, social, and economic injustice committed by the rich against the poor can easily cause the poor to become resentful and to stumble. Jesus warns his disciples, however to be on their guard (προσέχετε ἑαυτοῖς).[198] He exhorts them not allow the sins of their brother to cause them to stumble. Instead, when their brother sins they should rebuke him, and if he repents (ἐὰν μετανοήσῃ), they should forgive him.[199] No matter what the sin is or how many times it is committed against them, if the person committing the sin comes and says, "I repent (μετανοῶ)," then the disciples are obligated to forgive that person (17:4).[200] Just as Jesus came in order to call sinners to repentance and to forgives sinners who do repent, so the disciples are instructed to forgive sinners who repent, even those who repeatedly sin against them.[201] While the sins committed by the rich

---

[197] Fitzmyer states that "Luke now continues his travel account with further sayings of Jesus, which are completely unrelated to the foregoing chapter or parable" (*The Gospel*, 2:1136). If by this statement, Fitzmyer means that in their historical context the sayings were made by Jesus apart from the sayings and parable in chapter 16, then Fitzmyer very well may be correct, but if Fitzmyer means that in their present literary context the statements are unrelated to the sayings and parable in chapter 16, then I see no reason to make such an assertion. As I will show, the sayings of 17:1–4 may very well be related to the parable of the rich man and Lazarus.

[198] This is the same advice Jesus gives his disciples when he warns them to beware of the hypocrisy of the Pharisees (12:1) and when he warns them not to allow their hearts to be weighed down with dissipation and drunkenness and the worries of this life (21:34).

[199] While Fitzmyer understands 17:1–3a and 17:3b–4 to be two sets of isolated sayings that are unrelated to each other (cf. *The Gospel*, 2:1138), the context suggests to me that 17:1–4 represents a single unit. Fitzmyer has taken the imperative προσέχετε ἑαυτοῖς (17:3a) to serve as the conclusion to the preceding sayings; however, on the two other occasions where the author uses the construction it serves as an introduction to what follows (12:1; 21:34). The imperative of 17:3a should be seen as a transitional statement connecting the sayings of 17:1–2 with 17:3b–4.

[200] The point is not to harbor resentment or a grudge toward those who sin against you, whereby you yourself end up stumbling and falling into sin. This point is explicitly made in *T. Gad*, where it is written, "Therefore, love one another from the heart, and if a man sins against you, speak to him in peace, after having cast away the poison of hatred; and do not hold guile in your soul. And if he confesses and repents (μετανοήσῃ), forgive him; and if he denies, do not get into a passion with him, lest, when he starts swearing, you sin doubly" (6:3–4).

[201] Recognizing the difficulty of such a task, the apostles say to Jesus, "Increase our faith" (17:5). Jesus assures them that they have the faith necessary to do what's required of them. He also demonstrates to them the type of forgiveness required. In vv. 11–19 Jesus passes between Samaria and Galilee on his way to Jerusalem where ten lepers beg for mercy. Jesus heals them and gives them instructions to follow. One of the lepers returns to give thanks; he is a Samaritan, an enemy of the Jews. Earlier in the narrative, the disciples were prepared to call down fire from heaven to destroy an entire village of Samaritans who refused to allow Jesus to pass through their village on his way to Jerusalem (9:51–55). Even though the Samaritans had previously rejected Jesus, in the cleansing of the ten lepers, Jesus heals at least one Samaritan who begs Jesus to have mercy on him. This type of compassion

man and his brothers against Lazarus were severe, had the rich man or his brothers come to Lazarus and repented, Lazarus would have been required to forgive them, and if the rich man's brothers do repent (as the rich man desires) then they should be forgiven.

Repentance requires forgiveness,[202] and it is the forgiveness extended to repentant sinners that enables them to receive the salvation of God and that helps once estranged and alienated people to live together as a genuine community of God's people. In keeping with this notion that repentance requires forgiveness, in the last reference made to repentance in Luke—as in the first reference made to repentance—repentance is once again associated with the forgiveness of sins. The Lukan gospel tradition begins with John the Baptist "preaching a baptism of *repentance for the forgiveness of sins* (μετανοίας εἰς ἄφεσιν ἁμαρτιῶν)," and it ends with Jesus declaring to his disciples that "*repentance for the forgiveness of sins* (μετάνοιαν εἰς ἄφεσιν ἁμαρτιῶν) is to be preached in his name to all nations."[203] The notion that those who repent of their sins are to be responded to with forgiveness forms an inclusio for the entirety of Luke.[204]

Repentance in the Preaching of the Disciples

According to Luke, one of the last commands given by Jesus to his disciples was for them to preach a baptism of repentance for the forgiveness of sins. John the Baptist preached a baptism of repentance for the forgiveness of sins; Jesus came in order to call sinners to repentance, and as Jesus was departing he commissioned his disciples to preach a baptism of repentance for the forgiveness of sins. The preaching of repentance is clearly central in the ministries of John the Baptist, Jesus, and the disciples. However, as was the case in the Lukan portrayal of the preaching of Jesus, there is an obvious omission of μετανοέω from the preaching of the disciples in Luke's gospel.

The Second Obvious Omission

All three of the Synoptic gospels record the sending out of "the twelve" by Jesus.[205] According to tradition, Jesus called the twelve together and gave them authority over spirits and power to cure diseases. As he sent them out, he commanded them to take no provisions for their journey: their needs would be met

---

toward one's enemies is the same type of forgiveness the disciples should display.
[202] Luke 1:77; 3:3; 5:20–24; 7:47–49; 11:4; 24:47; Acts 2:38; 5:31; 10:43; 13:38; 26:18
[203] Luke 24:47; 3:3.
[204] The notion of repentance being responded to with forgiveness of sins is also associated with the first and last references to repentance in the book of Acts (cf Acts 2:38; 26:12–20).
[205] Mark 6:7–13; Matt 10:1, 5–15; Luke 9:1–6.

by those with whom they stayed in the various towns and villages. He also instructed them to move on from the places where they were not welcomed and to shake the dust off of their feet as a testimony against such places.

According to Mark's gospel, after receiving such instructions the twelve "went out and proclaimed that all should repent (ἵνα μετανοῶσιν). They cast out many demons, and anointed with oil many who were sick and healed them."[206] While Matthew's gospel completely lacks any such concluding remarks, Luke's gospel presents these remarks differently. The concluding remarks of Luke's gospel clearly suggest that the author is familiar with the remarks found in Mark's gospel and that he is following the order of his Markan source; however, instead of declaring that the twelve went out preaching repentance, casting out demons and anointing the sick with oil, Luke simply states that "they departed and went through the villages, preaching good news and healing everywhere (πανταχοῦ)."[207]

In many ways the summary statement used by the author here is similar to the summary statement used by the author when he began his account of the beginnings of Jesus' public ministry. In both Mark and Matthew, Jesus began his public ministry in Galilee by exhorting the people to repent (μετανοεῖτε) because the kingdom of God had drawn near. In Luke's gospel, however, the author omits the reference to repentance. Instead of identifying what it was Jesus said to the people when he began his ministry in Galilee, the author simply states that Jesus "began to teach in their synagogues and was praised by everyone (πάντων)."[208] The author makes no reference to repentance in the initial preaching of Jesus nor in the initial preaching of the twelve; instead he simply notes that Jesus and the twelve began their ministry preaching and teaching; going everywhere (πανταχοῦ) and impacting everyone (πάντων).

As stated earlier, as predominant as μετανοέω and μετάνοια are in Luke-Acts, the omission of μετανοέω from an inherited tradition would seem to suggest a conscious and deliberate decision on the part of the author. As in the case of the initial preaching of Jesus, there is most likely a literary justification for the author's omission of μετανοέω from the initial preaching ministry of the disciples.[209] In Luke 9:2, the author adds to his account of the sending out of the twelve the statement, "and he [i.e. Jesus] sent them out to proclaim the kingdom of God and to heal." This statement represents the Lukan version of the Markan statement that the author omitted from his account of Jesus' choosing of the twelve.[210] Mark records that when Jesus called his disciples together he appointed twelve, whom he also called apostles, "to be with him, and to be sent out to proclaim the message,

---

[206] Mark 6:12–13.
[207] Luke 9:6.
[208] Luke 4:14–15.
[209] Possible explanations for the omission of μετανοέω from the initial preaching of Jesus have already been discussed above.
[210] Luke 6:12–16.

and to have authority to cast out demons."[211] Luke, however, moves this comment from the choosing of the twelve to the actual sending out of the twelve.[212] The author does, however, state in Luke 8:1–3 that Jesus went through the cities and villages, "proclaiming and bringing the good news of the kingdom of God. The twelve were with him, as well as some women who had been healed of evil spirits and infirmities: Mary, called Magdalene, from whom seven demons had gone out." This Lukan addition is a depiction of what Mark alludes to in Mark 3:14–15. The twelve also remained with Jesus as he healed the Gerasene demoniac (8:26–39) and both the woman with the flow of blood and Jairus' daughter (8:40–56). Now, after being with Jesus while he preached the good news of the kingdom of God and casted out demons and healed diseases, the twelve are sent out by Jesus "to proclaim the kingdom of God and to heal."

Luke 9:1–6 is clearly meant to be read in close connection with chapter 8.[213] Chapter 8 begins with Jesus "preaching the good news of the kingdom of God," and continues with him casting out demons and healing diseases. The "kingdom of God" has been Luke's favored designation for the preaching of Jesus,[214] and now it is to be understood as the content of the preaching of the twelve. The author is intent on using the vocabulary of "preaching the kingdom of God," "demons" and "healing" to connect the ministry of the twelve in 9:1–6 with the ministry of Jesus in Chapter 8. A reference to repentance in Luke 9:1–6 might possibly disrupt and distract the reader from the connection being made with chapter 8.

It may also be, however, that the author was influenced by an additional source that does not mention repentance, but only speaks about the kingdom of God.[215] The missing reference to Jesus preaching repentance in Luke 4:14–15 is found in the parallel passages from Mark and Matthew. The missing reference to the disciples preaching repentance in Luke 9:6, however, is also missing from the parallel passage in Matthew. The reference to the disciples preaching repentance is only found in Mark; therefore the reference may have been missing from the additional source used by Luke and Matthew.[216]

---

[211] Mark 3:14–15.

[212] The influence of Mark 3:14–15 on Luke, as well as the moving of the verses to the Lukan version of the sending out of the twelve, most likely caused the author to replace the Markan "unclean spirits" in Mark 6:7 with "demons" in Luke 9:1.

[213] The Lukan addition of "power" to Mark's "authority" in Luke 9:1 immediately links the passage with Luke 8:46 and foreshadows both Luke 24:49 and Acts 1:8.

[214] Luke 8:1 (cf. 4:43; 6:20; 7:28; 8:10; *et. al.*).

[215] Cf. Matt 10:7; Luke 10:8, 11.

[216] This additional source most likely inspired Luke's closely related mission account in 10:1–20, which clearly influenced his account in 9:1–6 (In 9:3 Luke drops the Markan mention of sandals, which are prohibited in Luke 10:4, and in 9:5 the author uses this additional source to clarify Mark's "whichever place" (Mark 6:10–11) by specifically mentioning "town," which is found in Luke 10:8, 10, 11, 12). Elements from Luke 10:1–20 are also found in Matthew's fragmented mission account (cf. Matt 9:37–38; 10:7, 8, 11–16), which clearly suggests the existence of an additional source (Luke 10:7 also adds a degree of clarity to Luke 9:4 as well as Mark 6:10 and Matt 10:11: it is appropriate for the physical needs of the disciples to be provided for by others; however, they are not to take advantage

Finally, the author may have been reserving any mention of a ministry of repentance until the period of Jesus ended and the period of the disciples and the Church officially began. As the period of Jesus' earthly ministry was coming to an end, he told his disciples that "repentance for the forgiveness of sins (μετάνοιαν εἰς ἄφεσιν ἁμαρτιῶν)" was to be preached (by them) in his name.[217] In making the disciples responsible for preaching repentance for the forgiveness of sins, Jesus is passing on to them a task that was central to the ministry of both John the Baptist and himself. Of the five occurrences of the noun ἄφεσις, usually translated "forgiveness" in 24:47, the term is used to describe John's mission in 1:77; 3:3, Jesus' mission in 4:18, and now the future mission of the disciples.

Jesus informed the disciples that they were to wait in Jerusalem until they were "clothed with power from on high."[218] According to the author's second volume, the disciples received that power on the day of Pentecost, and they immediately began preaching repentance in the name of Jesus.[219] The disciples began their ministry of repentance after they had received the promised power from on high—marking the beginning of the period of the Church.[220] The gospel story begins with John the Baptist preaching repentance during his period of ministry. After the period of John the Baptist ends, Jesus preaches repentance during his period of ministry, and after the period of Jesus ends, the disciples preach repentance during their period of ministry.

The Commission to Preach Repentance

While Jesus' final commissioning of his disciples is found in all three of the Synoptic accounts, the commission in each account is formulated to reiterate and reinforce major themes in the theology of each Gospel.[221] In the Markan appendix—which is universally accepted to have not been written by the author, but which echoes Markan themes—the disciples are commissioned to "Go into all the world and proclaim the gospel (κηρύξατε τὸ εὐγγέλιον) to the whole creation."[222] While any explicit reference to the "gospel" (εὐγγέλιον) is

---

of people or try to upgrade on the hospitality received by going from house to house).

[217] Luke 24:47–48 (The preferred reading here is μετάνοιαν εἰς ἄφεσιν ἁμαρτιῶν [P⁷⁵, ℵ, B, syᵖ, co], which matches Luke 3:3. In both cases the phrase is dependent on the verb κηρύσσω. The variant καί instead of εἰς would mean "repentance **and** forgiveness of sins" [A, C, D, L, W, Θ, Ψ, 063, ƒ¹³, the Koine text tradition, and many ancient versions], which, although attested in Acts 5:31, most likely represents the emendation of a copyist (cf. Fitzmyer, *The Gospel*, 2:1584)).

[218] Luke 24:49.

[219] Acts 2:1–4, 38; 3:18–19; 5:31.

[220] The period of the ministry of Jesus officially began after the Holy Spirit descended upon him at his baptism in bodily form like a dove, and the period of the ministry of the disciples and the Church officially began when the Holy Spirit descended upon the disciples in the form of tongues of fire.

[221] Cf. Fitzmyer, *The Gospel* 2:1578.

[222] Mark 16:15.

completely missing from the Lukan message and occurs only four times in the Matthean message, the notion of the "gospel" (εὐγγέλιον) plays a prominent role in the Markan message.[223] It would seem that within the gospel tradition itself the use of the term εὐγγέλιον is a Markan contribution. For Mark, the "gospel" (i.e. the "good news") is the summation of the message of Jesus Christ (1:1), which he has recounted for his audience.[224]

Furthermore, the notion of casting out demons (δαιμόνια ἐκβάλλειν), which is only found in the Markan version of Jesus' final commissioning of his disciples, reiterates a theme found throughout Mark. While Mark is the shortest of the canonical gospels, there are more references in Mark to the casting out demons than in any of the other canonical gospels.[225] From the very beginning of his ministry in Mark, Jesus is involved in casting out demons and unclean spirits.[226] The Markan Jesus explicitly appoints the twelve apostles to "cast out demons" (ἐκβάλλειν τὰ δαιμόνια).[227] Immediately following this appointment is an elaborated pronouncement story whose core is a controversy over the source of Jesus' power to cast out demons.[228] Later, when the twelve are sent out by Jesus, only Mark records that "they cast out many demons" (δαιμόνια πολλὰ ἐξέβαλλον).[229]

The healing of the "sick" (ἄρρωστος) in 16:18 also echoes a Markan theme. In the final commission given by the Markan Jesus, those who believe will "lay their hands on the sick (ἐπὶ ἀρρώστους χεῖρας ἐπιθήσουσίν), and they will recover." Immediately before Jesus' sending out of the twelve, Mark records that Jesus could do no deeds of power in Nazareth, "except that he laid his hands on a few sick people (ὀλίγοις ἀρρώστοις ἐπιθεὶς τὰς χεῖρας) and cured them" (6:5). Mark also asserts that when the twelve apostles were sent out by Jesus, they cast out many demons and anointed with oil "many that were sick (πολλοὺς ἀρρώστους) and healed them" (6:13). Three of the five New Testament occurrences of ἄρρωστος are found in Mark.[230] The casting out of demons and unclean spirits, the healing of the sick, and the preaching of the gospel are major themes in the theology of Mark,

---

[223] Cf. Mark 1:1, 14, 15; 8:35; 10:29; 13:10; 14:9 (The use of the term εὐγγέλιον is also missing from the Johannine gospel).

[224] Mark calls his account "the gospel (τοῦ εὐγγελίου) of Jesus Christ" (1:1), while Luke calls his account a "narrative" (διήγησις; 1:1).

[225] There are nine references to the casting out of demons in Mark (1:34, 39; 3:15, 22; 6:13; 7:26, 29, 30; 9:38; 16:9, 17), while there are seven in Matthew, seven in Luke and none in John. There are also 11 references to "unclean spirits" (πνεῦμα ἀκάθαρτος) in Mark (1:23, 26, 27; 3:11; 30; 5:2, 8, 13; 6:7; 7:25; 9:25), while there are only two references in Matthew, five in Luke and none in John.

[226] Mark 1:23–27, 34 (cf. 1:39, 3:11–12, 22; 5:2, 8, 13; 7:25–26, 29–30; 9:25; 16:9).

[227] Mark 3:15 (cf. 6:7).

[228] Mark 3:19b–35.

[229] Mark 6:13.

[230] The other two occurrences are found in Matt 14:14 and I Co 11:30.

and they are all reiterated by the Markan Jesus in his final commissioning of his disciples.[231]

In Matthew's gospel, Jesus' final commission to his disciples is not formulated in terms of the "gospel" (εὐγγέλιον), casting out demons or healing the sick; instead, Jesus commissions his disciples to "Go therefore and make disciples (μαθητεύσατε) of all nations... teaching them to observe (τηρεῖν) all that I have commanded (ἐνετειλάμην) you."[232] The thematic issues in the Matthean commission are teaching, the observance of commandments, and the making of disciples.

Not only is there a massive amount of teaching material in Matthew that has been systematically arranged and presented, but it has been repeatedly noted by many New Testament scholars that the Matthean Jesus is depicted as a teacher.[233] Unlike the Markan Jesus, who is primarily depicted as one who casts out demons and heals the sick, the Matthean Jesus is portrayed primarily as a teacher. Matthew tends to bring the material pertaining to Jesus' teaching together into blocks. There are five major teaching discourses by Jesus that end with the phrase, "When Jesus had finished saying these things." (7:28; 11:1; 13:53; 19:1; 26:1).[234] Jesus' most prominent activity in Matthew is teaching.

In Jesus' first major teaching discourse, commonly referred to as the "Sermon on the Mount," Jesus is depicted as an interpreter and teacher of Torah.[235] He

---

[231] The healing of the "sick" (ἄρρωστος) in 16:18 also echoes a Markan theme. In the final commission given by the Markan Jesus, those who believe will "lay their hands on the sick (ἐπὶ ἀρρώστους χεῖρας ἐπιθήσουσίν), and they will recover." Immediately before Jesus' sending out of the twelve, Mark records that Jesus could do no deeds of power in Nazareth, "except that he laid his hands on a few sick people (ὀλίγοις ἀρρώστοις ἐπιθεὶς τὰς χεῖρας) and cured them" (6:5). Mark also asserts that when the twelve apostles were sent out by Jesus, they cast out many demons and anointed with oil "many that were sick (πολλοὺς ἀρρώστους) and healed them" (6:13). Three of the five New Testament occurrences of ἄρρωστος are found in Mark (the other two occurrences are found in Matt 14:14 and I Co 11:30).
[232] Matthew 28:19–20.
[233] For a discussion of Jesus as the unique teacher in the christology of Matthew, see Marinus de Jonge, *Christology in Context* (Philadelphia: Westminster Press, 1988) 91–93.
[234] It has been repeatedly suggested that the author has deliberately structured his gospel into five sections corresponding to the five books of the Pentateuch—portraying Jesus, therefore, as a teacher equivalent to Moses (This hypothesis was developed most fully by B. W. Bacon, *Studies in Matthew* (New York: Henry Holt, 1930). While it is tempting to correlate the five-part division of Matthew to the Pentateuch, attempts to work out the correlation in detail have often appeared somewhat forced, and have unnecessarily brought the five-part division of the Matthean gospel into disrepute. The five-part division clearly displays an intentionality behind wanting to depict Jesus as a teacher (cf. T. Keegan, "Introductory Formulae for Matthean Discourses," *CBQ* 44 (1982) 415–30), and is consistent with the five-part division of literary works common in the Jewish and Greco-Roman world at that time (John P. Meier, "Matthew, Gospel of," *ABD* 4:629–635).
[235] Throughout this discourse one of the ways the Matthean Jesus interprets and teaches Torah is by employing the antithetical statement, "You have heard it said," followed by a text of Torah, "But I say to you," followed by his interpretation (5:21, 27, 31, 33, 38, 43).

informs his disciples that he has come to fulfill the law, and instructs them saying, "Therefore, whoever breaks one of the least of these commandments (τῶν ἐντολῶν), and teaches others to do the same, will be called least in the kingdom of heaven; but whoever does them and teaches them will be called great in the kingdom of heaven" (5:19). Not only is the Matthean Jesus a teacher, but as in his final commissioning of his disciples, the Matthean Jesus instructs his disciples throughout the gospel to observe and to teach others to observe what has been commanded.

Throughout Matthew, the author stresses this notion of observing what has been commanded. The verb τηρέω ("observe, keep, guard") occurs six times in Matthew, but only once in Mark and never in Luke. Similarly, the verb ἐντέλλομαι ("command, order, give orders") occurs five times in Matthew, but only twice in Mark and once in Luke. When a rich young man approached Jesus and said, "Teacher, what good deed must I do to have eternal life?" Jesus responded, "Why do you ask me about what is good? There is only one who is good. If you wish to enter into life, *keep the commandments* (τήρησον τὰς ἐντολάς)."[236] Observing what has been commanded is a prominent theme in Matthew, and it is reiterated in the Matthean Jesus' final commission.

The notion of discipleship is also a major theme in Matthew. In Jesus' final commission, the disciples are instructed to go and "make disciples (μαθητεύσατε) of all nations." Matthew is the only one of the canonical gospels to use the verb μαθητεύω ("become a disciple, make a disciple of"). Of the four occurrences of the verb in the New Testament, three of those occurrences are found in Matthew.[237] A few verses before the commission to go and make disciples, Matthew records that immediately after the death of Jesus, "When it was evening, there came a rich man from Arimathea, named Joseph, who had also become a disciple (ἐμαθητεύθη) of Jesus."[238] As a disciple, Joseph went to Pilate and asked for the body of Jesus. He took the body, wrapped it in a clean linen shroud, and laid it in his own new tomb. After being cared for in death by a rich man who had become a disciple, the resurrected Jesus now commissions his own disciples to go and make disciples of all nations. The increased importance of discipleship in Matthew is also reflected by the fact that μαθητής is used seventy-three times in Matthew, but only forty-six times in Mark, and thirty-seven times in Luke.

Clearly the accounts of Jesus commissioning his disciples in both Mark and Matthew were formulated to reiterate and reinforce major themes in the theology of each of these two gospel. Similarly, the commissioning account in Luke was also formulated to reiterate and reinforce major themes in the theology of Luke. In Luke's commissioning account there is no reference to preaching the gospel or

---

[236] Matthew 19:16–17 (the explicit command to "keep the commandments" is missing from the Synoptic parallels; cf. Mark 10:17–22; Luke 18:18–23).
[237] Matt 13:52; 27:57; 28:19 (the only other occurrence is Acts 14:21).
[238] Matt 27:57.

healing the sick; neither is there any reference to making disciples or teaching them to observe what has been commanded. In the commissioning statement of the Lukan Jesus, the disciples are informed that "repentance for the forgiveness of sins (μετάνοιαν εἰς ἄφεσιν ἁμαρτιῶν)" is to be proclaimed (by them) "in his name (ἐπὶ τῷ ὀνόματι αὐτοῦ) to all nations (εἰς πάντα τὰ ἔθνη)." This of course is consistent with the major themes of repentance, forgiveness of sins, and universalism, which are found throughout the Lukan gospel.[239] That which characterized the mission of John the Baptist and of Jesus in Luke, will now characterize the mission of the disciples.

The Period of the Disciples

Volume two of the Lukan narrative begins by overlapping much of Luke 24, thereby bridging the transition from the period of Jesus to the period of his disciples. In the first chapter of Acts, the reader is reminded of Jesus' final commissioning of his disciples and of his ascension into heaven. After selecting a successor to Judas, the twelve—along with a number of other disciples—receive

---

[239] The commissioning statement in Luke not only reiterates and reinforces major themes found throughout Luke, it also explicitly connects the gospel with volume two of this narrative and it foreshadows themes that will play a major role in the second volume. In Jesus' final commissioning of his disciples he instructs them to wait in Jerusalem until he sends them what the Father has promised and they receive power from on high. He also informs them that they are to be "witnesses" (μάρτυρες)—beginning from Jerusalem—of both Jesus' suffering, death and resurrection and of the preaching of repentance "in his name to all nations." Volume two of the narrative opens with a reiteration of both the command to wait in Jerusalem and of the promise of power (Acts 1:4, 8). There is also a repeating—in what serves as a programmatic verse in the book of Acts—of the statement to the disciples that they will be "witnesses" (μάρτυρες), beginning in Jerusalem (Acts 1:8). The noun μάρτυς (witness) is only used one other time in Luke (11:48), and is therefore not a major theme in the gospel; the noun does, however, occur thirteen times in Acts (more than in any other New Testament writing). The use of μάρτυς in Luke 24:48, therefore, foreshadows a theme that will play a prominent role in the second volume of the author's narrative (Acts 1:8, 22; 2:32; 3:15; 5:32; 10:39, 41; 13:31; 22:15, 20; 26:16). On at least four occasions being a witness in Acts is also associated with proclaiming repentance (2:32–38; 3:14–19; 5:30–32; 26:15–20). Furthermore, the notion of preaching in the name of Jesus occurs nowhere in the gospel outside of 24:47; however, preaching "in the name of Jesus" recurs throughout Acts (2:38; 3:6, 16; 4:10, 12, 17–18, 30; 5:28, 40–41; 8:12; 9:16, 21, 27, 28; 15:16; 16:18; 19:13, 17; 21:13; 22:16; 26:9; The first three occurrences of repentance in Acts are associated with preaching done "in his name," 2:38; 3:16–19; 5:27–32). Finally, while the use of ἔθνος in Luke 24:47 does reiterate the eleven other occurrences found in Luke, it also foreshadows the 43 occurrences found in Acts (at least three of those occurrences are also associated with repentance; Acts 11:18; 17:26–30; 26:20). (For a detailed analysis of the Lukan commissioning statement, see J.-M. Guillaume, *Luc interprète des anciennes traditions sur la résurrection de Jésus* (Études Bibliques; Paris: Gabalda, 1979) 181–187; also cf. B. J. Hubbard, "Commissioning Stories in Luke-Acts; A Study of Their Antecedents, Form and Content," *Semeia* 8 (1977) 103–126.)

what Jesus had previously identified as "the promise of my Father."[240] Peter then delivers the first of several speeches in Acts.

In this first speech, he explains the meaning of the outpouring of the Holy Spirit and testifies about the life, suffering, death, and resurrection of Jesus. When the crowd responds to Peter's speech with the same question that was asked of John the Baptist—"What shall we do (τί ποιήσωμεν)?"—Peter answers, "Repent (μετανοήσατε), and be baptized every one of you in the name of Jesus Christ for the forgiveness of your sins (εἰς ἄφεσιν τῶν ἁμαρτιῶν ὑμῶν); and you will receive the gift of the Holy Spirit."[241] Through the disciples' Spirit inspired outburst of speech that communicated to "Jews from every nation under heaven" and through Peter's speech explaining this phenomenon and his preaching of repentance for the forgiveness of sins (in the name of Jesus), the final commission given by Jesus to his disciples is beginning to be fulfilled. Peter's apostolic preaching of repentance is clearly in continuity with the preaching of John the Baptist, in fulfillment of scripture, and in response to the command of the risen Jesus.

As in Luke, μετανοέω and μετάνοια in Acts are used to depict a change of thinking that usually leads to a change of behavior and/or way of life. However, whereas the change of thinking in the gospel deals directly and primarily with a change in the way people think about and interact with other people, the change of thinking in Acts most often has to do with a change of thinking regarding Jesus of Nazareth. This change of thinking regarding Jesus, however, also results in a change in the way people think about and interact with other people.

The Lukan Jesus explicitly stated that he was sent in order "to preach good news to the poor, to proclaim release to the prisoners and recovery of sight to the blind, to send away the oppressed released, and to proclaim the acceptable year of the Lord." However, as it became apparent to those in the synagogue at Nazareth that Jesus was not referring to them but to those they considered outsiders, the

---

[240] Luke 24:48; Acts 2:1–4, 32–33. In addition, the words spoken by John the Baptist regarding baptism "in the Holy Spirit and fire" in Luke 3:16 and reiterated by Jesus in Acts 1:5 are also fulfilled.

[241] Acts 2:37–38. (It is interesting to note that the first two occurrences of μετανοέω in Acts seem to echo the first two references to repentance in Luke. The use of language such as "repent," "baptized," and "forgiveness of sins" in Peter's Pentecost speech, as well as the question asked of Peter, "What shall we do?," clearly connects the Pentecost scene with the scene depicting John the Baptist's preaching of repentance (Luke 3:3–14). The second occurrence of μετανοέω in Acts (3:19) is preceded by an account of the healing of a lame man. Many of the linguistic details of that story resemble those found in the account of Jesus' healing of the paralytic (Luke 5:17–26), a story which precedes the Lukan Jesus' statement that he had "not come to call the righteous but sinners to repentance." Not only do the scenes share linguistic similarities (e.g. "rise and walk," Luke 5:24; Acts 3:6; "immediately," Luke 5:25; Acts 3:7; "glorifying/praising God," Luke 5:24–25; Acts 3:8–9; "amazement" among onlookers, Luke 5:26; Acts 3:10), but both incidents explicitly raise the issue of "what authority" is at work in the performance of these healings (Luke 5:21–24; Acts 4:7))

people became hostile toward Jesus and rejected him.[242] Their rejection of Jesus symbolized and foreshadowed the rejection and opposition his ministry would evoke among his own people. By rejecting Jesus, they were rejecting the notion of God's acceptance of all people, especially those people they considered to be outsiders—therefore unworthy of repentance. However, the Lukan Jesus informed the people that he had not come to call the righteous, but sinners to repentance.[243]

Throughout Luke, Jesus preaches and teaches about the acceptance of all people: he teaches about the proper use of possessions and the just, merciful and equitable treatment of the poor, alienated, outcast and downtrodden. Jesus seeks to fulfill God's plan of universal salvation and to encourage a community comprised of all people In Acts, repentance for the Jewish people involves a change of thinking regarding Jesus; however, if they are going to change their thinking regarding Jesus, they are also going to have to change their thinking regarding Jesus' teachings concerning the acceptance of all people and the proper use of possessions.

Jewish Repentance in Acts

In Acts, the resurrected Jesus orders the apostles not to leave Jerusalem, but to wait there for the promise of the Father. He tells them, "This is what you have heard from me; for John baptized with water, but you will be baptized with the Holy Spirit not many days from now."[244] In Peter's speech at Pentecost, he identifies Jesus' declaration with the outpouring of the Spirit that has just taken place and with the Old Testament prophecy of Joel: "In the last days it will be, God declares, that I will pour out my Spirit upon all flesh."[245] Clearly Peter is depicting Jesus as a prophet whose prophecy is not only coming to pass but is also consistent with the prophecies of Old Testament Jewish prophets such as Joel. In the very next speech delivered by Peter, he once again exhorts the Jewish people to repent so that God might:

> send the Christ appointed for you, that is Jesus. . . . Moses said, "The Lord your God will raise up for you from your own people a prophet like me. You must listen to whatever he tells you. And it will be that everyone who does not listen to that prophet will be utterly rooted out of the people." And all of the prophets, as many as have spoken, from Samuel and those after him, also predicted these days.[246]

---

[242] Luke 4:18–30.
[243] Luke 5:32.
[244] Acts 1:4–5.
[245] Acts 2:16–17a. The use of the phrase "all flesh" (πᾶσαν σάρκα) is also meant to echo the promises of worldwide salvation in Luke 2:30–32; 3:6.
[246] Acts 3:19–20, 22–24.

In an effort to change the Jewish peoples' thinking regarding Jesus, the author portrays Peter depicting Jesus as and numbering him among Israel's prophets of old.[247]

In his speech at Pentecost, Peter not only depicts Jesus as a prophet whose prophecy is consistent with that of the Old Testament prophet Joel, he also depicts Jesus as one whose suffering, death and resurrection was according to the plan and foreknowledge of God and was foretold by the patriarch and prophet David.[248] The people of Israel should not think that the suffering and death of Jesus indicates that he is not "the one to redeem Israel." His suffering, death and resurrection were foretold in scripture by all that the prophets had spoken.[249] They serve, therefore, as proof that he actually is the one to redeem Israel.[250] Not only have the people of Jerusalem betrayed and murdered the prophet spoken of by Moses and others, but their ancestors persecuted and killed those prophets "who foretold the coming of the Righteous One."[251]

The speeches of Peter are meant to convict those involved in the persecution of Jesus and to cause them to change their minds regarding Jesus.[252] The people are repeatedly rebuked for having denied and persecuted the "Righteous One."[253] They are repeatedly reminded of their involvement in the persecution and murder of an

---

[247] The author places this same quote from Moses—regarding God's raising up of a prophet like himself—on the lips of Stephen (7:37). Other depictions of Jesus as a prophet or as one spoken of by Israel's prophets are found in Acts 8:34–35; 10:42–43; 13:27; 26:22–23; 28:25.

[248] Acts 2:23, 29–31.

[249] Luke 24:21, 25–27.

[250] Acts 1:6 (That redemption, however, is dependent on repentance (Acts 3:19–21)).

[251] Acts 7:52.

[252] Speeches were commonly used in the Hellenistic world in order to provoke repentance among listeners (e.g. Seneca *Epistles* 95.65; Dio Chrysostom *Discourses* 1.8, 57; 18.2–3; 19.3; 32.12, 14, 21; 34.4–5; 38.9–51; 45.1; 49.3; Epictetus *Discourses* 3.1.36–37; 3.21.11–18; 3.22.2, 23, 53; Plutarch *On Listening to Lectures* 38A–B; 42A–C; 46E; *How to Tell a Flatterer from a Friend* 55C–56A; 59D–E; 67A–68F; 69C; *Progress in Virtue* 82A–E; *Precepts of Statecraft* 810C; Lucian *Philosophies for Sale* 8; *Peregrinus* 18). Throughout Acts, it is in the speeches of Peter, Stephen, Philip and Paul that the call for repentance is repeatedly made (for an examination of the speeches in Acts see, H. J. Cadbury, "The Greek and Jewish Traditions of Writing History," and "The Speeches in Acts," *The Beginnings of Christianity*, 2.7–29, 5.402–427; E. Schweizer, "Concerning the Speeches in Luke-Acts," *Studies in Luke-Acts*, 208–216; M. Dibelius, "The Speeches in Acts and Ancient Historiography,: *Studies in the Acts of the Apostles* (trans M. Ling; New York: Scribner's, 1956) 138–185; R. C. Tannehill, "The Function of Peter's Mission Speeches in the Narrative of Acts," *NTS* 37 (1991) 400–414).

[253] Acts 3:14; 7:52; 22:14 (Not only is Jesus identified as the "Righteous One," whereby creating a sense of guilt among those who denied and persecuted him, but he is also identified by several other titles, including: "a man attested by God" (2:22); "the Holy One" (ὁ ὅσιος: 2:27; 13:35; ὁ ἅγιος: 3:14; 4:30); "the Christ" (2:31, 36; 3:18; 4:26; 5:42; 8:5; 9:22; 17:3; 18:5, 28; 26:23); "the Lord" (1:21; 4:33; 8:16; 10:36; 11:17; 15:11, 26; 16:31; 19:5, 17; 20:21, 35; 21:13; 28:31); "the Author of Life" (3:15; cf 5:31); "Savior" (5:31; 13:23); etc. . . and on two occasions it is explicitly stated that God is the one who has made Jesus "Lord and Christ" and "Leader and Savior" (2:36; 5:31)).

innocent man. They are repeatedly made aware of the fact that despite their rejection and murder of Jesus, God has raised him up and exalted him.[254] All of this rebuke is meant to cause those Jews who had at one time rejected Jesus to recognize the error of their way and to change their thinking about Jesus.[255] This change of thinking regarding Jesus, however, is from the outset depicted in the context of human interaction and manifested by the just, merciful and equitable treatment of the poor and needy.

Immediately after Peter's rebuke of the Jewish people for crucifying and killing Jesus and his exhortation to them to repent and to save themselves from their "crooked (σκολιᾶς)" generation,[256] The author writes, "So those who welcomed his message were baptized, and that day about three thousand persons were added. . . . All who believed were together and had all things common (ἅπαντα κοινὰ); and they sold their possessions and goods and divided the proceeds among all, as any had need."[257] While repentance for Peter's Jewish audience clearly entails a change of thinking regarding Jesus, once again—as in the gospel—repentance is associated with establishing a community of all people, where individuals treat each other justly, mercifully and equitably.[258] Repentance is the key in helping to fulfill God's plan of universal salvation and in helping to establish a community comprised of all people. Over three thousand Jews "from every nation under heaven" (2:5) responded to Peter's preaching by welcoming his word (ἀποδεξάμενοι τὸν λόγον αὐτοῦ), receiving God's salvation and coming together as a community, living peacefully and sharing their individual possessions for the common good.[259] The act of sharing "all things common" mirrors the "fruits worthy of repentance" presented in the gospel.[260]

---

[254] Acts 2:22–36; 3:13–15; 4:10–12; 5:30–32; 7:51–53; 10:39–40; 13:27–41.

[255] There appears to have been much initial success among the Jews (see Acts 2:41; 4:4; 21:20). A discussion of the role and function of "recognition scenes" as dramatic devices can be found in Boris Uspensky, *A Poetics of Composition: The Structure of the Artistic Text and Typology of a Compositional Form* (trans. by Valentina Zavarin and Susan Wittig; Los Angeles: University of California Press, 1973) 1450a–54a.

[256] As mentioned earlier, the only other Lukan occurrence of σκολιός is found in connection with John the Baptist's preaching of repentance (Luke 3:5).

[257] Acts 2:41, 44–45. The phrase καθότι ἄν τις χρείαν εἶχεν ("as any had need"), suggests that **whenever** there was a financial need among the poor in the congregation, those with property and or other goods would sell something and distribute the proceeds among those with the need (BDF §367 states that the augmented tenses of the indicative with ἄν are used in an iterative sense; cf Acts 4:35).

[258] The ethical and communal aspects of repentance are closely associated with the religious aspects.

[259] The expression ἀποδέχεσθαι τὸν λόγον was commonly used by Greek authors to describe a favorable response to a messages (cf. Plato *Symposium* 194D; *Laws* 642D; *Theaetetus* 162E; Lucian *The Goddess of Syria* 22).

[260] The phrase "all things common" (ἅπαντα κοινὰ), is clearly an allusion to the Hellenistic *topos* concerning friendship. The Greek proverb, "friends hold all things common" (τοῖς φίλοις ἅπαντα κοινὰ) was widely known (see, e.g. Ovid, *Metamorphoses* 1:88–111; Plato, *Republic* 449C; *Critias* 110C–D; Aristotle, *Nichomachean Ethics* 1168B; *Politics* 1263A; Plutarch, *The Dialogue on Love* 767E; Philo, *On Abraham* 235). Such

Immediately after the author's depiction of the early Christian community as one in which everyone had all things common, the author portrays Peter and John healing a lame beggar outside of the gate of the Temple.[261] Seeing the people's amazement, Peter delivers his second speech, in which he once again rebukes the people for denying and crucifying Jesus. He informs his Jewish listeners that it is by faith in Jesus' name that the lame man has been healed. He also informs them that he knows that they acted out of ignorance, like their rulers, when they crucified Jesus. He commands them, "Repent (μετανοήσατε) therefore, and return (ἐπιστρέψατε), so that your sins might be wiped out."[262] As Peter and John continue speaking to the people about Jesus and his resurrection, the Jewish religious leaders become annoyed and have them arrested.[263] Despite the arrest of Peter and John, however, many of the Jews believe and over five thousand people are added to the Christian community.[264]

After the author's account of Peter's and John's imprisonment and release, he turns his attention back to the growing Christian community. As was the case when three thousand were added to the community of believers, the author asserts that the five thousand new believers were also of "one heart and soul (καρδία καὶ ψυχὴ μία), and no one claimed private ownership of any possessions, but they had all things common (ἅπαντα κοινά). . . . There was not a needy person among them, for as many as owned lands or houses sold them, and brought the proceeds of what was sold, and laid it at the apostles' feet, and it was distributed to each as any had need."[265]

---

sharing of possessions reflected the ideal state (Plato, *Republic* 420C–422B; 462B–464A; *Laws* 679B–C; 684C–D; 744B–746C; 757A). For a discussion of the use of this type of communal language in the writings of Aristotle, Plato, and others, see David Mealand, "Community of Goods and Utopian Allusions in Acts II–IV," *Journal of Theological Studies* 28 (1977) 96–99 (It is prophesied in the *Sibylline Oracles* that when the ideal future is realized, "Lives will be in common and wealth will have no division" (2.321)).

[261] Acts 3:1–10.

[262] As in his first speech, repentance is again associated with forgiving sins. Despite the attempt of many biblical scholars to portray μετανοέω and ἐπιστρέφω as synonymous, the use of both terms in this passage indicates that the author did not necessarily consider them synonymous. Repentance here should apparently lead to a "returning" of some sort (Elsewhere this type of "returning" is explicitly identified as a returning "to God," 26:18, 20; see also 9:35; 11:21; 14:15; 15:19; cf. Luke 1:16). While the change in thinking and living conveyed by repentance is often closely associated with turning from a life of unbelief and evil to a life of faith and righteousness, μετανοέω and ἐπιστρέφω as not necessarily synonymous in Luke-Acts (cf. Luke 2:39; 8:55; 17:4, 31; 22:32; 9:40; 15:36; 28:27).

[263] Acts 4.

[264] Peter's first speech resulted in about three thousand people being added, and now over five thousand are added to the Christian community.

[265] Acts 4:32–35. While the Hellenistic *topos* regarding friends having "all things common" has been discussed above, the idea that friends are of "one soul" (μία ψυχή) is attested by Euripides, *Orestes* 1046 and cited as a proverb by Aristotle, *Nichomachean Ethics* 1168B. The phrase "no one claimed private ownership of any possessions" is similar to Plato, *Critias* 110C–D. The statement that "there was not any needy person among them" (4:34) appears to be an allusion to Deut 15:4–5.

In the first two speeches of Peter, repentance clearly implies a change of thinking regarding Jesus. In both speeches, however, this change of thinking regarding Jesus is associated with establishing an ideal community, where individuals treat each other justly, mercifully and equitably.[266] As in Luke, the "fruits worthy of repentance" are still depicted in the context of human interaction and manifested through the just, merciful and equitable treatment of the poor and needy. Since those who had previously rejected Jesus had also rejected his teachings regarding the acceptance of all people and the proper use of possessions, a change of thinking regarding Jesus required them to now embrace his teachings regarding the acceptance of all people and the proper use of possessions.[267]

In the next speech, which is shorter and delivered exclusively to the high priest, Sadducees, captain of the temple, and chief priests, Peter and the rest of the apostles again rebuke the Jerusalem leaders for crucifying Jesus.[268] They inform the leaders that despite their rejection and murder of Jesus, God has exalted Jesus "at his right hand as Leader and Savior, to give repentance (μετάνοιαν) to Israel and forgiveness of sins (ἄφεσιν ἁμαρτιῶν)."[269] Not only does repentance suggest a change of thinking regarding Jesus, but Peter and the rest of the apostles make it clear to the Jerusalem leaders that the same Jesus they "killed by hanging him on a tree" is now the one extending to Israel both the opportunity to repent and forgiveness of sins.[270] Just as the earthly Jesus came in order to forgive sins and to

---

[266] Both Acts 2:42–47 and 4:32–37 serve as summaries that depict the everyday life of Jewish believers who accept the message of Peter and change their thinking regarding Jesus (For a discussion of the role and importance of the alternation between "scene" and "summary," see Gérard Genette, *Narrative Discourse*, 109–110).

[267] In Acts 4:34–35, after selling (πωλοῦντες) their land and houses, these Jewish believers distributed (διεδίδετο) the proceeds within the community as any had need. In Luke Jesus told the rich ruler, "Sell (πώλησον) all that you have and distribute (διάδος) to the poor" (18:22). He also told the disciples, "Sell (πωλήσατε) your possession and give (δότε) alms" (12:33). There was also a member of the Christian community of Acts 4:32–37 named Barnabas, who sold (πωλήσας) a field that he owned and laid the proceeds at the apostles feet (vv 36–37). Clearly the early Christian community in Acts is observing the teachings of Jesus found in Luke (cf Acts 5:1–11).

[268] As in Peter's first two speeches, the teaching and preaching (in the name of Jesus; 5:28) of "repentance" and "forgiveness of sins," as well as the declaration "we are witnesses (μάρτυρες) of these things" (5:32), are clearly meant to echo the final commission of the Lukan Jesus (Luke 24:47–48).

[269] Acts 5:31 (The fact that repentance is divinely given is stated again by Peter at 11:18; and that Israel is among the recipients of such repentance is stated in 13:24; cf. 20:21; 26:20. Throughout the Jerusalem section of Acts, the author maintains a steady focus on the offer of salvation made to Israel (1:6; 2:36; 4:10, 27; 5:21)).

[270] The phrase "hanging him on a tree" (5:30) is drawn from the book of Deuteronomy: "When someone is convicted of a crime punishable by death and is executed, and you hang him on a tree, his corpse must not remain all night upon the tree; you shall bury him that same day, for anyone hung on a tree is under God's curse" (Deut 21:22–23). The religious leaders, therefore, became "enraged and wanted to kill them" when they heard the apostles' declaration that a crucified man—a man under God's curse—had been exalted by God as "Leader and Savior" (5:33). Not only was such a declaration blasphemous, but the fact that Jesus was exalted by God in order to give Israel a chance to change her mind (i.e. repent)

call sinners to repentance, so now the heavenly Jesus has been exalted by God in order to give repentance and forgiveness of sins.

After the message of repentance was preached throughout Jerusalem and "the number of the disciples increased greatly in Jerusalem" (6:7), "a great persecution arose against the church in Jerusalem, and all except the apostles were scattered throughout the countryside of Judea and Samaria" (8:1).[271] While in Samaria, Philip proclaimed the Christ to the people, and a large number of them—including an influential magician named Simon—became believers.[272] After witnessing several people receive the Holy Spirit as a result of the "laying on of hands" by Peter and John, Simon offered the Jerusalem apostles money so that he might have the power to lay hands on people and they receive the Holy Spirit. Peter, however, rebuked Simon for thinking that the gift of God could be purchased with money. He informed Simon that his heart was not right before God, and he ordered him, "repent (μετανόησον) therefore of this wickedness of yours and pray to the Lord that, if possible, the intent of your heart may be forgiven (ἀφεθήσεται) you."[273] Repentance here clearly involves a change of thinking, but unlike in his preaching to the Jerusalem leaders, Peter's command to Simon to repent does not entail a change of thinking about someone Simon had previously rejected and murdered.[274] Instead, Peter is demanding Simon to change his thinking regarding the proper use of money.[275] As the message of repentance moved out of Jerusalem and was no

---

about Jesus suggests that Israel was responsible for shedding the blood of an innocent man (5:28c; Frank Matera states that the author suggests that it is "the inhabitants of Jerusalem and their leaders," and not the Jews in general, who were responsible for the death of Jesus [cf. Acts 13:27]; Matera, "Responsibility for the Death of Jesus according to the Acts of the Apostles," *JSNT* 39 (1990) 77–93, especially 86).

[271] The persecution initiated the fulfillment of the prophesy, "and you shall be my witnesses in Jerusalem, *and in all Judea and Samaria* and to the end of the earth" (Acts 1:8b).

[272] Acts 8:5–13 (this is the only ancient source that depicts Simon being baptized as a believer).

[273] Acts 8:18–22 (Once again repentance and forgiveness go hand in hand). Since Simon had already been baptized as a believer, this passage indicates that repentance is possible for post-baptismal sins (contra. Heb 6:4; it does remain uncertain, however, whether the 'intent of Simon's heart' will be forgiven him). Repentance, therefore, is not only appropriate for those seeking to become believers, it is also appropriate for believers. Repentance is the means by which believers who sin are restored to fellowship with God and the community (cf Luke 17:3–4).

[274] In the first seven chapters of Acts, where the setting is primarily in Jerusalem and the focus is primarily on the Jerusalem Jews, repentance essentially entails recognizing the error of ones ways and changing ones thinking about Jesus. As shall been seen in the section dealing with the Gentiles, the repentance demanded of the Gentiles essentially entails recognizing the errors of idolatry and immorality and changing ones thinking about ones religious, moral, and ethical practices and lifestyle.

[275] Simon was still thinking as a magician—as one who charges a fee for the use his powers (see, C. K. Barrett, "Light on the Holy Spirit from Simon Magus (Acts 8, 4–25)," *Les Actes des Apôtres: Traditions, rédaction, théologie* (ed. J. Kremer; Bibliotheca Ephemeridum Theologicarum Lovaniensium 48. Gembloux: Leuven University Press, 1979) 287–88). The proper use of money and possessions in Luke-Acts has already been discussed

longer directed toward those who had denied and murdered Jesus, the expressed rationale for repentance also began to change.[276]

Toward Gentile Repentance

The mission to Samaria should not be regarded as the church's first attempt to evangelize Gentiles.[277] The Jews did not think of the Samaritans as Gentiles; instead they thought of them as apostates (i.e. 'lost sheep of the house of Israel'). The Samaritans shared a common heritage with the Jews: they were descendants of Abraham and adherents of the Torah. The Samaritans were the children of those who had intermarried with the mixed population that settled in Israel after the Assyrian conquest of the northern kingdom (2 Kgs 17:24–41). Most Jews considered the Samaritans to be idolatrous, back-slidden Jews.[278] The mission to the Samaritans is part of the progressive fulfillment of Acts 1:8. It also serves as the first step in the narrative toward a mission to the Gentiles.

Another step toward this mission to the Gentiles is immediately depicted in Philip's encounter with the Ethiopian eunuch. Many scholars—classical and contemporary—consider Philip's baptism of the Ethiopian finance minister as the beginning of the Gentile mission.[279] While I will not attempt to assess the historical accuracy of such a claim, it is quite clear that the author is not suggesting that Philip's baptism of the Ethiopian eunuch marks the beginning of the Gentile mission. As Ernst Haenchen points out, the author is intentionally ambiguous about the Ethiopian's identity as a Jew or a Gentile.[280]

---

at length; however, money as a factor in the corruption of religion also receives special attention in Acts (cf 1:18; 5:1–11; 16:16–19; 19:24–27).

[276] By "expressed rationale" I am referring to the reasons for repentance given by those demanding repentance. While the reasons for which repentance are demanded may change, the literary rationale for repentance remains the same throughout Luke-Acts: the fulfillment of God's plan of universal salvation and the establishment of a community comprised of all people.

[277] The reaction of the Jerusalem apostles to the salvation of the Samaritans was much more favorable than their reaction to the salvation of the Gentiles (cf. 8:14–25; 11:1–18).

[278] Cf. Amos 3:9, 12; 8:14; Hos 8:5–6; Isa 8:4; Mic 1:5–6 (For a discussion of the Jewish perspective on Samaritans, see J. Jervell, *Luke and the People of God*, 113–132).

[279] Irenaeus, *Contra haereses* 3.12.8; 4.23.2; Eusebius, *Historia ecclesiastica* 2.1; Jerome, *Commentarii in Isaiam prophetam* 14.53; 790; M. Hengel, *Acts and the History of the Earliest Christianity* (Philadelphia: Fortress Press, 1980), 79; I. H. Marshall, *Acts of the Apostles* (Grand Rapids, MI: Eerdmans, 1980)160–61; R. Tannehill, *Narrative Unity* 2:108–110; C. H. Felder, *Stony the Road We Trod: African American Biblical Interpretation* (Minneapolis: Augsburg Fortress, 1991), 142; C. H. Talbert, *Reading Acts: A Literary and Theological Commentary on the Acts of the Apostles* (New York: Crossroad, 1997).

[280] Ernst Haenchen *The Acts of the Apostles: A Commentary* (Oxford: Basil Blackwell, 1971) 314. The author's depiction of the Ethiopian eunuch as possessing his own copy of the prophet Isaiah and returning from Jerusalem, where he had gone to worship, suggests that the author wanted the eunuch to be perceived as a diaspora Jew (the ban against a eunuch's entering the assembly of the Lord (Deut 23.1) is by no means conclusive here (cf. Isa 56:3–5; Wis 3:14). Nowhere in the narrative does the author give the impression that the

While the cultural, social, sexual, and financial identifiers associated with the Ethiopian eunuch all serve to highlight the universalism of the mission in Luke-Acts, it is clearly the Lukan scene with Peter and Cornelius rather than the scene with Philip and the Ethiopian eunuch that signifies a new (Gentile) mission.[281] As with the baptism of Simon and the Samaritans, the baptism of the Ethiopian eunuch represents the extension of the salvation of God to those who are marginalized within the people of God. Taken together, both scenes highlight the universality of salvation: the community of God's people is open to Samaritans, magicians, those impressed by magic, men, women, Ethiopians and eunuchs.[282] The scenes are also employed by the author to move his reader closer to the anticipated Gentile mission.[283]

In continued preparation of his introduction of the Gentile mission, the author gives an account of Paul's Damascus road experience.[284] In this first account of Paul's revelatory experience, the Lord appears to a disciple named Ananias and tells him to go to Paul and lay his hands on Paul in order that Paul might regain his sight. The Lord tells Ananias, "he is an instrument whom I have chosen to bring my name before Gentiles and kings and the sons of Israel."[285] As a result of the Lord's

---

eunuch was excluded from worshiping in the Temple; see Josephus, *War* 6.9.3; *Antiquities* 3.15.3. The inclusion of the eunuch continues a Lukan motif; cf Luke 14:12–14, 21; 5:27–30; 15:1–2; 7:36–50). There are also references in Isaiah to the gathering of "the remnant," "the outcast of Israel," "the dispersed of Judah" from Ethiopia and the four corners of the earth (Isa 11:11; cf. Zeph 3:9–10). While the eunuch could have been a so-called "God-fearer," the absence of the term φοβούμενος with reference to the eunuch, and the fact that Cornelius is the first explicitly identified φοβούμενος (10:2, 22, 35), suggests that the author wants Cornelius not the Ethiopian eunuch to be recognized as the first Gentile convert (in Acts 15:14, James refers to the Cornelius episode as God's "first" visit with the Gentiles). Within the narrative, the Ethiopian eunuch represents the ingathering of the outcast and scattered people of Israel, while Cornelius represents the beginning of the Gentile mission.

[281] The fact that the author depicts the Jerusalem apostles validating Philip's ministry in Samaria by sending Peter and John, also suggests that the author most likely marked the beginning of the Gentile mission with Peter's encounter with Cornelius rather than with Philip's encounter with the Ethiopian eunuch. Furthermore, in light of the inconsequential nature of Philip's encounter with the Ethiopian eunuch, the enormous amount of attention given by the author to the Cornelius encounter (chapters 10–15) makes little sense at all if the Cornelius encounter is not meant to represent the beginning of a new missionary endeavor.

[282] As stated earlier, however, such inclusivity requires a radical change of thinking on the part of all who wish to participate in the community of God's people.

[283] As Tannehill has pointed out, Ethiopia was thought to be on the edge of the known world (*Narrative Unity* 2:108–9). The Ethiopian eunuch scene, therefore, "anticipates the power of the gospel to reach 'the end of the earth' (1:8)" (*Narrative Unity* 2:107).

[284] While the author does not use the name Paul until chapter 13, for the sake of consistency I will use the name Paul throughout this work rather than switching back and forth between Saul and Paul.

[285] Acts 9:10–15. While the ordering of the words "Gentiles and kings and sons of Israel" does not represent the order in which Paul actually preaches, the phrase is programmatic for Paul's preaching, just as Acts 1:8 is programmatic for the movement of the church's preaching. The ordering of the words "Gentiles and kings and sons of Israel"

statement to Ananias, the reader is made aware that the mission to the Gentiles is part of God's will.[286] All the preparations have now been made for the decisive and definitive step forward toward the Gentile mission.

Gentile Repentance

While neither μετανοέω nor μετάνοια are used in connection with Paul's Damascus experience, Paul's behavior after the experience clearly reveals a radical change of thinking by Paul regarding Jesus (9:19–31). Most scholars talk about Paul's Damascus road experience in terms of a conversion.[287] There are, however, many scholars who insist that it is inappropriate to speak of Paul as having experienced a conversion.[288] Krister Stendahl argues that a conversion is a "change of 'religion'" and Paul did not experience a change of religion.[289] According to the author's portrayal of Paul's defense before Felix the governor, Paul declared, "according to the Way, which they call a sect, I worship the God of our ancestors, believing everything laid down according to the law or written in the prophets."[290] Paul is not depicted as experiencing a conversion; instead he is depicted as experiencing an enlightenment and a "calling"—an assignment to a new task. In his classic study of conversion, Arthur Darby Nock defined conversion as "the

---

is meant to emphasize Paul's calling to go to the Gentiles—which marks a new development at this point in the narrative—while not ignoring his mission to the sons of Israel (cf. 13:44–47; 18:6; 28:23–28). (It should be pointed out that just as Paul experienced a change in thinking as a result of a visit from the Lord, so also Ananias experienced a change in thinking as a result of a visit from the Lord. Ananias, who once feared Paul because of all the evil Paul had done to the saints in Jerusalem, went and laid his hands on Paul and addressed him as "Brother" (9:13–17). The use of μαθητὰς τοῦ κυρίου (9:1) to identify those being persecuted by Paul and the use of μαθητής (9:10) to identify Ananias emphasizes that a change in thinking on the part of both Paul and Ananias leads to reconciliation between two men who once thought of each other as enemies. The formation of God's all inclusive community requires a fundamental change of thinking on the part of virtually everyone who desires to be a part of that community. Even the Jerusalem disciples (μαθηταῖς) and apostles had to change their thinking about Paul, and as a result, "The church throughout Judea, Galilee, and Samaria had peace and was built up. Living in the fear of the Lord and in the comfort of the Holy Spirit, it increased in numbers" (9:31))

[286] In the second account of Paul's Damascus experience—which is told by Paul himself—Ananias tells Paul, "The God of our ancestors has chosen you to know **his will** . . . for you will be his witness to all the world." (22:14–15a). In the third and final account, Paul tells King Aggripa (note in the first account Ananias is told that Paul will bring the Lord's name before kings) that the Lord told him directly that he was being sent to the Gentiles (26:15–17).

[287] Cf. Beverly Gaventa, *From Darkness to Light: Aspects of Conversion in the New Testament* (Philadelphia: Fortress Press, 1986) ch. 1; A. F. Segal, *Paul the Convert: The Apostolate and Apostasy of Saul the Pharisee* (New Haven: Yale University Press, 1990).

[288] The unclarity that surrounds the English word "conversion" complicates many of the discussions regarding Paul's Damascus road experience.

[289] Krister Stendahl, *Paul Among Jews and Gentiles and Other Essays* (Philadelphia: Fortress Press, 1976) 7–23.

[290] Acts 24:14.

reorientation of the soul of an individual, his deliberate turning from indifference or from an earlier form of piety to another, a turning which implies a consciousness that a great change is involved, that the old was wrong and the new is right."[291]

While the "reorientation of the soul" and the conscious awareness referred to by Nock very well may have accompanied Paul's change, the author of Acts—unlike most contemporary New Testament scholars—does not engage in a psychological or even a spiritual analysis of Paul's soul or consciousness. The author is not concerned with depicting the Damascus road event as some sort of introspective conversion experience. While the multiple accounts of Paul's Damascus road experience clearly indicate the importance of the experience to the author's narrative, in none of the accounts does the author focus on Paul's conscious thoughts or motivations before or after the Damascus road experience. Instead, all three accounts focus on the fact that Paul has been "called" by God to be a witness for Jesus to all people—Gentiles and Jews.[292]

Paul is clearly an important character in the narrative; however, neither Paul nor the Damascus experience itself is as important as what the experience introduces at this point in the development of the author's narrative.[293] Paul's Damascus road experience introduces the notion of a divinely initiated change in thinking about Jesus that leads to a new understanding regarding the status of Gentiles and their place within the community of God's people. Paul experiences a fundamental change in thinking about Jesus—as well as Jesus' disciples—at this point in the narrative because the author now wants to direct the reader's attention to the fact that the Lord has chosen Paul to be an instrument to carry the Lord's name before Gentiles and kings, as well as before Jews.

From a literary perspective, this first depiction of Paul's Damascus road experience, the Lord's declaration to Ananias that Paul has been chosen to carry his name before Gentiles, and Paul's radical change in thinking about Jesus and his disciples all foreshadow the change in thinking that will be required of Peter and the Jerusalem Jews regarding the status of Gentiles and their place within the community of God's people. These events also assure the reader that the changes

---

[291] *Conversion*, 7.
[292] Acts 9:15; 22:15; 26:16. Like Stendahl, Luke Johnson assets, "the 'conversion' of Paul was in reality the call of a prophet" (L. T. Johnson, *The Acts of the Apostles* (Collegeville, Minnesota: Liturgical Press, 1992) 167).
[293] While the reader was informed earlier that Paul consented to the stoning of Stephen and that Paul ravaged the church—dragging off men and women and committing them to prison—the reader at this point in the narrative knows nothing else about Paul. The author's introduction of Paul at this point in the narrative is abrupt and uninformative. The author simply tells the reader that Paul persecuted the disciples of the Lord. The author mentions nothing about Paul's background, education, religious beliefs or motives for persecuting the disciples of the Lord. While this may be because the author assumes that the reader already knows all of this information about Paul, it is most likely because the author is not really concerned with introducing Paul. Unlike many misguided modern readers of Acts, the author is not concerned with Paul as a person nor with assessing Paul's personal and religious beliefs and psychological motivations before and after the Damascus road experience.

in thinking regarding Gentiles, as well as the Gentile mission itself, have all been ordained by the Lord.

Shortly after Paul's revelatory experience, the author records that a Roman centurion named Cornelius, a Gentile who feared God (φοβούμενος τὸν θεὸν) and gave alms generously to the people, had a vision in which an angel of God appeared to him and instructed him to send for Peter.[294] The next day Peter also had a vision in which he saw the heaven opened and a large sheet lowered to the ground. On the sheet were all kinds of four-footed creatures, reptiles and birds. A voice told Peter to get up, kill and eat. Peter, however, responded, "By no means, Lord; for I have never eaten anything that is common and unclean (κοινὸν καὶ ἀκάθαρτον)."[295] The voice replied, "What God has made clean (ἐκαθάρισεν) you must not call common (κοίνου)." This happened three times, and the vision ceased.[296]

While Peter was trying to figure out the meaning of the vision, the men sent by Cornelius arrived looking for him. The Spirit told Peter to go with the men because they had been sent by God. The men lodged with Peter that night, and the next morning they all left for Caesarea, where Cornelius resided. Through his speech to Cornelius, Peter reveals to the reader of Acts the meaning of his visionary experience. Peter reminded Cornelius and his household how it was unlawful for a

---

[294] The description of Cornelius is reminiscent of the centurion who was highly regarded by the Jews of Capernaum because he had generously built a synagogue for them. Jesus himself praises the centurion saying, "not even in Israel have I found such faith" (Luke 7:1–10). Unlike in Matthew's parallel account (8:5–13), in which the centurion approaches Jesus, in Luke Jesus never actually meets the Gentile centurion. The Lukan scene, in which the centurion sends Jewish delegates to Jesus to request Jesus to come, clearly foreshadows the Peter/Cornelius episode. While Jesus went with the Jewish delegation to the centurion's house, the centurion sent friends to intercept Jesus, saying, "Lord, do not trouble yourself, for I am not worthy to have you come under my roof" (7:6). Jesus, therefore, never enters the centurion's house nor meets the centurion. The author most likely withheld any interaction between Jesus and the centurion and prevented Jesus from entering the centurion's house in order to emphasize the newness and significance of what occurs between Peter, the Gentile delegation and Cornelius. Peter is authorized and instructed by the Holy Spirit to go with the Gentile delegation to meet with Cornelius because the Spirit has arranged the meeting (Acts 10:20).

[295] It is interesting to note that while Peter has a problem with the idea of eating meat that is unclean, he seems to have no problem residing with a tanner (9:43). While Leviticus 11 offers a lengthy and detailed list of clean and unclean animals, 11:39–40 pronounces unclean anyone who touches the carcass of an animal that dies. A tanner, therefore, would be perpetually unclean (cf. *m Ketubim* 7:10; *b. Kiddushin* 82a Bar.). Since there seems to be no apparent reason for the author to identify Simon as a "tanner" (9:43; 10:6, 32; the only mention of this occupation in the New Testament), the author is most likely using Peter's residing with Simon to foreshadow God's revelation to Peter that he should not call any man unclean.

[296] Acts 10:1–16. The importance of this vision to the author's narrative is reflected in the fact that the narrator states that the exchange between Peter and the heavenly voice happened three times and in the fact that the author records this event twice. When Peter gives his report to the church at Jerusalem, he recounts the details of this event in full (Acts 11:4–10).

Jew to associate with or to visit a Gentile.²⁹⁷ He informed them, however, that God had shown him that he should not call anyone "common or unclean (κοινὸν ἢ ἀκάθαρτον)."²⁹⁸ After Cornelius informed Peter about his own visionary experience, Peter gained additional insight regarding his earlier vision, declaring what is clearly one of the defining programmatic statements, not only for the remainder of Acts, but for the entirety of Luke-Acts: "Truly I perceive that God is not one who shows partiality, but in every nation anyone who fears him and does what is right is acceptable (δεκτὸς) to him."²⁹⁹

The use of "acceptable" (δεκτὸς) here echoes Jesus' programmatic statement in which he declared that he had been sent to proclaim the "acceptable (δεκτόν)" year of the Lord.³⁰⁰ This allusion to Jesus' programmatic statement is strengthened by Peter's reference to the good news of peace preached by Jesus "beginning in Galilee after the baptism which John declared: how God anointed (ἔχρισεν) Jesus of Nazareth with the Holy Spirit (πνεύματι)."³⁰¹

---

²⁹⁷ Peter's statement appears to have been an exaggeration, because there is no evidence that it was unlawful for Jews "to associate with or to visit a Gentile." It is also interesting to note that Peter didn't seem to have a problem lodging the Gentile delegation that came to Joppa to request his presence. Apparently Gentiles visiting Jews was thought of differently than Jews visiting Gentiles (cf. 11:2–3).

²⁹⁸ Acts 10:17–28. Clearly the meaning of the vision was revealed to Peter progressively as the Spirit instructed Peter to go with the Gentiles who would come looking for him, as the delegation informed Peter of Cornelius' status as an upright and God-fearing man who had been directed by a holy angel to send for Peter, and as Peter talked to Cornelius and found a house full of Gentiles there waiting to hear from him.

²⁹⁹ Acts 10:34–35. The notion of God's acceptance of all people has been alluded to throughout Luke-Acts (e.g. Luke 1:14–17, 32–33, 50; 2:10, 14, 30–32; 3:6, 10–14; 4:18–19, 25–27, 43; 5:30–32; 6:36; 7:39–48; 9:51–56; 10:29–37; 13:29–30; 14:11, 21b–23; 15; 18:9–14; 19:9–10; 20:21; 23:34, 42–43; 24:46–47; Acts 1:8; 2:5, 16–18, 21, 39; 8:5, 12–15, 25, 26–38; 9:15), and after the Peter/Cornelius episode the presence and acceptance of all people—especially Gentiles—dominates Acts (11:18, 20–26; 13:1, 16, 26, 38–39, 43, 46–49; 14:1, 8–18, 27; 15:1–35; 16:1–5, 14–15, 29–34; 17:12, 22–34; 18:4–6; 19:10, 17–20, 26; 20:21; 21:19, 25; 22:14–15, 21; 26:16–23; 28:28). While the notion of God being impartial was not a novel idea in the ancient world (cf. Jouette Bassler, "Luke and Paul on Impartiality," *Biblica* 66 [1985] 546–552), and while it may not have been an alien concept within ancient Judaism (Deut 10:17), Peter's statement, "*truly I understand* that God shows no partiality" emphasizes that the traditional Jewish understanding of the impartiality of God was not sufficient (cf. Luke 10:21). Ancient Jewish tradition asserted that God had chosen and favored Israel above all nations (cf. Exod 19:5–6; Deut 7:6–8; 26:19). Peter's new understanding of the impartiality of God, however, challenged the Jewish notion of the inferiority of non-Jews, as well as the notion of "clean" and "unclean"—not only with regard to food but also with regard to people. As demonstrated by the initial Jewish response in chapter 11, Peter's new understanding required a major change of thinking on the part of the typical first century Jew.

³⁰⁰ Luke 4:19 (The importance of "acceptable" (δεκτὸς) in the gospel passage is emphasized by its use again in Jesus' declaration to the Jews at Nazareth, "Truly, I say to you, no prophet is acceptable (δεκτός) in his own country" (4:24); Luke 4:19, 24, and Acts 10:35 are the only three occurrences of δεκτός in Luke-Acts).

³⁰¹ Acts 10:36–37. After the baptism of John, Jesus declared in Nazareth of Galilee that he had been anointed (ἔχρισεν) by the Spirit (πνεῦμα) to preach (Luke 4:16–18b). (Note: The last occurrence of an indeclinable nominative form of "Nazareth" occurs in Luke 4:16,

Peter then informs his Gentile audience that the Jerusalem Jews were responsible for killing Jesus "by hanging him on a tree."[302] He also tells them, however, that God raised Jesus from the dead in order to give "forgiveness of sins (ἄφεσιν ἁμαρτιῶν) through his name" to everyone who believes in him.[303] Before Peter could say anything else, the Holy Spirit fell on all who heard the word, and the Gentiles began speaking in tongues and extolling God, just as the apostles and disciples had on the day of Pentecost. Seeing that the Gentiles had received the Spirit, Peter ordered them to be baptized in the name of Jesus, and he resided there with them for several days.

When Peter returned to Jerusalem, he was greeted by Jews who had heard that the Gentiles had accepted the word of God.[304] Surprisingly, these Jerusalem Jews did not express disbelief over the Gentiles accepting the word of God, nor did they attack Peter for baptizing Gentiles; instead, they criticized Peter for going to the Gentiles and for eating with them. The issue, as they posed it, was clearly one of table-fellowship.[305] Peter responded to the criticism by recounting the entire story—from his vision in Joppa to the Holy Spirit's falling on Cornelius and his entire household. The key point in Peter's defense is that if the Lord, through visions and by pouring out the Spirit upon the Gentiles, demonstrated that there is no distinction between Jews and Gentiles, how could he oppose God by trying to maintain such a distinction?[306] When the Jewish leaders heard Peter's account, they

---

and the only occurrence in Acts is found here in 10:38)

[302] 10:39 (cf. 5:30). Although Peter is unable in this sermon to address and accuse the Jews directly of killing Jesus, he makes it known—as he does in all of his other sermons—that the Jerusalem Jews were responsible for killing Jesus.

[303] Acts 10:40-43 (Peter's speech to Cornelius and the rest of the Gentiles ends on the same note of universalism with which it began). The reader will quite naturally associate "forgiveness of sins (ἄφεσιν ἁμαρτιῶν) though his name" with the "repentance for forgiveness of sins" that is to "be preached in his name to all nations" (cf. Luke 24:46-48). The author confirms this association through the declaration of the Jerusalem Jews, "then to the Gentiles also God has granted repentance (μετάνοιαν) unto life" (11:18).

[304] Not only had the apostles and Jewish believers in Jerusalem heard that the Gentiles had accepted the word of God, but believers throughout Judea had heard the news. What occurred at the house of Cornelius is clearly being depicted by the author as a major event (cf. 10:45) and a turning point (cf. 15:7, 14).

[305] Acts 11:1-3. While no eating is depicted during Peter's visit with Cornelius, the fact that he resided in Caesarea with Cornelius for several days suggests that he must have eaten there with them. The response of the Jerusalem Jews is not so surprising when the reader recognizes that, as has been the case throughout Luke's gospel, the author's focus has not been so much on theological issues as it has been on social issues that keep people separated from one another (As mentioned earlier, accounts of eating with and visiting with the wrong kinds of people form "type scenes" in Luke; cf. 5:30; 15:2; 19:7). Apparently, the fact that "the Gentiles had also accepted the word of God" (11:1) did not change their status of being "unclean" in the minds of these Jerusalem Jews. These Jews were still thinking the way Peter used to before Peter changed his thinking as a result of insight from God.

[306] 11:12 (cf 15:9). If that which has been given by God to both Jews and Gentiles is a *gift* (δωρεά; 11:17; cf. 2:38; 8:20; 10:45), and if it is that gift rather than ethnic origin or ritual practices that establishes membership into the family of God, then the community of God's people must learn to change its thinking and accept all people as they are into the

ceased their criticism of Peter and began praising God, declaring, "Then even to the Gentiles God has given the repentance (μετάνοιαν) that leads to life."[307]

The sheer length of the Peter/Cornelius episode, the details with which the story is told and the fact that the account is referenced three times in the narrative, indicates the importance of the story in the context of Acts as a whole.[308] The story initiates the debate about Jewish/Gentile relations as well as the debate about the place of Gentiles within the community of God's people and their responsibilities as members of that community. The issues raised by the Peter/Cornelius episode are ones that will remain at the forefront for the remainder of Acts.

The greatest obstacle to the mission to the Gentiles was that it brought law-abiding Jews into contact with people they considered to be unclean, and with food they considered to be unclean as well. However, both Peter's residing with Simon the tanner and his vision regarding so-called unclean animals seem to have prepared both Peter and the reader for what would happen in Caesarea at the house of Cornelius. The Peter/Cornelius episode also makes it clear that Gentile inclusion was not simply a human decision, but the result of God's initiative and guidance.[309]

While the author's depiction of the Jerusalem Jews declaring, "Then even to the Gentiles God has granted repentance unto life," may cause the modern reader to think that repentance for the Gentiles was the same as repentance for the Jews, such was not the case. Unlike the Jews in Acts, Cornelius and the other Gentiles are not depicted as changing their thinking about Jesus. As a matter of fact, no indication is ever given as to what Cornelius and the others thought about Jesus or even if they knew anything about Jesus before Peter's arrival. Repentance for Cornelius and the other Gentiles is presented here simply as believing in Jesus.[310]

---

community—a notion that will be addressed in ch. 15.

[307] Acts 11:4–18.

[308] The importance of this encounter between Peter and Cornelius to the narrative of Acts is apparent by its repetition. First the events are narrated (10:1–49); then they are recounted (11:1–18); and later they are recalled (15:7–11, 14). Like the threefold repetition of Paul's Damascus road experience, this reiteration is for emphasis.

[309] The reader, however, is already a privileged observer who knows far more than the characters in the narrative about the will of God. The Peter/Cornelius episode depicts what the reader has been anticipating throughout Luke-Acts. Since the beginning of the narrative, the reader has been aware of the promise that Jesus would be a "light of revelation to the Gentiles" (Luke 2:32). Only in Luke was John's preaching accompanied by a text from Isaiah that promised, "all flesh shall see the salvation of God" (Luke 3:6; Isa 40:5, LXX). At the end of the gospel, Jesus declared to the apostles that repentance for the forgiveness of sins would preached "to all nations" (Luke 24:47), and finally in Acts 1:8 Jesus told his apostles that they would be his witnesses "to the ends of the earth."

[310] According to the author, while Peter was still saying, "every one who *believes* in him receives forgiveness of sins through his name," the Holy Spirit fell upon the Gentiles (10:43–45). Because of the association previously made between repentance and forgiveness of sins in his name (Luke 24:47), when the author depicts the Jews as declaring, "Then even to the Gentiles God has given the repentance that leads to life," he is suggesting that repentance for the Gentiles is synonymous with believing in Jesus.

The change in thinking implied by repentance appears to be associated with a change of religion, a turning from an earlier form of piety to a new form.[311]

While Cornelius and the other Gentiles are the ones depicted as repenting, as was the case with the tax collectors and soldiers in the preaching of John the Baptist and Levi and Zacchaeus in the preaching of Jesus, the acceptance of the Gentiles into the community of God's people requires a fundamental change of thinking on the part of those who consider themselves members already and seek to deny the acceptance of Gentiles into the community of God's people. If God has accepted the Gentiles into the family of God, then the community's reception of them needs to follow.[312] The repentance of tax collectors, soldiers, and other so-called sinners and undesirables, as well as Samaritans, eunuchs, and Gentiles gains them forgiveness of sins and helps to fulfill God's plan of universal salvation; however, it is the repentance of those who consider themselves to be the only ones worthy of membership in the community of God's people that leads to the establishment of a community comprised of all people.[313]

With the mission to the Gentiles prepared and legitimized by the precedent set by Peter, and with God's acceptance of the Gentiles now an established fact within the narrative, the church in Jerusalem sends Barnabas to Antioch where many Greeks are believing in and turning to the Lord Jesus.[314] Barnabas, pleased with the work that is occurring in Antioch, encourages those in Antioch to remain faithful to the Lord. After more and more people are "added to the Lord,"[315] Barnabas goes to Tarsus to look for Paul, who—as the reader knows—has been chosen by God to carry the Lord's name before the Gentiles.[316] Paul and Barnabas worked with the

---

[311] As seen in our examination of repentance in Jewish literature (e.g. *Joseph and Aseneth* 9–13; 15:6; 16:7; Philo, *On the Virtues* 175–186), repentance for non-Jews is closely associated with what is commonly thought of as "conversion." While Cornelius is identified as a devout man who feared God, he was still a Gentile, with whom the reader would still associate idolatry and pagan practices (cf Acts 10:25; 12:22; 14:11–18; 15:19–20; 17:16–34; 19:18–19a, 26–28, 35–37; 28:6). Repentance for the Gentiles entailed a change in thinking about their idolatrous and pagan practices.

[312] This is why Peter asks the question, "Can anyone withhold water for baptizing these people who have received the Holy Spirit even as we have" (10:47)?

[313] Although utilizing the language of "conversion" rather than "repentance," B. R. Gaventa makes the same point by declaring, "Luke demonstrates that the conversion of the first Gentile required the conversion of the church as well" (*From Darkness to Light*, 109).

[314] While the Peter/Cornelius episode legitimizes the Gentile mission and sets the stage for what follows, the arrival of the gospel in Antioch is not the result of the conversion of Cornelius. Instead, it is the continuation of the spreading of the gospel resulting from the scattering of believers after the persecution of Stephen (cf 8:4; 11:19). The Peter/Cornelius episode does, however, prepare the church in Jerusalem (as well as the reader) to receive the news of Greeks believing in and turning to the Lord (11:20–21).

[315] 11:24. The Antioch church experiences a period of rapid growth similar to that of the Jerusalem church (cf. 2:41, 47; 5:14).

[316] This of course is the first mention of Paul since his abrupt departure from the narrative in 9:30, where he was sent off to Tarsus. Now that Peter has prepared the way for Paul's Gentile mission, Paul is brought back on the scene from Tarsus. It is also Barnabas who once again introduces Saul to a community of believers (cf. 9:26–29). As one sent to

church in Antioch for a year, and, according to the author, "it was in Antioch that the disciples were first called 'Christians.'"[317] With the ministry of Paul and Baranabas suggesting that the future growth of the church lies with the Gentiles,[318] the issue of the status and responsibilities of the Gentiles within this predominantly Jewish movement begins to take center stage.

Before having Paul and Barnabas begin their missionary outreach, the author very skillfully makes another connection between Peter and the mission of Paul and Barnabas The author records that while Paul and Barnabas were working in Antioch, prophets came down from Jerusalem to Antioch. A particular prophet named Agabus predicted by the Spirit that there would be a great famine over all the world. When the famine occurred, the disciples in Antioch sent relief to those in Judea by the hand of Barnabas and Saul.[319] The author further records that king Herod was persecuting those who belonged to the church. He had killed James the brother of John and imprisoned Peter. Miraculously, an angel of the Lord delivered Peter from prison and Peter went "to the house of Mary, the mother of **John, whose other name was Mark**, where many were gathered." Shortly thereafter, the author records. "And Barnabas and Saul returned, having fulfilled their mission to Jerusalem, bringing with them **John, whose other name was Mark**.[320]

Antioch by the Jerusalem church, Barnabas' recruitment of Saul to work in the church at Antioch suggests that Paul was indeed acceptable to the Jewish leadership.

[317] With the appearance of Antioch, two mission bases now appear in the narrative, Jerusalem and Antioch. In B. N. Kaye's, "Acts' Portrait of Silas," *Novum Testamentum* 21 (1979) 13–26, Kaye asserts, "The focus of the story shifts in Acts xi 19 ff. from Jerusalem (with excursions from there) to Antioch (with excursions from there)." 16.

[318] Acts 13:46–49 (cf. 18:6; 28:28).

[319] Acts 11:27–30. Like the Jerusalem believers who shared their wealth with other members of the community who were in need (cf. 2:44–47; 4:32–37), those in Antioch—"each one according to his ability"—shared not only with those in the Antioch community but also with believers throughout Judea (Note: Barnabas was used as a model of the Jerusalem church's sharing (4:36–37), and he now plays a central role in Antioch's sharing with Jerusalem (11:30)).

[320] Acts 12:12, 25 (emphasis added). Since 12:25 has spawned much debate over whether or not Saul and Barnabas are returning "to" Jerusalem or "from" Jerusalem (cf. RSV and NRSV), many scholars miss the connection being made between vv. 12 and 25. The fact that the first place Peter goes when released from prison is to the house of Mary, the mother of "John, whose other name was Mark," and the fact that Paul and Barnabas take with them "John, whose other name was Mark," establishes another connection between the ministry of Peter and that of Paul and Barnabas. The narrative suggests that Paul and Barnabas went to Jerusalem carrying financial aid for those stricken by the famine (11:29–30). After they finished their mission to Jerusalem (the author has placed εἰς 'Ιερουσαλήμ ahead of the participial phrase in which it belongs; cf Haenchen, *Acts* 387), they returned to Antioch with John/Mark (12:25–13:3), who played an active role in their ministry (13:5). Because of the connection between 12:12 and 12:25, the author may be trying to suggest that Paul and Barnabas were among the "many" gathered at the house of Mary, the mother of John/Mark, when Peter arrived. In any case, John/Mark clearly functions as a link between Peter and Paul (It is interesting to note that John/Mark assists Paul and Barnabas as they proclaim "the word of God in the synagogues of the Jews," but he leaves them before their declaration that they are turning to the Gentiles (cf. 13:5, 13, 46). This departure by John/Mark later becomes a source of contention between Paul and Barnabas. On their next missionary journey,

After Paul and Barnabas returned to Antioch, their missionary journeys were initiated by the Holy Spirit, who instructed the church there to "Set apart for me Barnabas and Saul for the work to which I have called them."[321] Paul and Barnabas began their journeys by preaching throughout Cyprus, then on to Antioch of Pisidia, where the author presents Paul's first speech. Like Stephen in his speech, Paul works through the history of Israel. The author is careful, however, to focus Paul's speech on the areas of Israel's history not focused on by Stephen.[322] The ministry of John the Baptist is depicted as an historical event in the life of Israel, and Paul summarizes John's ministry as the preaching of a "baptism of repentance to all the people of Israel."[323]

Paul preaches to both the men of Israel—sons of the family of Abraham—and to those among them "who fear God (φοβούμενοι τὸν θεόν)."[324] Paul's speech

---

Barnabas takes John/Mark with him but Paul takes Silas, a leader in the Jerusalem church who had been sent by the apostles and elders of the Jerusalem church to Antioch with Paul and Barnabas to declare to the Gentiles the decisions made at the Jerusalem Council regarding the Gentiles (15:22–41). Barnabas is replaced by another representative from the Jerusalem church who, like Barnabas, accompanies Paul in his mission to Jews and Gentiles).

[321] Acts 13:1–2 (see also v 4). The reader of course is keenly aware that Paul has been "called" by God to carry the Lord's name before Gentiles and kings, as well as the people of Israel. The reader will also very shortly find out that Barnabas shares that call when he and Paul declare, "Behold we turn to the Gentiles. For so the Lord has commanded (ἐντέταλται) us, saying, 'I have sent you to be a light for the Gentiles, that you may bring salvation to the ends of the earth'" (13:46c–47. Since the phrase "to the ends of the earth" is identical to that found in Acts 1:8, Paul and Barnabas' mission is meant to be understood as fulfilling the initial and driving programmatic statement of Acts. The verb ἐντέλλομαι is used in Acts only at 1:2, with reference to the apostle's commission, and 13:47, with reference to Paul and Barnabas' commission). Even though Paul and Barnabas continued to preach in synagogues and among the Jews after declaring they were turning to the Gentiles, the summary statement at the end of their first missionary journey (14:27)—"When they arrived, they called the church together and related all that God had done with them, and how he had opened a door of faith for the Gentiles"—demonstrates that the focus is on the mission to the Gentiles. The statement also implies that the "work" alluded to in the commissioning scene of 13:1–3 has been (or at least is being) fulfilled.

[322] Whereas Stephen's speech focused on Abraham, Joseph, and Moses, Paul's speech ignores the patriarchs altogether and focuses on the kingship of Saul and David.

[323] Acts 13:24. John's baptism of repentance is depicted as an historical event in the life of Israel that demanded a change of thinking among the Jewish people in order that they might be able to receive the teachings and believe in the person of Jesus (v. 25; cf. Acts 19:4). Repentance in the preaching of Paul will demand a similar change in thinking among the Gentiles regarding their pagan and idolatrous practices, in order that they might be able to receive the teachings and believe in the person of Jesus. The author presents Paul in continuity with the history of salvation that preceded him, including the preaching of repentance by John the Baptist.

[324] Acts 13:16, 26. Since the phrase φοβούμενος τὸν θεόν was recently used in the narrative for the first time to refer to Cornelius (cf. 10:2, 22, 35), it is most likely being used here to refers to God-fearing Gentiles, rather than being used in apposition to either "Men of Israel" or "sons of the family of Abraham" (this seems to be supported by the authors use of "devout proselytes" in 13:43). The speech is intended to show how Paul's missionary endeavors began by addressing a synagogue audience. Paul's next major speech, however, will be addressed exclusively to Gentile pagans (17:22–31).

provides an excellent parallel to the speech delivered by Peter to Cornelius.[325] Like Peter's speech, Paul's speech contains statements regarding the Jewish rejection of Jesus and God's vindication of him.[326] Furthermore, just as Peter declared that "*every one who believes* in him receives *forgiveness of sins* through his name," so also Paul declares, "that through this man *forgiveness of sins* is proclaimed to you, and by him *every one who believes* is freed from everything."[327] In both cases, the 'forgiveness of sins' received 'through Jesus' is clearly meant to be associated with the message of "repentance for the forgiveness of sins" that was to be preached in Jesus' name by his disciples.[328] Since the Jews in the city did not believe but instead rejected the word of God preached by Paul, they did not receive forgiveness of sins, and Paul and Barnabas declared that they were turning to the Gentiles.[329]

While Paul declared that he was turning to the Gentiles, he continued to work among the Jews, preaching to both Jews and Gentiles.[330] The remainder of the narrative, however, focuses on his work among the Gentiles. The next major speech of Paul is directed exclusively to a pagan Gentile audience. While waiting for Silas and Timothy to join him in Athens, Paul delivered a speech in the Areopagus before Epicurean and Stoic philosophers, as well as before other Athenians and foreigners who lived in Athens. Paul acknowledged to the people of Athens that their idols and altars and inscriptions testified to the fact that they were indeed more religious than most.[331] Paul through his speech, however, sought to challenge their religious thinking and to persuade them to change their way of thinking. Paul proclaimed to the people of Athens a God who created all things, who does not live in shrines built by people nor is able to be depicted by gold, or silver, or stone, or by the art and imagination of humanity, a God who is lord of heaven and earth and who has given life to all people and has caused all the nations of the world to spring forth from one common ancestor, in order that everyone might seek after and serve the same God, who "is not far from each one of us" because humanity finds its existence in this God.[332]

---

[325] There are also similarities with Peter's Pentacost speech, especially the reference to Psalm 15:10: "You will not let your Holy One experience corruption" (13:35; 2:25–28), as well as with Peter's speech in Solomon's portico. In the latter, both Paul and Peter declare that what happened in Jerusalem was due to Jewish ἄγνοια (3:17; 13:27). Despite their ignorance, however, what they did fulfilled the plan and will of God (3:18; 13:29–33a).

[326] Acts 10:39–40; 13:27–30.

[327] Acts 10:43; 13:38–39.

[328] Luke 24:47; see also Acts 2:38; 5:31–32; 10:42–43.

[329] Acts 13:46. The extension of God's salvation that has been implied throughout the Gospel (cf. 2:32) and Acts (cf. 9:15), and has been initiated by Peter's encounter with Cornelius, is now declared by Paul in a programmatic statement.

[330] Acts 14:1; 17:1–4, 10–12, 17; 18:4, 19; 19:8–10; (cf. 18:5–6; 28:28).

[331] Acts 17:22. The comparative δεισιδαιμονέστερος (δεισιδαίμων) conveys the notion of being "more religious" (or more superstitious) than usual.

[332] Acts 17:24–29. While Paul here is critical of the numerous religions of the Greco-Roman world (cf. 19:23–27), he is not critical of Greco-Roman philosophy. Many of Paul's views resonate with such philosophy (cf. Dibelius, *Studies in the Acts*, 42–54).

Like the Jews who acted out of ignorance (ἄγνοια) with regard to Jesus,[333] the Gentiles acted out of ignorance with regard to God.[334] While God at one time overlooked such ignorance, God is no longer "unknown;" therefore, God now commands everyone everywhere to repent (μετανοεῖν).[335] God demands a change in thinking from everyone because God has appointed a day on which the world will be judged in righteousness by Jesus (v. 31; cf. 10:42), and in order to survive that judgment everyone will need to make fundamental changes in their ways of thinking.[336] These changes, however, are not simply changes in the way Gentiles worship and think about God, but also changes in the way people think about each other. Paul's speech testifies to both the sovereignty of God and the oneness of humanity. God is the creator of all human beings; therefore, all human beings have a universal relationship with each other that transcends all ethnic and cultural distinctions. Every human being is a member of the same family—the family of God.[337] The author combines in this one speech of Paul's the two aspects of repentance that are central to the overall purpose and mission of Luke-Acts: 1) a change in thinking about God or Jesus that enables all people to receive the salvation of God, and 2) a change in thinking about others than enables diverse groups of people to live together as a community of God's people.

In the third of three major speeches attributed to Paul during his three recorded missionary journeys, the notion of universal repentance once again plays a prominent role.[338] The author also revisits the notion suggested in Paul's previous speech: that ignorance is no longer overlooked by God because God is no longer unknown. In his farewell speech to the elders of the Ephesian church, Paul reminds them how he lived among them, serving the Lord with humility.[339] He proclaims,

---

[333] Acts 3:17; 13:27.

[334] Acts 17:23, 30 (cf. 14:16). While the Athenians were "ignorant" regarding God, they did wish "to know" (γνῶναι) what Paul was teaching (17:19, 20).

[335] As shall be demonstrated below, the notion that humanity no longer has an excuse is confirmed in Paul's next speech to the Ephesian elders.

[336] While the theme of universal repentance is announced in Luke 24:47, this is by far its most explicit expression.

[337] Luke, in contrast to Matthew, traces Jesus' genealogy all the way back to Adam—who was "the son of God" (Luke 3:38)—emphasizing the universal relatedness of all people. It is most likely the biblical story of the origin of all people from Adam that lies behind Acts 17:26.

[338] In his mission speech to Jews in Antioch of Pisidia (13:16–41), Paul says that John preached a baptism of repentance "to all the people of Israel" (v. 24). In his mission speech to Greeks in Athens (17:22–31), he declares that God "commands all people everywhere to repent" (v. 30). Finally, in his farewell speech to the elders of the Ephesian church (20:18–35), he proclaims that he bore witness "both to Jews and to Greeks" about repentance (v. 21). Being that μετανοέω and μετάνοια only occur four times in all of the Pauline epistles (Rom 2:4; 2 Cor 7:9, 10; 12:21), the emphasis on repentance in the Pauline speeches of Acts is clearly the work of the author.

[339] Paul's farewell speech has many elements resembling farewell speeches in the Old Testament and other ancient Jewish literature (cf. Hans-Joachim Michel, *Die Abschiedsrede des Paulus and die Kirche Apg 20, 17–38: Motivgeschichte und Theologische Bedeutung.* SANT 35. (Munich: Kösel-Verlag, 1973) 48–54, 68–71; C. K. Barrett, "Paul's Address to

"how I did not shrink from declaring to you (οὐδὲν ὑπεστειλάμην... τοῦ μὴ ἀναγγεῖλαι ὑμῖν) anything that was helpful or from teaching you publicly and from house to house, bearing witness both to Jews and to Greeks about repentance (μετάνοιαν)."[340] This is why he later says, "Therefore I declare to you this day that I am clean of the blood of all of you, for I did not shrink from declaring to you (οὐ γὰρ ὑπεστειλάμην τοῦ μὴ ἀναγγεῖλαι... ὑμῖν) the whole purpose of God."[341] Those in the Ephesian community have no excuse for not repenting and serving God because Paul has testified about repentance "both to Jews and to Greeks" among them, teaching them all about the "whole purpose of God."[342]

The theme of universal repentance was announced by Jesus to his disciples in Luke 24:47. In Paul's previous speech to the Greeks in Athens, he makes the most explicit reference to universal repentance by telling them that God "commands all people everywhere to repent." Now in his farewell speech to the Ephesian elders, Paul concludes his ministry among them by stressing that he has played a major role in helping fulfil God's plan of universal repentance. Through Paul's preaching of repentance "both to Jews and to Greeks," God is accomplishing the task of "commanding all people everywhere to repent."

Paul reiterates this point regarding universal repentance in his last speech, which is a defense before King Agrippa. Paul tells Agrippa that he had been sent by God to both Jews and Gentiles, "to open their eyes so that they may turn from darkness to light and from the power of Satan to God, so that they may receive forgiveness of sins (ἄφεσιν ἁμαρτιῶν) and a place among those who are sanctified by faith in me." He then informs Agrippa that he has been obedient to the call of God by declaring "first to those in Damascus, then in Jerusalem and throughout all the country of Judea, and also to the Gentiles, that they should repent

---

the Ephesian Elders," *God's Christ and His People* (eds. J. Jervell and W. Meeks; Oslo: Universitetsforlaget, 1977) 107–121; J. Lambrecht, "Paul's Farewell Address at Miletus (Acts 20:17–38)," *Les Actes des Apôtres: traditions, rédaction, théologie* (ed. J. Kremer; Gembloux: Leuven University Press, 1979) 307–337).

[340] Acts 20:18–21a. While the author is surely intentional in presenting two balanced positions—1) repentance toward God and 2) faith toward the Lord Jesus—it is unclear as to exactly what the author means by these two positions. It may be that repentance is thought of as being in response to the will of God, while faith is thought of as being in response to the teachings of Jesus. What can be said about "repentance toward God and faith toward our Lord Jesus" is that the phrase is a part of the rhetorical word pairs used by the author throughout vv. 20–21 in order to emphasize the fullness of Paul's efforts (e.g. "to announce and to teach"; "publicly and from house to house"; "to Jews and to Greeks").

[341] Acts 20:26–27. This Pauline declaration echoes an earlier declaration made by Paul to the Jews of Corinth. Immediately after Paul's speech to the people of Athens, he testified to Jews in Corinth that the Christ was Jesus. However, when they opposed him he declared to them, "Your blood be upon your heads! I am clean" (18:6).

[342] The phrase "both to Jews and to Greeks" recalls Paul's Ephesian ministry in which he reached "all the residents of Asia... both Jews and Greeks" (19:10, 17). Teaching them about the "whole purpose of God" prepares the elders to protect the "whole congregation" (Jews and Gentiles) from the false teachers who will arise and teach perverse things in order to entice the disciples to follow after them (vv. 28–32).

(μετανοεῖν) and turn to God and perform deeds worthy of repentance (ἄξια τῆς μετανοίας ἔργα πράσσοντας).[343]

Through Paul's preaching of repentance to Jews in Damascus, Jerusalem and throughout Judea, as well as to Gentiles everywhere, God's demand for universal repentance is being accomplished. Furthermore, Paul's declaration that he is "saying nothing but what the prophets and Moses said would take place: that the Christ must suffer, and that, by being the first to rise from the dead, he would proclaim light both to the people and to the Gentiles" is clearly meant to echo Jesus' declaration to his disciples, "that everything written about me in the law of Moses and the prophets and the psalms must be fulfilled. . . . Thus it is written, that the Christ should suffer and on the third day rise from the dead, and that repentance for the remission of sins should be preached in his name to all nations."[344]

Paul's defense is not only the last speech made by Paul and the last speech recorded in Luke-Acts, it also marks the last reference to repentance in Luke-Acts. Like the first reference to repentance, the author once again associates repentance with "forgiveness of sins" and "deeds/fruits worthy of repentance."[345] The author brings the reader back to that which is consistent and universal about repentance—whether it is Jewish repentance or Gentile repentance—that is that repentance always secures the forgiveness of sins (no matter what the sins) and that repentance is always accompanied by the manifestation of deeds/fruits that attest to one's repentance.

Summary

Clearly the meaning of μετανοέω and μετάνοια—and therefore the meaning of repentance—in Luke-Acts is essentially the same as that found in Greco-Roman, Jewish, and early Christian literature. Both μετανοέω and μετάνοια are used to convey a change in thinking that usually leads to a change in behavior and or way of life. The motif of repentance plays a central role in both the development of the story in Luke-Acts and the message conveyed by Luke-Acts. Repentance is not simply a change in thinking that represents an appropriate response to inappropriate thoughts and or actions; repentance is the necessary change in thinking and behavior

---

[343] Acts 26:17–20. The fact that Paul cites his preaching of repentance to those in Damascus, Jerusalem, and throughout Judea, as well as to Gentiles, as evidence that he did not disobey the call of God (vv. 19–20), suggests that the antecedent of "to whom (εἰς οὓς)" in v. 17b is not simply "the Gentiles" but "the people and the Gentiles" (Contra. Haenchen, *Acts*, 686; Johnson, *Acts*, 436–437). While the references to opening eyes, turning from darkness to light, turning to God, and receiving forgiveness of sins (v. 18) do fit the contexts of religious conversion (Johnson, *Acts*, 437), they are not limited to Gentiles in Luke-Acts (e.g. Luke 1:16, 77–79; 4:18). Furthermore, Paul's speech ends by declaring the resurrected Christ's mission of proclaiming light both to Jews and to Gentiles (v. 23).

[344] Acts 24:22–23; Luke 24:44–47.
[345] Luke 3:3, 8.

required of individuals in order to help fulfill God's plan of universal salvation and to help establish a community composed of all people.

As demonstrated throughout this chapter, the author of Luke-Acts is not only concerned with emphasizing the universality of salvation, he is also concerned with emphasizing the required change in thinking and living that enables diverse individuals to receive the salvation of God and to live together as a community of God's people. Since the plan of God involves making salvation accessible to all flesh, everyone is eligible for membership in the community of God's people. Such inclusivity, however, requires a fundamental change in thinking on the part of many in the emerging religious community of Luke-Acts. Repentance in Luke-Acts represents a fundamental change in thinking that enables diverse individuals to receive the salvation of God and to live together as a community of God's people. Repentance is therefore an essential element in the preaching of all of the prominent characters of Luke-Acts: John the Baptist, Jesus, and the apostles whom Jesus commissioned as messengers of repentance. Among the apostles, repentance plays an especially important role in the ministry of both Peter and Paul.

In the author's narration of the appearance of John the Baptist, he extends the prophetic reference from Second Isaiah found in Mark and Matthew, suggesting that he understands repentance to represent a fundamental change in thinking that permanently and radically alters the way things use to be. The author seeks to make this point very early in his telling of the gospel. As a result of the preaching of John the Baptist, the author also immediately establishes that he wants his implied reader to associate repentance with ethical social behavior that enables once alienated people to live together as a community of God's people. The addition of the ethical preaching activity of John the Baptist to Luke's gospel clearly makes the "fruits worthy of repentance" the focus of the Lukan baptist preaching unit (Luke 3:7–18).

The inquiries made by the "crowds," as well as by the tax collectors and soldiers, as to what they needed to do in order to "bear fruits worthy of repentance," not only indicates that repentance is expected of everyone but that God has afforded everyone an opportunity to repent, even those who may be considered by many as unworthy of repentance. The author depicts John the Baptist as a preacher of hope and encouragement, even to the most despised segments of the population at that time. Part of the hope and encouragement that John brings is that repentance, which delivers people from the wrath to come, is available to all people and that repentance requires the just, merciful and equitable treatment of all people by all people, enabling diverse individuals to receive the salvation of God and to live together as a community of God's people.

In Luke's Gospel, μετανοέω and μετάνοια occur quite frequently in the preaching and teaching of Jesus. In a small but significant redaction to one of the sayings of Jesus, Luke records Jesus informing the Pharisees and their scribes that he has "not come to call the righteous, but sinners to repentance (εἰς μετάνοιαν)." This declaration is clearly meant to function as a programmatic statement. Since Jesus has come to call sinners to repentance, the teachings of Jesus and the actions of those who respond favorably to the call and teachings of Jesus further demonstrate what the author considers to be "fruits worthy of repentance."

Jesus' declaration that he has "not come to call the righteous, but sinners to repentance," immediately follows his calling of Levi, Peter, James and John. It is therefore their abandonment of their former ways of thinking and living—their willingness to leave "everything" and to follow Jesus in a new way of living that he will prescribe for them—that serves as a paradigm for repentance. The author seeks to make it clear that Jesus is not simply calling sinners to follow him; he is calling them to repentance, which not only includes following Jesus but also includes changing one's way of thinking and living and adopting a new way of thinking and living consistent with the lifestyle prescribed in the teachings of Jesus. By adopting this new way of thinking and living, an environment is created in which diverse individuals are able to live together as a community of God's people.

In the first detailed preaching section of Jesus, commonly referred to as The Sermon on the Plain/Mount, Jesus is depicted as preaching good news to the poor. The good news is an eschatological promise to the poor (6:20–21; cf. 14:21), which is accompanied, as in the preaching of John the Baptist, by an ethical challenge to those with resources to share those resources with the poor in order to help meet their needs and/or relieve their poverty (6:24–25; cf. 14:12–14). Throughout this extensive sermon, as throughout Luke's gospel, most of the teachings of Jesus, like those of John the Baptist, emphasize ethical social behavior that focuses on abandoning greed and treating all people fairly, justly and equitably. Like John the Baptist, the Lukan Jesus suggests that the fruits worthy of repentance are those that are manifested in the context of human interpersonal relationships and that demonstrate ethical social concern for the well being of others. Such fruits represent the "good fruit" produced by the "good tree."

The preaching of Jesus also conveys that while sin is part of the human condition, people are not condemned because of their sin, but because of their failure to repent.[346] Repentance delivers sinners from destruction, enabling them to receive the salvation of God. This is one of the reasons why rejoicing and celebrating are appropriate expressions of and responses to repentance.[347] The offer of repentance is part of the good news preached by both John the Baptist and Jesus, and as good news it should be responded to with rejoicing. Furthermore, since repentance secures forgiveness of sins from God, it should be responded to by human beings with forgiveness. Just as Jesus came in order to call sinners to repentance and to forgives sinners who do repent, so the disciples are instructed to forgive sinners who repent, even those who repeatedly sin against them.[348] Repentance requires forgiveness, and it is the forgiveness extended to repentant sinners that enables them to receive the salvation of God and that helps once

---

[346] Luke 10:13–14; 11:32; 13:1–9; 15:1–32.
[347] Luke 5:27–39; 15:5–7, 9–10, 22–24, 32.
[348] Luke 17:1–4.

estranged and alienated people to live together as a genuine community of God's people.

Not only are the disciples instructed to forgive sinners who repeatedly sin against them, they also are commissioned by Jesus to preach repentance for the forgiveness of sins to all nations. Whereas repentance in Luke deals directly and primarily with a change in the way people think about and interact with other people, the change of thinking in Acts, most often has to do with a change of thinking regarding Jesus of Nazareth. This change of thinking regarding Jesus, however, also results in a change in the way people think about and interact with other people.

Repentance for the Jews in Acts primarily involves a change of thinking regarding Jesus; however, if they are going to change their thinking about Jesus, they are also going to have to change their thinking regarding Jesus' teachings concerning the acceptance of all people and the proper use of possessions. The speeches in Acts that are directed to Jewish listeners are meant to convict those involved in the persecution of Jesus and to cause them to change their minds regarding Jesus. The people are repeatedly reminded of and rebuked for their involvement in the persecution and murder of Jesus. They are also repeatedly made aware of the fact that despite their rejection and murder of Jesus, God has raised him up and exalted him. All of this is meant to cause those Jews who had at one time rejected Jesus to recognize the error of their way and to change their thinking about Jesus. This change of thinking regarding Jesus, however, is from the outset depicted in the context of human interaction and manifested by the just, merciful and equitable treatment of the poor and needy.

As the message of repentance moved outside of Jerusalem and was no longer directed exclusively toward those who had denied and murdered Jesus, the expressed rationale for repentance also began to change. Simon the magician was not rebuked for rejecting and persecuting Jesus, but for thinking that the gift of God could be purchased with money. He was told that his heart was not right before God, and he was ordered to repent of his wickedness in order that the intent of his heart might be forgiven. While Simon's repentance clearly involved a change of thinking, it did not entail a change of thinking about someone Simon had previously rejected and murdered. His repentance, however, was still meant to result in the forgiveness of his sin.

The two most prominent preachers of repentance in Acts are Peter and Paul. Not only do they preach repentance inside and outside of Jerusalem, both men experience changes in their own thinking that determine the direction of the Christian ministry outside of Jerusalem. While neither μετανοέω nor μετάνοια is used to describe the change in thinking resulting from Paul's Damascus road experience, Paul's behavior after the experience clearly reveals a radical change of thinking by Paul regarding Jesus. This change in thinking about Jesus also leads to a radical and fundamental change in thinking regarding the status of Gentiles and their place within the community of God's people.[349] Likewise, while neither μετανοέω nor μετάνοια is used to describe the change in thinking resulting from Peter's visionary experience and his encounter with Cornelius, Peter's declaration, "Truly I perceive that God shows no partiality" clearly indicates a fundamental change of thinking by Peter. The radical change in thinking by Paul and Peter foreshadows the change in thinking required of the Jerusalem Jews regarding the status of Gentiles and their place within the community of God's people.

As Peter, Paul and Barnabas carry the message of Jesus outside of Jerusalem, everyone—especially the Gentiles—is commanded to repent. While God at one time overlooked the ignorance of the Jews and the Gentiles, God now demands everyone everywhere to repent. Repentance for the Gentiles however, is not the same as repentance for the Jews. The Gentiles are not depicted as changing their thinking about Jesus. As a matter of fact, no indication is ever given as to what the Gentiles thought about Jesus or even if they knew anything about Jesus before the preaching of Peter and Paul. Repentance for the Gentiles is depicted simply as believing in Jesus. The change in thinking implied by repentance appears to be associated with a change of religion—a conversion.

While most—if not all—of the discussions regarding repentance in Luke-Acts focus on the explicitly identified repentance of Jews and Gentiles, very little is said about the implicit changes in thinking demanded by the notion of universal salvation. Tax collectors, soldiers, harlots, sinners, Samaritans, eunuch, Gentiles, and other so-called undesirables are explicitly depicted as repenting; however, the acceptance of such people into the community of God's people requires a fundamental change of thinking on the part of those who consider themselves members already and seek to deny the acceptance of such people into the community of God's people. If God accepts tax collectors, soldiers, harlots, sinners, Samaritans, eunuchs, Gentiles, and other so-called undesirables into the family of God, then the community's reception of such people needs to follow. The repentance of such individuals clearly gains them forgiveness of sins and helps to fulfill God's plan of universal salvation; however, it is the repentance of those who consider themselves to be the only ones worthy of membership in the community of God's people that leads to the establishment of a community composed of all people.

---

[349] Cf. Acts 22:21–22.

APPENDIX

Table 1: Occurrences of βουλή, βούλομαι and βούλημα in Luke-Acts

	Mk	Mt	Jn	Lk	Change made in parallel passage[1]	Acts	Total NT	Total Lk-Acts
βουλή	–	–	–	2	Yes	8	13	10
βούλομαι	1	2	1	2	Yes	14	37	16
βούλημα	–	–	–	–	–	1	3	1

[1] Parallel passage changes are as followed (the changes involve Luke's addition of the word in question):

βουλή – **Lk 7:24–30** ≈ Mt 11:7–11 (21:31b–32); **Lk 23:50–52** ≈ Mk15:42–43; Mt 27:57–58; Jn 19:38

βούλομαι – **Lk 22:41–42** ≈ Mk 14:35–36; Mt 26:39; Jn 18:1 (12:27)

Table 2: προ- compounds in Acts that convey the idea of a divine plan

προ- Compounds	NT Gospels	Acts	Total NT
πρόγνωσις "foreknowledge"	None	1	4
προεῖπον "foretell"	None	1	3
προκαταγγέλλω "announce beforehand"	None	2	2
προκηρύσσω "proclaim beforehand"	None	1	1
προοράω "foresee"	None	3	4
προορίζω "decide beforehand"	None	1	6
προχειρίζομαι "appoint" (destine)	None	3	3
προχειροτονέω "appoint beforehand"	None	1	1

Table 3: New Testament occurrences of μετανοέω and μετάνοια

	Mk	Mt	Lk	Acts	Rev	Rest of NT	Total NT	Total Lk-Acts
μετανοέω	2	5	9	5	11	1	33	14
μετάνοια	1	2	5	6	0	8	22	11

SELECTED BIBLIOGRAPHY

Reference Works

Abrams, Meyer Howard. *A Glossary of Literary Terms*. 4th ed. New York: Holt, Rhinehart and Winston, 1981.

Balz, Horst, et. al. eds. *Exegetical Dictionary of the New Testament*. 3 vols. Grand Rapids, MI: W. B. Eerdmans, 1990–1993.

Barnet, Sylvan, Morton Berman and William Burto, eds. *A Dictionary of Literary Terms*. 2nd ed. Boston: Little Brown, 1971.

Bauer, W. A. *Greek-English Lexicon of the New Testament and Other Early Christian Literature*. Translated and revised by W. F. Arndt, F. W. Gingrinc, and F. W. Danker. 2nd ed. Chicago: University of Chicago Press, 1979.

Blass, F. and A. Debrunner. *A Greek Grammar of the New Testament and Other Early Christian Literature*. Translated and revised by R. W. Funk. Chicago: University of Chicago Press, 1961.

Boisacq, E. *Dictionnaire etymologique de la Langue Grecque*. 4th ed. Heidelberg: C. Winter, 1950.

Brown, Colin, ed. *New International Dictionary of New Testament Theology*. 2 vols. Exeter: Paternoster Press, 1975–1978.

Brown, Francis, S. R. Driver, and Charles A. Briggs. *The New Brown-Driver-Briggs-Gesenius Hebrew and English Lexicon*. Peabody, MA: Hendrickson, 1979.

Freedman, Noel, et. al. eds. *Anchor Bible Dictionary*. 6 vols. New York: Doubleday, 1992.

Gingrich, W. and F. Danker, eds. *A Greek-English Lexicon of the New Testament and Other Early Christian Literature*. 2nd ed. Chicago: University of Chicago Press, 1958.

Hatch, E. and H. Redpath. *Concordance to the Septuagint and Other Greek Versions of the Old Testament*. 3 vols. Oxford: Oxford University Press, 1897. Reprint, Grand Rapids: Baker, 1983.

Kittel, G. ed. *Theological Dictionary of the New Testament*. 10 vols. Translated by W. Bromiley. Grand Rapids: Eerdmans, 1964–1976.

Liddell, Henry, and Robert Scott, eds. *Greek-English Lexicon*. Revised and edited by Henry Jones and Roderick McKenzie. Oxford: Clarendon, 1996.

Metzger, Bruce. *A Textual Commentary on the Greek New Testament*. London: United Bible Society, 1971.

Strack H. and P. Billerbeck, *Kommentar zum Neun Testament*. 6 vols. Munich: Beck, 1922–1961.

Ancient Sources: Texts, Editions, and Translations

Aeschylus. *Prometheus Vinctus*. Revised and edited by Henry Silvester Richmond. London: W. Pickering, 1846.
Aesop. *Corpus Fabularum Aesopicarum*. Edited by Augustus Hausrath. Leipzig: Teubner, 1940.
Apostolic Fathers. Edited and translated by Kirsopp Lake. LCL. 2 vols. Cambridge, MA: Harvard University Press, 1917.
Appian. Edited and translated by H. White. LCL. 4 vols. Cambridge, MA: Harvard University Press, 1912–1931.
Apuleius. *Metamorphoses*. Translated with introductions and explanatory notes by P. G. Walsh. Oxford: Clarendon, 1994.
Aspasii in ethica Nicomachea quae supersunt commentaria. Edited by G. Heylbut. Berlin: Reimer, 1889.
Callimachus. Edited by Rudolf Pfeiffer. 2 vols. Oxonii, Italy: E Typographeo Clarendoniano, 1949–1953.
Chariton. *Callirhoe*. Edited and translated by G. P. Goold. LCL. Cambridge, MA: Harvard University Press, 1995.
Cicero. Edited and translated by E. Winstedt, et al. LCL. 28 vols. Cambridge, MA: Harvard University Press, 1912–1977.
Comicorum Graecorum fragmenta. Edited by G. Kaibel. Berlin: Weidmann, 1899.
Corpus Hermeticum. Edited by A. D. Nock and A. J. Festugière. 4 vols. Paris: Collection Budé, 1945–1954.
The Didache. Ancient Christian Writers 6. Edited by J. A. Kleist. Westminster, MD: The Newman Press, 1948.
La Didachè. Instructions des apôtres. Edited by J. P. Audet. Paris: J. Gabalde, 1958.
Dio Chrysostom. Edited and translated by J. W. Cohoon and H. L. Crosby. LCL. 5 vols. Cambridge, MA: Harvard University Press, 1932–1951.
Diodorus Siculus. Edited and translated by C. H. Oldfather, et al. LCL. 12 vols. Cambridge, MA: Harvard University Press, 1933–1967.
Diogenes Laertius: Lives of Eminent Philosophers. Edited and translated by R. D. Hicks LCL. 2 vols. Cambridge, MA: Harvard University Press, 1925.
Dionysius of Halicarnassus. Edited and translated by Earnest Cary. LCL. 7 vols. Cambridge, MA: Harvard University Press, 1937–1950.
1 (Ethiopic Apocalypse of) Enoch. Edited and translated by E. Isaac. In *The Old Testament Pseudepigrapha*, ed. J. H. Charlesworth, 1:5–89. Garden City, NY: Doubleday, 1983.
Epictetus. Edited and translated by W. A. Oldfather. LCL. 2 vols. Cambridge, MA: Harvard University Press, 1925–1928.
I Esdras. A Critical Edition. Edited by S. S. Tedesche. Ph.D. Dissertation, Yale University, 1928.
The Fourth Book of Ezra. Edited and translated by Bruce Metzger. In *The Old Testament Pseudepigrapha*, ed. J. H. Charlesworth, 1:517–559. Garden City, NY: Doubleday, 1983.
Fragmenta Comicorum Graecorum. 4 vols. Edited by A. Meineke. Berlin: Reimer, 1841.
Die Fragmenta der Vorsokratiker. 6th ed. 3 vols. Edited by H. Diels and W. Kranz. Berlin: Weidmann, 1952.
The Greek New Testament. 4th ed. United Bibles Societies, Stuttgart: Deutsche Bibelgesellschaft, 1993.

Harpocrations lexicon in decem oratores Atticos. Edited by W. Dindorf. Oxford: Oxford University Press, 1853.
Joseph and Aseneth. Edited and translated by C. Burchard. In *The Old Testament Pseudepigrapha,* ed. J. H. Charlesworth, 2:177–247. Garden City, NY: Doubleday, 1985.
Josephus. Edited and translated by H. St. J. Thackeray, et al. LCL. 10 vols. Cambridge, MA: Harvard University Press, 1926–1965.
Josephus. *The Works. New Updated Edition.* Edited and translated by W. Whiston. Peabody, MA: Hendrickson, 1987.
Juvenal and Persius. Edited and translated by G. G. Ramsay. LCL Cambridge, MA: Harvard University Press, 1918.
The Letter of Aristeas. Edited and translated by H. St. J. Thackeray. In *An Introduction to the Old Testament in Greek,* ed. H. B. Swete. Cambridge: Cambridge University Press, 1902.
Lucian. Edited and translated by A. M. Harmon et. al. LCL. 8 vols. Cambridge, MA: Harvard University Press, 1913–1967.
Macrobius. *Saturnalia.* Edited and translated by Percival Davies. New York: Columbia University Press, 1969.
The Communings with Himself of Marcus Aurelius Antoninus, Emperor of Rome. Edited and translated by C. R. Haines LCL. Cambridge, MA: Harvard University Press, 1970.
Menander: Epitrepontes. Edited and translated by W. G. Arnott. LCL. Cambridge, MA: Harvard University Press, 1976.
Menandri sententiae. Edited by S. Jaekel. Leipzig: Teubner, 1964.
Minor Attic Orators. Edited and translated by G. Maidment. LCL. 2 vols. Cambridge, MA: Harvard University Press, 1941.
The Old Testament Pseudepigrapha. 2 vols. Edited by J. H. Charlesworth. Garden City, NY: Doubleday, 1983–1985.
Orientis Graeci Inscriptiones Selectae. Edited by W. Dittenberger. Leipzig: Teubner, 1905.
Origenis Hexaplorum Fragmenta. 2 vols. Edited by F. Field. Oxford: Oxford University Press, 1875.
Ovid. Edited and translated by G. P. Gould, et al. LCL. 6 vols. Cambridge, MA: Harvard University Press, 1924–1979.
Patrology. 4 vols. Edited by Johannes Quasten. Ultrecht, Holland: 1950. Reprint, Westminster, MD: Christian Classics, 1992.
Pausanias. Edited and translated by W. Jones and H. Ormerod. LCL. 5 vols. Cambridge, MA: Harvard University Press, 1918–1935.
Philo. Edited and translated by F. H. Colson, et al. LCL. 10 vols. Cambridge, MA: Harvard University Press, 1929–1962.
Philo. The Complete Works. New Updated Edition. Edited and translated by C. D. Yonge. Peabody, MA: Hendrickson, 1993.
Plato. Edited and translated by R. G. Bury, W. R. M. Lamb, et al. LCL 12 vols. Cambridge, MA: Harvard University Press, 1914–1935.
Plutarch: Moralia. Edited and translated by F. C. Babbitt, et al. LCL. 16 vols. Cambridge, MA: Harvard University Press, 1927–1969.
Plutarch: The Parallel Lives. Edited and translated by Bernadotte Perrin. LCL. 11 vols. Cambridge, MA Harvard University Press, 1914–1926.
Polybius. Edited and translated by W. R. Paton. LCL. 6 vols. Cambridge, MA: Harvard University Press, 1922–1925.

Rhetores Graeci. Edited by L. Spengel. Frankfurt: Minerva, 1966.
Seneca. Edited and translated by J. W. Basore, et al. LCL. 10 vols. Cambridge, MA: Harvard University Press, 1917–1972.
Septuaginta, id est Vestus Testamentum Graece iuxta LXX interpretes. Edited by A. Rahlfs. Stuttgart: Deutsche Bibelgesellschaft, 1935.
The Sibylline Oracles. Edited and translated by J. J. Collins. In *The Old Testament Pseudepigrapha*, ed. J. H. Charlesworth, 1:317–472. Garden City, NY: Doubleday, 1983.
The Sibylline Oracles of Egyptian Judaism. Edited and translated by J. J. Collins. Society of Biblical Literature Dissertation Series 13. Missoula, MT: Scholars Press, 1974.
The Hebrew Text of Sirach: A Text-Critical and Historical Study. Edited by Alexander Di Lella. London: Mouton and Co., 1966.
The Book of Ben Sira: Text, Concordance and an Analysis of the Vocabulary. Edited by Z. Ben-Hayyim. Jerusalem: Academy of the Hebrew Language, 1973.
Stoicorum Veterum Fragmenta. 4 vols. Edited by J. Von Arnim. Stuttgart: Teubner, 1966.
Sylloge Inscriptionum Graecarum. 3rd ed. 3 vols. Edited by W. Dittenberger. Leipzig: Teubner, 1924.
The Tabula of Cebes. Edited and Translated by J. Fitzgerald and M. White. SBL Text and Translations 24. Graeco-Roman Religion Series 7. Chico, CA: Scholars Press, 1983.
The Testament of Abraham. Edited and translated by E. P. Sanders. In *The Old Testament Pseudepigrapha*, ed. J. H. Charlesworth, 1:871–902. Garden City, NY: Doubleday, 1985.
The Testament of Abraham: The Greek Recensions. Edited and translated by M. E. Stone. Text and Translations 2. Missoula, MT: Society of Biblical Literature, 1972.
The Testament of Moses. Edited and translated by J. Priest. In *The Old Testament Pseudepigrapha*, ed. J. H. Charlesworth, 1:919–934. Garden City, NY: Doubleday, 1983.
Testaments of The Twelve Patriarchs. Edited by R. H. Charles. Oxford: Oxford University Press, 1908.
Testaments of The Twelve Patriarchs. A Critical Edition of the Greek Text. Edited and translated by M. de Jonge, H. W. Hollander, H. J. de Jonge, and T. Korteweg. Pseudepigrapha Veteris Testamenti Graece I 2. Leiden: E. J. Brill, 1978.
Thucydides. Edited and translated by C. F. Smith. LCL. 4 vols. Cambridge, MA: Harvard University Press, 1919–1923.
Xenophon. Edited and translated by C. L. Brownson et al. LCL. 7 vols. Cambridge, MA: Harvard University Press, 1918–1968.

Secondary Literature

Alter, Robert. *Art of Biblical Narrative*. New York: Basic Books, Inc., 1981.
Ambrozic, A. *The Hidden Kingdom: A Redactional-Critical Study of the References to the Kingdom of God in Mark's Gospel*. CBQ Monograph Series 2. Washington: Catholic Biblical Association of America, 1975.
Arnold, E. V. *Roman Stoicism*. Cambridge: Cambridge University Press, 1911.
Attridge, Harold W. *The Epistle to the Hebrews*. Hermeneia. Philadelphia: Fortress, 1989.
Aubin, Paul. *Le problème de la 'conversion': Étude sur un terme commun a l'hellenisme et au christianisme des trois premiers siècles*. Paris: Beauchesne, 1962.
Aune, D. E. *The New Testament in its Literary Environment*. Philadelphia: Westminster, 1987.
Bacon, B. W. *Studies in Matthew*. New York: Henry Holt, 1930.
Badian, E. *Publicans and Sinners: Private Enterprise in the Service of the Roman Republic*. Ithaca, NY: Cornell University Press, 1976.
Bagwell, Timothy J. *American Formalism and the Problem of Interpretation*. Houston: Rice University Press, 1981.
Bailey, Jon N. "*Metanoia* in the Writings of Philo Judaeus." *Society of Biblical Literature Papers 1991*. Edited by E. H. Lovering, Jr. *SBLSP* 30. Atlanta: Scholars Press (1991) 135–141.
———. *Repentance in Luke-Acts*. Ph.D. Dissertation, University of Notre Dame, 1993.
Bailey, K. E. *Poet and Peasant. A Literary Cultural Approach to the Parables in Luke*. Grand Rapids, MI: Eerdmans, 1976.
Barnett, A. E. *Paul Becomes a Literary Influence*. Chicago: University of Chicago Press, 1941.
Barrett, C. K. *Luke the Historian in Recent Study*. London: Epworth, 1961.
———. "Paul's Address to the Ephesian Elders." In *God's Christ and His People*, ed. J. Jervell and W. Meeks, 107–121. Oslo: Universitetsforlaget, 1977.
———. "Light on the Holy Spirit from Simon Magus (Acts 8, 4–25)." In *Les Actes des Apôtres: traditions, rédaction, théologie*, ed. J. Kremer, 281–95. Bibliotheca Ephemeridum Theologicarum Lovaniensium 48. Gembloux: Leuven University Press, 1979.
Barton, J. *Oracles of God: Perceptions of Ancient Prophecy in Israel after the Exile*. London: Darton, Longman and Todd, 1986.
Bassler, Jouette. "Luke and Paul on Impartiality," *Biblica* 66 (1985) 546–552.
Bauckham, Richard J. *Jude, 2 Peter*. Word Biblical Commentary, 50. Waco Texas: Word, 1983.
Baumeister, A. *Denkmäler des klassischen Altertums zur Erlauterung des Lebens der Griechen und Rome*. 3 vols. Leipzig: R. Oldenbourg, 1885.
Beckford, James A. "Accounting for Conversion," *British Journal of Sociology* 29 (1978) 249–262.
Berger, Peter. *Sacred Canopy: The Social Reality of Religion*. London: Faber, 1969.
Bohak, Gideon. *Joseph and Aseneth and The Jewish Temple in Heliopolis*. SBL Early Judaism and Its Literature 10. Atlanta: Scholars Press, 1996.
Booth, Wayne. *The Rhetoric of Fiction*. 2nd ed. Chicago: University of Chicago Press, 1983.
Borgen, P. "Philo of Alexandria. A Critical and Synthetical Survey of Research since World War II." *ANRW* II.21.1 (1991) 97–154.

———. "Philo of Alexandria." In *Jewish Writings of the Second Temple Period*, ed. M. Stone, 233–282. CRINT 2. Philadelphia: Fortress, 1985.
———. *Philo, John, Paul*. Brown Judaica Series. Atlanta: Scholars Press, 1986.
Borig, R. *Der wahre Weinstock*. Munich: Kösel, 1967.
Bovon, François. *Luke the Theologian. Thirty-Three Years of Research (1950–1983)*. Translated by K. McKinney. Allison Park, PA: Pickwick, 1987.
Brawley, R. L. *Luke-Acts and the Jews: Conflict, Apology, and Conciliation*. SBLMS 33. Atlanta: Scholars Press, 1987.
———. *Centering on God: Method and Message in Luke-Acts*. Louisville, KY: Westminster/John Knox, 1990.
Bréhier, É. *Les Idées philosophiques et religieuses de Philon d´Alexandrie*. 3rd ed. Paris: Librairie philosophique J. Vrin, 1950.
Brownlee, W. R. "John the Baptist in Light of Ancient Scrolls." In *The Scrolls and the New Testament*, ed. Krister Stendahl and James Charlesworth, 33–53. New York: Crossroad, 1992.
Bultman, R. *The History of the Synoptic Tradition*. Revised Edition. Translated by John Marsh. New York: Harper and Row, 1963.
Cadbury, Henry J. *The Style and Literary Method of Luke*. Harvard Theological Studies 6. Cambridge, MA: Harvard University Press, 1919–1920.
———. "The Summaries in Acts." In *The Beginnings of Christianity*, ed. F. J. Foakes Jackson and Kirsopp Lake, 5:269–277. London: Macmillan and Co., 1933.
———. *The Book of Acts in History*. New York: Harper and Brothers, 1955.
———. *The Making of Luke-Acts*. 2nd ed. London: SPCK, 1958.
Campbell, G. *The Four Gospels*. New York: Gould and Newman, 1837.
Carlston, C. E. *Metanoia and Church Discipline in the New Testament*. Ph.D Dissertation, Harvard University, 1958.
Chamberlain, William. *The Meaning of Repentance*. Philadelphia: Westminster Press, 1943.
Chang, Sang. "Justice of Jubilee in Luke," *Reformed World* 45, 2 (1995) 87–96.
Chatman, Seymour. *Story and Discourse: Narrative Structure in Fiction and Film*. Ithaca, NY: Cornell University Press, 1978.
Chestnutt, R. D. "The Social Setting and Purpose of Joseph and Aseneth," *Journal for the Study of the Pseudepigrapha* 2 (1988) 21–48.
Coggins, Richard J. *Sirach*. Sheffield, England: Sheffield Academic, 1998.
Collins, J. J. "The Development of the Sibylline Tradition," *ANRW* II.20.1 (1987) 421–459.
Conzelmann, H. *The Theology of St. Luke*. Translated by Geoffrey Buswell. Philadelphia: Fortress, 1961.
Corwin, Virginia. *St. Ignatius and Christianity in Antioch*. New Haven: Yale University Press, 1960.
Cosgrove, Charles. "The Divine ΔEI in Luke-Acts. Investigations into the Lukan understanding of God's Providence," *Novum Testamentum* 26 (1984) 168–190.
Cousar, Charles B. "Luke 5:29–35," *Interpretation* 40 (1986) 58–63.
Dahl, N. A. "The Story of Abraham in Luke-Acts." In *Studies in Luke-Acts*, ed. L. Keck and J. Martyn, 139–158. Philadelphia: Fortress, 1980.
Davis, R. *Service in the Roman Army*. New York: Columbia University Press, 1989.
Dawsey, James. *The Lukan Voice. Confusion and Irony in the Gospel of Luke*. Macon, GA: Mercer, 1987.
Denney, J. "Three Motives to Repentance, Luke XIII. 1–9," *Expositor* 4/7 (1893) 232–237.

Derrida, J. *Margins of Philosophy*. Translated by Alan Bass. Chicago: University of Chicago Press, 1982.
Dibelius, M. *Studies in the Acts of the Apostles*. Translated by M. Ling. New York: Scribner's, 1956.
Dirksen, Aloys H. *The New Testament Concept of Metanoia*. Washington, D.C.: The Catholic University of America, 1932.
Donahue, J. R. "Tax Collectors and Sinners: An Attempt at Identification," *Catholic Biblical Quarterly* 33 (1971) 39–71.
———. "Two Decades of Research on the Rich and the Poor in Luke-Acts." In *Justice and the Holy: Essays in Honor of Walter Harrelson*, eds. D. Knight and P. Paris, 129–144. Atlanta: Scholars Press, 1989.
Donfried, K. P. *The Setting of Second Clement*. Novem Testamentum Supplements 38. Leiden: Brill, 1974.
———. "Attempt at Understanding the Purpose of Luke-Acts. Christology and the Salvation of the Gentiles." In *Christological Perspectives*, eds. R. F. Berkey and S. A. Edwards, 112–122. New York: Pilgrim, 1982.
Douglas, Mary. "Deciphering a Meal," *Daedalus* 101 (1972) 61–81.
Dunn, J. D. G. *Romans*. 2 vols. Word Biblical Commentary. Waco, TX: Word, 1988.
Dupont, J. "Repentir et conversion d'après les Actes des Apôtres," *Science Ecclesiastiques* 12 (1960) 137–173.
———. "La conversion dans les Actes des Apôtres," *Lumière et Vie* 9 (1960) 48–70.
———. *The Salvation of the Gentiles*. Translated by J. R. Keating. New York: Paulist Press, 1979.
Edwards, R. A. *A Theology of Q: Eschatology, Prophecy, and Wisdom*. Philadelphia: Fortress, 1976.
Eltester, W., ed. *Jesus in Nazareth*. BZNW 40. Berlin: de Gruyer, 1972.
Esler, Philip F. *Community and Gospel in Luke-Acts: The Social and Political Motivations of Lukan Theology*. SNTSMS 57. Cambridge: Cambridge University Press, 1987.
Etzioni, Amitai and David Carney, eds. *Repentance: A Comparative Perspective*. Center for Communitarian Policy Studies. Lanham, MD: Rowman and Littlefield, 1997.
Evans, R. *Soldiers of Rome: Praetorians and Legionnaries*. Cabin John, MD: Seven Locks, 1986.
Felder, Cain H. *Stony the Road We Trod: African American Biblical Interpretation*. Minneapolis: Augsburg Fortress, 1991.
Feldman, Louis H. and G. Hata, eds. *Josephus, the Bible, and History*. Detroit: Wayne State University Press, 1989.
Finn, Thomas M. *From Death to Rebirth: Ritual and Conversion in Antiquity*. New York: Paulist Press, 1977.
Fitzmyer, J. *The Gospel According to Luke*. 2 vols. Anchor Bible. Garden City, NY: Doubleday 1981–1985.
———. *Luke the Theologian*. London: Geoffrey Chapman, 1989.
Flanagan, N. M. "The What and How of Salvation in Luke-Acts." In *Sin, Salvation, and the Spirit*, ed. D. Durken, 203–213. Collegeville, MN: Liturgical Press, 1979.
Frank, T., ed. *An Economic Survey of Ancient Rome*. 6 vols. Baltimore, MD: Johns Hopkins Press, 1933–1959.
Fritzsche, O. F. *Libri apocryphi veteris testamenti graece*. Leipzig: Teubner, 1871.
Frye, N. *Anatomy of Criticism*. Princeton, NJ: Princeton University Press, 1957.

Garnsey P. and R. Smaller. *The Roman Empire: Economy, Society, and Culture* London: Duckworth, 1987.

Garrett, Susan R. "Beloved Physician of the Soul? Luke as Advocate for Asetic Practice." In *Asceticism in the New Testament*, ed. Leif Vaage and Vincent Wimbush, 71–95. New York: Routledge, 1999.

Gaventa, Beverly, R. *From Darkness to Light: Aspects of Conversion in the New Testament*. Philadelphia: Fortress, 1986.

Genette, Gérard. *Narrative Discourse: An Essay in Method*. Translated by J. Lewin. Ithaca, NY: Cornell University Press, 1980.

Giblin, Charles, H. "Structural and Theological Consideration on Luke 15," *Catholic Biblical Quarterly* 24 (1962) 15–31.

Giles, K. N. "Salvation in Lukan Theology," *Reformed Theological Review* 42 (1983) 10–16.

González, J. *Faith and Wealth: A History of Early Christian Ideas on the Origin, Significance, and Use of Money*. San Francisco: Harper and Row, 1990.

Goody, J. *Cooking, Cuisine and Class: A Study in Comparative Sociology*. Cambridge: Cambridge University Press, 1982.

Green, Joel B. "Good News to Whom? Jesus and the 'Poor' in the Gospel of Luke." In *Jesus of Nazareth: Lord and Christ. Essays on the Historical Jesus and New Testament Christology*, eds. Joel Green and Max Turner, 59–74. Grand Rapids, MI: Eerdmans, 1994.

———. "'Salvation to the End of the Earth' (Acts 1347): God as Savior in the Acts of the Apostles." In *The Book of Acts in its Theological Setting*, vol. 6, eds. I. H. Marshall and David Petersen. The Book of Acts in it First Century Setting. Edited by Bruce W. Winter. Grand Rapids, MI: Eerdmans, 1997.

Green, Joel B. and Michael C. McKeever. *Luke-Acts and New Testament Historiography*. Grand Rapids, MI: Baker Books, 1994.

Gressmann, H. "Vom reichen Mann und armen Lazarus: Eine literargeschichtliche Studie," *Abhandlungen der königlichen preussischen Akademie der Wissenschaften* phil.-hist. Kl. 7 (1918) 63–68.

Griffith, F. L. *Stories of the High Priests of Memphis*. Oxford: Clarendon, 1900.

Guillaume, J.-M. *Luc interprète des anciennes traditions sur la résurrection de Jésus*. Études Bibliques. Paris: Gabalda, 1979.

Haenchen, Ernst. *The Acts of the Apostles: A Commentary*. Oxford: Basil Blackwell, 1971.

Hamm, Dennis. "Zacchaeus Revisited Once More: A Story of Vindication or Conversion?" *Biblica* 72, 2 (1991) 249–252.

Harnack, A. von. *The Date of the Acts and of the Synoptic Gospels*. New Testament Studies, IV. London: William and Norgate, 1911.

Hengel, M. *Property and Riches in the Early Church: Aspects of a Social History of Early Christianity*. Translated by J. Bowden. Philadelphia: Fortress, 1974.

———. *Acts and the History of the Earliest Christianity*. Philadelphia: Fortress, 1980.

Hercher, R. *Epistolographi Graeci*. Paris: Didot, 1873. Reprint, Amsterdam: Hakkert, 1965.

Herrenbrück, F. "Wer waren die 'Zöllner'?" *Zeitschrift für die neutestamentliche Wissenschaft* 72 (1981) 178–194.

Hezel, Francis. "'Conversion and 'Repentance' in Lucan Theology," *The Bible Today* 37 (1968) 2596–2602.

Hirsch Jr., E. D. *The Aims of Interpretation*. Chicago: University of Chicago Press, 1976.

Hock, Ronald F. "Lazarus and Micyllus: Greco-Roman Backgrounds to Luke 16:19–31," *Journal of Biblical Literature* 106, 3 (1987) 447–463.

Holladay, W. L. *The Root of "Shub" in the Old Testament*. Leiden: E. J. Brill, 1958.
Hollander, H. W. *Joseph as an Ethical Model in the Testaments of the Twelve Patriarchs*. Studia in Veteris Testamenti Pseudepigrapha 6. Leiden: E. J. Brill, 1981.
Hollenbach, P. "Social Aspects of John the Baptizer's Preaching Mission in the Context of Palestinian Judaism," *ANRW* II.19.1 (1979) 850–875.
Hubbard, B. J. "Commissioning Stories in Luke-Acts; A Study of Their Antecedents, Form and Content," *Semeia* 8 (1977) 103–126.
———. "The Role of Commissioning Accounts in Acts." In *Perspectives on Luke-Acts*, ed. Charles H. Talbert, 187–98. Perspectives in Religious Studies Special Studies Series 5. Danville, VA: Association of Baptist Professors of Religion, 1978.
Jäger, Werner. "Review of Eduard Norden's *Agnostos Theos*," *Göttingische gelehrte Anzeigen* 175 (1913) 569–610.
Jellicoe, S. *The Septuagint and Modern Study*. Cambridge: Cambridge University Press, 1968.
Jeremias, J. *Jerusalem in the Time of Jesus*. Translated by F. H. and C. H. Cave. London: SCM, 1969.
———. *The Parables of Jesus*. Translated by S. H. Hooke et al. 3rd ed. London: SCM, 1972.
Jervell, J. *Luke and the People of God: A New Look at Luke-Acts*. Minneapolis: Augsburg, 1972.
———. "The Church of Jews and Godfearers." In *Luke-Acts and the Jewish People: Eight Critical Perspectives*, ed. J. B. Tyson, 11–20. Minneapolis, MN: Augsburg, 1988.
Johnson, L. T. *The Literary Function of Possessions in Luke-Acts*. SBLDS 39. Missoula, MT: Scholars Press, 1977.
———. *Sharing Possessions: Mandate and Symbol of Faith*. Philadelphia: Fortress, 1981.
———. *The Writings of the New Testament*. Philadelphia: Fortress, 1986.
———. *The Acts of the Apostles*. Sacra Pagina 5. Collegeville, Minnesota: Liturgical, 1992.
Jolly, R. *Le dossier d'Ignace d'Antioche*. Brussels: Éditions de l'université, 1979.
Jones, A. *The Roman Economy: Studies in Ancient Economic and Administrative History*. Edited by P. A. Brunt. Oxford: Basil Blackwell, 1974.
Jones, F. S. "The Pseudo-Clementines: A History of Research," *Second Century* 2 (1982) 1–33, 63–96.
Jonge, M. de, ed. *Studies on the Testaments of the Twelve Patriarchs. Text and Interpretation*. Studia in Veteris Testamenti Pseudepigrapha 3. Leiden: E. J. Brill, 1975.
———. *Christology in Context*. Philadelphia: Westminster Press, 1988.
———. *Jewish Eschatology, Early Christian Christology and the Testament of the Twelve Patriarchs: Collected Essays*. Supplements to Novum Testamentum. Leiden: E. J. Brill, 1991.
Karris, Robert. *Luke: Artist and Theologian. Luke's Passion Account as Literature*. New York: Paulist, 1985.
Kaye, B. N. "Acts' Portrait of Silas," *Novum Testamentum* 21 (1979) 13–26.
Keck, L. E. and J. L. Martyn, eds. *Studies in Luke-Acts: Essays Presented in Honor of Paul Schubert*. Nashville, TN: Abingdon, 1966.
Kee, Alistair. "The Old Coat and the New Wine: A Parable of Repentance," *Novum Testamentum* 12 (1970) 13–21.
Kee, Howard C. "The Ethical Dimensions of the Testament of the XII as a Clue to Provenance, *New Testament Studies* 24 (1978) 259–70.

Keegan, T. "Introductory Formulae for Matthean Discourses," *Catholic Biblical Quarterly* 44 (1982) 415–430.
Keppie, L. *The Making of the Roman Army: From Republic to Empire*. London: Batsford, 1984.
Kilgallen, John. "Social Development and the Lucan Works," *Studia Missionalia* 39 (1990) 21–47.
King, N. Q. "The 'Universalism' of the Third Gospel." In *Studia Evangelica Vol I: Papers presented to the International Congress on 'The Four Gospels in 1957' held at Christ Church, Oxford, 1957*, edited by Kurt Aland, et. al., 199–205. Berlin: Akademie-Verlag, 1959.
Koch, Robert. "Die religiöse-sittliche Umkehr nach den drei ältesten Evangelien und der Apostelgeschichte," *Anima* 14 (1959) 296–307.
Kraeling, C. H. *John the Baptist*. New York: Scribner, 1951.
Kümmel, W. G. *Introduction to the New Testament*. Translated by H. C. Kee. 17th ed. Nashville: Abingdon Press, 1975.
Lambrecht, J. "Paul's Farewell Address at Miletus (Acts 20:17–38)." In *Les Actes des Apôtres: traditions, rédaction, théologie*, ed. J. Kremer, 307–337. Bibliotheca Ephemeridum Theologicarum Lovaniensium 48. Gembloux: Leuven University Press, 1979.
———. *Once More Astonished: The Parables of Jesus*. New York: Crossroad, 1981.
Latte, K. "Schuld und Sünde in der griechischen Religion," *ANRW* 10:281 (1920) 250–261.
Lown, John S. *Toward a Morphology of Repentance: A Study of Conversion Terminology in the Pauline Epistles against the Background of the Book of Acts and Selected Graeco-Roman Literature*. Ann Arbor, MI: UMI, 1977.
Maddox, R. J. *The Purpose of Luke-Acts*. Edinburgh: Clark, 1982.
Malina, B. *Windows on the World of Jesus: Time Travel to Ancient Judea*. Louisville: Westminster/John Knox, 1993.
Manson, T. W. *The Sayings of Jesus as Recorded in the Gospels according to St. Matthew and St. Luke Arranged with Introduction and Commentary*. London: SCM, 1971.
Marshall, I. H. *Luke: Historian and Theologian*. Grand Rapids, MI: Zondervan, 1971.
———. *Gospel of Luke. A Commentary on the Greek Text*. NIGTC. Grand Rapids, MI: Eerdmans, 1978.
———. *The Acts of the Apostles*. Grand Rapids, MI: Eerdmans, 1980.
Martin, R. P. "Salvation and Discipleship in Luke's Gospel," *Interpretation* 30 (1976) 366–380.
Matera, F. J. "Responsibility for the Death of Jesus according to the Acts of the Apostles," *Journal for the Study of the New Testament* 39 (1990) 77–93.
Mealand, David. "Community of Goods and Utopian Allusions in Acts II–IV," *Journal of Theological Studies* 28 (1977) 96–99.
Merrill, E. T. *Essays in Early Christian History*. London: Macmillan, 1924.
Mette, H. J., ed. "Die 'kleinen' griechischen historiker heute," *Lustrum* 21 (1978) 31.
Michaelis, W. "Zum jüdischen hinterfrund der Johannestaufe," *Judaica* 7 (1951) 81–121.
Michel, Hans-Joachim. *Die Abschiedsrede des Paulus und die Kirche Apg 20, 17–38: Motivgeschichte und Theologische Bedeutung*. Studien zum Alten und Neuen Testament 35. Munich: Kösel-Verlag, 1973.
Michel, Otto. "Die Umkehr nach der Verkündigung Jesu," *Evangelische Theologie* 5 (1938) 403–413.

Michiels, R. "La conception lucanienne de la conversion," *Ephemerides Theologicae Lovanienses* 41 (1965) 42–78.
Minear, Paul. "Luke's Use of the Birth Stories." In *Studies in Luke Acts*, eds. Leander Keck and J. Louis Martyn, 111–130. Nashville, Abingdon, 1966.
Moessner, David P. "Paul in Acts: Preacher of Eschatological Repentance to Israel," *New Testament Studies* 34 (1988) 96–104.
———. "The 'script' of the Scriptures in Acts: suffering as God's plan (βουλή) for the world for the 'release of sins'." In *History, Literature, and Society in the Book of Acts*, ed. Ben Witherington, III, 56–72. Cambridge: Cambridge University Press, 1996.
Montefiore, C. G. "Rabbinic Conceptions of Repentance," *Jewish Quarterly Review* 16 (1904) 209–257.
Moore, Stephen. *Literary Criticism and the Gospels: The Theoretical Challenge*. New Haven, CT: Yale University Press, 1989.
Morgan, Robert and John Barton, *Biblical Interpretation*. Oxford Bible Series. New York: Oxford University Press, 1988.
Moscato M. "Current Theories Regarding the Audience of Luke-Acts," *Currents in Theology and Missions* 3 (1976) 355–361.
Neal, David A. *None but the Sinners: Religious Categories in the Gospel of Luke*. JSNT Supplement Series 58. Sheffield, England: Sheffield Academic Press, 1991.
Neusner, Jacob. "Repentance in Judaism." In *Repentance: A Comparative Perspective*, eds. Amitai Etzioni and David Carney, 60–75. Lanham, MD: Rowman and Littlefield, 1997.
Neyrey, J. H. "The Form and Background of the Polemic in 2 Peter," *Journal of Biblical Literature* 99 (1980) 407–31.
Nock, Arthur D. *Conversion: The Old and New in Religion from Alexander the Great to Augustine of Hippo*. London: Oxford University Press, 1933.
Nolland, J. *Luke 1–9:20*. Word Biblical Commentary. Dallas: Word, 1989.
Norden, Eduard. *Agnostos Theos*. Stuttgart: B. G. Teubner, 1912.
Nussbaum, Chaim. *The Essence of Teshuvah: A Path to Repentance*. Northvale, NJ: Jason Aronson Inc., 1993.
O'Neill, J. C. *The Theology of Acts in its Historical Setting*. London: SPCK, 1961.
O'Toole, Robert F. *The Unity of Luke's Theology: An Analysis of Luke-Acts*. Wilmington, DE: Glazier, 1984.
Parke, H. W. and D. E. H. Wormell, *The Delphic Oracle*. 2 vols. Oxford: Blackwell, 1956.
Parsons, Mikeal. *The Departure of Jesus in Luke-Acts: The Ascension Narratives in Context*. Journal for the Study of the New Testament Supplement Series 21. Sheffield: JSOT Press, 1987.
Perkins, P. "Taxes in the New Testament," *Journal of Religious Ethics* 12 (1984) 182–200.
Perrin, Norman. *The Kingdom of God in the Teaching of Jesus*. Philadelphia: Westminster, 1963.
———. *Rediscovering the Teachings of Jesus*. New York: Harper and Row, 1967.
Pervo, Richard. *Profit with Delight: The Literary Genre of the Acts of the Apostles*. Philadelphia: Fortress Press, 1987.
Petersen, Norman. *Literary Criticism for New Testament Critics*. Guides to Biblical Scholarship. Philadelphia: Fortress, 1978.
Pfeiffer, Rudolf. "The Image of the Delian Apollo and Apolline Ethics," *Journal of the Warburg and Courtauld Institutes* 15 (1952) 20–32.
———. *Ausgewählte Schriften*. Oxford: Clarendon, 1968.

Plummer, A. *A Critical and Exegetical Commentary on the Gospel According to St. Luke.* ICC. 5th ed. Edinburgh: T&T Clark, 1922.
Powell, Mark A. *What is Narrative Criticism.* New Testament Series. Minneapolis, MN: Fortress, 1990.
Ramaroson, L. "Le coeur du troisième évangile: Lc 15," *Biblica* 60 (1979) 348–360.
Ramsey, George W. "Plots, Gaps, Repetitions, and Ambiguity in Luke 15," *Perspectives in Religious Studies* 17 (1989) 37–41.
Reese, J. M. *Hellenistic Influences on the Book of Wisdom and its Consequences* Rome: Biblical Institute Press, 1983.
Rhoads, David. "Narrative Criticism and the Gospel of Mark," *Journal of the American Academy of Religion* 50 (1982) 411–434.
Rhoads, David and Donald Michie. *Mark as Story: An Introduction to the Narrative of a Gospel.* Philadelphia: Fortress Press, 1982.
Richard, Earl. "The Divine Purpose: The Jews and the Gentile Mission (Acts 15)." In *Luke-Acts: New Perspectives from the Society of Biblical Literature Seminar*, ed. C. H. Talbert, 188–209. New York: Crossroad Publishing Co., 1984.
Richardson, James T. *Conversion Careers: In and Out of the New Religions.* Beverly Hills, CA: Sage, 1978.
Ricour, Paul. "Toward a Hermeneutic of the Idea of Revelation." Translated by David Pellauer. *Harvard Theological Review* 70 (1977) 1–37.
Rimmon-Kenan, Shlomith. *Narrative Fiction: Contemporary Poetics.* London: Methuen, 1983.
Ringe, Sharon H. *Jesus, Liberation, and the Biblical Jubilee.* OBT 19. Philadelphia: Fortress, 1985.
Rist, J. M. *Stoic Philosophy.* Cambridge: Cambridge University Press, 1969.
Rius-Camps, J. *The Four Authentic Letters of Ignatius, the Martyr.* Christianismos 2. Rome: Pontificium Institutum Orientalium Studiorum, 1979.
Robinson, J. A. T. "The Baptism of John and the Qumran Community," *Harvard Theological Review* 50 (1957) 175–194.
———. *Redating the New Testament.* Philadelphia: Westminster, 1976.
Roche, E. "Pénitence et Conversion dans l'evangile et la vie Chrétienne," *La nouvele revue théologique* 79 (1957) 113–134.
Rordorf, W. and A. Tuilier, *La doctrine des douze apôtres (Didache): Introduction, Texte, Tradition. Notes, Appendice et Index.* Sources chrétiennes 248. Paris: Éditions du Cerf, 1978.
Rostovtzeff, M. *The Social and Economic History of the Roman Empire.* 2nd ed. Revised by P. M. Fraser. 2 vols. Oxford: Oxford University Press, 1957.
Safrai, S and M. Stern, eds. *The Jewish People in the First Century: Historical Geography, Political History, Social, Cultural and Religious Life and Institutions.* Philadelphia: Fortress, 1974.
Saggs, H. W. F. *The Greatness that Was Babylon: A Sketch of the Ancient Civilization of the Tigris-Euphrates Valley.* New York: Hawthorn Books,1962.
Sahlin, J. "Die Früchte der Umkehr: Die ethische Verkündigung Johannes des Taüfers nach Lk 3:10–14," *Studia theologica* 1 (1948) 54–68.
Salmon, M. "Insider or Outsider? Luke's Relationship with Judaism." In *Luke-Acts and the Jewish People*, ed. J. B. Tyson, 76–82. Minneapolis, MN: Augsburg, 1988.
Sanders, E. P. *Jesus and Judaism.* Philadelphia: Fortress, 1985.
———. *The Historical Figure of Jesus.* London: Penguin, 1993.

Sanders, J. T. *The Jews in Luke-Acts*. Philadelphia: Fortress, 1987.

———. "The Jewish People in Luke-Acts." In *Luke-Acts and the Jewish People*, ed. J. B. Tyson, 51–75. Minneapolis, MN: Augsburg, 1988.

———. "Who is a Jew and Who is a Gentile in the Book of Acts." *New Testament Studies* 37 (1991) 434–455.

Schechter, Solomon. *Aspects of Rabbinic Theology*. New York: Schocken Books, 1961. Reprint, Woodstock, VT: JEWISH LIGHTS, 1993.

Scheffler, E. H. "The Social Ethics of the Lukan Baptist," *Neotestimenica* 24, 1 (1990) 21–36.

Schnackenburg, Rudolf. "The Demand for Repentance." In *The Moral Teaching of the New Testament*. Translated by J. H. Smith and J. W. J. O'Hara, 25–33. New York: Herder and Herder, 1962.

Schoedel, W. "Are the Letters of Ignatius of Antioch Authentic?" *Religious Studies Review* 2 (1980) 195–201.

———. *Ignatius of Antioch*. Hermenia. Philadelphia: Fortress, 1985.

Schubert, Paul. "The Final Cycle of Speeches in the Book of Acts," *Journal of Biblical Literature* 87 (1968) 235–61.

Schürmann, H. *Das Lukasevangelium*. HTKNT. 2 vols. 2nd ed. Freiburg: Herder, 1982.

Seccombe, D. P. *Possessions and the Poor in Luke-Acts*. Linz: Fuchs, 1982.

Segal, Alan F. *Paul the Convert: The Apostolate and Apostasy of Saul the Pharisee*. New Haven: Yale University Press, 1990.

Shepherd, William H. Jr. *The Narrative Function of the Holy Spirit as a Character in Luke-Acts*. Atlanta: Scholars Press, 1994.

Sloan, R. B., Jr., *The Favorable Year of the Lord. A Study of Jubilary Theology in the Gospel of Luke*. Austin, TX: Schola Press, 1977.

Smith, D. E. *Social Obligation in the Context of Communal Meals*. Ph.D. Dissertation, Harvard University, 1980.

———. "Jewish Proselyte Baptism and the Baptism of John *Restoration Quarterly* 25 (1982) 13–32.

———. "Table Fellowship as a Literary Motif in the Gospel of Luke," *Journal of Biblical Literature* 106 (1987) 613–38.

Sparks, H. F. D. "Review of O'Neil's *The Theology of Acts*," *Journal of Theological Studies* 14 (1963) 454–466.

Squires, John. *The Plan of God in Luke-Acts*. Cambridge: Cambridge University Press, 1993.

Stegemann, W. "The Following of Christ as Solidarity between Rich, Respected Christians and Poor Despised Christians (Gospel of Luke)." In *Jesus and the Hope of the Poor*, eds. L. Schottroff and W. Stegemann, 5–25. Maryknoll, NY: Orbis Books, 1986.

Steinleitner, F. S. *Die Beicht im Zusammenhange mit der sakralen Rechtspflege in der Antike*. München: Oldenbourg, 1913.

Stendahl, Krister. *Paul Among Jews and Gentiles and Other Essays*. Philadelphia: Fortress, 1976.

Stowers, S. *The Diatribe and Paul's Letter to the Romans*. SBLDS 57. Chico, CA: Scholars Press, 1981.

Swete, H. B. ed. *An Introduction to the Old Testament in Greek*. Cambridge: Cambridge University Press, 1902.

Talbert, C. H. *Literary Patterns, Theological Themes, and the Genre of Luke-Acts*. Society of Biblical Literature Monograph Series 20. Missoula, MT: Scholars Press, 1974.

———. "Prophecies of Future Greatness: The Contributions of Greco-Roman Biographies to an Understanding of Luke 1:5–4:15." In *The Divine Helmsman*, 129–41. Edited by J. L. Crenshaw and S. Sandmel. New York: KTAV, 1980.

———. *Reading Acts: A Literary and Theological Commentary on the Acts of the Apostles*. New York: Crossroad Publishing Co., 1997.

———. "Conversion in the Acts of the Apostles: Ancient Auditors' Perceptions." In *Literary Studies in Luke-Acts: Essays in Honor of Joseph B. Tyson*, eds. Richard P. Thompson and Thomas Phillips, 141–153. Macon, Georgia: Mercer University Press, 1998.

———. ed. *Perspectives on Luke-Acts*. Perspectives in Religious Studies Special Studies Series 5. Danville, VA: Association of Baptist Professors of Religion, 1978.

———. ed. *Luke-Acts: New Perspectives from the Society of Biblical Literature Seminar*. New York: Crossroad Publishing Co., 1982

Tannehill, R. C. "The Mission of Jesus according to Luke IV 16–30." In *Jesus in Nazareth*, ed. W. Eltester, 51–75. Berlin: de Gruyer, 1972.

———. "Attitudinal Shift in Synoptic Pronouncement Stories." In *Orientation by Disorientation: Studies in Literary Criticism and Biblical Literary Criticism Presented in Honor of William A. Beardslee*, ed. Richard A. Spencer, 183–197. Pittsburgh: Pickwick Publications, 1980.

———. *The Narrative Unity of Luke-Acts. A Literary Interpretation*. 2 vols. Philadelphia: Fortress Press, 1986–1990.

———. "The Function of Peter's Mission Speeches in the Narrative of Acts," *New Testament Studies* 37 (1991) 400–414.

———. *Luke*. Abingdon New Testament Commentaries. Nashville: Abingdon, 1996.

Taylor, V. *The Gospel According to St. Mark*. 2d ed. New York: Macmillan, 1966.

Temple, P. J. '"House" or "Business" in Lk 2.49?', *Catholic Biblical Quarterly* 1 (1939) 342–52.

Thiselton, Anthony. *New Horizons in Hermeneutics*. Grand Rapids, MI: Zondervan, 1992.

Thompson, E. F. "Μετανοέω and Μεταμέλει in Greek Literature until 100 A.D. In *Historical and Linguistic Studies in Literature related to the New Testament*. Chicago: The University of Chicago Press, 1908.

Thompson, Richard and Thomas Phillips, eds. *Literary Studies in Luke-Acts: Essays in Honor of Joseph B. Tyson*. Macon, GA: Mercer University Press, 1998.

Tov, Emanuel. *The Text-Critical Use of the Septuagint in Biblical Research*. Jerusalem Biblical Studies. Jerusalem: Simor Ltd., 1981.

Turner, N. "The 'Testament of Abraham': Problems in Biblical Greek," *New Testament Studies* 1 (1954/55) 219–23.

Tyson, J. B. *Luke-Acts and the Jewish People: Eight Critical Perspectives*. Minneapolis, MN: Augsburg, 1988.

Uspensky, Boris. *A Poetics of Composition: The Structure of the Artistic Text and Typology of a Compositional Form*. Translated by Valentina Zavarin and Susan Wittig. Los Angeles: University of California Press, 1973.

van Unnik, W. C. *Sparsa Collecta. The Collected Essays of W.C. van Unnik*, I. Supplements to Novum Testamentum 29. Leiden: E. J. Brill, 1973.

———. "Luke-Acts, A Storm Center in Contemporary Scholarship." In *Studies in Luke-Acts: Essays Presented in Honor of Paul Schubert*, eds. Leander Keck and J. Louis Martyn, 15–32. Philadelphia: Fortress, 1980.

Vermes, G. *The Dead Sea Scrolls: Qumran in Perspective*. Philadelphia: Fortress, 1977.

Vökel, M. "Exegetische Erwägungen zum Verständnis des Begriffs κατεξῆς im lukanischen Prolog." *New Testament Studies* 20 (1973–74) 289–299.

Vokes, F. E. "The Didache—Still Debated," *Church Quarterly* 3 (1970) 57–62.

Walasky, Paul. *'And so we came to Rome': The Political Perspectives of St. Luke.* Society for New Testament Studies Monograph Series 49. Cambridge: Cambridge University Press, 1983.

Watkins, O. D. *History of Penance.* 2 vols. London: Longmans and Green, 1920.

Welborn, Lawrence. "On the Date of First Clement," *Biblical Research* 29 (1985) 35–54.

Wellek, René and Warren Austin. *Theory of Literature.* 3rd ed. San Diego: Harcourt, Brace, Jovanovich, 1975.

Wilamowitz-Moellendorf, U von. *Glaube der Hellenen.* 2 vols. Dormstadt: Wissenschaftliche Buchgesellschaft, 1952.

Wilken, W. R. *Repentance as a Condition for Salvation in the New Testament.* Ph.D. Dissertation, Dallas Theological Seminary, 1985.

Williamson, R. *Jews in the Hellenistic World: Philo.* Cambridge, MA: Harvard University Press, 1989.

Wilson, S. G. *The Gentiles and the Gentile Mission in Luke-Acts.* London: Cambridge University Press, 1973.

Wimsatt, William and Monroe Beardsley, "The Intentional Fallacy." In *The Verbal Icon: Studies in the Meaning of Poetry.* New York: Noonday, 1954.

Windisch, H. *Der Zweite Korintherbrief.* Göttingen: Vandenhoeck and Ruprecht, 1924.

Winston, D. "Judaism and Hellenism: Hidden Tensions in Philo's Thought," *The Studia Philonica Annual: Studies in Hellenistic Judaism* 2 (1990) 1–19.

———. "Philo's Doctrine of Repentance." In *The School of Moses: Studies in Philo and Hellenistic Religion*, ed. John Peter Kenney, 29–40. Studia Philonica Monographs. Atlanta: Scholars Press, 1995.

Wolfson, H. *Philo: Foundations of Religious Philosophy in Judaism, Christianity, and Islam.* Revised Edition. 2 vols. Cambridge, MA: Harvard University Press, 1962.

Wrede, W. "Μετάνοια—Sinnesanderung?" *Zeitschrift für neutestamentliche Wissenschaft* 1 (1900) 66–69.

York, J. O. *The Last Shall be First: The Rhetoric of Reversal in Luke.* JSNTSup 46. Sheffield: JSOT, 1991.

Zeller, E. *The Stoics, Epicureans and Sceptics.* Translated by O. J. Reichel. New Revised Edition. New York: Russell and Russell, 1962.